An Introduction to Continental Philosophy

An Introduction to Continental Philosophy

David West

Polity Press

Copyright © David West 1996

The right of David West to be identified as author of this work has been asserted in accordance with the Copyright, Designs and Patents Act 1988.

First published in 1996 by Polity Press in association with Blackwell Publishers Ltd.

2 4 6 8 10 9 7 5 3 1

Editorial office:
Polity Press
65 Bridge Street
Cambridge CB2 1UR, UK

Marketing and production:
Blackwell Publishers Ltd
108 Cowley Road
Oxford OX4 1JF, UK

Published in the USA by
Blackwell Publishers Inc.
238 Main Street
Cambridge, MA 02142, USA

ISBN 0-7456-1184-2
ISBN 0-7456-1185-0 (pbk)

A CIP catalogue record for this book is available from the British Library and the Library of Congress.

Typeset in 10.5 on 12 pt Times
by Best-set Typesetter Ltd., Hong Kong
Printed in Great Britain by Hartnolls, Bodmin, Cornwall

This book is printed on acid-free paper.

Contents

Preface

One of the most important and persistent features of continental philosophy, as we shall see, is its emphasis on the social, cultural and historical conditions of thought and existence. Continental philosophy is self-consciously historical. On the other hand, a major complaint against an Enlightenment too impressed by natural science is its wilful ignorance of history. Not surprisingly, any adequate understanding of contemporary thinkers in the continental tradition requires at least some knowledge of the history of that tradition. Thus, although the emphasis in what follows is on the ideas of currently influential thinkers and schools, their ideas are presented within a broad historical account. Whereas analytical philosophers of the twentieth century can be regarded as the Enlightenment's reasonably direct heirs, continental philosophy is the outcome of a series of critical responses to dominant currents of modern western and Enlightenment philosophy. Of course, it is impossible given the scope of this work to provide any reasonably complete account of even the major contributors to continental philosophy. Rather the aim here is to describe only the most important ideas of some of the tradition's most influential representatives.

In this spirit, the first chapter briefly characterizes continental philosophy in terms of the opposition between continental and analytical philosophy and the historical and philosophical roots of this opposition. It seems inevitable that some statement of the distinctiveness of continental philosophy must, in this way, come first. But as Hegel recognized, such (and perhaps also these) prefatory remarks are more likely to be understood at the end than at the beginning. Chapter 2 presents a somewhat more detailed account of modernity, modern and Enlightenment philosophy and some of the continental critics of these tendencies. This chapter acts as a kind of hub for the rest of the book. Subsequent continental thinkers and schools of thought are considered as developments of, or reactions against, the ideas of these continental critics. Later chapters aim to provide succinct introductions to major philosophical approaches and thinkers, including Marxism and the Frankfurt School, hermeneutics and phenomenology, existentialism, structuralism and poststructuralism. Finally, postmodernism can be seen as the most determined attempt yet to escape the fundamental assumptions of modern western philosophy. Unavoidably, there are overlaps and sideways connections between some of the chapters. For example, Heidegger is surely best understood in the context of hermeneutics and phenomenology, in the company of Husserl and Gadamer (chapter 4). But Heidegger also exerted a major influence on Sartre, who is discussed in chapter 5. Again Nietzsche, discussed here in the company of Kierkegaard and Sartre, was a major contributor both to the thought of the Frankfurt School and to Heidegger and the poststructuralist critique of humanism, and so also to postmodernism.

It remains for me to acknowledge the invaluable contributions of colleagues and friends. Philip Pettit and Robert Goodin commissioned an extended chapter for Blackwell's *Companion to Political Philosophy* on the 'Continental Contribution', which was the germ of the present project. John Thompson and Gill Motley, my editors at Polity Press, offered enthusiastic and patient support throughout its completion. Sue Fraser provided frequent and valuable assistance with research and referencing. An anonymous reader gave me a number of very helpful and timely comments for which I am very grateful. Finally, I would like to thank all those who read and commented on earlier drafts of individual chapters and in some cases, heroically, the whole manuscript, in particular: Nils Bubandt, Terrell Carver, Bruin Christensen, Tom Clarke, Frances Daly, Penelope Deutscher, Moira Gatens, John Hart, Barry Hindess, Peter McCarthy, Paul Patton, Philip Pettit, Scott Simon, Andrew Vincent, Caroline West, Glenn Worthington and Norbert Zmijewski.

David West
Canberra, 1995

1. Introduction: What is Continental Philosophy?

Before engaging with at least some of the complexities and controversies that surround the term 'continental philosophy', it is helpful to give a more straightforward definition. Continental philosophy includes a range of thinkers and philosophical approaches usually contrasted with the 'analytical philosophy', which has dominated academic philosophy in the English-speaking world for most of the twentieth century. Continental philosophy in this sense includes thinkers such as Hegel, Marx, Kierkegaard, Nietzsche, Husserl, Heidegger, Sartre, Gadamer, Habermas, Derrida, Foucault, Lyotard and Baudrillard. It involves such currents of thought as Hegelian idealism, Marxism, the 'critical theory' of the Frankfurt School, existentialism, hermeneutics, phenomenology, structuralism, poststructuralism and postmodernism. This description should make clear, even at this early stage, that there is no single, homogeneous continental tradition. Rather, there is a variety of more or less closely related currents of thought. There are thinkers who, in one way or another, work in an identifiably continental mode.[1]

For the purposes of this book, the identification of a distinctly continental array of approaches in philosophy will be made primarily in historical terms. It will be useful not only to identify some of the members of a group of thinkers who bear certain family resemblances to one another, but also to trace some of the more obvious lines of descent, to sketch an intellectual family tree. Thus a number of contrasts of both substance and style will be traced to the emergence of distinctively continental currents of thought in response to the main direction taken by modern European philosophy and, in particular, the Enlightenment. The dominant temper of that intellectual upheaval combined scepticism about the claims of traditional metaphysics, religion and morality with considerable (and, in the opinion of some, inordinate) admiration for the methods of the natural sciences. If science is nonetheless exposed to scepticism or doubt, then it is challenged as the most convincing example of human knowledge.[2] In comparison with natural science other claims to knowledge seem insecure to the characteristic philosophers of the Enlightenment, who typically seek to place artistic, moral and even religious truths on more rationally defensible, more scientific and thus more secure foundations.

For a number of continental critics of the Enlightenment, however, the efforts of these thinkers were doomed from the start. The failures and difficulties they met with in their attempts to provide secure, rational foundations for the moral, religious and artistic dimensions of human knowledge were not so much signs of an uncompleted project as the inevitable consequences of a distorted, one-sided philosophical approach. The Enlightenment's critics saw the need for a very different response to questions which neither scientific method nor Enlightenment philosophy appeared equipped to answer. The result was a number of novel intellectual approaches, which together make up what we are here calling continental philosophy. The main contours of this continental critique can be traced to the writings of Herder and Rousseau, but it is expressed most systematically and ambitiously in the philosophy of Hegel. Subsequent contributors to the continental tradition are almost invariably 'post-Hegelians', in the sense that they either develop or react against, but rarely simply ignore the thought of Hegel. Their ideas bear the marks of the Hegelian system, even when they vigorously oppose or reject it. In what follows, we shall examine some of the most important of these ideas.[3]

However, before going on to this task, it is perhaps necessary to ward off a possible objection to our whole enterprise.[4] Even if we set aside straightaway those objections habitually raised against any attempt to express a large subject in relatively few words or to make difficult ideas more accessible, we are left with a more substantial worry. This is that the isolation of a separate tradition of continental philosophy is contentious or even perverse. The project may seem particularly odd to readers from continental Europe itself – Europe, that is, considered apart from those mainly English-speaking islands at its western extremity. After all, the various currents of western philosophy share a common history from the pre-Socratics, Plato and Aristotle, through the significant influence of Christianity, Judaism and Islamic scholarship to such central figures of modern European philosophy as Descartes, Locke, Hume, Leibniz, Spinoza and Kant. With some justice the term 'continental philosophy' can even be accused of ethnocentrism, since evidently only the European continent is intended. Continental philosophy can only be a variant of western philosophy.

In fact, continental philosophy began life as a category of exclusion. Until recently the analytical philosophy prevailing within the English-speaking countries of the West, including the United States, Britain, Australia, Canada and New Zealand, has almost completely ignored philosophical work produced on the continent of Europe since Kant – or, in other words, continental philosophy. As recently as the 1970s a course in philosophy that failed to mention Hegel or Nietzsche, Husserl, Heidegger or Sartre, was not considered in the least deficient. In this respect Kant, whose significance is acknowledged within both analytical and continental traditions, represents a decisive point of transition or even rupture. His philosophy was, in part, a response to the radical scepticism of David Hume, one of the central figures of the Scottish Enlightenment and a significant influence on analytical philosophy. Kant's response is still taken very seriously by analytical philosophers. But the work of Hegel, whose most important ideas arise directly from criticism of Kant, has been largely ignored. So it is with and after Hegel that it begins to make sense to speak of continental and analytical rather than simply of European or western philosophy. A whole series of subsequent nineteenth- and twentieth-century continental thinkers, usually either directly influenced by or reacting against Hegel or Hegelian ideas, have either been ignored altogether by analytical philosophers or, like Sartre and Camus, valued mainly for their more literary works.

The genealogy of continental philosophy can, then, be traced to Hegelian and associated responses to Kant. But, as a category of exclusion, continental philosophy was first identified as a distinct tradition from the perspective of an emergent analytical philosophy. The latter development was given major impetus around the start of the twentieth century by such figures as Gottlob Frege, Bertrand Russell and G. E. Moore, who were engaged at the time in a protracted battle with what was then, both in Britain and the rest of the English-speaking world, an overwhelmingly idealist and Hegelian (or in other words, 'continental') ascendancy.[5] The rise of analytical philosophy dates from this time. Russell and Whitehead's *Principia Mathematica* was an important watershed.[6] Ironically, continental

Europe was then dominated by positivist and neo-Kantian philosophies, both much closer in spirit to analytical than to contemporary continental philosophy.

In effect, analytical philosophy revived the sceptical, scientific spirit of the Enlightenment with the help of technical developments in logic and mathematics. The resulting principles and techniques were deployed, initially with great enthusiasm, against the 'usual suspects' or, at least, their direct descendants: the claims of 'continental' metaphysical idealism, traditional religion and dogmatic morality. At its most rigorous (or rigid), analytical philosophy applies what is sometimes called Hume's fork. Hume claims that 'All the objects of human reason or enquiry may naturally be divided into two kinds, to wit, *Relations of Ideas*, and *Matters of Fact*.' The former include principally the truths of mathematics and logic, which are 'discoverable by the mere operation of thought, without dependence on what is anywhere existent in the universe'. The latter are contingent truths about the world which 'seem to be founded on the relation of *Cause and Effect*.'[7] Of course, Hume has in mind those truths most systematically expressed in the natural sciences of his day. Anything that belongs to neither category, including scholastic philosophy or 'metaphysics' and religion, is revealed *ipso facto* as worthless from the point of view of reason or genuine knowledge. Although analytical philosophers relax this principle somewhat in practice – if only to make sense of their own activity, which itself does not fall clearly into either category – they continue to work very much in its spirit. Since philosophy is neither a branch of logic or mathematics nor a natural science comparable to physics or biology, it must restrict itself austerely to the careful analysis of concepts. The only scientifically respectable philosophy is henceforth analytical. According to the 'linguistic turn' taken by twentieth-century philosophers more generally, this task is then interpreted as involving first and foremost the analysis of language. Michael Dummett's statement is representative: 'the goal of philosophy is the analysis of the structure of *thought*' and 'the only proper method for analysing thought consists in the analysis of *language*.'[8]

Continental philosophers, on the other hand, can be regarded as the distant relatives of those metaphysicians, moralists and believers so caustically dismissed by Hume, at least in the sense that they are unwilling to abandon the concerns and insights intimated by these modes of experience. Similarly, they continue to address questions which ordinary common sense has never ceased to regard as important elements of the philosopher's task. These are, above all, existential, moral or ethical and aesthetic questions: questions about the nature of existence and the meaning of life, questions of right and wrong or of the meaning of art and beauty. From the point of view of analytical philosophy, however, continental philosophers continue to employ dubious metaphysical methods, which have been superseded by their own more precise, rigorous and scientific tools of conceptual analysis. In these terms the continental approach has been subjected to frequent criticism, from 'logical positivist' diatribes against the 'senseless' utterances of 'metaphysics' to the continuing, though recently abating, concern to demarcate 'science' from 'nonsense'. When A. J. Ayer reiterates Hume's complaint that metaphysics comprises neither verifiable statements of fact nor analytical or logical truths and should therefore be dismissed as nonsense, he chooses the eminently continental figure of Heidegger as target.[9] There is some irony again here, since Heidegger, as we shall see, was also preoccupied with the need to overcome metaphysics, albeit in a very different sense.[10]

In other words, 'continental philosophy' is no innocent, and for that matter not just a boring, classificatory label, but rather begins life as something closer to a term of abuse. The opposition between continental and analytical philosophy thus resembles that other, more worldly and now increasingly obsolete opposition between East and West. The observer of politics soon realizes that 'East' and 'West' are ideological rather than geographical terms. The West is free, capitalist and prosperous, and celebrates human rights and the American way. The East has been totalitarian, stagnant and oppressive. Despite their geographical locations Japan and Australia are, for most purposes, regarded as belonging to the West, whereas Cuba belongs to the East. Similar anomalies beset any straightforwardly geographical interpretation of the distinction between analytical and continental philosophy.

Thus Frege played a significant role in the development of analytical philosophy despite being German, as did the logical positivists of the Vienna Circle and Ludwig Wittgenstein, who were Austrian.[11] On the other hand, there are obvious affinities between such nineteenth- and twentieth-century British idealists as T. H. Green, Bradley, Collingwood and Oakeshott and their idealist contemporaries across the Channel. Even John Stuart Mill, an honoured figure within the analytical tradition, was deeply influenced by the ideas of Wilhelm von Humboldt, a friend of Goethe and Schiller, and by German romanticism. Gilbert Ryle, author of *The Concept of Mind* (a classic of analytical philosophy) studied for a time with Husserl.[12] Contemporary English-speaking philosophers such as Richard Rorty, Alasdair MacIntyre and Charles Taylor, working mainly in North

America, self-consciously develop continental themes, albeit in the idiom of analytical philosophy. Again, there are now thriving schools of analytical philosophy in France and Germany, where there have in the past also been periodic revivals of neo-Kantianism, which is not so very different in its fundamental claims.[13] Logical and analytical approaches to philosophical questions, finally, have a long tradition in Poland (for example, the Lvov–Warsaw school) as well as in other eastern European countries.

Certainly, then, a straightforwardly geographical basis for the identification of two mutually isolated traditions in western philosophy cannot be found and, in any case, would be unlikely to be philosophically interesting. To adapt Derrida's apt phrase, the Continent is 'the nonempirical site of a movement'.[14] On the other hand, although there is evidence that the distinction between analytical and continental philosophy is more the product of antagonism between distinct philosophical camps, it is not easy to identify clear and substantial doctrinal differences or to define the two approaches reliably in terms of divergent topics, styles or even moods.[15] Certainly, it would be premature to attempt a firm distinction at this stage. Like all ideologically tinged oppositions, the distinction between analytical and continental philosophy has served as much to prevent serious intellectual engagement as to identify genuine differences. Intellectual traditions reflect social and historical allegiances as much as strictly intellectual considerations. It will surely prove more fruitful, therefore, to go on directly to a consideration of continental philosophy and the intellectual approaches and thinkers with which it is associated.

2. Modernity, Enlightenment and their Continental Critics

From Modernity to Enlightenment

Continental philosophy is a significant and continuing strand of western philosophy. It can be traced to a series of reactions to what have become known as modernity and Enlightenment. The Enlightenment was a philosophical as well as more broadly intellectual and cultural movement of the eighteenth century, but it can also be regarded as the culmination in the intellectual sphere of a series of events and developments transforming European society, particularly from the onset of the 'modern' period around 1500 AD. As we shall see, these social, economic and cultural developments were interwoven both with longer-term processes of 'modernization' and with the emergence of the West's self-consciousness as 'modern'. By the time of the Enlightenment, the West had formed a strong, though not uncontested, belief in the superiority of its own thought, institutions and values. It boasted the successful completion of a number of modernizing processes of development, including the emergence of the modern state and the rise of a capitalist market economy. Intellectually, autonomous scientific, artistic and moral spheres were demarcated from what had previously been an overwhelmingly religious worldview that made no such clear distinctions. The West had come to see itself as modern.

In its own eyes at least, then, western society was modernized by a series of social and cultural developments, which can be traced back to ancient Greece and Rome and which continue into modern times. The characterization of these apparently unplanned, or at least uncoordinated, developments as processes of modernization, rather than simply as change, relies on the role allegedly played in them by rationality. Western society is more modern because it is more rational. This is brought out clearly in Max Weber's sociological account of the evolution of western society as a process of 'formal' rationalization.[1] Rationalization, in Weber's sense, involves the abandonment or reform of traditional practices in favour of procedures designed to achieve more efficiently the goals identified with these practices. The result is what has also been described as the 'instrumental' rationalization of society: institutions are fashioned into more effective *means* for the realization of particular *ends*. In this sense, for example, Roman law significantly rationalized the legal and administrative systems of the Empire. Legislators produced a more ordered and consistent legal code, removing anomalies and incoherencies inherited from traditional practice and the precedents of the common law. Roman law then served as a model for the reform of many of the legal systems subsequently adopted in continental Europe.[2]

Significantly, although Roman law itself was far from secular in the contemporary sense, rationalization in the West was increasingly associated with processes of secularization, or what Weber calls 'disenchantment'.[3] The reform of traditional institutions and practices in the interest of greater efficiency disrupts the authority of religious beliefs and values.[4] For the rationalizing spirit, tradition and religion are no longer sufficient reasons for acting in a particular way. In this spirit, throughout the medieval period the gradual separation of state from church freed both laws and decision-making from the restrictions of religious belief and traditional morality, producing states and the political sphere in their modern sense for the first time. The secularization of the state allowed a politics and an administration more pragmatically attuned to temporal 'reasons of state' or, in later democratic variants, the secular interests of the community. Machiavelli's *The Prince* is a notoriously unsentimental exploration of the implications of the separation of politics from morality.[5] What is more, alongside the development of a relatively autonomous politics and state, the mode of operation of the state could also be rationalized. Traditional arts of government were displaced by a more systematically organized administration or 'bureaucracy'. The bureaucratic state is run by officials, who are selected according to criteria of professional expertise rather than family ties or wealth. Decisions are made according to fixed and predictable rules rather than at the discretion of trusted individuals. Each case must be recorded in a detailed and systematic manner. The rationalization of politics and state advanced throughout the medieval period, despite its subsequent characterization by a later and self-consciously more enlightened time as the 'Dark Ages'. William I's 'Domesday Book' of 1086, a systematic record of the land for purposes of taxation, is just one example.[6]

Similar processes of formal or instrumental rationalization occurred in the economic sphere, with the gradual spread of capitalist relations of production. Capitalism, a mode of economic organization that allows the free circulation and unlimited private accumulation of capital, begins to emerge with the rise of free cities from the thirteenth and fourteenth centuries. Capitalism, too, erodes traditional ways of organizing production and challenges the customary regulation of prices and wages. An increasingly free market intensifies competition between enterprises and unleashes the profit motive, creating a dynamic mechanism for greater productive efficiency and accelerating rates of economic growth. At the same time, broader social transformations are set in train. Traditional ties of authority are weakened as large numbers of peasants are displaced from country to town. New wealth provides a powerful base for the political and intellectual aspirations of the 'bourgeoisie' – the rising, middling classes of traders and merchants, small manufacturers, bankers and moneylenders, lawyers and accountants. This class will eventually be able to play a significant role in subsequent cultural, intellectual and political developments associated with modernity and Enlightenment.

This rationalization of state and economy sets the scene for a significant transformation of thought and culture. What has been described as the arrival of an explicit and self-conscious 'discourse of modernity' marks a further stage in the evolution of the West.[7] From around 1500, there is a recognizable break from the past and, for the self-consciousness of the West, a new sense of time. One aspect of the new consciousness is that the chauvinism by which Hellenes, Jews and then Europeans had regarded themselves as superior, is reinterpreted in world-historical terms. The West claims henceforth that its institutions and thought bear a privileged relation to a uniquely valid rationality, markedly reinforcing pretensions to universal truth already present in Epicurean and Stoic thought. Europeans come to see themselves as more modern, more advanced or more developed than peoples they now describe as traditional, backward or primitive – and whom they sometimes even see as being incapable of such development. A number of historic events contributed to the appearance of this self-conscious modernity and 'openness to the future'. In Habermas's words, 'The discovery of the "new world", the Renaissance, and the Reformation – these three monumental events around the year 1500 constituted the epochal threshold between modern times and the middle ages.'[8] Although, according to Habermas's account, the self-consciousness of modernity is not fully articulated until the eighteenth century with the Enlightenment, the moment of transition is then fixed in the past: 'Only in the course of the eighteenth century did the epochal threshold around 1500 become conceptualized as this beginning.'[9] The Enlightenment, as its name intimates, understands this threshold as the first dawning of an age of reason and light.

Voyages of discovery, Renaissance and Reformation, these 'monumental events' helped trigger a profound transformation of the social, cultural and intellectual life of Europe. In the process, the view of the world still dominant at the end of the Middle Ages, essentially a synthesis of Christian doctrine and classical Greek science and cosmology, was unravelled. By the sixteenth century philosophers, moralists and political thinkers had begun to cast doubt on traditional beliefs and religious authority in search of surer, more rational foundations for our knowledge of nature, our moral beliefs and the political order. The voyages of discovery had put Europeans into contact with previously unknown and (to them) evidently primitive peoples. Travellers' tales of encounters with 'uncivilized' or 'savage' natives were popular and would continue to figure in the fictions and moral treatises of the Enlightenment.[10] The interest of these encounters was heightened by the evident contrast between these peoples and what was being learned of the civilizations of ancient Greece and Rome. The rediscovery of these cultures, made possible in part by the contributions of Islamic scholars who had translated and so preserved many of the texts of classical antiquity, inspired a 'renaissance', a rebirth or reawakening, of both arts and sciences. Artists and architects imitated ancient temples and sculptures, and revived classical subjects, techniques and literary genres. The revival of these forms encouraged the flourishing of humanism, which placed greater emphasis on human interests, capacities and concerns and less on the supernatural or divine. The art of the Renaissance paid more attention to secular themes and, in the works of Michelangelo or Leonardo da Vinci, unashamedly celebrated the perfection of the human form. Even the religious art of the Renaissance accorded greater space to human experience and emotion. Humanism was also associated with a more realistic employment of artistic techniques – sometimes to the advantage of the newly developing sciences, for example with the more accurate anatomical representation of the human body – and the systematic application of linear perspective for the representation of objects in three-dimensional space.[11]

Parallel to the humanism of the cultural and artistic spheres were developments in philosophy and science that opened ever deeper fissures in a hitherto overwhelmingly religious worldview. Philosophical humanism helped to legitimate what Francis Bacon (1561–1626) termed 'learning' as opposed to the 'wisdom' of traditional morality and religion. Still, Bacon's defence of unaided human knowledge of 'God's works' depends on theological premises:

> let no man upon a weak conceit of sobriety or an ill-applied moderation think or maintain, that a man can search too far, or be too well studied in the book of God's word, or in the book of God's works; divinity or philosophy: but rather let men endeavour an endless progress or proficience in both . . .[12]

Achievements in the natural sciences provided an important spur to this new self-confidence. From now on there was less emphasis on the limitations of human knowledge, more on its actual or potential achievements. Human beings can investigate the world unaided. They no longer need to reconcile their findings with either revealed religion or established authority. Even the appropriation of classical Greek and Roman texts had to be critical. Ideally the pursuit of knowledge should 'begin anew from the very foundations'.[13] In other words, with philosophers such as Bacon, the modern conception of science as a systematic, critical and unconditional enterprise is clearly formulated for the first time.

Not surprisingly, knowledge produced on this humanist basis soon contradicted the teachings of established religion. A notable example is the confrontation of Galileo Galilei (1564–1642) with the Catholic Church. Galileo's astronomical observations led him to support the 'heliocentric hypothesis' of Copernicus, that the sun rather than the earth is at the centre of the universe. Copernicus' hypothesis would eventually greatly simplify calculations of the movements of the planets.[14] Heliocentrism was in sharp conflict with the orthodox view of the Church, adopted from the second-century Egyptian, Ptolemy, that the home of God's most important creature must be the centre of the universe. The Church refused to separate the moral and religious issue of the importance of 'man' and 'his' earth from more purely scientific questions of astronomical calculation and prediction. In a striking scene of Bertolt Brecht's play, dramatizing this historic confrontation, senior figures of the Church are invited to confirm Galileo's revolutionary observations with the help of his telescope, but they simply refuse to look. The Inquisition shows Galileo the instruments of torture and he recants. Although Galileo was condemned by the Inquisition in 1616 and remained in confinement for the rest of his

life, his ideas could not be contained so easily, and the victory of the
Church was to prove short-lived. Galileo is able to arrange for a copy
of his *Dialogue on Two World Systems* to be smuggled across the
border to safety in Holland.[15] The events described in Brecht's play
are representative of the broader historical transformation. The scientific discoveries of 'natural philosophers' like Galileo and Newton
eroded the worldview of medieval Christendom. Constructed under
the domination of the Catholic Church, this worldview was a complex
synthesis of classical and Christian doctrine. Perhaps at the heart of
the medieval picture is a view of the world as an ordered and meaningful cosmos – a very old idea already present in the thought of
Pythagoras and other pre-Socratics. All the elements of nature, including humanity, are understood according to their place in a coherent, ordered and meaningful universe. The Church reconciled this
cosmology with Christian doctrine. The world is seen as God's creation and as the expression of his will, as something visibly imbued
with both meaning and purpose. Similarly, evidence for the existence
and power of God is to be found throughout a natural world whose
perfection and complex interdependence so clearly seem the product
of intelligent and beneficent design. This view also accorded well with
Aristotle's 'teleological' biology, which explained the development of
plants and animals by the final goal or form, the *telos* that they strive
to achieve.[16]

For the medieval worldview, then, the central categories are purpose, meaning and divine will. By contrast, the world that comes into
view with the science and philosophy of the modern period is radically disenchanted. The world is no longer a meaningful order replete
with moral and religious significance but, as Charles Taylor puts it, 'a
world of ultimately contingent correlations to be patiently mapped by
empirical observation'.[17] The dualist philosophy of René Descartes
(1591–1650) is one important source of this picture of the physical
world. For Aristotle, *psyche* (in Greek, 'breath', 'life' or 'soul') is
what makes a body alive and so is essentially embodied. There is no
strict separation between mind and matter; therefore what seem to us
almost animistic explanations of biological development, as 'striving'
or 'aiming' for a final goal, are not clearly ruled out. Descartes's
dualism of mind and matter, on the other hand, serves to drive a
wedge between the scientific explanation of bodies in space and what
become strictly 'mental' categories of purpose and will. A purely
mechanical model of the material world as matter extended in space
is combined with a picture of mind as essentially immaterial and
disembodied.[18] Although God is invoked as the ultimate guarantor of
the truth of our experience of the external world, he plays no substan-

tive role in the explanation of events within it. The sufficient reason for every event in nature can be found within nature itself.

The revised view of the external world of nature also implies a novel account of the human 'subject'. In the terms of Descartes's dualism, the self is conceived as a non-physical subject of experience, essentially distinct both from its physical embodiment and its place in a meaningful order of nature. The self is no longer defined or constrained by an essential purpose, bound simply to realize an intrinsic nature or *telos*. The characteristic self of modern philosophy is an abstract and disembodied subject of consciousness. Descartes's account of this self emerges from the attempt to find indubitable foundations for knowledge. He pursues his famous method of radical scepticism or doubt, confident only of those beliefs that it is impossible to doubt. By this method Descartes soon arrives at the conclusion that the only thing that is certain is that 'I am, I exist.' I can doubt the evidence of my senses, the existence of an external world, even the existence of my own body. But when I doubt that I exist, it seems that I unavoidably presuppose my own existence. When I am doubting, I am thinking, and if I am thinking then I must exist. This train of reasoning delivers the famous *cogito ergo sum* or 'I think, therefore I am' of Cartesian philosophy. Descartes proceeds apace to the more controversial conclusion, that what I am 'essentially' is a thing that thinks. An essential property or attribute of a thing is one that is indispensable to its being that thing. An 'accidental' or 'contingent' property, on the other hand, is one that a thing may or may not have and still be the thing that it is. In this specific philosophical sense, whales are essentially marine mammals but only accidentally victims of human aggression. Descartes reasons that if I can doubt the existence of my body, then my physical attributes cannot be essential ones. I could be who I am without my body. The self is only accidentally physical, but essentially mental: 'I am not more than a thing which thinks, that is to say a mind or a soul, or an understanding, or a reason.'[19] If I am essentially a thing that thinks, then the connection between my self and my body can only be a non-essential or accidental one. Those features of a human being deriving from its physical embodiment are merely accidental or contingent features of a self that is essentially disembodied. By implication, purpose and meaning can no longer be derived from our place in an ordered cosmos. In future, the self must find its purpose, the meaning of its existence, from within itself. The self must become, in Taylor's terms, a 'self-defining subject'.[20]

This disembodied, self-defining subject corresponds to a very different picture of the nature of human knowledge. For the most influential currents of modern philosophy the goal of knowledge is no longer to decipher meanings woven into the fabric of the world, in order either to fulfil God's design or to live more in harmony with the purposes of nature. Rather, the value of knowledge is principally instrumental. Knowledge is something that makes our lives more certain, and perhaps more comfortable, by improving our ability to predict and control nature. Bacon expresses this view of knowledge in the clear, but explicitly patriarchal, terms of a relationship between man and a female nature: 'that knowledge may not be, as a curtesan, for pleasure and vanity only, or as a bondwoman, to acquire and gain to her master's use; but as a spouse, for generation, fruit, and comfort'.[21] The ambition, even arrogance, of these aspirations was encouraged by the combination of theoretical elegance and predictive success soon achieved by the natural sciences and, perhaps most impressively, in the mechanics and astronomy of Isaac Newton (1642–1727).[22] At the same time, a less optimistic subcurrent of European culture began to express fears at the excess of these ambitions. Expressions of this sentiment ranged from dramatizations of the Faust legend by Marlowe and Goethe to nineteenth-century Gothic tales about the potentially monstrous products of scientific hubris, like *Frankenstein*.[23] Still, the dominant currents of modern thought admire mathematics and natural science as the most impressive and most obviously useful examples of human knowledge.

A corollary of the modern view of knowledge is scepticism about other forms of human knowledge and experience. Religion, in particular, would suffer in the longer term. That said, early modern thought was not dominated by 'free thinkers', whether agnostic or atheist. Philosophers continued to profess belief in God, whether out of genuine conviction or fear of the consequences of unbelief. Descartes's 'ontological' proof of the existence of God is necessary, if he is to escape from the predicament of 'solipsism' – the belief that we can only be certain of the existence of our own mind or consciousness and cannot know that anything or anyone else exists. We can trust the evidence of our senses only on the assumption of a benign deity, who would not allow us to be permanently deceived by an 'evil demon'.[24] Other thinkers maintain the compatibility of faith and reason or, like Bacon and Locke, insist on the value of religious 'wisdom' or 'revelation' as opposed to mere human 'learning'.[25] Still, the world of the modern period is significantly disenchanted. Nature is essentially nothing more than a mechanistic system of extended matter without religious or moral significance. By the same token, our knowledge of this disenchanted world no longer provides unequivocal or immediate support for either morality or religion.

The culmination of the tendencies implicit in modern philosophy is reached with the Enlightenment in the eighteenth century. Most notably in France, the so-called 'Encyclopaedists', including such figures as d'Alembert, Diderot, Voltaire, Helvétius and d'Holbach, produced an influential dictionary or 'encyclopaedia' of contemporary arts and sciences. These Enlightenment figures argued for liberal and anti-clerical views, which found dramatic expression in the French Revolution of 1789. In Germany Kant espoused Enlightenment as the transition from 'immaturity' and dependence to the 'spirit of freedom' and autonomy, the ability 'to use one's understanding without guidance from another'.[26] Enlightenment thinkers conducted a more confident and open assault on the Church and traditional morality. However, the typical profession of these thinkers is still a form of deism, a religious faith shorn of 'superstitious' elements unacceptable to reason. A mature and rational humanity no longer requires either the distraction of miracles or the crude motivation of visions of hell and damnation.[27] On the other hand, Enlightenment thinkers are even more convinced of the value of science. After the Enlightenment, scepticism about science carries the hint of bravado previously attached to atheism.

A rather different 'Scottish Enlightenment' is associated with the more conservative, sceptical philosophy of David Hume (1711–76) and the moral and economic writings of Adam Smith (1723–90). David Hume, about a century after Descartes was writing, brings out the full implications of the Cartesian view of nature. Hume ridicules the medieval worldview's conception of nature as a teleological system of entities propelled by inner necessity to fulfil their essential purpose or goal. Even if such essential purposes or 'powers' existed, we could never have knowledge either of them or of the 'necessary connection' between events that they are supposed to imply. Knowledge of reality can only be derived from a careful observation of the 'constant conjunction' between contingent events. Where such a constant conjunction is observed, we are inclined (though for Hume not necessarily entitled) to attribute a causal relationship between events designated 'cause' and 'effect'.[28] The recent successes of natural scientists can only be accounted for in these terms. Scientific knowledge depends on the conscientious observation of the regularities of nature. Hume, like Hobbes some hundred years earlier, also seeks to apply the method of science to the 'science of man', to what are now known as human or social sciences.[29]

Certainly, scientific knowledge has nothing to do with either knowledge of canonical texts (whether Aristotle or the Bible) or a sensitive reading of nature considered as the manifestation of God's will. Hume challenges all attempts to base religious belief on our experience of the world, whether in the form of the argument from design or from the alleged evidence of miracles.[30] Overall, he directs some of his most biting irony at religion, in particular its dogmatic morality and the high-flown claims of theology. But Hume's scepticism also challenges the claims of moral and aesthetic judgement more generally. His classic statement of the distinction between facts and values announces that 'virtue is not founded merely on the relations of objects'.[31] There can be no derivation of an 'ought' from an 'is'; no collection of facts, however exhaustive, implies an evaluative conclusion. Judgements of value, whether of good and evil or of 'beauty and deformity', simply reflect our sentiments, our inclinations or taste.[32] Morality and aesthetics are based not on reason or knowledge but on feelings of pleasure and pain: 'Pleasure and pain, therefore, are not only necessary attendants of beauty and deformity but constitute their very essence . . . An action, or sentiment, or character is virtuous or vicious; why? because its view causes a pleasure or uneasiness of a particular kind.'[33] A variety of different accounts of moral and aesthetic value are provided by Enlightenment thinkers. But characteristically, value is something that must be added by human subjects to an evaluatively neutral world. Morality might be explained in terms of feelings of pleasure and pain or the impressions of a 'moral sense', as it is with Hume. Utilitarians like Jeremy Bentham developed Hume's picture of moral and aesthetic judgement as a projection of human desire or the capacity for pleasure and suffering. Moral laws are explained by Kant as the decrees of self-legislating rational beings.[34] With subjectivism values are regarded, in desperation, as the unchallengeable expressions of arbitrary will. In general, the self-defining subject must seek moral guidance from within. Values, previously manifest in every facet of a meaningful world, must now be justified. Values must be provided with foundations.

The Critical Philosophy of Immanuel Kant

There are, of course, many variants of Enlightenment philosophy within the broad constellation of ideas just described. However, the philosopher Immanuel Kant (1724–1804) occupies a pivotal position in their development.[35] He is respected as a major figure by later philosophers from both analytical and continental traditions, though different aspects of his works are highlighted and differing interpretations favoured within them. Kant's 'critical philosophy' seeks to establish the limits and underlying structure of human knowledge and experience, a project that has from the outset both negative and positive intentions, reflecting the dilemma faced by human reason in its relation to philosophical or 'metaphysical' questions: 'Human reason has this peculiar fate that in one species of its knowledge it is burdened by questions which, as prescribed by the very nature of reason itself, it is not able to ignore, but which, as transcending all its powers, it is also not able to answer.'[36] Kant's critical philosophy is able to play a pivotal role in the subsequent development of European philosophy, because it draws together most of the central issues of Enlightenment thought in a suggestive way. Most influentially, his critique of 'pure reason', which concerns the kind of knowledge of the external world most clearly demonstrated in the natural sciences, provides an imaginative synthesis of empiricism and rationalism, opposing camps in what was perhaps the central philosophical dispute of the period.[37] Both empiricism and rationalism are characteristically modern philosophies, seeking to place human knowledge on firm and indubitable foundations and to resist spurious claims to religious knowledge. Of course, this stance was not incompatible with a religious belief purified of unjustifiable pretensions and superstitious remnants. Sceptical empiricists, who regarded human knowledge as a very inadequate instrument, were sometimes open to alternative sources of wisdom.

Empiricists such as John Locke (1632–1704), George Berkeley (1685–1753) and David Hume hold that all human knowledge is ultimately based on experiences – on our 'impressions' or 'sensations' or observations of the external world. In the technical terms associated with the dispute between empiricists and rationalists, empiricists hold that all worthwhile knowledge is *a posteriori*, or something we can only achieve *after* having the appropriate experiences. Our knowledge is not based on any innate ideas: when we are born the mind is a blank slate or *tabula rasa*. By contrast, rationalists maintain that important, possibly the most important, instances of human knowledge are available to us prior to or independently of our experience. Rationalists are closer to the Platonic tradition in philosophy. Taking pure mathematics and logic rather than natural science as their favoured models, rationalists argue that such knowledge can only be understood as something we have *a priori* or *before* experience. Already Plato's dialogues contained arguments for this position. In the dialogue *Phaedo*, Socrates defends the view that 'what we call learning is just recollection' in order to prove the immortality of the soul.[38] In the *Meno* he uses the example of proofs in geometry to

portray the process of learning as a kind of recollection or remember-
ing of what we must have already known before.[39] The truths of
mathematics and logic can be demonstrated without appeal to experience and could never be contradicted by it. No number of observations could ever persuade us that '2 + 2 = 5' or that 'It is raining
and it is not raining' is ever true. Abstract mathematical entities, such
as perfectly straight lines, points that occupy no space or perfect
circles and triangles, are never met with in experience. So how can we
have knowledge of these entities, the kind of knowledge demonstrated in Euclid's geometry, unless it is somehow innate? Rationalists are
unconvinced by empiricist attempts to explain this knowledge in
some other way, whether as the product of generalization from experience or as made of ultimately contentless truths by definition.

Kant seeks to combine the insights of both empiricism and rationalism. He agrees with the rationalists that there are important truths
we can know *a priori*, but he seeks to provide a more adequate
explanation for the possibility of such knowledge than any provided
by rationalism. He agrees with empiricists that much of our knowledge depends on experience but, according to Kant, empiricists
neglect the 'formal' contribution, which the mind makes to the empirical 'content' it receives from sensation or 'intuition'. Although we
rely on experience, on 'receptivity' or intuition, for the particular
contents of our knowledge, the structure or form of that experience is
provided by the human mind or 'understanding'. Experience of an
external world would not be possible at all without the form contributed by the mind. For Kant, in other words, the views of both rationalists and empiricists are similarly one-sided. Rationalists undervalue
the contribution of experience or intuition, which is essential for any
genuine scientific knowledge. Empiricists realize this, but fail to recognize the importance of the formal structure, or 'concepts', by which
our experience is organized. A famous remark sums up Kant's position: 'Thoughts without content are empty, intuitions without concepts are blind. It is, therefore, just as necessary to make our concepts
sensible, that is, to add the object to them in intuition, as to make our
intuitions intelligible, that is, to bring them under concepts.'[40] Experience is necessarily made up of a combination of 'thoughts' or
concepts, which contribute the form of experience, and 'intuitions',
which contribute its content. Kant's basic insight allows a distinctive solution to the problem of accounting for human knowledge.
Self-consciously alluding to the impressive achievements of natural
scientists such as Galileo, Torricelli and Stahl, Kant describes his
contribution as a 'Copernican revolution' in metaphysics, a dramatic

overturning of previous philosophical assumptions comparable to that achieved in astronomy by Copernicus:

> Failing of satisfactory progress in explaining the movements of the heavenly bodies on the supposition that they all revolved round the spectator, [Copernicus] tried whether he might not have better success if he made the spectator to revolve and the stars to remain at rest. A similar experience can be tried in metaphysics, as regards the *intuition* of objects. If intuition must conform to the constitution of the objects, I do not see how we could know anything of the latter *a priori*; but if the object (as object of the senses) must conform to the constitution of our faculty of intuition, I have no difficulty in conceiving such a possibility . . . experience is itself a species of knowledge which involves understanding; and understanding has rules which I must presuppose as being in me prior to objects being given to me, and therefore as being *a priori*.[41]

It is possible for us to have *a priori* knowledge of the form or structure of experience – the form that all experience must share, if it is to be possible experience for us – because it is our mind or understanding that contributes that form to experience. Kant calls this special kind of knowledge 'transcendental', because although it concerns the nature of our experience it does not derive from it in the way that the empiricists had supposed.

Kant also expresses his claims about the necessary structure of our experience with a further distinction, which has become important for subsequent philosophy. The distinction, intended to cut across that between *a priori* and *a posteriori* knowledge, is between 'analytic' and 'synthetic' truths. Analytic truths, like straightforward definitions, can be found to be either true or false simply in virtue of the meanings of the terms they contain or, in other words, by analysis. For example, the proposition that 'A bachelor is an unmarried male' is, on at least one obvious interpretation of the terms it contains, simply true by definition. In Kantian terms, the concept of the predicate ('. . . is an unmarried male') is included in the concept of the subject ('A bachelor'). The truth of synthetic propositions, on the other hand, cannot be decided in this way. That 'No woman has ever been President of the USA' is a truth that can be known only synthetically. In this case the concept of the predicate is clearly not included in the concept of the subject (being male is not part of the definition of President). Analytic truths, which depend simply on the meanings of the terms we use and tell us nothing about the real world, are plausible examples of *a priori* knowledge. We don't find out that they are true by observation or experience. The most obvious examples of synthetic truths, on the other hand, appear to be factually informative and to depend on actual evidence or experience and therefore to be *a posteriori* truths. For Kant, crucially, transcendental knowledge of the basic form or structure of experience involves the less obvious possibility of truths that are both synthetic and *a priori*. Kant's philosophy, in other words, implies that we can have substantive or non-trivial knowledge of the structure of experience independently of all experience.

Kant describes his novel approach as 'transcendental idealism', a description that has often been misunderstood. In philosophical terms idealism is usually associated with the belief that there is no external, material reality. There are only ideas. Empiricism provides an obvious sceptical route to this belief. If all our knowledge of the external world comes from sensations that are seemingly 'in the mind', how do we know that anything 'out there' corresponds to our sensations? After all, when we dream or hallucinate we have similar sensations, but they prove to be merely illusory. The only way we can check the veracity of our experience is through other sensations, but the same problem applies to them as well. *Sceptical* idealists maintain that we can have no certain knowledge of the existence or nature of an external world; we can only have knowledge of our sensations. *Dogmatic* idealists, such as the 'good bishop' Berkeley, go one step further, claiming that they can know that reality is essentially mental, because the very idea of a material reality is incoherent or self-contradictory. In its contemporary version all our statements about reality are disguised statements about 'sense data'. For what is now usually called 'phenomenalism', statements about physical objects are logical constructs of statements about sense data. So when I make a statement about a tree, it can in principle be reduced to a complex series of statements about my sensations – what I see and what, under certain conditions, I would see. It is the latter series of statements that express what I *know* as opposed to what common sense usually asserts about an external material world.

Kant's transcendental idealism has been misunderstood, particularly by philosophers of analytical persuasion, as a version of idealism or phenomenalism in the above sense. But in fact, Kant's *transcendental* idealism is designed to refute all forms of what he calls 'empirical' idealism. Briefly, Kant claims that the world as it appears to us, the 'world of appearances' or 'phenomenal world', is inevitably experienced as a material world of causally interacting objects in space and time. We cannot know that the world as it is 'in itself' or the 'things in themselves' of the 'noumenal' world are actually organized in this way. We only have knowledge of the world of appearances; we cannot assume that the world really is exactly as it appears. But crucially, this does not mean that we only have knowledge of the contents of our minds or that there is no basis for a distinction between seeming and reality – the conclusion drawn by empirical idealists. As Allison points out, Kant maintains a distinction between mere 'semblance' (*Apparenz*) or 'illusion' (*Schein*) and reality.[42] That distinction is maintained *within* the 'world of appearances' (*Erscheinungen*), which is the only possible object of human knowledge. In his own terms, Kant is an *empirical* realist: we can achieve an objective knowledge of reality. The point of Kant's transcendental distinction between appearances and reality is of a different order. As Allison puts it,

> At the transcendental level . . . the distinction between appearances and things in themselves refers primarily to two distinct ways in which things (empirical objects) can be 'considered': either in relation to the subjective conditions of human sensibility (space and time), and thus as they 'appear', or independently of these conditions, and thus as they are 'in themselves.'[43]

The point of Kant's transcendental distinction is to undercut what he sees as the source of much metaphysical confusion, including scepticism and empirical idealism, namely transcendental *realism*. The transcendental realist regards appearances as things in themselves or, in other words, independently of the 'universal, necessary, and, therefore, a priori conditions of human knowledge'.[44] In effect, the transcendental realist understands human knowledge as an inferior or confused imitation of the perfect or absolute knowledge available to an infinite intelligence or God.[45] According to Kant, scepticism and empirical idealism are the natural results of attempting to understand human knowledge in this way.

Kant's rejection of transcendental realism thus also helps to make more sense of his Copernican revolution. Copernicus helped to overcome a cosmology, which insisted, essentially on religious grounds, that the earth must be at the centre of the universe because humanity is God's most important creation. Similarly, the essential task Kant sets for his critical philosophy is to expunge the ultimately religious sources of previous metaphysical confusion. Human knowledge must be understood in purely human terms rather than according to the misleading and unattainable standard of divine intuition. Kant's further demonstration of the usefulness of transcendental idealism lies in his discussion of the metaphysical paradoxes which result from a transcendentally realist perspective. The attempt to say something substantive about reality in abstraction from the inescapable conditions of human knowledge inevitably leads to the contradictions or 'antinomies' of previous or 'dogmatic' metaphysics. In the second part of the *Critique of Pure Reason*, the Transcendental Dialectic, Kant discusses the paradoxes which result from transcendentally realist assumptions. These include cosmological attempts to understand the world through 'an initially plausible but ultimately incoherent conception of the sensible world as a whole existing in itself'.[46] Kant also discusses theological arguments for the existence of God and claims of 'rational psychology' about the real nature of the human soul. In each case, he argues that opposed and seemingly irrefutable metaphysical positions stem from shared but mistaken assumptions of a transcendentally realist kind.

Kant's attempts to *prove* his claims about the necessary structure of our experience have, however, turned out to be a source of controversy. In particular, his 'transcendental deduction' of the 'categories' has been subjected to much scrutiny. The transcendental deduction is designed to establish the necessity of those basic features of our experience that Kant claims to be transcendental conditions of all possible experience. Briefly, it is designed to establish the necessity of space and time as 'forms of intuition' and the necessity of the 'pure concepts of the understanding', which define a material world of causally interacting objects and a unitary subject of experience, the 'I think' that must be able to 'accompany all our representations'. The difficulty of Kant's argument is notorious and I shall not attempt to reconstruct it here.[47] For the mainstream of analytical philosophy, though, it seems clear that Kant's transcendental arguments cannot amount to successful logical deductions. As arguments, they are either unconvincing or they can be reduced to analytical claims of no great significance.[48] Accordingly, for analytical philosophers Kant's crucial class of synthetic *a priori* truths turns out to be empty. Only analytical truths, which are ultimately contentless or 'tautological' truths by definition, can be known *a priori*. Analytical philosophy then sets out from an austere interpretation of Kant's critical philosophy, taking his strictures against traditional metaphysics to close off all further 'speculative' discussion of such questions. In effect, the analytical tradition reverts to Hume's claim that anything that cannot be understood as consisting either of 'matters of fact' (*a posteriori* and synthetic) or 'relations of ideas' (*a priori* and analytic) is not genuine knowledge but a species of nonsense. This tradition emphasizes the negative pole of Kant's dilemma, maintaining that philosophy should ignore those questions which 'it is not able to answer'. In this spirit, analytical philosophers have paid less attention to those fundamental questions that, according to Kant, human reason and, indeed, the living and acting human individual, 'is not able to ignore'.[49]

The continental tradition, on the other hand, places greater emphasis on Kant's recognition that there are nevertheless metaphysical, moral and aesthetic questions that we are unable to ignore. Continental philosophers have also been more sympathetic to Kant's transcendental deductions. From their perspective it is not surprising that these arguments are not strict logical deductions. For Kant logical deduction and observation or experiment (corresponding to Hume's two legitimate categories of truth) are central features of theoretical reason in its normal empirical employment within the bounds of knowledge. His own critical philosophy, which is designed to establish the limits of 'understanding' (*Verstand*) in that sense, must itself inevitably venture beyond these limits. Philosophical reflection cannot be reduced to the more limited and no doubt more reliable methods of the understanding. Evidently, Kant did not understand his transcendental arguments as strict logical deductions either. Dieter Henrich has argued that a juridical paradigm and legal standards of proof were in fact uppermost in his mind. Philosophical explanations are never incontrovertible demonstrations but 'probations' (*probationes*), which are necessarily holistic and never as clear and rigorous as 'the forms of discourse for whose sake the justification is undertaken'.[50] Philosophical reflection, as an exercise of 'reason' (*Vernunft*), necessarily operates beyond the safe but limited confines of knowledge or understanding. Subsequent continental philosophers, in diametrical opposition to the tendency of empiricist and later analytical readings of Kant, place even greater value on philosophical reason as opposed to 'mere' understanding.

Accordingly, too, for the continental tradition the second and third critiques, dealing with moral or practical reason and judgement, play a greater role. Certainly, moral and political questions are central to Kant's understanding of Enlightenment, which he defines as a process of maturation or escape from dependency: 'Enlightenment is man's emergence from his self-imposed immaturity. Immaturity is the inability to use one's understanding without guidance from another.'[51] He makes it quite clear, however, that he is not thinking only of the unfettered pursuit of factual or scientific understanding. Not only a 'book to serve as my understanding' but also 'a pastor to serve as my conscience' and 'autocratic despotism' are mentioned as obstacles to maturity. Freedom of public speech within responsible limits, freedom in religious matters and free discussion of legislation are all essential elements in the unfinished process of Enlightenment. 'Free thinking' is a 'kernel' which 'gradually reacts on a people's mentality' so that 'they become increasingly able to act freely'.[52] Those of Kant's successors who had a more critical stance towards the Enlightenment project tended to focus more on questions of morality and politics as well as artistic, aesthetic and religious areas of thought and experience.

Unlike some of his contemporaries, Kant was certainly aware that Enlightenment philosophy created a serious problem for morality and religion. Above all, a purely mechanistic view of the world as a concatenation of material causes and effects seems to undermine notions of freedom and moral responsibility. If, as a work like La Mettrie's (1709–51) *L'Homme machine* suggests, human beings are simply the playthings of causal forces, their actions the result of either biology or social conditioning, then it seems to make little sense to regard them as free and responsible agents.[53] It is also not obvious how the scientific rationality of the Enlightenment can support moral principles or imperatives at all (in Hume's terms, how an 'ought' can be derived from an 'is'). Any basis for the objective moral evaluation of human actions is apparently undermined.[54] Kant's response is a dual strategy designed to establish a secure basis for moral judgement independent of scientific reason. In the first place, the critique of pure reason sets limits to the pretensions of scientific rationality or understanding, not to rule out of court the claims of morality and religion (as some empiricist readings of Kant would suggest) but, precisely, to 'make room for faith'. In the Preface to the second edition, Kant remarks:

> I have therefore found it necessary to deny *knowledge*, in order to make room for *faith*. The dogmatism of metaphysics, that is, the preconception that it is possible to make headway in metaphysics without a previous criticism of pure reason, is the source of all that unbelief, always very dogmatic, which wars against morality.[55]

His own religious convictions were influenced by Pietism, a Lutheran movement that emphasized acts of worship rather than theological doctrine. The second, more positive part of Kant's strategy is to provide a firm foothold for morality and religion consistent with his critique of pure theoretical reason. In fact, he follows the same basic pattern of argument. His alternative account of the objectivity of moral judgement is based on an examination of the transcendental conditions of our *practical* experience. If we regard morality as a fact of human existence, then what are the necessary conditions for its possibility? What are the necessary 'postulates' of moral experience and judgement?

Kant's reply is that the fundamental postulate of morality is freedom, since if we are not free, we cannot be held responsible for our actions, and moral judgements cannot be applied to them. But freedom must also be reconciled with causal necessity, which Kant has shown to be an essential feature of the physical world. To achieve this reconciliation, he exploits the distinction between phenomenal and noumenal realms. Freedom is understood as an attribute of the noumenal or intelligible self rather than the causally determined empirical or phenomenal self. Put another way, freedom is an essential feature of the way we understand ourselves as self-conscious persons, who are also *agents* in the world, even though we are at the same time physical and therefore causally conditioned entities. Kant takes his account of morality to imply that free or moral action must be something completely purified of the 'empirical' motivations, the desires and impulses, of particular human individuals or phenomenal selves. A moral action must be motivated purely by the intention to do what is right, not by any particular interest or desire of the individual. The 'synthetic *a priori*' principles of morality must be derived, therefore, from the abstract notion of a rational will or agent, from which all distinguishing individual features have been expunged. The individual acts freely and morally when he or she acts purely in obedience to a universal moral law that is the product of reason alone.

Accordingly, Kant's famous 'categorical imperative' invites agents to 'universalize' the maxim of their actions: 'Act only on that maxim through which you can at the same time will that it should become a universal law.' This is Kant's version of the more familiar 'golden rule', that you should do to others what you would have them do to you. The examples Kant uses to illustrate the categorical imperative are designed to show that immoral actions are self-defeating when they are considered as examples that everyone might follow. Thus, lying is effective (the lie is believed and the agent's ulterior motives are served) only if most people tell the truth. If everyone lies (the hypothesis we entertain if we universalize the maxim of this action), then no one is believed, and both the purposes served by the institution of truth-telling and the purposes of the liar are inevitably frustrated. In another of Kant's formulations, intended to be equivalent to the first, the categorical imperative is expressed as the injunction never to treat others merely as means but always as ends in themselves:

> man, and in general every rational being, *exists* as an end in himself, *not merely as a means* for arbitrary use by this or that will: he must in all his actions, whether they are directed to himself or to other rational beings, always be viewed *at the same time as an end*.[56]

We should never use other people merely as instruments to our own ends (though we can, of course, enter into voluntary and mutually advantageous transactions, as long as these respect the autonomy of both parties). To act morally is to treat others as intelligible or rational beings and therefore as moral ends.

Some of Kant's most suggestive and, unfortunately, also most obscure remarks are contained in the third of his critiques, *The Critique of Judgement*, which contains the interrelated critiques of aesthetic and teleological judgement. As well as making an influential contribution to the philosophy of art, Kant provides what has been described as a bridge between the critiques of pure and practical reason. In Stuart Hampshire's words, 'there is a bridge that conducts us from unreclaimed nature to rational freedom.'[57] Aesthetic experience mitigates the stark opposition between two seemingly incommensurable dimensions of human life: on the one hand, our bodily existence within the deterministic realm of physical nature (the object of our empirical or scientific knowledge); and on the other hand, our existence as autonomous rational agents obeying the universal dictates of pure practical reason alone. Our aesthetic experience of natural beauty delivers an awareness of the meaningfulness or 'purposiveness' of nature, which mirrors the successful work of art's apparently natural inevitability – our sense that it could not have been otherwise, even though, as an 'end in itself', it serves no determinate function. As a result, we are more able to feel 'at home in nature':

> For the judgment of taste a beautiful work of art has the self-forming liveliness of a living organism in nature. The gap between the formative powers of nature, with their own indeterminate purposiveness, and the free, formative powers of human beings, has been closed. Human beings can to this extent feel at home in nature, in spite of the strain of their divided selves in moral endeavor.
> ... Closing the threatened gap between moral man and natural processes from the other side, we recognize natural beauty as involving a view of natural things 'after the analogy of art, and not as aimless mechanism'.[58]

Kant does not, at least after 1787, regard the purposiveness of nature as the actual product of God's intentional design.[59] But our aesthetic appreciation of the universe *as if* it were created or designed for some purpose makes it easier for us to reconcile the uncompromising demands of morality with the factual indifference of the material world. Kant's suggestive remarks are taken up by other thinkers in the continental tradition. Friedrich Schiller, for example, in his essay 'On the Aesthetic Education of Man', sees art as means to the recovery of a harmonious, organic unity for humanity. Beauty is the path from the 'state of nature' (*Naturstaat*) to an ethical state (*sittlicher Staat*) more adequate to the needs of the moral as opposed to merely physical individual. Beauty is the path to freedom.[60] In that spirit, too, there would be affinities between Kant's third critique and the criticisms of Enlightenment and modernity expressed by romanticism, by Hegel and by other continental thinkers.

Continental Critics of Enlightenment

As we shall see, Kant's philosophy provides an important point of departure for a number of influential critics of modernity and Enlightenment. The intellectual and cultural movement we have talked about as the Enlightenment was not unopposed. Its sober and often even moralistic 'free thinkers' were frequently condemned as atheists and corrupters of society. There were, of course, conservative defenders of traditional morality and orthodox religion. From the modernizing perspective of the Enlightenment, these defenders of the old intellectual order were conservatives or even reactionaries, struggling in vain against the inevitability of historical 'progress' or 'improvement'.[61] But other critics could not be categorized or dismissed so straightforwardly. Although they rejected some of the central tenets of Enlightenment thought, they also appreciated the value and force of its onslaught on superstition, dogma and arbitrary authority. They did not wish to return to the world that had existed before, but they also recognized one-sidedness and even dangers in the quickening tide of modernization. Their criticisms sought to divert rather than to reverse or halt this social and intellectual movement.

Jean-Jacques Rousseau (1712–78) was a complex and contradictory figure, who made a fertile contribution to the continental critique of Enlightenment. He also exerted a considerable influence on Kant, especially his moral philosophy and conception of autonomy. Rousseau was vividly aware of the ongoing social and cultural transformation of western society, but he was strongly critical of the direction of 'civilization', of what we are calling modernity. Some of his most powerful passages concern the degraded existence of 'civilized' as opposed to 'savage man':

> The savage and the civilised man differ so much in the bottom of their hearts and in their inclinations, that what constitutes the supreme happiness of one would reduce the other to despair. The former breathes only peace and liberty; he desires only to live and be free from labour; even the *ataraxia* of the Stoic falls far short of his profound indifference to every other object. Civilised man, on the other hand, is always moving, sweating, toiling, and racking his brains to find still more laborious occupations: he goes on in drudgery to his last moment, and even seeks death to put

himself in a position to live, or renounces life to acquire immortality. He pays his court to men in power, whom he hates, and to the wealthy, whom he despises; he stops at nothing to have the honour of serving them; he is not ashamed to value himself on his own meanness and their protection; and, proud of his slavery, he speaks with disdain of those, who have not the honour of sharing it.[62]

'Savage' or natural man is healthy and vigorous, has little foresight or fear of death and has no command, because little need, of language. He also exists without morality, for 'having no moral relations or determinate obligations one with another', 'men in a state of nature . . . could not be either good or bad, virtuous or vicious.'[63] The natural man has a healthy 'love of self' (*amour de soi*), the 'natural feeling which leads every animal to look to its own preservation, and which, guided in man by reason and modified by compassion, creates humanity and virtue'.[64] The natural love of self is contrasted with the more competitive and destructive concern with one's position in comparison to others. The characteristic *amour propre* of man in civilized society is 'a purely relative and factitious feeling, which arises in the state of society, leads each individual to make more of himself than of any other, causes all the mutual damage men inflict one on another, and is the real source of the "sense of honour"'.[65] The evils of 'society' flow inexorably and, as Rousseau significantly admits, irreversibly from economic and demographic trends associated with the development of society. As population increases and more intensive forms of agriculture become possible, human beings come into closer and more frequent contact with one another. Language develops, because it is useful to this intercourse. People start to compare themselves with one another and develop 'ideas of beauty and merit'. Alongside love and friendship develop their opposites, 'jealousy', 'discord' and 'impetuous fury'.[66] With settled agriculture, private property becomes inevitable, and from private property, with equal inevitability, arise ever greater economic and political inequalities and ultimately despotism.

Rousseau's condemnation of the evils of civilized existence is forceful and unambiguous. It stands in sharp contrast to the universalistic pretensions of uncritical partisans of Enlightenment and modernity. Where the ancient Greeks formed their sense of themselves in contrast to the inferiority of 'barbarians' and his contemporaries were imposing the 'benefits' of civilization on the inhabitants of newly discovered or newly accessible regions of the globe, Rousseau celebrates the simpler and healthier existence of the peoples colonized or enslaved. Indeed, a double slavery was involved. Colonized peoples were often literally enslaved by representatives of a civilization, which Rousseau regarded as itself little better than slavery. He makes considerable use of what we would now call anthropological reports about the 'Caribs of Venezuela', the 'Hottentots of the Cape of Good Hope' or the 'Oroonoko Indians' and the inhabitants of the Caribbean.[67] But significantly, Rousseau does not propose that we 'resume' an 'ancient and primitive innocence'. To advocate the abolition of private property or society and the 'return to nature', often associated with his name, would be 'a deduction in the manner of my adversaries'. For those, like Rousseau himself, 'whose passions have destroyed their original simplicity', there is no choice but to participate critically in their respective communities, mitigating where possible the deleterious effects of civilization.[68]

In this sense, it is misleading to associate Rousseau with the Romantic idea of the 'noble savage' – the view that humanity is naturally good and that we should return to nature.[69] In fact, Rousseau's 'conditional and hypothetical reasonings' are directed against any assumption of an original human nature, whether good or bad, altruistic or selfish.[70] The state of nature figures frequently in modern political philosophy as a hypothetical condition of human society prior to the institution of political authority. Thomas Hobbes (1588–1679) had exploited this device in pursuit of rational foundations for his newly scientific 'civil philosophy'. Hobbes assumes the natural selfishness and rapacity of individuals and reasons that only a sovereign or 'Leviathan', equipped with near-absolute powers, can impose order and prevent the destructive 'war of each against all'.[71] Political authority is justified, because the only alternative is chaos. But according to Rousseau, Hobbes, like other such philosophers, 'in speaking of the savage' has 'described the social man'.[72] Greed, pride and rapacity are products of society rather than attributes of the natural man. We are deceived if we believe we can ever make reliable statements about a state of nature. All we can ever hope to describe are forms of humanity corresponding to earlier or later stages of social development. The state of nature presupposed by philosophers like Hobbes is more accurately seen as such a stage in the development of society. Generalizations about a state of nature are impossible, because the life of human individuals depends not on a universal human nature but rather on the social, economic and cultural character of society. The individual is, as one jargon has it, socially constituted.

Rousseau's insight into the social constitution of individuality is reflected in the more constructive political philosophy of his *Social Contract* (1762). Rousseau regards the state's maintenance of order, which is Hobbes's prime justification of political authority, as a rudimentary achievement, which barely compensates for our loss of natural liberty. But although Rousseau is scathing about civilized society, he recognizes that the sacrifices individuals make on entering society also bring significant gains. What the individual loses in natural liberty, he gains in 'civil' and 'moral liberty':

> The passage from the state of nature to the civil state produces a very remarkable change in man, by substituting for instinct in his conduct, and giving his actions the morality they had formerly lacked. Then only, when the voice of duty takes the place of physical impulses and right of appetite, does man, who so far had considered only himself, find that he is forced to act on different principles and consult his reason before listening to his inclinations.

Although this transition involves the loss of 'some advantages which he got from nature', in society the individual is compensated by a stimulation and extension of his faculties, an ennobling of feeling and an uplifting of the soul. It is only in society that the individual becomes a responsible moral agent as opposed to a creature of impulse; it is only in society that the individual is truly free. It is the individual's 'moral liberty' which 'alone makes him truly master of himself; for the mere impulse of appetite is slavery, while obedience to a law which we prescribe to ourselves is liberty.'[73] In other words, the loss of natural liberty, which is lamented (at least 'conditionally' and 'hypothetically') in the 'Discourse on Inequality', is now recognized as a necessary sacrifice, if we are to achieve a more fully human moral liberty. Significantly, Rousseau's idea of moral liberty is taken up in Kant's moral philosophy, in particular the notion of autonomy as the subjection of will to a rational law of its own making.[74]

Rousseau's distinctively social account of human individuality is also at the heart of his famous notion of the 'general will'. In common with modern philosophers such as Locke and Hobbes, Rousseau is not satisfied with 'unenlightened' justifications of the state by 'divine right' or tradition. Instead, he derives the sovereignty of the state from the people. Although he has little liking for actual democracies – preferring the more aristocratic rule of ancient Sparta or Livy's Rome – his justification of the state is, in an important sense, still a democratic one. In whatever way the government is constituted (e.g. democratically or aristocratically), it should act in accordance with the 'general will' of the citizens. But for Rousseau, the general will is not simply equivalent to the 'will of all' or the sum of particular wills. It must express the general interest, which may be very different. That is why democratic political institutions may not be the best way of finding out what the general will is. Democratic institutions are only guaranteed to reflect the sum of all (or the majority's) particular wills. The general will in Rousseau's sense can only be reached through a process of negotiation and deliberation, designed to discover the common interest of society as a whole. Crucially, reaching the general will may involve the transformation of the particular wills of some or even all of those involved. But in fact the realization of the general will is compatible with, even a condition of, individual freedom, as genuine moral freedom consists not simply in the absence of interference by other individuals or by society, but in the positive transformation of the individual within society. Critics of Rousseau have seen this equation of liberty with subjection to the general will as a large step towards totalitarianism. It has been seen as licence for the tyrannical view that individuals can, in Rousseau's words, be 'forced to be free'.[75] Many contemporaries saw his political philosophy as justification of the radical but authoritarian Jacobinism of the French Revolution and even of the Terror. For much subsequent political thought, however, Rousseau's ideas nevertheless contain the valuable insight that, whatever the defects of existing societies, it is only within society that individuals can exist as fully rational, purposive moral beings. It is only in society that individuals have access to a full range of values, interests and forms of life. The life of the human individual is consequently far richer than the meagre repertoire of instinctive responses and biological needs of the hypothetical 'natural man'.[76]

The social constitution of the individual plays an important role for another contributor to the critique of Enlightenment thought, Rousseau's near-contemporary, Johann Gottfried von Herder (1744–1803). Central to Herder's thought is his view of language as the essential medium of our humanity.[77] Language underlies the distinctively human powers of memory and anticipation implicit in consciousness or 'reflection'. These powers compensate for the relative paucity and weakness of human as compared to animal instincts. In place of the fixity and certainty of the animal's instinctual responses they allow human beings both greater freedom and an enhanced ability to cooperate with one another. For Herder, crucially, language, as the essential medium for human thought and consciousness, is not just a vehicle for the expression of thoughts or ideas, which might have existed without it. Language is what makes thought possible and, as such, is inseparable from it. By the same token, different languages are not simply alternative instruments for the expression of the same ideas, but rather correspond to different ways of thinking and feeling, different thoughts and feelings. One result of this is that it may sometimes be difficult or even impossible to translate satisfactorily from one language to another. This 'constitutive role' of language for human thought and culture is also incompatible with the idea of a universal human essence, whether natural, intellectual or spiritual, independent of particular societies, an implication which further undermines universalist assumptions of human nature or historical progress favoured by the Enlightenment. Herder's views argue, instead, for the importance of the specific histories of distinct peoples. They also provided inspiration for nationalism, which was to become perhaps the most powerful ideological force of the nineteenth century. The languages of different peoples or nations correspond to differences of culture and sensibility, defining a distinct national identity.

In fact, in some ways Herder departs even more radically than Rousseau from Enlightenment assumptions. Although Rousseau is sceptical of universal histories and notions of inevitable progress, he does not hesitate to offer sharply critical advice to his contemporaries. He is ambivalent about the apparent direction of social development and the benefits of modernity, but he does not think that this process of development could have been avoided or could now be reversed. Rousseau's social and political philosophy is explicitly, if not unambiguously, prescriptive. Herder's thought, on the other hand, tends towards relativism. His account of human society seems to imply the incommensurability of the values and 'qualities of character' of different peoples and cultures.[78] The unique way of life of a nation or people cannot be measured against any other, let alone definitively evaluated in terms of some universal human essence or single model of the ideal society. Even though Herder does suppose an underlying, shared 'humanity' (*Humanität*), it is overlaid by differences of language and culture. Other Enlightenment philosophers, such as Hume and Montesquieu, had acknowledged the diversity of human societies, but they saw the variety of laws and customs as alternative means to the satisfaction of common human wants.[79] Herder's account of the self, on the other hand, suggests that even human wants are inseparable from the concrete forms of life of particular communities. In other words, Herder's appreciation of national and cultural difference provides an alternative to the universalizing tendencies of the Enlightenment, and indeed with ambiguous implications. On the one hand, the recognition of diversity was liberating in a German-speaking world resentful of the dominance of French culture throughout the eighteenth century. Germans should look for their own way through the thickets of modernity. On the other hand, relativism is for some only a few steps from nihilism. If there is no universal moral standard, then there might as well be no standard at all. Any value can be defended as an essential component of a discrete cultural tradition. As we shall see, the apparently short path from the social constitution of the individual through relativism to nihilism sets a stubborn and recurrent problem for subsequent thinkers in the continental tradition.

Although not himself a member of the Romantic movement, Herder's ideas also played an important role in the rise of romanticism towards the end of the eighteenth century. German thinkers, in part motivated by nationalist resentment at a predominantly French Enlightenment, cultivated the more 'devout, inward vision of the German soul'.[80] There was a widespread concern to defend religion or, more cautiously, the truths expressed through religion, against the lifeless and homogenizing materialism of French thought.[81] Romanticism celebrates the emotional, spiritual and aesthetic qualities of humanity. The Romantics were influenced by Kant's moral philosophy, particularly its message that moral life must be understood in terms other than the deterministic and reductive categories of natural science. They were less attracted to Kant's austere conception of autonomy as the rational self's subjection to a universally valid moral law and independence from 'empirical' motives of desire or inclination. They valued sincerity, authenticity and self-expression instead, qualities apparent in Goethe's extremely popular epistolary novel, *The Sorrows of Young Werther* (1774). At the same time, Romantics were not simply sentimentalists. After all, the treatment of feeling and emotion in both thought and fiction was hardly something which began with the Romantic movement.[82] It was the uninspired nature of this treatment, particularly in what was seen as the exhausted classicism of the eighteenth century, which was objectionable. Romantics advocated originality and individuality, the defiance of artistic and sometimes also social norms, and a contempt for all merely conventional feeling and action. They were, in Isaiah Berlin's words, 'champions not of feeling against reason, but of . . . the proud, indomitable, untrammelled human will'.[83]

For romanticism, value and beauty belong above all to the unique and the original. Like artists fashioning a work of art, individuals should cultivate their particular attributes, their individuality. Taylor describes the idea of the human subject implicit in the Romantic view as 'expressivism'. Expressivism understands the subject in terms of categories of expression rather than the mechanistic categories of natural science. Expressivism is identified with two ideals. It involves, first, the pursuit of self- as opposed to other-dependence – 'an inner force imposing itself on external reality'. This idea is associated with Rousseau and Kant as well as with Leibniz and Spinoza. This notion of autonomy combines, secondly, with the Herderian insight that expression is an essential rather than a merely accidental feature of the individual's autonomous self-development. Just as language is inseparable from the thoughts it communicates, so expression more generally does not leave unchanged whatever is expressed. Expressivism involves, in other words, 'the notion that the realisation of a form clarifies or makes determinate what that form is'.[84] The analogy between the individual human life and the work of art encapsulates this conception:

> man as a conscious being achieves his highest point when he recognises his own life as an adequate, a true expression of what he potentially is – just as an artist or writer reaches his goal in recognising his work as a fully adequate expression of what he wanted to say . . . The specific property of human life is to culminate in self-awareness through expression.[85]

Life is like art, hence art is important for life. Some would go even further, asserting that life *is* art.

The Hegelian Synthesis

The elaborate philosophical system of Georg Wilhelm Friedrich Hegel (1770–1831) attempts an ambitious synthesis of both Enlightenment and counter-Enlightenment themes. It has been the inspiration or at least a significant reference point for most subsequent contributions to a distinctively continental tradition of philosophy. Hegel was influenced by Rousseau and Herder, by Goethe, Hölderlin and romanticism, but he was also deeply imbued with Greek culture and philosophy and the ideals of classicism. Kant's philosophy too is an important point of departure. Hegel takes much further Kant's distinction between 'reason' (*Vernunft*) and mere 'understanding' (*Verstand*). Hegel claims much greater scope for the fluid, synthesizing capacities of speculative and practical reason as against the more prosaic defining, fixing and ordering activities of the understanding. He associates the latter unflatteringly with the rigid categories and lifeless abstractions of Kant's philosophy. In the same spirit, Hegel recognizes the force of criticisms levelled at the abstractly rational principles of Enlightenment rationality by thinkers such as Rousseau and Herder, and shares their scepticism at attempts to found an adequate view of human life, particularly life's moral, political and aesthetic dimensions, upon them. On the other hand, he is equally hostile to any Romantic or irrationalist abandonment of the achievements of modernity. Like the Romantics, Hegel sees Kant's complex system of separate faculties of pure and practical reason and aesthetic judgement as ultimately dry and dehumanizing. He pursues the Romantic goal of an ultimate resolution of the divisions embodied in Kant's philosophy and, relatedly, the recovery of the community, wholeness and harmony associated with classical antiquity. Hegel also appreciates the threat, vividly demonstrated in the excesses of the French Revolution, of the tyrannical rationalism that he regards as the political expression of the Enlightenment's limited and one-sided rationality. But Hegel is equally determined to preserve the characteristic gains of modernity including individual freedom, the constitutional state and critical reason.

Hegel's philosophical synthesis is all-encompassing, but it can be introduced most pointedly in terms of his reaction to Kant's moral philosophy and what Hegel sees as its expression in the French Revolution. Hegel is sceptical about the possibility of deriving concrete moral judgements from the abstract commitment to universality alone. It has become a familiar criticism of Kant to point out that simply universalizing the maxims of one's actions does not enable us to distinguish between moral and immoral ones. The principle of universality does not by itself rule out the possibility of a consistently evil agent, since any action, even the most immoral, can be described in such a way that its maxim can be universalized without contradiction. A powerful and brazen individual might maintain the maxim that might is right without falling into inconsistency. These considerations suggest that the purely formal and abstract categorical imperative is without content.[86] A second problem concerns the motivation of the moral agent. We have already seen that Kant defines genuinely moral action as action performed not simply in accordance with duty but for the sake of duty alone: 'For if any action is to be morally good, it is not enough that it should *conform* to the moral law – it must also be done *for the sake of the moral law*.'[87] But he finds it difficult to explain how ordinary human beings can be motivated by the moral law as such, without support from, or even against, their desires and inclinations.

What is worse, finally, Hegel believes that the abstraction of Kant's account of morality is more likely to lead to evil than good. He sees the French Revolution as a historical demonstration of the dangers inherent in the purely abstract rationality of Kant's moral philosophy. Hegel describes how, when 'each individual consciousness rises out of the sphere assigned to it' and 'grasps itself as the notion of will', it finds that 'its purpose is the universal purpose, its language universal law, its work universal achievement.'[88] But universal consciousness finds itself unable to produce any positive content, and 'there is left for it only negative action; it is merely the rage and fury of destruction', which aims only for death.[89] The French revolutionary Terror is the characteristic manifestation of the 'absolute freedom' and abstract universality of Kant's moral philosophy. In fact, this outcome is similar to what might be expected from the irrationalism of the Romantic celebration of pure, unconstrained and defiant will. Indeed, Hegel sees both as variants of the same erasure of 'otherwise valid duties':

> Once self-consciousness has reduced all otherwise valid duties to empti- ness and itself to the sheer inwardness of the will, it has become the potentiality of either making the absolutely universal its principle, or equally well of elevating above the universal the self-will of private partic- ularity, taking that as its principle and realising it through its actions, i.e. it has become potentially evil.[90]

For Hegel there are dangers in any account of morality, which ig- nores the tissue of moral values, duties and social practices in existing communities. It is characteristic of Enlightenment rationalism, pre- cisely, to ignore these established, merely traditional values and prac- tices of society in order to start again from scratch and design new and more rational principles. Hegel suggests that Kantian universal- ization reconstructs the intersubjective dimension, the relationship to others which is obviously essential to any understanding of morality, only in an abstract and ultimately empty way. The categorical imper- ative is a reconstruction of universal 'morality' (*Moralität*), but can- not ground the concrete intersubjectivity of 'ethical life' (*Sittlichkeit*). For Hegel, as for both Rousseau and Herder, ethical life can only be sustained through involvement with the culture, values and practices of an existing community.[91] Again, it is worth emphasizing that from Hegel's perspective the individual autonomy celebrated in Kant's moral philosophy is not rejected but reconciled with the values of organic wholeness and community. But genuine freedom – freedom that is not destructive for both individual and society – must be grounded in the ethical life of a community.

Hegel's account of the concrete intersubjectivity of ethical life also responds to the problem of the relationship between what is right and what is natural, between the 'moral' or 'rational' will on the one hand and what we want or desire as particular human individuals on the other. With Kant's view of morality, as we have seen, it is never clear why particular human individuals (as opposed to God or angels) should ever act in accordance with the moral law. There is an apparently unbridgeable gulf between nature and morality. For Hegel, on the other hand, the individual can only exist as such within particular communities. The individual is a product rather than a premise of the social order. As a result, not only will even the most rational reflections of the abstract individual never produce an adequate basis for ethical life, but without a concrete moral community there would be no individuals capable of such moral deliberation in the first place. But the social constitution of the individual also means that the moral or rational will is not so absolutely opposed to natural inclination. The moral will results from rationalizing or socializing rather than simply ignoring or overriding natural inclinations. The will, as opposed to mere impulse, is 'particularity reflected into itself and so brought back to universality, i.e. it is individuality'.[92] Whereas the 'wilful' impulses of the particular human organism bear no intrinsic relation to the interests of others, the socially constituted 'will' of the mature human individual reflects the demands of community though, of course, this does not mean that the wills of all members of society will necessarily be in complete harmony. The rational will, like Rousseau's general will, is not equivalent to the will of all.

At first sight Hegel's position, like that developed by Herder and the Romantics, seems to imply relativism. Without timeless and universal moral principles, it seems that we cannot criticize the values of different cultures or times, however repugnant they may seem. Enlightenment rationalism might lead to the revolutionary Terror, but without universal principles how can the Terror be condemned? Hegel seeks to avoid relativism with the help of an ambitious philosophy of history. The diversity of cultural forms are conceived as stages in a process of historical development, moments in an unfolding 'dialectic of spirit'. The term dialectic derives from the Greek word for debate or discussion. Classically, in Plato's Socratic dialogues the argument advances through the opposition of conflicting points of view. For example, a particular answer to the question 'What is justice?' is proposed and then criticized. But criticism does not simply erase the initial proposal, but rather leads to an alternative and presumably better suggestion. In Hegelian terms, it produces a determinate rather than merely abstract negation of the original view. In parallel terms, Hegel understands particular historical societies and their associated worldview or 'spirit' (*Geist*) as dialectically transcending previous ones, incorporating their positive features whilst eliminating negative ones. The tensions within one way of thinking are left behind in the transition to a more adequate one, though the new way of thinking will have tensions of its own.[93]

History can be reconstructed as a dialectical progression of structures of consciousness or 'spirit', embodied in particular historical societies.

Furthermore, Hegel thinks that the overall direction of the spirally ascending dialectic can be understood as the progress of freedom. 'The History of the world is none other than the progress of the consciousness of Freedom.'[94] Through the dialectic of history, according to Hegel, spirit – the concrete community considered as the embodiment of a particular worldview or conception of life – becomes increasingly rational and self-conscious. World history is boldly sketched in these terms. The 'stationary' civilization of the 'Orient', which allows freedom only to the despotic ruler, is eclipsed by the classical world and republican liberty of ancient Greece and Rome. Medieval Christendom enthrones a religion which assumes the equal worth of all before God and sets the stage for the further development of freedom. The 'Germanic' world of Protestantism asserts the rights of the individual conscience to a direct relationship with God.[95] At the same time, the spectre of relativism is exorcized. Hegel retains what amounts to a universal standard for the critical evaluation of societies without resorting to abstract arguments from nature or pure practical reason. Societies or cultures can be evaluated by locating them in the ascending series of dialectically unfolding forms. Significantly, Hegel's philosophy of history never questions the ultimate value of western civilization or modernity. But his dialectical account of the historical development of the West is considerably more nuanced than conventional Enlightenment narratives. In effect, processes of modernization are reconstructed not as a linear 'progress' of uninterrupted development, but an uneven and conflict-ridden series of one-sided but improving manifestations of spirit.

Hegel's dialectical method is also applied in his early and most famous attempt to escape from the central conundrum of Enlightenment epistemology, *The Phenomenology of Mind*. The characteristic approach of the Enlightenment sees knowledge as a medium or instrument by which the subject, understood in Cartesian terms, gains access to an external reality. This approach faces a series of well-known and intractable difficulties. How can we overcome sceptical doubts about the reliability of this instrument or doubts whether the external world exists at all? How can we know that there are other minds? How, Hegel is inclined to add, do we know that this view of knowledge is itself accurate? If we adopt the stance of Cartesian radical doubt, then even this view must itself be questioned. According to Hegel, Kant's transcendental idealism relies on a similar view of mind or 'understanding' as the unavoidable funnel of our experiences of the outside world. The positing of an unknowable 'thing-in-itself' or 'noumenon' is an immediate and, for Hegel, unsatisfactory consequence of this picture of knowledge. Kant is forced into the embarrassing position of postulating the existence of something of which, by definition, we can know nothing at all. Hegel's radical alternative to the inherently problematic approach of modern epistemology is to begin from a position that is genuinely without presuppositions. He proposes 'an examination of consciousness from the inside as it appears to itself – in other words, a phenomenology of mind'.[96] The phenomenology aims to produce 'an exposition of knowledge as a *phenomenon*, as it actually *appears*, not insofar as it conforms to some preconceived model'.[97] Hegel's argument assumes that when the problem of knowledge is put to consciousness, consciousness itself will be able to provide the solution.

Starting with 'sense certainty', the most basic form of sensory consciousness, Hegel shows how consciousness evolves through a series of transformations towards increasingly developed forms. Each form of consciousness (like each stage of history) contains tensions or contradictions, which render it incomplete and unstable, so that it is ultimately bound to give way dialectically to more adequate forms. The scope of Hegel's enterprise is daunting. He not only traces the development of sensory or empirical consciousness but also the emergence of self-consciousness and reason through a variety of forms of moral, religious and philosophical thought. In fact, he manages to compress the history of morality, art, religion and philosophy into the stages of his phenomenology of mind. The ethical community of the modern state, art and religion are identified as stages on the way to 'absolute knowledge'. The dialectic culminates with the self-reflective appropriation of the whole process of spirit's dialectical development by philosophy or, more precisely, Hegel's own philosophy. Philosophy brings spirit to the fullest and most fully rational self-consciousness – a self-consciousness equivalent to the highest possible realization of freedom. Philosophical knowledge is absolute because it is a form of consciousness without further internal contradiction or incompleteness: 'The terminus is at that point where knowledge is no longer compelled to go beyond itself, where it finds its own self, and the notion corresponds to the object and the object to the notion.'[98] In Hegel's terms, our knowledge of the world turns out to be just one moment in the unfolding self-consciousness of spirit in its manifold forms.

The outcome of Hegel's novel approach to philosophy is thus a form of idealism. Starting from the 'mind as it appears to itself' Hegel, perhaps not surprisingly, arrives at a view of reality as a whole as 'Mind as it appears to Itself'. Hegel's position is best understood as a radicalization of Kant's transcendental idealism. If the only world we can know is one which conforms to the form of our understanding, then it is not surprising that that world has features which align it more with mind than with the 'merely material'. However, this does not mean that Hegel denies the existence of external or material reality any more than did Kant's transcendental idealism. Hegel's idealism has the rather different implication that what is rational is real or actual and what is real is rational. As Taylor puts it,

> Hegel's idealism, far from being a denial of external material reality, is the strongest affirmation of it; it not only exists but necessarily exists . . . Absolute idealism means that nothing exists which is not a manifestation of the Idea, that is, of rational necessity. Everything exists for a purpose, that of the coming to be of rational self-consciousness, and this requires that all that exists be the manifestation of rational necessity.[99]

Reality is not 'merely ideal', as Berkeley's empirical idealism had implied, made up of Cartesian or Humean ideas without any underlying substance or materiality. Rather, reality is ideal in the sense that its elements are related in an intellectual or rational rather than a purely mechanical way. As Findlay puts it, Hegel's idealism is essentially teleological: reality can only be understood in terms of its ultimate purpose or goal, the realization of self-conscious spirit. It implies that 'nothing whatever in our world or our thought can have any meaning or function but to serve as a condition for the activities of self-conscious Spirit.'[100] At the limit of philosophical reflection, mind feels at home and at one with the world again.

Hegel's philosophy exerted considerable influence throughout the nineteenth century and beyond, at first mainly in Germany and then more widely. Hegelianism was the dominant philosophical school in Germany until the 1840s and gave rise to an influential movement of British idealists in the latter part of the century, including such philosophers as T. H. Green (1836–82), Bernard Bosanquet (1848–1923) and F. H. Bradley (1846–1924). In Italy Giovanni Gentile (1875–1944) and Benedetto Croce (1866–1952) were both prominent Hegelians. More broadly, the Enlightenment's apotheosis of scientific reason was significantly qualified though not entirely reversed – Hegel also knew a great deal about the natural sciences of his day. Both Hegel's philosophical understanding of history and his historical understanding of morality, art, religion and philosophy as essential stages on the road to absolute knowledge encouraged a whole range of cultural developments and intellectual disciplines. But the Hegelian synthesis was to prove an unstable amalgam and, as a dominant philosophical school, it soon became a popular target of criticism. Ironically, the more faithful expositors of Hegel's ideas have had less impact on the subsequent history of thought than some of his harshest critics. Hegel would be attacked for his idealism and political conservatism, for his excessive rationalism and for the overweening ambition of his philosophical system. In Britain, at the start of the twentieth century, the attacks of Bertrand Russell, G. E. Moore and others revived the empiricist approach and, in effect, founded analytical philosophy. Others, through their distinctive responses to what they were inclined to see as yet another manifestation of the distorted rationality of the Enlightenment, gave rise to a further series of approaches defining a distinctly continental tradition in philosophy.[101]

3. Dialectics of Emancipation: Marx, the Frankfurt School and Habermas

---

Feuerbach, Marx and Marxism

Hegel's philosophy was dominant in Germany at least until the 1840s, but a major division soon emerged, essentially over the question of whether the dialectic of history was substantially complete or incomplete.[1] The so-called 'Old Hegelians' were both politically and philosophically more conservative. They interpreted Hegel's philosophy as a sophisticated reconciliation of religion and philosophy, which overcame the destructive scepticism of the Enlightenment and established a new basis for faith. They saw both the existing political order in Prussia under Frederick William III and its intellectual expression in Hegelian idealism as the culmination of the dialectical unfolding of 'spirit' and, therefore, as moments of the Absolute. On the Old Hegelians' reading, Hegel's *Philosophy of Right* (1821) demonstrated, above all, the obligations of the individual to the community and the state. A variety of currents of continental and British idealism and conservatism continued to work essentially within this philosophical framework.[2] However, Hegel's 'Young Hegelian' successors were to have greater impact both on subsequent continental philosophy and on the world. They interpreted Hegel's writings rather differently, asserting the incompleteness of the historical process and the need for a further turn of the dialectical spiral. Both the existing political order and the prevailing philosophy and religion must be transformed or even abolished. Through radical social and intellectual criticism, philosophers must bring about intellectual and political revolution. Of the Young Hegelians Ludwig Feuerbach, in particular, was to exert long-lasting influence, mainly through his influence on the thought of Karl Marx and Friedrich Engels. From these origins a series of important contributions to continental philosophy can be traced. These range from the ideas of Marx himself and the intellectual and ideological system of historical materialism and Marxism constructed in his name to a variety of critical renewals of Marxian thought, including the 'Western Marxism' of the Frankfurt School and Habermas. Finally, Marxism continues a somewhat subterranean existence as a prime object of postmodernist critique.[3]

The three influences which contributed most to the formation of Marx's ideas were described by his collaborator, Friedrich Engels, as German idealist philosophy, French socialism and English economics.[4] The philosophy Engels had chiefly in mind was, of course, Hegel's, but his contribution was significantly mediated by Ludwig Feuerbach (1804–72).[5] The critique of religion plays the central role in Feuerbach's philosophy, but in a manner strongly influenced by Hegel. Feuerbach's critique of religion, presented in his most famous work *The Essence of Christianity* (1841), is more complex and nuanced than earlier expressions of Enlightenment rationalism. The Enlightenment's 'free thinkers' were mostly hostile to what they saw as the superstitious and unscientific elements of traditional Christianity. They also bemoaned the role played by the Church in shoring up authoritarian regimes in Europe. But reactions to religion took a variety of forms. Relatively few espoused an openly atheist position, even fewer explored the possibly radical, even nihilistic, moral and political implications of unbelief.[6] A more common response was an abstract deism, defended either as a rational religion purified of superstitious and dogmatic elements or, more pragmatically, as the only alternative to the social chaos, which seemed the most likely result of widespread atheism. As Voltaire remarked, 'If God did not exist, it would be necessary to invent Him.'[7]

By contrast, although Feuerbach denies the literal truth of religious belief, he still finds much truth in religion, indeed much truth even in the detail of doctrine and faith, which to the Enlightenment was indefensible. Feuerbach's critique of religion is dialectical, in the sense that he argues for a 'determinate' rather than a merely 'abstract negation' of religion. If religion is false, it is not for that matter worthless. The negation of religion does not leave us with nothing, but rather suggests a positive, determinate outcome – in effect, a higher dialectical stage. According to Feuerbach, although religion is literally false, it is nevertheless deeply rooted in human needs. If religion is not the product of divine revelation but of humanity itself, then it must also reflect human needs and aspirations. Adapting

Hegel's understanding of the process of human self-realization through history, Feuerbach understands the divine as an externalization or 'objectification' of human nature: 'The divine being is nothing else than the human being, or, rather, the human nature purified, freed from the limits of the individual man, made objective – i.e. contemplated and revered as another, a distinct being. All the attributes of the divine nature are, therefore, attributes of the human nature.'[8] God is understood in terms of human qualities of goodness, love or power, but these qualities are considerably amplified: God is perfectly good, all-loving and infinitely powerful. The human qualities projected, in this way, on to an imaginary being are, in the term which comes to play a significant role in Marx's ideas, 'alienated'. In comparison with a perfect and omnipotent God, humanity sees itself in negative terms as lacking the qualities it has alienated to God. Religion 'can enrich God only by impoverishing man'.[9]

Thus, religion must be reinterpreted as a species of human knowledge, albeit not of the divine or supernatural but of humanity itself. Religion is distorted human self-knowledge: 'religion is man's earliest and also indirect form of self-knowledge'.[10] It is an indirect or distorted self-knowledge, because as believers we are ignorant of the true essence of religion as alienation of human capacities. Ignorance is clearly 'fundamental to the peculiar nature of religion', since as soon as we recognize the true meaning of religious faith, we lose it.[11] The same is true of the main function served by religious belief, namely the consolation it offers us in the face of our dependence on nature and fortune, our vulnerability to accident, sickness, suffering and death. Consolation is based on the illusion of a beneficent deity, who gives meaning to suffering and who will reward us in the end with eternal life. Religion solves the problems of human existence, if only in illusion. In Kamenka's words, 'Religion is a dream, a fantasy-picture which expresses man's situation and at the same time provides a fantasy gratification of man's wish to overcome that situation.'[12] Feuerbach, like Hegel, expresses his position in terms of history. He describes a historical progression from primitive polytheism to more advanced monotheistic religions such as Judaism and Christianity. Protestantism, with its emphasis on the inward experience of faith and the direct relationship between the individual and God, comes closest to recognizing as human what less advanced religions idolatrously worship as divine. Still, Feuerbach believes that it is only by means of a thoroughgoing demystification of all religion, that humanity can fully reappropriate its alienated capacities and concentrate on a real rather than merely illusory satisfaction of its needs.

In *The Philosophy of the Future* Feuerbach extends the critique of religious mystification to 'speculative philosophy' or, in other words, Hegelian idealism, as the final obstacle to the undistorted self-knowledge of humanity.[13] He accuses speculative philosophy of having 'torn philosophy out of its natural alliance with science' and 'subjected it to the religious impulse'. The Hegelian reconciliation of religion and philosophy is really the transformation of philosophy into theology (albeit the 'true, rational theology'), and theology is neither philosophy nor religion.[14] In fact, theology is by no means preferable to religion. Religion is the 'real essence' or 'content' which contains distorted truths about humanity, whereas theology is the 'false essence' or 'form' of religion and involves an even more intense and self-conscious alienation of human capacities. Philosophy should not imitate theology in its attempt to produce a systematic reconstruction of the universe in ideas, but should rather be critical and materialist. Idealism, with its abstract and universal notions, remains too close to religion. Like the empiricists, Feuerbach believes that 'the beginning of philosophy is the finite, the determinate, the actual.'[15]

But Feuerbach also recognizes the one-sidedness of previous empiricism. 'Man' is not just a passive receptacle for impressions, but is actively and productively involved in the constitution of his experience. What is more, this involvement is not just the abstract and disembodied activity of a pure self-consciousness or Kantian transcendental ego. It is the practical activity of the whole person, which therefore involves interests, passions, fears and hopes as well as understanding or intellect. Knowledge belongs to 'man' as a sensual, physical being, not as disembodied ego or mind. Nor is knowing the activity of an isolated cognitive subject: it necessarily involves other people. Knowledge requires the intersubjectivity of the 'I–Thou' relationship. As Hegel's philosophy also implied, knowledge is carried by historically situated cultures and societies, rather than by either the monadic or abstract universal subject of Enlightenment epistemology. Knowledge, in sum, is practical – knowledge is social and embodied activity. For Feuerbach, only if humanity successfully overcomes both religion and speculative philosophy can it begin to tackle the problems of its condition in a real rather than an illusory way. In common with other Young Hegelians, this would involve a combination of liberal politics and the application of natural science. Natural science furthers the development of technology and the gradual mastery of the natural world, reducing humanity's vulnerability to sickness, natural disaster and want. Liberal politics would eliminate the remnants of feudal despotism, modernize the institutions of European states and institute a broad programme of democratic reforms.

Both Feuerbach's philosophy and the political liberalism of the

Young Hegelian movement provide important starting points for the earlier thought of Karl Marx (1818–83). However, in two of his earliest works, Marx already expresses dissatisfaction with any exclusively political solution to the alienation of humanity manifest in religion and speculative philosophy.[16] In the first place, the constitutional monarchies of his time clearly did not represent such a solution. In his 'Critique of Hegel's Doctrine of the State', Marx is critical of Hegel's apparent satisfaction with the Prussian state. On the one hand, Hegel shows considerable insight into the defects of contemporary capitalist society. In *The Philosophy of Right* Hegel portrays 'civil society' as an antagonistic sphere of competitive market relations dominated by individual self-interest. This sphere, which had become increasingly important with the rise of capitalism, could not provide a satisfactory basis for a fully human existence. However, according to Hegel's characteristically dialectical solution, the antagonism and conflict of civil society is potentially transcended by the state, properly understood as the complex totality comprising civil society and political sphere. In the modern state, the political sphere represents and mediates the particular sectional interests of civil society. The bureaucracy is a 'universal class' without any selfish interest of its own, which reconciles the otherwise antagonistic atoms of society. However, Marx is far from satisfied with Hegel's solution. It seems obvious to Marx that, far from reconciling the particular interests of civil society, states themselves represent sectional interests. In his later writings, he reinforces this picture of the 'bourgeois' state as vehicle of the interests of the capitalist class.[17]

Again, in his essay 'On the Jewish Question', Marx argues against the sufficiency of any merely political solution. The political emancipation of the Jews would not ensure their full human emancipation, 'because political emancipation is not the complete and consistent form of *human* emancipation'. Even a secular state such as the United States, which guarantees religious toleration, does not resolve the underlying problem. The proliferation there of by no means moderate religious denominations suggests that, despite a liberal constitution, the underlying problem remains and, 'since the existence of religion is the existence of a defect, the source of this defect must be looked for in the nature of the state itself.'[18] Marx, at this stage, seems content to advocate radical democratic reforms as the means of bringing about a real rather than merely illusory transcendence of the opposition between state and civil society. Marx, in McLellan's words, 'expected universal suffrage to inaugurate the reform of civil society by bringing back to it the social essence of man as a communal being that had been stolen from him and transferred to the sphere of constitutions that had no effect on his real life'.[19] Liberal 'rights of man' (including freedom of conscience and the right to property) are inadequate reflections of bourgeois society. They are 'quite simply the rights of the *member of civil society*, i.e. of egoistic man, of man separated from other men and from the community'. On the other hand, he explicitly defends the democratic 'rights of the citizen', whose 'content is *participation* in the *community*'.[20] Electoral reform, however, is advocated not simply for its own sake, but because it will inevitably lead to a more radical resolution of the contradictions of civil society: '*electoral reform* in the *abstract political state* is the equivalent to a demand for its *dissolution* [*Auflösung*] and this in turn implies the *dissolution of civil society*.'[21]

It is not yet made entirely clear what is involved in the dual dissolution of state and civil society. However, even in these early essays Marx refers to the role of private property. Marx's ultimate diagnosis of the pathology of contemporary society as essentially economic was influenced by his reading, in the early 1840s, of French socialists like Fourier and Proudhon, who were fiercely critical of capitalism. But he was also influenced by 'classical economists' such as Ricardo and Smith. Adam Smith (1723–90) provides an early and largely enthusiastic account of 'commercial society'. A system of 'natural liberty', which allows individuals to pursue private interests in their own way, will, through the 'invisible hand' of the market, lead to the greatest possible expansion of the 'wealth of the nation' and so to the ultimate advantage of all. Though every individual 'intends only his own gain', he is 'led by an invisible hand to promote an end which was no part of his intention'.[22] However, even Adam Smith is aware of some of capitalism's defects. The division of labour is responsible for the immense productivity of commercial society, but it also leads to the stunting of workers, who have to perform only a few simple operations and have less and less say in the organization of the work process. Almost inevitably, too, wealth accrues to the owners of capital, leaving the working class in relative poverty. But the classical economists thought that such defects could be remedied without fundamentally transforming capitalism.

Marx and his friend Engels, on the other hand, whose condemnation of the baneful influence of commercial society was far stronger than the criticisms of the classical economists, came to accept the socialist aim of abolishing private property and the capitalist system of production altogether.[23] Only in this way would it be possible to overcome the contradiction between the 'perfect idealism of the state' and the 'perfect materialism of civil society' – the unmediated opposition between an only abstractly universal state and an antago-

nistic realm of individual competition and greed.[24] The socialists revealed that the economic system described by the classical economists is not the only possible one, let alone the most efficient and
rational mode of production. There is nothing inevitable about a
system which exploits workers and makes capitalists rich. By the
same token, once capitalism is defined as the problem, then it is
natural to look for the solution in the working class or 'proletariat'.
But the working class will overthrow capitalism not only in its own
interest, as the exploited class, but in the universal interest of humanity. Not only is the proletariat systematically excluded from the benefits of capitalism, but through its future role in a socialist revolution
it will liberate humanity from its alienated condition. As Marx says in
the *Economic and Philosophical Manuscripts* of 1844, the proletariat
is a revolutionary agent, 'not because it is only a question of their
emancipation, but because in their emancipation is contained universal human emancipation'.[25] The proletariat is the universal class
Hegel had mistakenly identified as the bureaucracy. Significantly,
Marx sees capitalism not just as the source of much human suffering
or strictly economic exploitation, but as the root cause of a deeper
and more far-reaching alienation. Under capitalism 'man' is es-
tranged or alienated from his true nature, or what Marx calls 'species
being'. Human species being is realized through labour understood as
'the practical creation of an *objective world*, the *fashioning* of inor-
ganic nature'.[26] The labour of the worker under capitalism is alienated in at least four ways. Workers are alienated from the products of
their labour, which accrue to the capitalist; from the act of production, which they no longer control; from labour, as the medium for
the expression of their species being as creative producers; and, finally, from other men, as a result of the antagonistic, atomized relationships of capitalist civil society.[27]

Marx's theory of alienation is, in fact, a direct application of his
materialist critique of Hegelian idealism, which transforms the dialectic of spirit or ideas into a materialist dialectic of labour and class
struggle. Marx saw great value in Hegel's philosophy. He shares
Hegel's disdain for the empiricists, the 'contemplative' materialists of
the Enlightenment, who 'left out the subjective, creative side of
man's interaction with nature'.[28] But he is also clearly inspired by
Feuerbach's critique of Hegel, with its emphasis on the intersubjective and embodied basis of human knowledge. In effect Marx combines Feuerbach's version of materialism with Hegel's historical
account of the dialectical progression of forms of knowledge. The
result transposes the dialectic to an explicitly social and embodied
context. In effect, the universal and eternal categories of the Kantian

transcendental subject are reinterpreted in terms of historically un-folding social forms. Our understanding of reality, what we take to be nature at a particular stage of our development, reflects the forms of social organization which prevail at that time:

> [Feuerbach] does not see how the sensuous world around him is, not a thing given direct from all eternity, remaining ever the same, but the product of industry and of the state of society; and, indeed, in the sense that it is an historical product, the result of the activity of a whole succes-sion of generations, each standing on the shoulders of the preceding one, developing its industry and its intercourse, modifying its social system according to the changed needs.[29]

It is not, as Hegel's philosophy had suggested, ideas which represent the essence of a particular epoch. Rather it is our historically pro-duced 'social being' which determines our ideas or consciousness. The 'human essence' is neither the abstract individual or disembod-ied subject of the Enlightenment nor the historically unfolding 'spirit' of Hegel, but 'the ensemble of the social relations'.[30] According to his own description Marx 'puts Hegel back on his feet', replacing the idealist dialectic of spirit with a materialist dialectic of work or labour.

Marx's materialist critique of Hegel corresponds to a materialist conception of history. Labour, as the true essence of humanity, is the activity through which humanity creates its own nature in a series of historical stages, which are the various ways human societies have organized the process of production. The meaning of history is not the coming to self-consciousness of absolute spirit, but the dialectical unfolding of a series of 'modes of production'. Like Rousseau in the 'Discourse on Inequality', Marx proposes a theory of history in terms of the evolving relationship between human beings and nature through which human beings must satisfy their material needs: 'life involves before everything else eating and drinking, a habitation, clothing and many other things. The first historical act is thus the production of the means to satisfy these needs, the production of material life itself.'[31] Marx describes the development of 'productive forces' (methods or techniques of production, technology, human resources and so on) and contradictions which result between forces and 'relations of production' (the forms of property ownership which define a particular economic system as feudalism, capitalism, commu-nism etc.). The relations of production within a particular economic system imply a particular division between social classes, essentially between those owning or controlling the means of production and those excluded from ownership and control. Contradictions between forces and relations of production are expressed in the form of class struggle. History as a whole is driven, not by the contradictions within particular ideas or worldviews, but by the conflict between social classes. This understanding of class struggle transposes into material-ist mode an important motif from Hegel's *The Phenomenology of Mind*, namely the dialectic of 'lordship and bondage'.[32]

In fact, according to this materialist conception of history the development of all aspects of human life, including ideas, 'all the different theoretical products and forms of consciousness, religion, philosophy, ethics, etc. etc.' are to be explained in terms of the 'real process of production'.[33] Marx's remarks on 'ideology' suggest that the development of ideas is determined by relationships of power deriving from the mode of production rather than the reverse:

> The ideas of the ruling class are in every epoch the ruling ideas, i.e. the class which is the ruling material force of society, is at the same time its ruling intellectual force. The class which has the means of material produc-tion at its disposal, has control at the same time over the means of mental production, so that thereby, generally speaking, the ideas of those who lack the means of mental production are subject to it.[34]

The materialist conception of history undermines 'idealist' explana-tions of historical change in terms of new ideas, great individuals or the 'spirit of the time' (*Zeitgeist*). It follows that, if the true basis of history is materialist, then neither philosophical critique nor moral and political exhortation are likely to bring about the next dialectical stage of history. Marx attacked the position of the Young Hegelians, who sought change through 'mental criticism'. Change will only come about as a result of developments at the level of the mode of produc-tion – 'not criticism but revolution is the driving force of history.'[35] Revolution will only come about, if the social conditions are already 'pregnant' with the new social order.

Thus, while Marx agreed in broad outline with the political goals of the French and English socialists, both he and Engels were highly critical of what they dubbed 'utopian socialism', which they thought was as little likely to bring about genuine social change as the meas-ures proposed by the likes of Adam Smith. These socialists fail to develop clear ideas about the actual means, including potential agents, of social transformation, relying instead on persuasion and small-scale utopian experiments. Although the ideals of the utopian socialists appealed to certain groups of workers, especially the skilled artisans who were being displaced by new machinery and the factory system, these groups were relatively small and declining in number. Their interests were not the same as those of the growing number of unskilled workers in the newly mechanized industries, who were taking their place. Marx is also contemptuous of any socialist doctrine which advocates equality as a simple levelling down of available resources, an approach which under conditions existing at the time could only universalize deprivation and need. Communism will only become possible with the help of the enormous productivity of capitalism, which has the power to eliminate material scarcity altogether.

The decisive implication of Marx and Engels's 'scientific socialism' is that communism cannot be achieved by halting or reversing the course of capitalist economic development, but only by bringing that development to completion. Marx's attitude to capitalism and the 'bourgeoisie' is accordingly ambivalent or 'dialectical'. He is unstinting in his condemnation of capitalism as an intensification of class conflict, bringing misery and alienation. Capitalism is a system of exploitation, which extracts wealth from workers for the sake of the capitalists. Even the abolition of capitalism will, in the short term, allow only the realization of the socialist principle of economic justice, that each should be rewarded according to her or his contribution to the social product, a principle which 'tacitly recognizes unequal individual endowment and thus productive capacity of the worker as natural privileges' and therefore remains *a right of inequality, in its content, like every right*.[36] Only the dynamic productivity of capitalist society, the fact that 'the bourgeoisie cannot exist without constantly revolutionizing the instruments of production', offers the prospect of a society in which everyone can have whatever they need.[37] For the first time goods will be distributed according to the communist principle, 'From each according to his ability, to each according to his needs!'[38] Equally, the dynamic expansionism of the capitalist market promises to draw other nations into an ultimately progressive worldwide transformation: 'The bourgeoisie, by the rapid improvement of all instruments of production, by the immensely facilitated means of communications, draws all, even the most barbarian, nations into civilization . . . it compels them to introduce what it calls civilization into their midst, i.e., to become bourgeois themselves.'[39] Overall, whereas utopian socialists simply oppose capitalism, both Marx and Engels see it, in effect, as a necessary evil. Capitalism's successor can only come about as a result of the complete development of capitalism. The vicissitudes of history, like the stages in the Hegelian dialectic, cannot be avoided simply by means of the good intentions of an enlightened politics.

Marx's later work focuses on the economic and sociological analysis of capitalism.[40] It is designed to uncover tendencies which might lead to the collapse of capitalism. The industrial revolution had already physically assembled large bodies of workers in huge factories and sprawling industrial cities. The mechanization of production had destroyed the special status of skilled artisans, such as the hand-loom weavers of the Luddite rebellions, and further automation seemed destined to lead to further levelling and homogenization. Trade unions were signs of the stirring self-consciousness and activism of the working class. Marx's economic theory suggests that capitalism will eventually succumb to contradictions of its own making. His 'labour theory of value' analyses capitalist exploitation as the extraction of 'surplus value' from workers. Wages only compensate workers for the value of their labour power (their capacity to labour), which is equivalent to the value of the commodities required to reproduce it – essentially, 'subsistence' or resources sufficient to keep workers alive. The difference between this value and the value of the actual labour workers can be made to perform is the ultimate source of 'surplus value' or profit. This theory implies that workers' wages will always tend to a subsistence level. A further factor, which Marx thinks will tend to reduce wages, is the rising 'organic composition of capital'. The proportion of 'fixed capital' (e.g. plant and machinery) rises, and the proportion of 'variable capital' (or labour) declines, with the seemingly irreversible trend toward greater mechanization and automation. Since labour rather than fixed capital is the source of profit, there must be a tendency for the rate of profit to fall, although this tendency may be counteracted by other tendencies. If the rate of profit falls, capitalists will be driven to increase the rate of exploitation by intensifying the pace of production or by reducing wages. The resulting 'pauperization of the proletariat' can only encourage a further escalation of class struggle. The self-consciousness and purpose of the proletariat as a class is all the more likely to come about as divisions between workers disappear. A united, impoverished and self-conscious working class can hardly fail to bring about communist revolution and the end of class society. Marx's undoubted revolutionary optimism would later be misinterpreted as a firm prediction of the inevitability of communist revolution.

Marx's critical appropriation of German idealist philosophy, classical economics and English and French socialism, produced an explosive amalgam of abstract intellectual speculation and political engagement. In his famously concise 'Theses on Feuerbach', Marx distinguishes his conception of materialism from that of the Enlightenment, which even Feuerbach does not leave completely behind. Whereas the 'old' materialism is 'the contemplation of single individuals and of civil society', the standpoint of the 'new' materialism is 'human society, or social humanity', which inevitably refers to the

future form of social existence, communism. The critique of religion
and philosophy leads ineluctably to the commitment to change existing society. In other words, in Marx's hands philosophy is inseparable
from political action. Most famously, until now 'The philosophers
have only *interpreted* the world, in various ways; the point is to *change*
it.'[41] This marrying of 'theory' and 'practice' tied Marx's ideas to
historical and political events in a novel way. But partly as a result,
the determining factor in the ultimate fate of these ideas would be the
fashioning, from Marx's diverse, fertile and not always consistent
writings, of Marxism as a systematic doctrine and even dogma –
Marxism as orthodoxy. Marx's critical 'surpassing' or 'transcending'
of philosophy was taken as unequivocal farewell, as sufficient prelude
to the down-to-earth and ultimately more useful pursuits of politics
and science. Marxism was the basis for a scientific politics without metaphysical illusions or moral pretensions, a politics without
philosophy.[42]

Two factors played a decisive role in the fate of Marxism as orthodoxy. In the first place, when Marx died in 1883 his long-time collaborator and financial supporter Friedrich Engels (1820–95) was left to
edit, interpret and popularize his friend's thought. A second factor
was that Engels's role coincided with the growing political influence
of Marx's ideas, which were 'beginning to become the official doctrine of a mass political movement'.[43] Both factors served to divert
attention from the complexities and tensions in Marx's own writings,
to precipitate the more systematic but somewhat one-dimensional
version of his thought dubbed 'the materialist conception of history',
later 'historical materialism'. This phrase, as Carver puts it, 'brought
Marxism into existence'.[44] Engels's contribution reflected his own
scientific and philosophical interests. In particular, Engels had considerable sympathy with the positivist climate of nineteenth-century
thought. Positivists such as Comte and Spencer restated the empiricist position in historical terms. Natural science is seen as the most
advanced form of human knowledge, supplanting both religion and
speculative philosophy.[45] Engels was also greatly influenced by recent
developments in the natural sciences, such as Darwin's theory of
natural selection, and even offered his own account of 'The part
played by labour in the transition from ape to man'. He praises
Darwin's theory in supposedly Hegelian terms as a 'grandiose' attempt to 'demonstrate historical evolution in Nature', despite its non-
dialectical method.[46]

By implication, historical materialism applies a similar method to
the evolution of society. In his widely read popularizations of Marx's
ideas, Engels exaggerates the similarities between Marxian political

economy and explicitly deterministic theories in natural science, stressing its rigorous grasp of the 'laws of motion' of capitalism and its ability to predict the outcome of historical processes of transformation. The Marxian dialectic is seen as the general science of the development of nature, human society, and thought. In fact, Engels sometimes also presents the materialist conception of history as a critical tool, revealing the inadequacy and one-sidedness of idealistic explanation, rather than as the rigidly mechanistic model of historical change that it would become. Economic determinism is qualified by the admission that material causes assert themselves 'only in the last resort': 'The economic situation is the basis, but the various elements of superstructure also exercise their influence upon the course of the historical struggle and in many cases preponderate in determining their form. There is an interaction of all these elements.'[47] Nevertheless, Engels's overall emphasis prepared the ground for further simplification of Marx's ideas, further assimilation to positivist principles. The seal was set on the emergence of Marxism as systematic but intellectually infertile doctrine by the central role it came to play in the politics of the working class.

From the start, however, the Marxist project was beset with difficulties. These have ranged from the non-occurrence of revolution in the West and the sustained efforts by capitalist powers to undermine communism to the degeneration and now collapse of socialist revolution in the East. On the one hand, revolution failed to occur in the most economically developed capitalist societies where, on Marxist assumptions, it was most to be expected.[48] Where revolutions were successful, the results have been, to say the least, disappointing. From the beginning they were attacked by western powers. With the events of 1989 and after, it is no longer obvious that Marxism has any contemporary historical significance. With the fall from power of the communist parties of the Soviet Union and eastern Europe, the break-up of the former 'evil empire' of the Soviet Union and the beleaguered state of the regimes in Cuba, Albania and North Korea, communist China is the only significant survivor – and then only by dint of substantial market reforms. Even the social democratic parties of many western countries are in ideological retreat, with major elements of their programmes in question. So it is perhaps not surprising that essays abound on the historic defeat of communism, the bankruptcy of social democracy and, on the other side, the apparent triumph of liberalism and democracy. Even the end of history has been enthusiastically proclaimed, though not all are convinced.[49]

The continuing relevance of the ideologies of communism and social democracy is an issue beyond the scope of this book. But

despite the fact that the organized workers' movement has, if anything, shown signs of a deficiency rather than an excess of philosophy,
the practical problems and failures of the socialist project have given
rise to some considerable contributions to continental philosophy. A
number of thinkers have made significant contributions to Marxist
theory. Although their relative importance is controversial, such
figures as Karl Kautsky, Rosa Luxemburg and Antonio Gramsci
deserve to be mentioned. Arguably, though, their importance is not
strictly philosophical. On the other hand, a more philosophical renewal of Marxism has been attempted. What has come to be known
as 'Western Marxism' assumes a variety of forms. Louis Althusser's
'structuralist' Marxism was influenced by Spinoza as well as Lenin.
The existentialist Jean-Paul Sartre, who had a complex relationship
with the French Communist Party, also left his mark. Sartre and
Althusser represent opposing 'humanist' and 'anti-humanist' approaches to Marxism.[50] But arguably the most comprehensive and
still influential body of thought has been produced by the Frankfurt
School and its contemporary representative, Jürgen Habermas.

The Critical Theory of the Frankfurt School

For a significant tradition of western Marxists the practical failures
and failed successes of revolutionary Marxism reflect inadequacies in
the theory of historical materialism itself. The Frankfurt School was
a group of theorists, originally associated with the Frankfurt Institute
for Social Research, who sought to rescue the valuable kernel of
Marx's theory from a rigid, increasingly hollow and ideological doctrine. In the spirit of the Marxian and Hegelian insight into the
historically situated nature of thought, they propose a renewal of
Marxism in the light of contemporary conditions and experience.
This renewal involves a threefold return – to Hegel, to the earlier and
more Hegelian Marx and to philosophy. The return to the more
Hegelian ideas of the early Marx was reinforced by the belated
publication of the *German Ideology* and, in 1932, of Marx's *Economic and Philosophical Manuscripts* (1844).[51] Where orthodox Marxism
understands Marx's materialist turn as the straightforward replace-
ment of philosophy by science and revolutionary practice, theorists
like Theodor Adorno (1903–69), Max Horkheimer (1895–1973) and
Herbert Marcuse (1898–1979) reclaim a central role for philosophy.
Marx's critique of philosophy was not anti-philosophical. On the
contrary, as Adorno and Horkheimer remark of their own account of

the dialectic of Enlightenment, 'It is a critique of philosophy, and therefore refuses to abandon philosophy.'[52] Central to their account is an awareness of the ambivalent legacy of modernity. They share Hegel's fears about the abstract rationalism of Kant and the Enlightenment. They also echo Marx's materialist retort to Hegel, that the logic of the historical process cannot be a predominantly intellectual or conceptual one. They regard capitalism as an important symptom of the pathology of modernity. However, the Frankfurt School sees the degeneration of Marx's ideas into the historical materialism of orthodox Marxism as another expression of the same pathology. Only a whole-hearted return to philosophical critique promises escape from the fateful dialectic of Enlightenment.

The Institute for Social Research was founded in Frankfurt in 1923 under Carl Grünberg, though the man who was director from 1930, Max Horkheimer, had a more lasting impact on its work.[53] The historical context of the Frankfurt School's formation was also to mark its future theoretical orientation. In Germany the thirties saw the rise to power of the national socialists under Hitler and the enforced migration of the Frankfurt Institute to Geneva in 1933 and then, in 1935, to the United States. Traces of the trauma of these years can be detected in much of their later work. Fascism was a dramatic demonstration that the transition to socialism and communism was far from imminent in the West. The degree of popular support for fascism, which included significant elements of the working class, cast doubt on Marx's casting of the proletariat as agent of universal emancipation. In addition, there was evidence of a structural transformation of capitalism, which had not been anticipated by Marx. This became particularly clear with the gradual recovery from the Great Depression of the thirties, which had seemed to herald the final collapse of capitalism predicted by Marx. Whether in the 'totalitarian' guise of fascism or in the more democratically accountable form of the New Deal in the USA, a mixture of Keynesian economics and neo-corporatism, what Frankfurt theorists variously termed 'monopoly' or 'state' capitalism demonstrated an unforeseen ability, by means of more extensive state intervention, to overcome the limitations of nineteenth-century liberal capitalism.[54]

There were also obvious similarities between the methods of propaganda pioneered by the national socialists and the burgeoning 'culture industries' of the western democracies. Other developments in the West cast further doubt on Marxist assumptions about the course of capitalist development. After the Second World War, under the relatively benign conditions of the long economic boom, the working classes of the western capitalist democracies appeared increasingly integrated and pacified. Working-class political activism was mostly channelled into either social democracy or trade unionism. As Horkheimer wrote in 1968, 'The revolutionary thrust of the proletariat has long since become realistic action within the framework of society.'[55] The 'affluent society' contradicted Marx's pessimistic predictions about the falling rate of profit and inevitable impoverishment of the working class. The experience of Soviet Marxism after the Bolshevik revolution, finally, demonstrated the bankruptcy of orthodox Marxism. Marxist-Leninist revolution did not ensure safe passage to communist utopia. The similarities between bureaucratic state socialism and the almost equally administered monopoly or state capitalism of the West were more striking than the differences.[56]

In their response to these historical developments the Frankfurt School theorists held on, at times desperately, to the politically engaged role of theory, encapsulated in Marx's famous remark that whereas until now 'philosophers have only *interpreted* the world, in various ways; the point is to *change* it.'[57] Social theorists should do more than simply describe or explain. They should provide a diagnosis of the faults of existing society and, beyond that, take part in the struggle for its transformation in the interest of the oppressed and exploited. At the same time they were dismayed by the actual development of Marxism as orthodoxy and dogma. The central task facing Frankfurt theorists, then, was the liberation of critical thought from the strait-jacket of historical materialism. In pursuing this goal they took their cue from Georg Lukács, who had argued that the commitment to Marx's critical *method* was more important than any of the particular *contents* of Marxism.[58] Marxism should be capable of self-criticism, capable of applying its critical method to itself. The increasing dogmatism of the revolutionary communist movement also belied Marx's own Hegelian insight into the social and historical constitution of thought. Engaged theory must develop and change in response to important social transformations which had occurred since the 1840s.

Many of the specific claims of Marxist orthodoxy had become vulnerable. Predictions about the falling rate of profit, the tendency for the proletariat to become impoverished and the imminence of socialist revolution in the West were no longer plausible.[59] Rather than being reduced to a level of uniform poverty, the industrial proletariat was divided by new hierarchies of status and skill. A 'new middle class' of technically skilled and professional workers had emerged.[60] Reformist social democratic politics and trade unionism looked more like long-term expressions of working-class activism than the first faltering steps of a still infantile revolutionary will, as they had been portrayed by the early Lenin.[61] But it was not the incorrectness of some of historical materialism's central sociological and economic claims (which, in any case, remain the object of considerable debate), but the degeneration of Marx's critical method which was most disturbing. Above all, it was the dogmatic petrification of the method, which made the revision of the specific claims so difficult. The movement had inherited the wise words of its founding father rather than his critical intellect and, contrary to the hopes of a genuinely scientific socialism, vehemently expunged all heresy. In fact, of course, a number of Marxist theorists continued to investigate the new historical reality in a critical spirit, including Karl Korsch, Rosa Luxemburg, Antonio Gramsci and Ernst Bloch. For the theorists who have become known as the Frankfurt School, the only possible response to a foreclosing of critical reflection in the name of science is the reinvention of Marx's critical method as 'critical theory'. An important instance of this method is Marx's critique of classical political economy. Economists like Adam Smith and Ricardo describe capitalism as if it were a natural system. However, what they describe is 'false nature', because capitalism is a socially and historically contingent mode of production, rather than something timelessly natural and rational, which western society happened to stumble upon. Describing capitalism as a natural system conceals, even if unintentionally, the possible transition to socialism and communism. Classical political economy is ideological rather than scientific, because despite its veneer of scientific objectivity it serves the sectional interests of the bourgeoisie rather than humanity as a whole. It closes off avenues of social development, which would emancipate the working class.

Marx's critique of political economy is taken as the model for a more general critique of 'positivism'. This term was first used by Auguste Comte (1798–1857) to refer approvingly to humanity's mature intellectual stage of 'positive or *scientific* understanding, based only on observable facts and the relations between them and the laws discoverable from observing them'.[62] The positive stage, effectively the Enlightenment seen from an empiricist point of view, follows more primitive 'theological' and 'metaphysical' stages of thought. Comte also coined the term 'sociology', and it is more particularly the application of 'positive' scientific methods to the study of human societies, which is usually described as positivism. A century earlier than Comte, Hume advocated the 'application of experimental philosophy to moral subjects' in order to lay the 'science of man' on the 'solid foundation' of 'experience and observation'.[63] Geuss provides a workable definition of positivism: 'In Frankfurt usage a "positivist" is a person who holds: (a) that an empiricist account of natural science is adequate, and (b) that all cognition must have essentially the same cognitive structure as natural science.'[64] By contrast, Frankfurt theorists emphatically resist the application of scientific method to human subjects as tantamount to the denial of human potentialities and freedom. By using natural scientific method to uncover laws of economy or society, positivist social theory portrays the regularities of oppressive societies as facts, which can only be accepted with resignation. To theorize alterable social relations as 'second nature' is to obscure possible alternatives to present society. In what came to be known as the 'positivism dispute' Adorno and Horkheimer take issue with any social theory which, under cover of scientific objectivity, effectively conspires with the existing order. In so far as contemporary social science is modelled on the methods and assumptions of natural science, it is, in their terms, a species of 'traditional' as opposed to critical theory.[65]

But the critique of positivism is directed, in the first place, against the positivist petrification of Marx's ideas. The notion that a deterministic science of society can identify 'iron laws' of capitalism and predict its imminent collapse is identified as an important source of the defects of both Stalinism in the East and the communist parties loyal to Stalinism in the West.[66] The scientific status of historical materialism insulates party intellectuals and leaders from 'uninformed' criticism. By turning moral or political issues into questions of theoretical or technical expertise, it justifies the 'democratic centralism' of the Bolshevik party. Surely decisions should be taken by those with a sophisticated knowledge of Marxist theory rather than ordinary workers and peasants? In this way, positivism paves the way for the bureaucratic authoritarianism of Soviet Marxism.[67] In some quarters, crudely deterministic versions of the primacy of the economic in the explanation of social change led to the 'economistic' belief in the centrality and sufficiency of struggles at the site of production as well as indifference to broader moral and political activism, considered merely utopian. In more 'voluntarist' style, Leninism exploits the scientific authority of the revolutionary activist, in order to underwrite an energetically political but no less authoritarian vanguardism. Expedient violations of 'bourgeois morality' can be excused, because there need be no fear that the scientifically certified advance towards communism will ever be diverted from its predetermined goal by the corruption of the revolutionary movement.[68]

From the point of view of Frankfurt theorists, therefore, Marx and Engels's critique of the utopian socialism of Owen, Fourier and Saint-Simon is distinctly ambivalent. Although Marx rightly emphasizes the importance of relating socialist ideals both to current social and historical conditions and to potential revolutionary agents, the outright rejection of utopian thought by subsequent Marxists was a mistake. The exploration of an alternative moral vision and the anticipation or 'prefiguration' of more emancipated social relations in experimental communities were valuable aspects of utopian socialism that were regrettably absent from the revolutionary communist tradition. A genuinely critical theory must identify human potentialities neglected within the existing social order, and so uncover the 'negative' moment of existing reality – that moment, in other words, which promises further dialectical transformation. Needless to say, it is this negative dimension of present society which is invisible to positive science. Critical theory requires more than the limited resources of the one-sided rationality of Enlightenment science. Utopian political thought, on the other hand, is an example of negative or critical thinking, if only in embryonic form, since it is insufficiently practical.

Even 'bourgeois' philosophy and art hold out a utopian promise which, though unfulfilled, preserves the 'general demand for human liberation'.[69] In an alienated society, suppressed human possibilities are expressed, albeit in politically innocent form, in works of art and in idealist philosophy. Beauty is the foretaste of a more harmonious existence. The dreams and fantasies of romanticism encode, and so protect, latent human aspirations and needs. In Marcuse's terms, the harmony, proportion and beauty of classical art is 'the sensuous appearance of the idea of freedom', and he advocates a 'permanent aesthetic subversion' of the status quo.[70] Art and art theory, in other words, are politically charged. Some of Adorno's most important works are in the area of aesthetics and musicology.[71] In effect, their account runs parallel to Feuerbach's demystification of religion and speculative philosophy as symptoms of a traumatized humanity, which contain hidden truth. And so, according to Herbert Marcuse, only a critical theory imbued with fantasy can fulfil its emancipatory potential: 'Without phantasy, all philosophical knowledge remains in the grip of the present or the past and severed from the future, which is the only link between philosophy and the real history of mankind.'[72] Critical theory should decode and so liberate the utopian potential of religion, art and philosophy, rather than seek, in positivist spirit, to certify them as irrational and unscientific.[73]

Both the Frankfurt School's emphasis on fantasy and imagination and its rejection of positivist or 'traditional' theory raise, with some urgency, the question of the epistemological grounding of critical theory. Horkheimer admits that critical theory, being directed to the future rather than based on the present and the past, 'appears, to prevailing modes of thought, to be subjective and speculative, one-sided and useless'.[74] This situation is made worse by loss of faith in the proletariat as privileged epistemological subject – 'even the situation of the proletariat is, in this society, no guarantee of correct knowledge.'[75] In their constructive attempts to ground critical theory, members of the Frankfurt School reveal their debt to the Hegelian dialectic but also their substantial departures from it. Horkheimer rejects Hegel's philosophy of history, the claim to understand history as a totality. Not only, as Marx and the Young Hegelians had complained, is the dialectic of history not yet complete, but we cannot regard the dialectic as 'closed' in the sense of having a foreseeable and final outcome.[76] Adorno resists all such attempts to 'represent the totality' as evidence of a 'desire to control the world'. He denies that there can be any final truth or even any assurance of a 'linear path from ignorance to knowledge'.[77] We should seek to avoid all 'hypostasis of mind', caused by speculative and positivist systems of thought.[78] The nineteenth-century German philosopher Friedrich Nietzsche, with his suspicion of all systematic thought, foundationalist epistemology, metaphysical systems and claims to absolute truth, was a significant source of these critical, anti-metaphysical themes.[79] The aphoristic style of many of Adorno's writings, as well as his belief that only such a style could resist recuperation by the system, also betrays the influence of Nietzsche. On the other hand, Frankfurt theorists seek to rebut charges of relativism by means of a continuing commitment to the dialectic, albeit one that is not closed and so not knowable in advance as a totality. The outcome of critique is not the blank rejection or 'abstract negation' of a particular position, but rather its 'determinate negation'. Through 'internal' or 'immanent' critique, the rejection of one position leads dialectically to an alternative position, which is presumed to incorporate the strengths whilst eliminating the inadequacies of the previous position. In this way a limited or one-sided perspective is replaced by a more complete one. An important model of immanent critique is Marx's demonstration of the discrepancy between bourgeois ideals of universal liberty and justice and the actual exploitation and injustice of capitalist society. On this interpretation, socialism promises to realize these values concretely rather than merely abstractly. In this sense critical theory retains a residue of faith in the dialectic. The determinate outcome of critique is presumed to be an advance towards a more emancipated society.

The Frankfurt theorists' anti-positivist critical theory, then, is embedded in a more sceptical philosophy of history, one which refrains both from the speculative ambitions of Hegelian philosophy and the predictive optimism of historical materialism. In their more modest attempts to tell the story of a highly ambivalent 'dialectic of Enlightenment' they were again influenced by Nietzsche. His critical assessment of the Enlightenment and the claims of modern scientific reason is reflected in their own 'primal history of a subjectivity that wrests itself free from the power of mythic forces'.[80] At first sight, Enlightenment rationalism is a simple victory of reason over all superstition and mythological thinking: 'The disenchantment of the world is the extirpation of animism.'[81] In fact, however, myth and enlightenment are interdependent. As Held puts it, 'myth is already enlightenment; and enlightenment reverts to mythology.'[82] On the one hand, myths and magic are already attempts to gain control over a dangerous and capricious natural world. Humanity's instrumental relationship to the natural world is not invented, only elaborated and intensified, with modern natural science. On the other hand, the victory of scientific rationality over superstition and myth is only partial and is won at a cost. Enlightenment becomes 'engulfed in mythology'.[83] At the same time as it liberates us from the animistic terrors and uncertainties of nature, scientific reason offers only a diminished and partial understanding of nature as an object to be manipulated and controlled: 'What men want to learn from nature is how to use it in order wholly to dominate it and other men', and 'Men pay for the increase of their power with alienation from that over which they exercise their power.'[84] Positivist reason is even dogmatic, because it assumes that nature can be understood in terms of quantitative categories – 'the process is always decided from the start . . . Mathematical procedure became, so to speak, the ritual of thinking.'[85]

In its attitude to society, on the other hand, the Enlightenment positivistically treats the existing order as everlasting. And so, to the disenchantment of nature there corresponds a 'sacralization of reality'. The extension of scientific reason to humanity's self-understanding comes at the cost of an 'introversion of sacrifice', a corresponding loss of our own humanity. An instrumental logic, initially applied to a world of objects, is extended to relations between persons, reducing them to the status of things. As a result, human relationships are impoverished and our access to a full, subjective life impaired. With capitalism, an application of instrumental rationality, human beings are subjected to a 'technical apparatus' originally designed to serve them. As Habermas puts it, 'The permanent sign of enlightenment is domination over an objectified external nature and a repressed internal nature.'[86] There is a further dialectical sting to this analysis. Suppressed 'internal nature' is always threatening to erupt destructively into modern life. National socialism, with its unique combination of organizational efficiency and atavistic barbarism, demonstrates with particular ferocity the interdependence of myth and rationality characteristic of modernity. In this sense, the Marquis de Sade's celebration of cruelty and unbridled passion is just an honest presentation of the moral implications of Enlightenment reason. De Sade's fantasies are a clear-sighted anticipation of totalitarian order, which 'gives full rein to calculation and abides by science as such', and whose 'canon is its own brutal efficiency'.[87]

The Frankfurt School's account of modernity and Enlightenment is deeply indebted to the sociologist, Max Weber (1864–1920). It is influenced, in particular, by his account of the rationalization of society.[88] Weber sees both capitalism and bureaucracy as instances of more general processes of rationalization characteristic of modern civilization. With bureaucracy the state organizes efficient administrative means for the realization of particular ends, in the same way that capitalism reorganizes productive resources for profit. However, both bureaucracy and capitalism represent only a one-sided, instrumental rationality. They rationalize society only in the sense of 'formal' rationality, which concerns the selection of efficient means for given ends. Rationalization is indifferent to the 'substantive' rationality of ends, the exercise of reason in the evaluation of the ultimate goals of human activity.[89] So the formal or instrumental rationalization of society is compatible with the occurrence of substantively irrational outcomes. States can be efficiently organized to realize undesirable or even obnoxious ends. Moreover, rationalization dislodges traditional religions and worldviews, offering little in return for a disenchanted world bereft of meaning. The one-sided rationalization of society confines human beings to an alienated and bureaucratically regulated 'iron cage'. But whereas Weber sees the process of rationalization as inevitable, Frankfurt theorists insist on searching for a way out of the iron cage.

In the Frankfurt School's analyses of contemporary society a significant role is also played by the psychoanalytic theories of Sigmund Freud (1856–1939). Freud's psychological explanations of the formation of character and desire promised to fill a gap in Marxism, for example by helping to explain the proletariat's considerable loyalty to an exploitative capitalist society. Freud's ideas, like Weber's, were again given an optimistic twist. Whereas Freud saw the frequent neuroses and occasional psychoses of *fin de siècle* Vienna as symptoms of an inevitable sacrifice of pleasure, or 'eros', for the sake of 'civilization', Frankfurt theorists blame rationalization and hold out the hope of a less repressed society.[90] Thus, Marcuse reckons the costs of modern society in terms of a repression of 'eros', which is now superfluous.[91] Just as the neurotic adult unconsciously repeats patterns of behaviour fixed by childhood trauma, so the members of contemporary society behave in ways more appropriate to the scarcities of the past. Affluent western societies impose a level of self-denial, a curtailing of the 'polymorphous perversity' of the 'pleasure principle' which is no longer necessary in an era of unprecedented productive potential. The pathological work ethic and equally obsessive and dutiful consumerism of the United States are expressions of a redundant but pathologically fixed 'performance principle'. But in contrast to Freud, Marcuse expects revolutionary release from the 'surplus repression' of an obsolete system. Written in the conformist 1950s in the United States, Marcuse's analysis would be taken up with enthusiasm in the 'permissive' decade of sexual revolution that was to follow.

Perhaps most influential have been the Frankfurt School studies of the 'culture industry'. In contrast to the high art or 'intellectual culture' of the bourgeoisie, which potentially subverts the existing order, the culture industry reinforces conformity. Popular or 'material' culture has been transformed by its integration with the capitalist mode of production. Walter Benjamin's (1892–1940) classic essay, 'The Work of Art in the Age of Mechanical Reproduction', sees progressive potential in the spread of mechanization and mass production to the area of culture. Drawing his examples mainly from photography, printing and film, Benjamin claims that the mechanical reproducibility of cultural artefacts destroys the magical, almost sacred 'aura' of works of high culture, detaching them from ritual and tradition: 'that which withers in the age of mechanical reproduction is the aura of the work of art.'[92] Benjamin associates this development with the 'increasing significance of the masses in contemporary life' with their 'sense of the universal equality of things' and sees it as potentially progressive:[93] 'Mechanical reproduction of art changes the reaction of the masses toward art. The reactionary attitude toward a Picasso painting changes into the progressive reaction toward a Chaplin movie.'[94] Referring to the role of ritual and propaganda in 1930s Germany, he claims that the insistence on the autonomy of art or 'art for art's sake' is 'consummated' with the 'introduction of aesthetics into political life' by fascism. The 'post-auratic' work of art, on the other hand, potentially connects with politics in a different way and 'Communism responds by politicizing art.'[95] Art should serve the revolution, though not by faithfully (and tediously) portraying the hardships and heroism of proletarian life or resorting to outright propaganda, as socialist realism and 'agitprop' set out to do.[96]

Other theorists associated with the Institute for Social Research are more pessimistic. They refer to the 'culture industry', not to 'mass culture', because the latter term gives the false impression that the capitalist organization of culture serves the needs of the masses rather than, as in reality, the needs of capital. Although the culture industry 'undeniably speculates on the conscious and unconscious state of the millions towards which it is directed', the masses are really an object of calculation, an appendage of the machinery.[97] Cultural artefacts are subjected more systematically to the logic of the profit motive and capital accumulation. The critical potential of intellectual culture is undermined by the conformist, or 'affirmative', products of the culture industry, which facilitate the individual's adaptation to capitalism. Affirmative culture provides an escape from reality, which requires little effort or concentration from workers demoralized and dulled by an alienating work process. The various techniques used to achieve these ends are also analysed. Adorno describes techniques of 'standardization' (e.g. the standardized plots of the Western), 'pseudo-individualization' (the introduction of insignificant differences of plot which obscure the 'formula'), and the use of 'response mechanisms' such as canned laughter, which are designed to guarantee the 'correct' response from the audience.[98] Like fascist propaganda these devices appeal unconsciously to the audience's emotions and discourage critical responses.[99] Even popular astrology has conformist implications. It reinforces fatalism and short-term pragmatism, reconciling people to a social system they can neither understand nor control:

> In as much as the social system is the 'fate' of most individuals independent of their will and interest, it is projected upon the stars in order to thus obtain a higher degree of dignity and justification in which the individuals hope to participate themselves. At the same time, the idea that the stars, if only one reads them correctly, offer some advice mitigates the very same fear of the inexorability of social processes the stargazer himself creates.[100]

Popular music encourages 'compulsiveness' and suggestibility. It can only be listened to in a state of 'deconcentration' or distraction: 'If the standardized products, hopelessly like one another except for conspicuous hit lines, do not permit concentrated listening without becoming unbearable to the listeners, the latter are in any case no longer capable of concentrated listening.'[101] In contrast to this attitude to popular culture, Adorno welcomes the more challenging, formally innovative products of contemporary intellectual culture. The music of Schoenberg and Webern 'gives form to that anxiety, that terror, that insight into the catastrophic situation which others merely evade by regressing'.[102] But Adorno's position is not just elitism. Rather, Adorno objects to the blurring of the boundaries between high and low art to the detriment of both. Popular art loses 'the rebellious resistance inherent within it as long as social control was not yet total'.[103]

The much vaunted liberties of liberal capitalism are also stifled by a parallel series of transformations. According to Marcuse's analysis, the potentially revolutionary conflict of liberal capitalism has been eliminated from the 'one-dimensional' societies of advanced capitalism, which lack genuine opposition. These societies appear to be free because of their free elections, free press, consumer choice and the apparent contrast with totalitarian communism. But the freedom of advanced capitalism is really 'repressive tolerance', which serves to divert attention from, and so entrench, the manipulation and conformism of an increasingly administered society.[104] The critical public sphere of early bourgeois societies (seen in the rapid expansion of newspaper and book publishing, coffee houses and salons of the late seventeenth and eighteenth centuries) has given way to a 'manipulated publicity'. Public opinion is something to be measured and managed by state and media, a mere reflection of the prevailing order. It is no longer an independent source of criticism or opposition.[105] Marcuse's bleak portrayal suggests a society of uninterrupted manipulation and control with few obvious grounds for hope. With the seamless mediocrity of its mass-produced entertainment, its overfed complacency and positivistically disarmed sociology and philosophy, contemporary western society either stifles or marginalizes genuine opposition, all but eliminating any possibility of revolution. In fact Marcuse, as the critical theorist most directly concerned with political practice, looks to those excluded from the system, to 'the substratum of the outcasts and outsiders, the exploited and persecuted of other races and other colours, the unemployed and the unemployable', for potential agents of transformation. But this turn to political practice seems artificial and, in the end, not that distant from Leninism. For these groups will bring about revolution only if they are led by the radical students and youth, who represent 'the most advanced consciousness of humanity'.[106] Although Marcuse's views were heard sympathetically by the New Left and student activists of the sixties, particularly in the USA and Germany, a critical theory, which accords such responsibility to critical intellectuals, renews fears of vanguardism.

From one point of view, then, the Frankfurt School's return to a broader, 'superstructural' agenda of aesthetic, cultural, psychological and sociological studies enriches the Marxist critique of ideology, opening the way to more adequate explanations of fascism, Soviet communism and advanced capitalism. It is less obvious whether any escape from the labyrinth of modernity is found. In the end, the Frankfurt School's exhaustive inventory of the subtlety and all-pervasiveness of mechanisms of power is double-edged. The more the conformity of contemporary society is explained, the more any upsurge of revolutionary enthusiasm seems unlikely. Reinforced by such a range of argument and research, the mood of pessimism haunting the Frankfurt School's account of contemporary society is not coincidental. The tendency to inspire resignation rather than revolt is exacerbated by a relative inattention to potential agents of social transformation. In Paul Connerton's phrase, there are no 'structural gaps within the system of repressive rationality'.[107] Adorno and Horkheimer soon lost faith in the revolutionary potential of the working class. Marcuse's identification of new revolutionary agents is, as we have seen, no less problematic. To adapt the phrase Gramsci made famous, pessimism of the intellect threatens optimism of the will.[108] For critical theory, which defines itself in terms of the essential relationship between radical theory and transformative practice, this problem is fundamental.

Habermas and the Renewal of Critical Theory

More recently the critical theory of the Frankfurt School has been renewed by the wide-ranging, ambitious and influential project of the German social theorist and philosopher, Jürgen Habermas (1929–).[109] Habermas combines a philosophically informed and critical sociology with a philosophy grounded in categories of social action. His project involves a protracted critical engagement with the distinct but inter-related ideas of Marx and historical materialism. In this sense, he can be understood as the most recent representative of the tradition of thought which can be traced from Kant, Hegel and Marx to the Frankfurt School. Habermas's work is also marked by a serious en-counter with analytical philosophy, particularly the speech act theory of J. L. Austin and John Searle and the later philosophy of Ludwig Wittgenstein. Habermas reworks the critique of positivism on what he sees as more secure epistemological foundations. This involves the explication of a fuller conception of rationality, one which is not reducible to instrumental rationality. He starts out from basically Hegelian and Marxian premises. Knowledge and values are not the timeless accomplishment of a transcendental subject. They can only

be understood in the context of the material history of human societies, the biological reproduction and social evolution of the human
species.

The direction of Habermas's critique and renewal of historical
materialism is signalled by an early distinction between two kinds of
action, 'labour' or 'work' and 'interaction'. The concept of work is
intended to correspond to Marx's concept of labour which, in the
form of historically developing modes of production, is the most basic
category of historical materialism. The act of satisfying human needs
by means of labour is, for Marx, distinctive of human as opposed to
merely animal existence and so the act which founds human history.
Marx's materialist conception of history charts a series of dialectically
unfolding modes of production, different ways of organizing labour.[110] Habermas defines labour to encompass all those forms of
'purposive-rational action', which can be explained in the limited
terms of instrumental rationality. Purposive-rational action simply
'realizes defined goals under given conditions'. It includes both 'instrumental action', which 'organizes means that are appropriate or
inappropriate according to criteria of an effective control of reality',
and 'strategic action', which 'depends on the correct evaluation of
possible alternative choices, which results from calculation supplemented by values and maxims'.[111] The significant point about strategic action is that, although values play a role, the form of rationality
involved is still merely calculative, having no bearing on the validity
of the values themselves. This is the familiar form of rationality most
clearly embodied in natural science and technology. Scientific knowledge and technological development follows 'a logic that corresponds
to the structure of purposive-rational action regulated by its own
results, which is in fact the structure of work'.[112]

Work is distinguished from 'interaction'. Interaction refers to the
pragmatic domain of relations between human subjects. Where work
involves an instrumental relationship of control over a realm of objects, interaction is defined in terms of communication or mutual
understanding between subjects. Where work involves the application of technical rules to external reality, interaction depends on
moral (or 'practical') norms. Interaction, which is also described as
'communicative action' or 'symbolic interaction', is 'governed by
binding *consensual norms*, which define reciprocal expectations
about behavior and which must be understood and recognized by at
least two acting subjects'.[113] If work is the domain of natural science,
technology and bureaucracy, interaction is the domain of values and
norms. Interaction is concerned with the validity of norms and values,

with 'substantive rationality' (Weber) or 'reason' (Hegel), rather than the instrumental assessment of means for the realization of particular ends ('formal rationality' or 'understanding'). Just as labour provides a pragmatic context for the explication of scientific knowledge, interaction is designed to provide a pragmatic context for the interpretation of norms and values.

According to Habermas, critical theory must shift its attention to the domain of interaction or communicative action, in order to reinforce the critique of an oppressive social reality. This is because the Marxist category of labour (which, as we have seen, is linked both to the mode of production and to natural science and technology) provides only a partial basis for understanding society. The limitations of the category of labour are reflected in the Marxist account of modernization. In fact, science and technology play a progressive role for Marxism equivalent to the role allotted to scientific rationality by the Enlightenment. The state of development of science and technology is closely related to the level of development of the forces of production, which include the human, natural but also technological resources available for production at a particular time. Clearly science and technology play an important role, because, as the industrial revolution demonstrated, they can dramatically affect the productivity of labour. But for Marx and Engels the development of the forces of production plays a progressive role. History progresses dialectically as a result of contradictions between forces and relations of production. Once the forces of production have grown beyond the limits of existing relations of ownership, they work to bring about the transition to a more advanced mode of production and society.[114] However, Habermas is sceptical of guarantees of progress based exclusively on a dialectic of labour of this kind. Progressive changes in the 'superstructural' spheres of law, politics, philosophy or morality cannot simply be predicated on developments within the economic base, or mode of production. In Habermas's terms, developments within the pragmatic context of work do not lead automatically to progress in the intersubjective context of interaction.

A change of emphasis is particularly necessary, because of the transformed role of science and technology within contemporary or advanced capitalism. This thesis is reflected in Habermas's distinctive reading of the Enlightenment. An initially critical Enlightenment rationality, deployed against dogma, religion and traditional authority, was able to occupy the space created by a new 'public sphere'. The public sphere of late seventeenth- and eighteenth-century Europe, with its clubs, salons, novels, newspapers and journals, allowed the formation of an informed and critical public opinion. The public expression of private opinion, which was forbidden in Prussia in the years before the French Revolution, was gradually gaining a foothold in Britain and France:

> The inhibited judgments were called 'public' in view of a public sphere that without question had counted as a sphere of public authority but was now casting itself loose as a forum in which the private people, come together to form a public, readied themselves to compel public authority to legitimate itself before public opinion.[115]

Although clearly bourgeois in its membership and perspectives, this sphere between civil society and the state was a locus of potential political opposition and critique as well as literary and aesthetic criticism.

However, in the industrially developed societies this critical public sphere has since been transformed by a series of developments, which turned a 'culture-debating' into a 'culture-consuming' public. Public opinion now takes the privatized form of opinion surveys and anonymous voting at elections. It is the object of scientific research, designed to make it more easily manipulable. At the same time, there is an increasingly pervasive 'technocratic' consciousness. In place of bourgeois ideology, which still claimed intersubjective validity for certain moral values, there is a progressive depoliticization of issues. A greater role is accorded to technical experts and expertise. For example, economic rationalism interprets issues of social justice as technical issues of economic management. Prevailing scepticism about the possibility of 'intersubjectively binding' discussion concerning moral or aesthetic values – in the form of ethical relativism, subjectivism or 'decisionism' – reinforces technocratic consciousness.[116] These developments, which undermine the possibility of an evaluatively grounded political opposition to the existing order, manifest the changed role of scientific rationality from a critical to a conservative one. With what Habermas describes as 'the expansion of the rational form of science and technology . . . to the proportions of a life form, of the "historical totality" of a life-world', science and technology become ideology.[117] Thus, in contemporary societies the expansion of the instrumental rationality of work and science, instead of being a progressive force, is an obstacle to emancipation.

In the light of this transformation of both the public sphere and the dominant ideology, Habermas proposes a reworking of critical theory and its critique of positivism. Both the later Marx and historical materialism are condemned for ultimately conspiring in the suppression of the dimension of interaction and the enthronement of labour, instrumental rationality and positivism. Of course, Marx assumes a duality of labour and interaction, in the sense that the category of labour or production includes relations as well as forces of production.[118] In Habermas's terms, relations of production, which obviously have legal, political and moral dimensions, occur within the realm of interaction. Significantly, too, the realm of interaction also extends beyond relations of production to include legal, political and moral dimensions of society in general. But then, the assumption made by historical materialism, that development of the forces of production will inevitably lead to revolution of the relations of production, and hence to changes in all other areas of society outside the mode of production, encourages the theoretical reduction of the latter to the former – or, in other words, of interaction to labour. If morality and politics are simply dependent variables of the economic base, then any autonomous logic of interaction is effectively denied. The situation is made worse by the fact that Marx also fails to make a clear *epistemological* distinction between labour and interaction. He fails, in other words, to distinguish clearly between the different kinds of knowledge and rationality, which correspond to these fundamental contexts of human action. This further weakens resistance to the eventual eclipse of interaction and hastens the positivist degeneration of Marxism. The later Marx's increasingly positivist interpretation of his own 'dialectical' method reinforces this tendency. The emphasis on the uncovering of general laws, analogies with natural science and the inevitability of the transition to communism emerges clearly with Engels and later versions of Marxism and historical materialism.[119]

Up to this point, Habermas's argument can be seen as a restatement of the Frankfurt School's core theoretical position. However, his 'reconstruction of historical materialism' also responds to a basic inadequacy in the position of these earlier theorists and of Weber, who was a major influence on them. It is apparent that Habermas's category of work corresponds to the Frankfurt School's conception of instrumental rationality and to Weber's concept of rationalization. However, although these theorists recognize the importance of an alternative or 'substantive' rationality of ends, they fail to provide any reconstruction of its basis or structure – in Habermas's terms, any reconstruction of interaction. Thus, Weber describes how processes of rationalization dissolve values and traditions and lead to disenchantment, but he sees no alternative basis for a substantive rationality of ends other than arbitrary choice or decision. Analogously, Horkheimer and Adorno describe how the unrestricted expansion of instrumental rationality suppresses internal nature, reducing human

beings to the status of objects. Marcuse describes the repression of
our instinctual life or 'eros' as the cost extracted by an unfettered
production process detached from real human needs. However, these
versions of the suppressed pole in the dialectic of Enlightenment
offer no politically or philosophically convincing alternative to instrumental rationality. There is a need, therefore, for a more persuasive
reconstruction of an alternative rationality. For Habermas, this alternative is communicative rationality.

Habermas's ambitious epistemological project is given fuller expression in *Knowledge and Human Interests* (1968), which develops
more explicitly and systematically the connection between work and
interaction on the one hand and distinct categories of knowledge and
rationality on the other. The outcome is a kind of transcendental
pragmatism. The achievements of the knowing subject are related to
historicized contexts of social action, which provide the categorial
framework for particular kinds of human experience. Natural scientific knowledge (including the application of science in the form
of technology) is understood in terms of the pragmatic context of
work or labour. The objectivity of the 'empirical-analytic sciences' is
grounded in purposive-rational action, and organized in terms of a
technical interest in the control of external reality: 'facts relevant to
the empirical sciences are first constituted through an *a priori* organization of our experience in the behavioural system of instrumental
action.'[120] Natural science does not, as realist accounts of science
suppose, describe reality as such but only from the point of view of an
underlying 'cognitive interest' in control. This is reflected in the
hypothetico-deductive structure of scientific theories and the essential role played in them by prediction and experiment.[121] Habermas's
account of natural science draws on the philosophy of science of the
American pragmatist, Charles Sanders Peirce (1839–1914). Peirce
understands that 'the task of methodology is not to clarify the logical
structure of scientific theories but the logic of the procedure with
whose aid we *obtain* scientific theories.'[122] Natural science can then be
conceived as a 'self-regulating, cumulative learning process' within
the framework of instrumental action.[123] Science self-consciously sys-
tematizes and formalizes activities of problem-solving necessary for
the reproduction of human societies.

However, Habermas argues against Peirce that natural science
cannot be understood in this way as a practical activity without breaking more radically with the 'scientistic self-understanding' of positivism. The practice of science depends on a scientific community and
so, inevitably, on the achievement of mutual understanding by means
of language and communication. In other words, science cannot be

understood without reference to the pragmatic context of interaction
or communicative action:

> the communication of investigators requires the use of language that is not
> confined to the limits of technical control over objectified natural pro-
> cesses. It arises from symbolic interaction between societal subjects who
> reciprocally know and recognize each other as unmistakable individuals.
> This *communicative action* is a system of reference that cannot be reduced
> to the framework of *instrumental action*.[124]

Reflection on science as a social activity implies a different kind of
knowledge, which is based on a different cognitive interest and different conditions of objectivity. Here Habermas draws on Dilthey's
'hermeneutic' account of the 'cultural sciences' (or *Geisteswissenschaften*), which emphasises the role of 'understanding' (or *Verstehen*).[125] What Habermas calls the 'historical-hermeneutic sciences'
find the basis of their objectivity in the pragmatic context of interaction or communication. History, literary criticism and other disciplines centrally concerned with the interpretation of texts, utterances
or meaningful symbols are all included in this category. These disciplines serve a cognitive interest in mutual understanding, providing
'interpretations that make possible the orientation of action within
common traditions'.[126] Unlike the empirical-analytic sciences, they do
not imply a manipulative or instrumental relationship with objects,
but a relationship of mutual understanding between subjects. Mutual
understanding is essential to the continuing life of any society, both
for the coordination of the activities of its members and for the
historical accumulation of experience and insight. Hermeneutics,
then, is the 'scientific form of the interpretive activities of everyday
life', just as the experimental method of natural science 'refines the
everyday pragmatic controls of rules of instrumental action'.[127]

  Habermas proceeds to identify a third kind of knowledge. The
'critically oriented sciences' are grounded in the further pragmatic
context of 'self-reflection' and are motivated by an 'emancipatory
cognitive interest'. No more than natural science can the hermeneutical sciences provide a full and satisfactory account of human knowledge. Habermas rejects the 'universality claims' of hermeneutics just
as, with the critique of positivism and scientism, he rejects the claim
to universal validity of natural scientific method. On the one hand,
Habermas does not deny that the methods of natural science have a
valid domain of application in the control of nature for the material
reproduction of human societies. Even the establishing of 'law-like
correlations' between social phenomena has a role in the social sciences. But here, as the critique of positivist social science implies,

critical social science must go beyond the identification of law-like correlations 'to determine when theoretical statements grasp invariant regularities of social action as such and when they express ideologically frozen relations of dependence that can in principle be transformed'.[128] The last phrase recalls Marx's critique of bourgeois economics as the prototype of a critical theory which uncovers and helps to dissolve the 'immutable' regularities of capitalism.

On the other hand, and parallel to this argument for the limited validity of the methods pioneered in the natural sciences, Habermas argues for the insufficiency of hermeneutic knowledge. As a consequence of its exclusive concern with the meanings of utterances, texts or symbols, hermeneutic knowledge is not equipped to uncover ideological forms of consciousness. Typically, the hermeneutic stance seeks to reconstruct the meaning of otherwise obscure or misleading human expressions. It is not concerned with the causal context of these expressions or, in other words, with ideology in the Marxist sense. Ideologies are systems of thought or value, which serve the interests of particular social groups (such as the bourgeoisie) and are, by some means, imposed on other groups, which they disadvantage (such as the proletariat). In Habermas's terms, hermeneutics is blind to forms of false consciousness or 'distorted communication', which bear the imprint of power or domination. There is thus an indispensable role for critical theories of interpretation. Habermas takes Freudian psychoanalysis as a methodological model of a critical theory in this sense. Mental disorders such as neuroses can be understood as obsolete defence mechanisms, resulting from past traumas, which inhibit the individual's transparent 'internal communication'. Crucially, for Freudian theory the neurosis can only be understood by looking beyond its explicit expression to both external interventions in the life of the child and the unconscious workings of the mind. Psychoanalytic interpretations penetrate beneath the surface complex to the underlying cause and so, once the psychoanalytic interpretation has been understood and accepted by the patient, help to dissolve the neurotic symptom. In both their Marxist and psychoanalytic variants, therefore, critically oriented theories serve an interest in emancipation, whether from relations of domination and the ideologies which sustain them, or from the inhibiting opacity of the disordered mind.

Having clarified the epistemological character of critical theories, Habermas seeks to provide more adequate foundations for values which inform the practice of critique. Previous members of the Frankfurt School advocated an immanent critique of society. Society would be transformed by rendering explicit the tensions and contradictions within it. The 'sham universality' of bourgeois justice provides the basis for its own transcendence. But the Frankfurt School's own analysis of contemporary society suggests that the enterprise of immanent critique is endangered, because universalistic bourgeois values have given way to technocratic consciousness. Bourgeois consciousness has, in the meantime, become too 'cynical', and its immanent critique can no longer be expected to lead to social transformation.[129] The alternative Habermas pursues is to ground critique in a theory of communication. The values of autonomy and responsibility or solidarity, which are deployed in the critique of society, are implicit in language:

> The human interest in autonomy and responsibility is not mere fancy, for it can be apprehended *a priori*. What raises us out of nature is the only thing whose nature we can know: language. Through its structure, autonomy and responsibility are posited for us. Our first sentence expresses unequivocally the intention of universal and unconstrained consensus.[130]

The way we use language (the 'pragmatics of language') provides the clearest picture of the structure of interaction or communication and reveals the fundamental values on which communication is based. Since communication between subjects is an unavoidable condition of human society, these values must have universal validity. It is crucial to Habermas's argument that his account is valid in every society (it is a theory of *universal* pragmatics), because otherwise the values he uncovers could not be regarded as the basis for the critique of every society. As McCarthy puts it, Habermas's argument is 'that the goal of critical theory – a form of life free from unnecessary domination in all its forms – is inherent in the notion of truth; it is anticipated in every act of communication.'[131]

Habermas's universal pragmatics identifies basic values or 'validity claims', corresponding to what he sees as the inevitable structure of communication. Every act of communication implicitly involves raising each of four validity claims. These validity claims reflect the relation of language (which must be comprehensible) to a realm of intersubjectivity or society (which involves relations of morality or rightness), to external reality or nature (raising the question of truth), and to the 'internal nature' of the speaker's own feelings, beliefs and intentions (which concerns the truthfulness or sincerity of the speaker). In other words,

> The speaker has to select a *comprehensible* expression in order that the speaker and hearer can *understand one another*: the speaker has to have the intention of communicating a *true* propositional content in order that the hearer can *share the knowledge* of the speaker, the speaker has to want

to express his intentions *truthfully* in order that the hearer can *believe in* the speaker's utterance (can trust him); finally, the speaker has to select an utterance that is *right* in the light of existing norms and values in order that the hearer can accept the utterance, so that both speaker and hearer can *agree with one another* in the utterance concerning a recognised normative background.[132]

Validity claims correspond to the various kinds of challenge an interlocutor can raise against a particular utterance. She or he can challenge the utterance as unintelligible, as false (or based on falsehood), as insincere or as inappropriate. To the extent that we are able to engage in communication with other subjects, we can be assumed to understand these values. Our communicative competence includes 'mastery of these values, the basis of our ideas of truth, freedom and justice'.[133]

Clearly decisive for Habermas's account is the way in which problematic validity claims are resolved. After all, challenges to particular utterances may be met with appeals to authority (of priests, oracles, sacred or scientific texts), or with the use of force or inducements (the Inquisition, psychiatric treatment, bribery or imprisonment). Indeed in some cultures, and in some regions and periods of western culture, these responses have been regarded as perfectly legitimate. But Habermas believes that a more rational or enlightened response is not only to be preferred but, in some sense, implicitly presupposed whenever people enter into communication. Truth, freedom and justice are to be understood in terms of consensus theories of theoretical (factual or scientific) and moral or practical truth (rightness). But a consensus is not valid if it is the result of inadequate information or external pressure or compulsion. A moral or factual claim is vindicated only when it is the object of a rational or unconstrained consensus. Consensus is valid only when the participants in discourse are subject only to 'the peculiarly unforced force of the better argument'.[134] Discourse is to be measured against the standard of an 'ideal speech situation', which is free from relations of power or domination, and which is undogmatically committed to the consideration of all available evidence and even alternative conceptual schemes. Consensus is always provisional. It is vulnerable to new evidence or ideas and to the perspectives of participants hitherto excluded from full and equal participation. An ideal speech situation is precisely what is ruled out whenever distorted communication prevails, whether within society as ideology or within the individual as some form of mental disorder. Critically oriented theories, in other words, uncover deviations from the ideal speech situation.

Universal pragmatics reconstructs a notion of communicative rationality, which is clearly different from the various manifestations of instrumental rationality associated with the Enlightenment. It is designed to ground more securely and more transparently the claims of critical theories. However, Habermas's claim to reconstruct a communicative competence universal to the human species has been criticized as a return to the doomed Enlightenment project of finding timelessly rational foundations for moral values. It has been seen as Kantian transcendentalism in new guise. Many critics have been sceptical of the universal status accorded to discourse ethics. How can we suppose that members of every culture, whatever its norms of communication, have always implicitly raised precisely the same validity claims, discursively redeemable in the way Habermas describes? Some postmodernist critics even see Habermas's commitment to consensus as constraining and potentially oppressive, although he stresses that it is only an idealized and anticipatory commitment.[135]

In the light of these criticisms Habermas has more recently qualified the status of his enterprise. In the spirit of Hegel's critique of Kant, Habermas now explicitly limits the scope of discourse ethics to the validation of universal norms of 'morality' (*Moralität*), as opposed to the values and forms of 'ethical life' (*Sittlichkeit*), which are inseparably linked to the particular identities of groups and individuals and, through these, to cultural traditions. He admits, in other words, that a universalistic morality in the style of Kant is unable to adjudicate between concrete life-forms and customs, which are inextricably bound to particular human communities.[136] Habermas claims credit, above all, for decisively opting for intersubjectivity in the face of the exhaustion of the 'philosophy of the subject'. Habermas returns to a theme which preoccupied a number of Enlightenment thinkers, when he claims that it is only the communicative use of language, as opposed to the use of signs or even propositions, which is distinctively human: 'it is . . . only the communicative use of propositionally differentiated language that is proper to our sociocultural form of life and is constitutive for the level of a genuinely social reproduction of life.'[137] It is this dimension of intersubjectivity which is threatened, too, by any relativist or postmodernist abdication of responsibility for the substantive or communicative rationality of ends. Overall, Habermas's renewal of critical theory is impressive for its range of theoretical concerns and intellectual sources. It has exerted considerable influence in the fields of social and political theory and philosophy. He has succeeded in integrating many of the characteristic methods and concerns of analytical philosophy, and his work has been taken up by some analytical philosophers. His is the most recent, and one of the most sophisticated of a series of related responses to the Enlightenment, which we have traced from Hegel, Feuerbach, Marx and Marxism to the Frankfurt School.

4. Historicism, Hermeneutics and Phenomenology

Dilthey, Philosophy of Life and Hermeneutics

A significant array of approaches in continental philosophy emphasize history, understanding, interpretation, meaning and subjectivity
as fundamental categories of knowledge in opposition to the dominance of natural scientific reason. This approach emerges most clearly in the context of nineteenth-century German philosophy, which
was dominated by two associated products of the decay of Hegelian
philosophy, 'historicism' and 'philosophy of life' (*Lebensphilosophie*). A number of related but not always consistent strands of
thought, loosely and sometimes confusingly referred to as historicism, reflect the central role played by history in the thought of some
of the most influential critics of the Enlightenment.[1] Both Herder and
Hegel were sceptical of Enlightenment assumptions of a universal
human nature, natural law or morality, stressing instead the 'spirit' of
different historical communities and, in Hegel's case, the 'world spirit' (*Weltgeist*) of history as such. For Herder, human beings differ
from other animals, because their behaviour is not determined by
natural instinct but rather is historical. Mind and language are related
expressions of a historically changing humanity. The languages of
different nations are manifestations of the unique temperament or
spirit of a people (*Volksgeist*). Again, for Hegel morality exists, above
all, as the expression of the distinctive culture, institutions and practices or 'ethical life' of a concrete community. By implication any
adequate understanding of human life, ideas and societies must be a
historical understanding. Mind or spirit, as opposed to physical na-

ture, can only be understood in terms of its genesis through the unfolding stages of development by which less adequate worldviews or forms of life give birth to more adequate ones.[2] Hegel sees the different manifestations of spirit as stages in the dialectical unfolding of a single world spirit to the ultimate *telos* or goal, the realization of Absolute knowledge. Hegel's philosophy, which seeks to express the truth of this Absolute as fully as possible, is inextricably linked to his philosophy of history, by which human history is accorded meaning and significance as the essential medium for the more complete articulation of reason.

In general, historicist currents of thought regard history as central to the understanding of human life. But in Hegel's speculative philosophy of history, the insight that the present can only be understood historically had, according to some critics, led to an interpretation of the past and of other cultures distorted by the concerns of the present. This was, in part, because Hegel thought history itself could only be properly understood in terms of philosophy. But historicists were sceptical of Hegel's philosophy of history, which made the cultural values of nineteenth-century Europe the ultimate goal of previous human history. Hegel's philosophy attributes an overall purpose to history, which the people who make history, playthings of the 'cunning of reason', necessarily ignore. Individuals 'are the living instruments of what is in substance the deed of the world mind and they are therefore directly at one with that deed though it is concealed from them and is not their aim and object'.[3] To a more sceptical historical consciousness, which ironically Hegel himself had also helped to inspire, other cultures could not be assessed from the perspective and against the standards of one's own time and philosophy in this way. This raised philosophical questions about the status of our knowledge of the past. One outcome of the decay of Hegelianism was thus the emergence of what is called 'critical philosophy of history', a tendency which also drew inspiration from Schleiermacher, Savigny and others. Where speculative philosophy of history assigns an overall purpose to human history as a whole, critical philosophy of history investigates the nature of historical knowledge and appropriate methods of historical research. It was associated with the emergence of history as a respectable academic discipline.[4] Many historicists drew the explicitly relativist conclusion, that the values and norms of different cultures are, in their particular social and historical context, equally valid. If moral values can only be understood in terms of the community to which they belong, and it is no longer plausible to locate different human societies within a historical dialectic, then there is no obviously rational way to decide between conflicting values. The validity of values can only be judged for a particular time rather than for all time. In this variant moral and cultural values are historicized.

For other critics, including the life philosophers, Hegel's grand system was, for all its dialectical sophistication and comprehensive synthesis, the product of an exclusively theoretical or intellectual consciousness. In response several currents of thought placed value on 'life' or 'existence', as opposed to the theoretical rationality demonstrated no less by Hegel than by more mainstream Enlightenment thinkers. Romantics defended spontaneity, emotion and individuality against the reductive categories of theoretical reason. Poetry rather than science provides the most adequate path to truth, the most adequate understanding of humanity. In this respect the mature Hegelian system is less adequate than the poetic achievement of the friend of his youth, Friedrich Hölderlin.[5] Again, for Søren Kierkegaard, now often regarded as the first existentialist, even the most impressive and dialectically mediated feats of theoretical reason must inevitably fail to capture the 'subjective truth' of human life or existence, which is essentially religious.[6] For these approaches a more adequate understanding of human life requires a radical break with cognitive or theoretical reason or the 'philosophy of consciousness'. Life philosophy, too, implied that the most important features of human life could not be captured with the abstract categories of theoretical reason. Life in this sense 'referred to the collected inner powers of man, especially the irrational powers of feeling and passion as over against the prevailing power of rational understanding'.[7] For life philosophers only a less reductive understanding of human life offers some hope of answering basic questions of philosophy and life, such as the nature of happiness or the good life. For these philosophers, both subjective experience and history, as the accumulated experience of humanity, are primary sources of genuine understanding.[8]

In his varied writings on philosophy, history and the human sciences, Wilhelm Dilthey (1833–1911) combines elements of both historicism and life philosophy with respect for the achievements of natural science. Historicism and life philosophy come together in the conviction that history is the key to the understanding of human life. Human individuals and societies can only be understood historically, so the study of history and the methods appropriate to this study must be of central concern. Like the life philosophers, Dilthey thinks that the positivist attempt to apply the methods of the natural sciences to the study and understanding of human life inevitably leaves out or distorts essential features of human existence. But criticisms of the mechanistic and reifying implications of scientific reason, made by the Romantics and the life philosophers, can easily degenerate into merely subjective and ultimately futile protest. The celebration of passion and will may even encourage a potentially dangerous irrationalism. Equally, the 'speculative idealism' of Hegelian reason, though opposed to the reductive rationalism of positivism, is dogmatic and ultimately unsustainable.[9] Even in less rationalistic variants of German idealism, the deification of will may encourage irrationalist tendencies similar to those inspired by romanticism.[10] Dilthey never underestimates the rationality, objectivity and rigour demonstrated in natural science. Overall, Dilthey seeks to do justice to the concerns of historicists, life philosophers and Romantics in an account of history and the 'human sciences' (*Geisteswissenschaften*) capable of reconciling scientific objectivity with an appreciation of the fullness of human life.[11]

As a convinced empiricist, then, Dilthey regards all knowledge as ultimately derived from experience. He is influenced in this by British empiricists such as Locke and Hume, but above all by the critical philosophy of Kant. He accepts the empiricist (or 'epistemological' view), that all knowledge is based on 'inner experience' or 'the facts of consciousness'. But the approach of previous empiricists overemphasizes intellectual or cognitive experience and neglects emotion and will:

> No real blood flows in the veins of the knowing subject constructed by Locke, Hume and Kant; it is only the diluted juice of reason, a mere process of thought. Cognition seems to develop concepts such as the external world, time, substance and cause from perception, imagination and thought. However, my historical and psychological studies of man as a whole led me to explain cognition and its concepts in terms of the powers of man as a willing, feeling and imagining being.[12]

The historical dimension of human experience, its 'historicity', is also a central aspect of what a positivist approach inevitably fails to capture:

> For [Dilthey] the present is not an extended instant but a small, structured, part of the flow in which the immediate experience is always enriched by awareness of the past and anticipation of the future. So every moment of life has a distinctive meaning according to its place in the temporal sequence . . . This connection between the temporal structure and the categories of life makes man a historical being.[13]

By implication, even intellectual or cognitive experience occurs within a flow of human experience which is irreducibly historical.

Dilthey's more full-blooded account of human experience suggests a resolution of the contradiction between romanticism, life philosophy and idealism on the one hand and positivism on the other. He hopes to provide a firm epistemological basis for a 'science' of humanity, which can both do justice to the irreducible qualities of mind or life and yet aspire to an objectivity and rigour equal to that of the sciences of nature. In order to secure the human sciences from the distorting influence of positivism, Dilthey clarifies the distinctive methodology and standards of objectivity within such disciplines as history, classical and literary studies, anthropology and psychology. In order to lay 'a foundation for the study of society and history',[14] it is important to recognize the different grounds of objectivity in the human sciences. Unlike the kind of objects studied by astronomy, mechanics or other physical sciences, human beings have both mental and physical attributes and must therefore be studied in a different way. Since the defining feature of human experience is its historicity, it is historical knowledge which is central to an understanding of the human sciences more generally. Recalling Kant's famous critique of pure or theoretical reason, Dilthey describes his project as a critique of historical reason, which is designed to set the limits and establish the fundamental principles of historical understanding.

Dilthey describes two contrasting approaches to the acquisition of knowledge as 'explanation' (*Erklären*) and 'understanding' (*Verstehen*). Explanation is the primary goal of the natural sciences and involves the formulation of general causal laws: 'By an explanatory science we understand the subsumption of a range of phenomena under a causal nexus by means of a limited number of unambiguously defined elements (i.e. constituents of the nexus).'[15] Explanatory science is obviously the main concern of Kant's critique of pure reason as well as the dominant model of knowledge for positivism. Explanation, however, is not by itself an adequate model for the human sciences, whose 'object' of study is humanity itself. Human beings have a physical existence and, to that extent, can be studied by the methods of explanatory science. But the human sciences are more concerned with the various expressions of mind or spirit. The human sciences deal with actions, utterances, institutions and artefacts which, unlike events in the physical world, have intrinsic meaning and so call for a different cognitive approach: 'We call the process by which we recognize some inner content from signs received by the senses *understanding* . . . Understanding is the process of recognizing a mental state from a sense-given sign by which it is expressed.'[16] Where understanding forms part of a 'systematic process with a controllable degree of objectivity', Dilthey talks about 'interpretation'.[17] Understanding is concerned with the recovery of meanings rather than the identification of causal regularities. It is not concerned with generalization but with the description of the individual in its full complexity and particularity. Overall, 'We explain nature; man we must understand.'[18]

In our attempts to understand human beings as opposed to physical events, we seem to have the advantage that we know how our own minds work already. Dilthey embraces 'Vico's principle that the mind can understand what the mind has created' and 'uses our immediate awareness of how our minds work as a key to unlock the impersonal world of mind'.[19] Certainly, it seems that we could never understand the emotions of others if we did not have emotions ourselves. But by the same token, our knowledge of ourselves is imperfect, if we cannot compare ourselves to others: 'the inner experience in which I become aware of my own states can never by itself make me conscious of my own individuality. It is only in comparing myself with others that I come to experience what is individual in myself . . .' But our access to the mental life of others is not direct. It is mediated by the various external manifestations of mind: 'the existence of others is in the first instance given to us only from without, in facts of sensation, in gestures, sounds, and actions. It is only by reconstructing that which thus falls under the observation of our senses in particular signs that we add this inner reality.'[20] The various 'expressions of life' are only encountered to the extent that they are externalized or objectified as 'objectifications of the mind'. These can take an immense variety of forms, including written documents, financial accounts and official reports, letters, works of literature or art, buildings, archaeological remains, gestures and so on. Together these form the basis of our knowledge of other human beings.

In order to analyse what is involved in the process of understanding objectifications of the mind, Dilthey builds on the discipline of 'hermeneutics'. In fact hermeneutics, in the sense of systematic reflection on the practice of interpretation or understanding, has a long history in western culture. The term derives from the ancient Greek word for interpretation (*hermeneuein*), which is related etymologically to the god Hermes – in Greek mythology, the bringer of messages and inventor of language and writing.[21] In the second century AD Artemidorus wrote a learned treatise on the interpretation of dreams, which were widely regarded as messages from the gods, and even then was able to draw on a considerable range of sources. Artemidorus describes how these often unhelpfully opaque messages from the gods can be deciphered.[22] With the advent of Christianity problems of biblical exegesis became the major spur to the development of hermeneutic principles. The spread of Protestantism, which encouraged a more critical attitude to the authority of the Church, made the interpretation of particular passages from the Bible a matter of widespread concern. Hermeneutic manuals, produced mainly for Protestant pastors, spread throughout Europe during the second half of the seventeenth century.[23] In Germany, Herder's thought helped to foster hermeneutic reflection, particularly in the work of Friedrich Ast (1778–1841) and Friedrich August Wolf (1759–1824).[24]

Dilthey, however, was most directly influenced by the philosopher and theologian, Friedrich Schleiermacher (1768–1834). Initially hermeneutic techniques were designed to overcome obvious difficulties or failures of understanding, typically when passages from a religious text were found obscure or inconsistent. Schleiermacher realized that the fact that we are unconscious of obscurities or inconsistencies in a text is no guarantee that our interpretation is correct. Understanding is always potentially mistaken. We cannot simply assume that familiar words mean what we think they do, when they occur in a historical text. As Linge puts it, 'Misunderstanding arises naturally because of the changes in word meanings, world views, and so on that have taken place in the time separating the author from the interpreter. Intervening historical developments are a snare that will inevitably entangle understanding unless their effects are neutralized.'[25] Hermeneutic principles are therefore called upon whenever we seek understanding, not just when we experience difficulties. Like Schleiermacher, too, Dilthey stresses the interdependence of parts and whole in his account of the process of interpretation:

> Here we encounter the general difficulty of all interpretation. The whole of a work must be understood from individual words and their combination but full understanding of an individual part presupposes understanding of the whole. This circle is repeated in the relation of an individual work to the mentality and development of its author, and it recurs again in the relation of such an individual work to its literary genre.[26]

What has become known as the 'hermeneutic circle' is a fundamental and unavoidable feature of interpretation as well as a recurring motif of continental philosophy. Evidently we cannot achieve an adequate understanding of the individual components of a text (words or phrases) without understanding the text as a whole. The same words or even sentences mean different things in different contexts. We only become confident of a particular interpretation when we see how it fits with the rest of the text. But obviously we cannot understand the text as a whole without some understanding of its parts. The interdependence of whole and parts reflects the fact that the elements making up a text cannot be analysed as discrete and independent parts in the way that the physical elements of a mechanical system seemingly can be. Meanings and words behave in significantly holistic ways. By implication, the practice of interpretation is irreducibly circular. As Dilthey's remark also makes plain, the 'wholes' in terms of which meanings must be understood are also various. Individual authors use language in distinctive or even idiosyncratic ways, so knowledge of the author's *oeuvre* is an indispensable aspect of interpretation. Similarly, we must know to which kind of discourse or *genre* the text belongs. The interpretation of a text depends on whether it is considered as philosophical treatise or comic novel, as camouflaged theology or political polemic. Nor can authors be understood in abstraction from their cultural milieu and historical context. For example, the interpretation of political writings may depend critically and in quite complex ways on assumptions about date of publication and relationship to contemporary events and ideological currents.[27]

To the pessimist, the inevitable circularity of hermeneutic practice might be thought to present an almost insuperable barrier to comprehension. The interpreter seems victim to a vicious and inescapable regress, since understanding the whole is impossible without understanding the parts and understanding of the parts impossible without understanding of the whole. Dilthey is more optimistic about the possibility of objectively valid interpretations. He believes that through 'honest subordination' to the text and extensive knowledge of the totality in which it occurs, it is possible for the interpreter to achieve an ever-improving if never perfect understanding. In fact, in principle it is even possible for interpreters to know the author better than they know themselves. A rigorous process of interpretation 'will enable the student to recover, re-enact, or even re-experience the original meanings, or at least come very close to this ideal'.[28] Dilthey's faith in the possibility of objectively true or valid interpretations depends on the assumption of a common humanity, underlying the variety of human language, culture and personality. In understanding, 'the personalities of the interpreter and his author do not confront each other as two facts which cannot be compared: both have been formed by a common human nature and this makes common speech and understanding among men possible.'[29] This assumption of a common human nature is not necessarily incompatible with Dilthey's belief in the historical constitution of humanity, since the characteristics he supposes universal to humanity are relatively abstract ones. He claims only that 'mind has an innate structure which gives rise to typical connections between mental processes', that 'our mental life is purposive', that we express 'our mental states by physical manifestations' and that we both perceive and evaluate the world around us.[30] According to his earlier, more psychologistic formulations, through a kind of empathy the historian can relive or re-experience the thoughts, intentions or feelings of past individuals. But this approach is vulnerable to charges of subjectivism. It is difficult to reconcile the apparent vagueness and insubstantiality of empathy with the aspiration to objective validity of interpretation. In later writings, influenced by Husserl's strictures against psychologism, Dilthey places more weight on 'the insight that experience itself is organized by symbolic structures' (such as language).[31] The task of hermeneutics is to decode these symbolic structures. Overall, Dilthey still believes that, although 'the results reached in interpretation can never have demonstrative certitude', it is possible for interpreters to overcome their historical situation and achieve valid interpretations.[32] However, even this qualified optimism would be substantially undermined by the subsequent development of hermeneutic theory and philosophy.

Husserl and Phenomenology

Throughout his philosophical career Edmund Husserl (1859–1938) was, like Dilthey, concerned to resist the imperialist tendencies of natural scientific reason, particularly in the area of moral and cultural value. Thus positivism and other forms of 'naturalism' attempt to derive an evaluative philosophy of the world and of life from the findings and methods of natural science alone. The naturalist makes claims to knowledge in questions of value, which cannot be sustained according to his own assumptions and so falls into contradiction: 'The naturalist teaches, preaches, moralizes, reforms ... But he denies what every sermon, every demand, if it is to have a meaning, presupposes.'[33] However, despite his hostility to naturalism, Husserl emphatically appreciates the achievements of the 'theoretical attitude' of the natural sciences, products of the strong 'will for rigorous science' that can be traced from Socrates and Plato to Galileo and modern science. For Husserl it is not the theoretical attitude itself which is suspect. Rather, what is to be resisted is the exclusive identification of rigorous science with the methods of the natural sciences, as a result of their undoubted successes within their proper sphere. 'Spirit' is not of the same order of 'being' as the objects of the natural world and should not be subjected to the same categories of explanation.

What particularly troubles Husserl about naturalism is the cultural

scepticism and relativism which, when properly understood, it implies. Husserl is equally unconvinced by Hegel's attempt to overcome
relativism by means of a dialectical philosophy of history. It is in this
respect that Husserl departs most clearly from Dilthey, whose relativist 'philosophy of worldviews' (*Weltanschauungphilosophie*) was one
of the by-products of the decay of the Hegelian system. Indeed,
Dilthey's relativism and historicism are held partly to blame for the
prevailing cultural atmosphere. He quotes Dilthey's remark that 'the
formation of a historical consciousness destroys more thoroughly
than does surveying the disagreement of systems a belief in the
universal validity of any of the philosophies that have undertaken to
express in a compelling manner the coherence of the world by an
ensemble of concepts'.[34] Husserl believes that Dilthey fails, in the
end, to provide a sufficiently firm bulwark against the relativist force
of historical consciousness, because he remains satisfied with a dualism of understanding and explanation, of human and natural sciences. Instead, Husserl believes that the category of understanding
can supply a new basis for a single and complete philosophy of the
knowing, feeling and acting subject. His strategy is no longer simply,
as it was for Dilthey, to secure an autonomous domain for the human
sciences free from the universalizing pretensions and reductive categories of the natural sciences. Attacking naturalism on its own
grounds, he wishes, as Dews puts it,

> [to] constitute a new, rigorously scientific philosophy which will place the
> empirical sciences themselves on an apodictic basis, while at the same
> time . . . preventing the 'objectivist' impetus of the sciences from leading to
> a culturally disastrous obliteration of awareness of the constituting role of
> subjectivity.[35]

A new understanding of the subject of consciousness will allow him to
refute the pretensions of both naturalism and historicism without
relapsing into either Hegelian idealism or irrationalism.

In this ambitious spirit, Husserl makes no concessions to a narrow,
positivist conception of rationality. But he is also equally unwilling to
relinquish the high aspirations towards rigorous truth implicit in the
critical spirit of rationalism. He seeks an account of truth and rationality capable of delivering a rigorously grounded philosophy and,
ultimately, a morality too. He asserts the 'imperishable demand for
pure and absolute knowledge (and what is inseparably one with that,
its demand for pure and absolute valuing and willing)'.[36] Husserl's
strategy involves turning the weapons of the sceptic against scepticism. If cultural scepticism is the main problem with both naturalism
and historicism, scepticism also provides the basis for a philosophical

response to this problem. The critical and sceptical attitude of Enlightenment rationalism must be radicalized. In other words, Descartes's methodical doubt is still the model:

> with the radicalism belonging to the essence of genuine philosophical science we accept nothing given in advance, allow nothing traditional to pass as a beginning, nor ourselves to be dazzled by any names however great, but rather seek to attain the beginnings in a free dedication to the problems themselves and to the demands stemming from them.[37]

A rigorous philosophy must be completely free of all presupposition, it can take nothing for granted. In addition, Husserl also accepts (with Descartes, Hume and Kant) the characteristic starting point of modern epistemology, the assumption that the contents of consciousness represent our only certain knowledge.[38]

But Husserl is dissatisfied with the answers of his philosophical forebears to the problem of knowledge, though their various approaches provide him with some important clues. If Descartes suggests the correct starting point and the overriding principle of a rigorous science free from presuppositions, Kant's transcendental idealism provides the nearest approach to a correct method. Kant, too, starts out from the epistemological premise that we can only have direct knowledge of a 'phenomenal' world of things as they appear to us and cannot know with certainty the nature of things as they are 'in themselves'. But Kant has the insight that sensations (or 'intuitions') must be organized in a certain way if they are to be possible objects of experience for us. Sensations must conform to certain formal features of the mind or subject of experience. Specifically, experience must be organized in terms of categories (e.g. causality and substance), which constitute the objective world as it appears to us. These features of the subject are transcendental, in that they are what make our experience of an objective world possible and so must be conceived as prior to that experience. Kant believes that we can know that we inhabit a world of causally interrelated objects in space and time, because as transcendental subjects of experience we must experience the world in that way.[39]

But Husserl is not satisfied with Kant's solution either. Kant's subject of experience is still no more than an abstract and unknowable 'unity of apperception', the mere basis for the attribution of 'my' experiences to an identifiable subject or 'I'. What Kant derives from this conception of the subject is an argument for the necessity of the structure of the objective world discovered by natural science. Once this 'transcendental deduction' has been achieved, no richer conception of consciousness or experience is pursued. Because he identifies the possibility of objective experience with the possibility of scientific knowledge Kant remains, according to Husserl, confined within a philosophical 'objectivism', which neglects the full contribution of consciousness and subjectivity. As a result, Kant still offers succour to positivism and naturalism.[40] With Kant's philosophical successors these tendencies become more obvious. Still, despite these criticisms, Husserl proposes to pursue Kant's transcendental exploration of the constitution of our experience. He is still a transcendental philosopher: throughout his philosophical career Husserl will investigate 'the relationship . . . between the subjectivity of knowing and the objectivity of the content known'.[41] All knowledge is founded on the achievements of an 'object-constituting subjectivity' (*leistende Subjektivität*). Husserl cites St. Augustine's dictum that 'The truth is not to be found in the external world; it resides in the interiority of Man.'[42]

In contrast to Kant, though, Husserl focuses much more fixedly, even obsessively, on the subject of experience, providing an elaborate description of the nature of consciousness in order to elucidate the notions of subject, object and the 'intentional' relation of the subject to the object. At first Husserl did not clearly distinguish his own approach from a psychological or, to his critics, 'psychologistic' approach. For the naturalistic temper of late nineteenth-century Europe, experimental psychology provided the obvious route to a scientific solution of philosophical problems. After all, psychology is the scientific study of conscious or psychic phenomena, and Husserl had come to the conclusion that the nature of consciousness was the key to the conundrum of epistemology. Husserl was forced to distinguish his own approach to consciousness from a psychological one, as a result of the response to his early work on the foundations of arithmetic. In his *Philosophy of Arithmetic* (1891) he provides a genetic account of the psychological processes through which the concept of number is acquired. Husserl's work was sharply criticized by Gottlob Frege (1848–1925), a major figure in the development of analytical philosophy, as a form of psychologism. Rather than provide an adequate analysis of the necessary truths of arithmetic, Husserl had psychologistically reduced them to the status of contingent and therefore falsifiable generalizations from experience.[43] It was soon obvious to Husserl that experimental psychology, which simply correlates mental or psychic states with physical or neurological ones, could never resolve the problem of epistemology. Naturalistic psychology presupposes nature as an objective external reality and so cannot, without circularity, support arguments for the existence of an external world: 'every psychological judgment involves the existential positing of physical nature, whether expressly or not.' A psychological epistemology can never be more than just another manifestation of naturalism.[44]

On the other hand, whilst accepting these criticisms of psychologism, Husserl still thought that Frege and others were neglecting the 'noetic conditions' or 'subjective aspect of knowledge'.[45] Husserl's attempt to provide a closer examination of the nature of consciousness without succumbing to psychologism takes advantage of the work of his former teacher, Franz Brentano (1838–1917). In *Psychology from an Empirical Standpoint* (1874), Brentano argues that the experimental psychology of his day inevitably fails to capture the specific and distinctive properties of consciousness. He is equally sceptical of 'introspectionist' psychology, which seeks to derive knowledge of consciousness from the psychologist's observation of his own mental states. Introspectionist psychology fails to recognize the essential difference between the observation of physical events and the introspection by the psychologist of her own mental states. With mental phenomena the act of observing inevitably distorts its object: 'the attempt to observe, say, our anger – to concentrate our attention upon it – at once, he says, destroys it.'[46] The reliability of introspection is also something which, by definition, cannot be checked by other observers, as is the case with our knowledge of external reality. As Husserl puts it, psychical phenomena are pure phenomena which have no possibility of 'presenting themselves in experience according to diversely varying "subjective appearances"'.[47] Brentano proposes instead what he calls 'descriptive psychology', which depends on a distinction between the 'perception' and the 'observation' of mental phenomena. The introspectionist psychologist simply observes his or her own mental states. The psychologist's observation amounts to a further mental state, which has the original mental state as its object and which, as we have seen, is intrinsically unreliable. Perception, on the other hand, is something which accompanies or is an element of every mental state and so does not involve this problematic supplement. According to Passmore's helpful explanation, 'each mental act perceives itself directly as its "second object" – not as an "appearance", not as something from which the real character of the mental act has to be inferred, but precisely as that mental act actually is.' Perception provides the psychologist with 'an immediate and direct apprehension of the realities which constitute his subject matter'.[48]

Brentano derives the related (and more graspable) principle of the 'intentionality' of consciousness from the scholastic tradition in which he trained as priest. According to this principle, it is distinctive of mental or psychic phenomena that they are 'directed towards an object', that they 'refer to a content' or 'object':

> Every mental phenomenon includes something as object within itself, although they do not all do so in the same way. In presentation something is presented, in judgement something is affirmed or denied, in love loved, in hate hated, in desire desired and so on . . .
>
> This intentional in-existence is characteristic exclusively of mental phenomena. No physical phenomenon exhibits anything like it.[49]

I remember my great-aunt, I am afraid of the bull, I decide to write a book – in each case the mental state cannot be described without reference to a particular object or content, indicated by the phrases 'my great-aunt', 'the bull' and 'to write a book'. Significantly, the intentional object is not the same as some physical thing in the world (e.g. the bull). This is obvious in the case of mental states whose objects do not, or even could not correspond to existing entities: consider thoughts about destroyed buildings, David Copperfield, unicorns or four-sided triangles. Thoughts about numbers, logical relations and abstract entities such as anger, jealousy or inventiveness present similar problems. In order to describe the special status of the objects of mental acts, Brentano speaks of their 'intentional in-existence' or 'immanent objectivity' in consciousness. But he also seeks to avoid any idealist misreading of such phrases, to the effect that even 'physical phenomena' are only thought to exist 'in the mind'.[50] The concern with the existential status of such abstract objects of mental states as numbers, relations, universals and impossible objects, provided the impetus for Husserl's work on the foundations of arithmetic and mathematics.[51]

Husserl applies Brentano's conception of descriptive psychology to what he regards as the only feasible approach to the epistemological problem. This is the examination of consciousness itself as the only thing which is indubitable. In order to understand the nature of consciousness as 'object-constituting subjectivity', we need to enter the realm of 'pure' or 'transcendental' consciousness, so that the world can then be described 'in all its essential aspects . . . and without bias'.[52] In Husserl's terms, we must examine consciousness 'phenomenologically' or, in other words, as it appears or as pure phenomenon.[53] At the same time, we must rigorously avoid all assumptions about the existence of physical objects in the world, to which our thoughts are normally taken to refer. This involves the 'bracketing' (*epoché*) of the 'natural attitude': the suspension of all those assumptions about existence, causality and so on, which occur in natural scientific and common-sense explanations of events in the physical world.[54] Phenomenology encourages us to distil what is really given in consciousness from what we normally assume as participants in the natural attitude. It is worth stressing, at this point, that

Husserl is not trying to answer the sceptic by identifying indubitable foundations for knowledge, as his Cartesian assumptions and admiration for Descartes might suggest. Rather, he believes that a more adequate understanding of consciousness will not allow the sceptical argument to get going.

Husserl takes Brentano's account of psychology to imply that the phenomenological project is a feasible one. Phenomenology involves perception rather than observation in Brentano's terms. Phenomenology is not another version of introspectionist psychology. The phenomenologist does not observe the individual mental components of an actual stream of consciousness. He 'intuits' the 'essence' or *eidos* of mental phenomena. If this is correct, then there is no intrinsic obstacle to a complete account of the distinctive 'being' of consciousness, because the mental phenomenon as essence is exactly what it appears to be. It does not belong to the order of ordinary physical existence, within which appearance and reality potentially diverge. The mental state as essence is pure phenomenon or appearance. In scholastic terms, mental phenomena have no existence (*Dasein* or *existentia*) but only an essence (*essentia* or *Sosein*) which, if it cannot be observed, can at least be intuited: 'if phenomena have no nature, they still have an essence, which can be grasped and adequately determined in an immediate seeing ... Intuition grasps essence as essential being, and in no way posits being-there.'[55] Consciousness can be intuited as pure phenomenon or 'eidetically'.

The method of 'pure intuition' (or 'ideation' or 'essential analysis') of the phenomena of consciousness 'by themselves, in pure immanence' is, in effect, the method of phenomenology. In contrast to 'the psychological point of view in which the glance is directed upon experience as the natural standpoint dictates, upon an experience of joy, for instance, as an *inner state* of feeling of a man or an animal', within the phenomenological point of view 'the glance is directed in reflection upon the absolute pure consciousness, giving us the apperception of an absolute experience in its intimate subjective flow.'[56] Although Husserl's technical terms for the phenomenological method are somewhat arcane, his examples are not always so intimidating. Thus it is pure or unmediated intuition which enables us to distinguish between the essences of sound and colour.[57] Phenomenology is also, as this example suggests, Husserl's solution to the problem of universals. The focus on consciousness as 'object-constituting subjectivity' is the other side of the recognition that 'nominalist' accounts of our ability to use certain concepts – the kind of account favoured by empiricism – are inevitably circular. Nominalist accounts of our ability to use concepts rely on our ability to generalize from experience.

Having experienced a number of sensations of, say, objects of a particular colour, we acquire the concept of that colour – the universal 'red'. But, as critics of nominalism have long pointed out, however many experiences we have of red objects, we could not acquire the concept of redness, unless we already possessed the ability to classify red objects together or, in other words, knew that all red objects have redness in common. But this presupposes that we already have the concept of redness. Husserl's approach at least has the advantage that it focuses our attention on this fundamental achievement of consciousness.[58]

A more extended description of the phenomenological method renders explicit the relationship Husserl finds between the notion of philosophy without presuppositions, intentionality and the distinctive being of consciousness as pure essence:

> if knowledge theory will nevertheless investigate the problems of the relationship between consciousness and being, it can have before its eyes only beings as the correlate of consciousness, as something 'intended' after the manner of consciousness: as perceived, remembered, expected, represented pictorially, imagined, identified, distinguished, believed, opined, evaluated, etc. It is clear, then, that the investigation must be directed toward a scientific essential knowledge of consciousness, toward that which consciousness itself 'is' according to its essence in all its distinguishable forms. At the same time, however, the investigation must be directed toward what consciousness 'means', as well as toward the different ways in which . . . it intends the objective . . .[59]

The reference here to what consciousness 'means' recalls Dilthey's use of the hermeneutic method for the understanding of mind or spirit and the meaning of its objectifications. By contrast, though, phenomenology applies concepts reminiscent of hermeneutic ones for more explicitly philosophical purposes. Husserl maintains that our perception and knowledge of the external world, even our most basic logical and mathematical categories, must be grounded phenomenologically in the realm of meanings. The 'contents' of consciousness are to be understood in terms of an order of essences or meanings, rather than, as is more typical within the empiricist tradition, reified as straightforwardly 'thing-like' stand-ins for material objects (as 'copies' or 'effects' of real things, as 'ideas' or 'impressions' or 'sense data' which are 'in the mind'). Hume, in this sense, comes close to the domain of phenomenology but remains within the ban of empiricist psychology – he is 'a psychological philosopher of the school of Locke' who 'almost enters its domain, but his eyes are dazzled'.[60]

Despite its evident rigour and ingenuity, Husserl's programme for philosophy as rigorous science has difficulty in fulfilling its more ambitious aims. Also ironic, perhaps, is the abstraction and abstruseness of Husserl's increasingly refined attempts to grapple directly with 'the things themselves'. The difficulty of realizing the project of pure phenomenology is reflected in some of Husserl's last lectures and writings, collected in *The Crisis of European Sciences and Transcendental Phenomenology*. In a piece written after Hitler's national socialists had seized power in Germany, Husserl returns to themes which preoccupied him throughout his life. As a result of the 'positivistic reduction of the idea of science to mere factual science', factual science is incapable of grounding human values, explaining human freedom or distinguishing reason from unreason. Scientific reason in the sense both of the objectivist natural sciences and of the humanistic sciences devoted to value-freedom 'excludes in principle precisely the questions which man, given over in our unhappy times to the most portentous upheavals, finds the most burning: questions of the meaning or meaninglessness of the whole of this human existence'.[61] However, this loss of meaning is now expressed in the rather different terms of a gulf between the practice of science and a historically unfolding 'life-world'. As Pivcevic puts it, 'bewilderment about the meaning of science is due to science being divorced from its historical human context.' As a result of this separation, the human world itself is becoming increasingly opaque to us: 'modern science, although helping us to understand nature better and to dominate it more successfully, tends to conceal from us the world as our world.'[62]

Husserl's response to the crisis of European sciences is now to focus on the role of the life-world as the basic presupposition of all thought and action. Science and philosophy, in particular, must be understood as practices, which are pursued against 'an unquestioned ground of presuppositions', a background of unreflective assumptions, values and practices, which make up the life-world. In all philosophical and scientific inquiry,

> the everyday surrounding world of life is presupposed as existing – the surrounding world in which all of us (even I who am now philosophizing) consciously have our existence; here are also the sciences as cultural facts in this world, with their scientists and theories. In this world we are objects among objects in the sense of the life-world, namely, as being here and there, in the plain certainty of experience, before anything that is established scientifically, whether in physiology, psychology, or sociology. On the other hand, we are subjects for this world, namely, as the ego-subjects experiencing it, contemplating it, valuing it, related to it purposefully . . .[63]

Positivism and factual science disrupt these pre-theoretical certainties, in whose terms we have previously led our lives, but without providing us with any more scientific or rigorous alternative. A more rigorous philosophical understanding of the life-world is not made available to us. It is the task of genuine philosophy to supply such a rigorous understanding, bridging the gulf between science and life-world. Husserl believed he could apply the phenomenological method to this task, providing a phenomenological analysis of the essence 'life-world'. But it is difficult to reconcile the notion of the life-world, as an intersubjective and historically situated background to the achievements of the knowing subject, with the perspective of transcendental consciousness, which is fundamental to Husserl's earlier formulations of phenomenology. Arguably, in his last works Husserl begins to move beyond the theoretical framework of transcendental phenomenology.[64]

In the end, Husserl's ambitious epistemological claims and the elaborate technical apparatus of transcendental phenomenology, with its relentless proliferation of neologistic terms and sometimes abstruse distinctions, have found few followers. It is perhaps Husserl's idea of going back to the things themselves, of going back to things as they are 'before science and philosophy', which proved germinal. As Bubner puts it, 'The inheritance of phenomenology has thus consisted for a long time in a certain attitude to the business of philosophizing, not in the completion of Husserl's system.'[65] Thus, for example, in the work of Maurice Merleau-Ponty (1908–61), a phenomenological description of the contents of experience and an original critique of experimental psychology provide a suggestive basis for the philosophical discussion of the body, perception, sexuality and gender.[66] In opposition to Husserl's intellectualism, Max Scheler (1874–1928) emphasizes emotions and will, the ethical and the intersubjective. His phenomenological anthropology is based on the interdependence of self and other and a notion of the person as something more than just a knowing subject. Alfred Schütz (1899–1959) adapts the notion of the life-world for a sociological investigation of the common-sense presuppositions of everyday life.[67] But it is above all in the 'ontological hermeneutics' of Heidegger that some of the ideas of Husserl and also Dilthey find their most fruitful continuation and development.

Heidegger's Phenomenology of Being

The writings of Martin Heidegger (1889–1976) represent a significant node within the development of the continental tradition in philosophy.[68] His earlier philosophy left its imprint on existentialism, particularly through the work of Jean-Paul Sartre. Heidegger is also a major point of reference for poststructuralism, deconstruction and postmodernism, but here it is his later work which tends to be most highly regarded. His philosophy affected the Frankfurt School's critique of instrumental reason. Perhaps the most direct lines of descent lead to the philosophical hermeneutics of Gadamer and Derrida's philosophy of deconstruction. Heidegger also brings together a number of important themes from previous philosophy. Like Hegel, he is committed to a view of life and philosophy as essentially historical. For him the practice of philosophy is inseparable from the interpretation of previous philosophical texts. Through the course of his career he wrote major studies of Kant, Nietzsche and Hegel, and his thinking returned continually to the ideas of Socrates, Plato, Aristotle and the pre-Socratics as well as to medieval thinkers such as Duns Scotus. A significant role in Heidegger's philosophy is also played by the history of language. He is not only extremely sensitive to nuances of meaning and association, but he also uses (some would say abuses) words in the light of their etymology (or what he takes their etymology to be).[69] A related dimension of his project is the attempt to recover meanings and insights lost over the course of the western metaphysical tradition. It is necessary to recover these meanings, in order to remedy a basic distortion of that tradition. Heidegger's attempt to overcome western metaphysical thought is influenced most directly by Husserl, and particularly his diagnosis of the naturalism and scepticism of western culture. It is also in phenomenology and hermeneutics that Heidegger finds the most useful starting point for an alternative philosophical method.

For Heidegger, the very character of western metaphysical thought is responsible for the all-pervasive influence of scientific reason and technology, which, in common with Husserl, he regards as an ultimately destructive influence on western culture. Specifically, Heidegger identifies a pathological distortion in the predominance of what he calls an 'ontotheological' conception of substance as something absolutely unconditional, something which depends on nothing else for its existence.[70] Western metaphysics is governed by the underlying conviction that there must be some being or beings, which are fundamental or 'truly real' in both an explanatory and a justificatory or normative sense. In other words, all other levels or kinds of being are causally dependent on them and all norms and values have their ground or justification in them. The history of western metaphysics consists of a number of attempts to identify such a fundamental being or beings, from Plato's 'Forms' and Aristotle's 'unmoved mover' to the God of medieval theology and Hegelian 'spirit'. According to Heidegger's account, western scientific reason sets out from the failure of these attempts. But scientific reason retains the underlying metaphysical conviction, that it makes sense to speak, if not of the normative, then at least of the causal foundations of things as absolutely or unconditionally real. The privileging of this scientific 'ontology' – the assumptions of natural science about what really exists – has led to our culture's prejudice in favour of science and scientific method as the only genuine knowledge. In order to challenge the hegemony of scientific reason, then, it is necessary to get down to the most fundamental assumptions of western metaphysics, where the idea of something as absolutely and unconditionally real first takes root. Heidegger thinks that by taking a different direction at this basic and original level, the level of ontology, it will be possible to exorcize the yearning for absolutes, the longing for ultimate metaphysical foundations.

A central problem with the ontology of scientific reason is the status of the subject. Heidegger believes this has been a problem for ontotheological conceptions of substance since Plato and Aristotle. But it becomes most clearly visible with the philosophers of the modern period and, in particular, with Descartes's dualist metaphysics of mind and matter. Descartes conceives the world as a mechanistic realm of extended material objects, which is mysteriously connected to a spiritual domain of mind or consciousness.[71] The difficulty of explaining how mind and matter can ever interact, already regarded as a major problem by Descartes's contemporaries, is just one consequence of this metaphysics. The inappropriateness of applying natural scientific method to the understanding of an essentially historical mind or spirit was a theme of Dilthey's philosophy of the human sciences. But, as Husserl realized, even human sciences governed by hermeneutic methodology cannot provide a satisfactory basis for values. Historicism is no more able to resist cultural scepticism and nihilism than is scientism. Philosophy, it seems, must provide a radically different account of the subject and subjectivity.

A direct attempt to found value on 'subjective truth' had been made by Søren Kierkegaard, in retrospect often described as the first existentialist.[72] Heidegger's reaction to Kierkegaard's attempt provides a useful introduction to some of his most important ideas. Heidegger acknowledges the importance of both Kierkegaard and life philosophy as responses to the limitations of scientific rationality. But despite their emphasis on the irreducibility of mind, life or existence, they are only 'on the way' to an understanding of life. Kierkegaard's championing of subjective truth, though valuable, is fundamentally limited, because he fails to make a sufficiently radical break with western ontology. In effect, Kierkegaard, like Dilthey, defends the subjective domain of mind or existence from the incursions of scientific reason and its ancestor, ontotheological metaphysical thinking, but he does not fundamentally challenge the ontological basis of science and metaphysics on their own ground. In Heidegger's terms, Kierkegaard does not address the 'question of Being' in all its 'existential' fullness and complexity, because his analysis is merely concerned with the 'existentiell' characteristics of subjective existence:

> In the nineteenth century, Søren Kierkegaard explicitly seized upon the problem of existence as an *existentiell* problem, and thought it through in a penetrating fashion. But the *existential* problematic was so alien to him that, as regards his ontology, he remained completely dominated by Hegel and by ancient philosophy as Hegel saw it.[73]

Heidegger uses the term 'existentiell' to refer to the subjective point of view intrinsic to the existence of conscious beings. An exploration of this perspective does not *ipso facto* illuminate what Heidegger sees as the crucial 'existential' question of 'the ontological structure of existence'.[74] In other words, although Kierkegaard provides important insights into one region of being (subjective existence), he nevertheless fails to pursue the implications of his insights for knowledge, truth and the ontological question of Being (*Sein*) as such.

Heidegger offers a similar diagnosis of Dilthey. He cites approvingly the view of Count Yorck von Wartenburg that Dilthey's investigations of the 'historical' are significant as contributions to a truer philosophical understanding of life, to 'raising up "life" into the kind of scientific understanding that is appropriate to it'. But Dilthey, like other life philosophers, was only 'on his way towards the question of "life"', because he does not mount the required challenge to western ontology.[75] Any attempt to break the grasp of scientific reason and the category of substance must do more than simply reassert the importance of subjectivity against but, as it were, alongside an objectifying positivism. It is necessary to rethink the fundamental categories of western thought for the understanding of matter and spirit, body and mind. Within western metaphysics, scientific rationality's 'objectivist' conception of nature as simply a collection of things is the counterpart of a 'subjectivist' view of mind as disembodied and isolated. In other words, subjectivism and objectivism are contrasting symptoms of the same underlying disorder of western thinking, what Gadamer has called the '"objectivistic" subjectivism of the modern age'.[76] It is not enough to reassert the 'subjective' pole of life or existence as a distinct order of being opposed to the 'objective' pole of the being of physical things in space. It is necessary to address the primordial question of Being in general.

In his best-known work, *Being and Time* (1927), Heidegger makes his first determined attempt to 'break away from the traditional domination of western thought by the category of substance (thinghood)'.[77] In effect, Heidegger restates Husserl's strategy in his own terms. Where Husserl sought a phenomenological understanding of consciousness as the means to a more adequate understanding of the nature of both 'physical' and 'mental' phenomena, Heidegger similarly attempts to reconcile the 'ontic' and the 'Historical'. To achieve an adequate understanding of life does not involve simply adding to our factual knowledge of the 'ontic' (which includes both everyday, pre-scientific knowledge and the kind of knowledge contributed by natural science). A truer understanding of life can only be achieved 'by bringing both the "ontical" and the "Historical" into a *more primordial unity*, so that they can be compared and distinguished'.[78] In order to realize this goal, Heidegger sets out to determine just what it means for something to be. Heidegger calls this the 'question of Being'. This question is so important for Heidegger because it allows him to connect both 'ontic' and 'Historical' dimensions of inquiry in the appropriate way: 'The idea of Being embraces both the "ontical" and the "Historical". It is *this idea* which must let itself be "generically differentiated".'[79]

In order to address the very abstract question of 'what it means to be', Heidegger believes (at least in his early work), that the question of Being can best be explored by asking what it means to be the kind of being which can ask that question. The question of what it means to be must be asked from the perspective of that 'being for whom Being is a question' or, in other words, from the perspective of human beings. The human being is unique in that he 'not only *is*, but has some understanding of and some responsibility for who he is'.[80] If we are able to pose the question of Being at all, then we must have some implicit understanding of Being already. Heidegger thinks that the content of this understanding is made manifest in human existence. Heidegger's term for human existence – '(T)his entity which each of us is himself and which includes inquiring as one of the possibilities of its Being' – is 'Dasein'. Literally 'being there' (but also 'being *here*'), Dasein is the German scholastic term for 'existence' as opposed to 'essence' (*Sosein* or 'being thus').[81] It was already apparent to the scholastic philosophy of the Middle Ages that the existence or 'substance' of a thing is different from its essence – its qualities or attributes. In the terms used by Kant (and taken up in the predicate calculus of modern symbolic logic), 'existence is not a predicate'.[82]

Heidegger's use of the term Dasein is, however, much more specific. He builds on the idea, already articulated by Kierkegaard and other thinkers, that human existence is something radically different from the mere subsistence of ordinary things. The term Dasein is reserved for distinctively human existence. Thus Dasein is to be the key to the meaning of Being in general.

In order to provide a description of Dasein as the key to the understanding of Being, Heidegger assumes the phenomenologist's stance of describing the world and reality as they are experienced. But he is concerned to avoid falling into the same traps as previous phenomenologists. In particular, he is determined to avoid any view of consciousness as simply the abstract bearer and organizer of experience. Accordingly, Heidegger describes Dasein as irreducibly situated and intersubjective. Dasein is from the beginning both 'Being-in-the-world' and 'Being-with-others'. Consciousness is not primarily or originally a detached and abstract bearer and organizer of experience. Rather, it is something which can only be such a bearer of experience against the background of a certain understanding of what it is to be, of the individual subject as person or individual. In other words, Heidegger is describing what Husserl discusses in his last work as the life-world. Dasein thus bears no resemblance to the detached and contemplative consciousness or 'theoria' of the western philosophical tradition.

The primary relationship of Dasein to the world is one of practical, personal involvement or 'care' (Sorge) – 'the Being of Dasein itself is to be made visible as care.'[83] We do not originally encounter the world as detached observers but as involved participants, for whom things in the world are 'ready-to-hand' (zuhanden) rather than simply 'present-at-hand' (vorhanden). Things exist originally as tools or 'equipment' we can use in particular ways. Equipment always exists in relation to other things in an 'arrangement' corresponding to a range of related practices.[84] The world is originally and, for Heidegger, fundamentally constituted as a practical totality. The objectivity of the world is first conveyed to us through its resistance to desire and will. On the other hand, the presence-at-hand of objects is a secondary or derivative mode of being, corresponding to the contemplative attitude of scientific theory – an attitude which is secondary to the originally practical relationship of care. In these terms, the western metaphysical tradition goes wrong by treating what is fundamentally readiness-to-hand as if it were presence-at-hand. Crucially, it is impossible to think of the situated Dasein of Heidegger's ontology as a detached observer of the world like the Cartesian ego: 'Being-in-the-world is a structure which is primordially and constantly *whole*.'[85] Dasein, as 'being-there', is inseparable from the world, and so it is essentially Being-in-the-world. It is equally important to realize that, by implication, the world is just as inseparable from the idea of conscious existence as Dasein is inseparable from the world. Heidegger's radical challenge to the objectivism of western metaphysics could not be more apparent.

By the same token, Dasein is primordially 'Being-with-others'. If our primary relationship to the world is the practical relationship typified by work, then in our encounters with ready-to-hand tools or products we also encounter the others, for whom these products are made or who supplied the materials we are using.[86] In his discussion of Being-with-others Heidegger again makes clear, that he wishes to avoid the solipsistic predicament. He does not propose to 'start by marking out and isolating the "I" so that one must then seek some way of getting over to the Others from this isolated subject': 'the world is always the one that I share with Others.'[87] Just as the fundamental relationship of Dasein to the world is care, the primordial relationship to others (as Dasein) is one of 'solicitude' (*Fürsorge*). The relationship of Dasein with others brings with it the possibility of 'inauthenticity'. Although it is possible for Dasein to be with others authentically, the relationship with others is also the basis for an inauthentic relationship of conformity to the 'they' (*das Man*).

> We take pleasure and enjoy ourselves as *they* [*man*] take pleasure; we read, see, and judge about literature and art as *they* see and judge; likewise we shrink back from the 'great mass' as *they* shrink back; we find 'shocking' what *they* find shocking. The 'they', which is nothing definite, and which all are, though not as the sum, prescribes the kind of Being of everydayness.[88]

In effect, Heidegger restates in ontological terms criticisms of mass society, which play a significant role in the writings of existentialists such as Kierkegaard and Nietzsche. When Dasein is subjected to an impersonalized other, its own authentic selfhood is lost.

The possibility of authentic or inauthentic relationships to others highlights a crucial dimension of Dasein, namely its directedness to future possibilities and projects. Unlike other entities Dasein has no determinate essence. Put another way, Dasein is distinguished by its freedom to make itself: 'Dasein always understands itself in terms of its existence – in terms of a possibility of itself: to be itself or not itself . . . Dasein is an entity whose Being has the determinate character of existence.'[89] In other words, human beings are free to make or remake themselves. They do not simply fulfil a predetermined 'essence' as, it seems, plants or animals must do. If human beings embrace their freedom, they have the possibility of authentic existence.

If they do not, they fall into inauthenticity and are, in Heidegger's terms, 'fallen'. Fallenness is absorption in the everyday, in the present and in the conformity of the 'they'. It involves abdication of that freedom and possibility intrinsic to authentic Dasein. It is that kind of Being-in-the-world 'which is completely fascinated by the "world" and by the Dasein-with of Others in the "they"'.[90] Free or fallen, authentic or inauthentic, these possibilities of Dasein reflect the historicity and temporality of human existence. Human projects are aimed at the future. It is a feature of consciousness, that we can formulate projects, that our actions are aimed at goals in the future. Equally, our projects are inevitably limited by the 'facticity' of the situation we inherit from the past. Our freedom is a situated one, not all projects are available to us as possibilities.

But why are we constantly tempted to relinquish authentic existence and to abdicate our freedom? The reason is that authentic existence – an existence lived in the full awareness of our freedom to act, to realize our own projects rather than the projects of the 'they' – is an extremely arduous state. Awareness of freedom is inseparable from anxiety. It is much easier simply to go with the flow, to conform to the everyday. Authentic Dasein is possible only with intense awareness of the ever-present possibility of death. In an important sense, 'Care is Being-towards-death.'[91] Like Kierkegaard, Heidegger sees awareness of the prospect of our own death as an important condition of a genuinely authentic existence. Death forces us to confront our evasion of the most important questions, our absorption in the trivia of everyday life. The awareness of death can awaken us from the conformist forgetfulness of the everyday, from our fallen state of 'fleeing in the face of death': 'Death is a possibility-of-Being which Dasein itself has to take over in every case. With death, Dasein stands before itself in its ownmost potentiality-for-Being . . . If Dasein stands before itself as this possibility, it has been *fully* assigned to its ownmost potentiality-for-Being.'[92] More prosaically, the prospect of death concentrates the mind wonderfully.

Being and Time exerted a profound influence on continental philosophy (at roughly the same time as it became, for the logical positivists, the favourite example of the meaninglessness of metaphysics). Ironically, though, this work was understood at first mainly as a sophisticated statement of existentialism and, as a result, it contributed substantially to the vocabulary of existentialist philosophers such as Jean-Paul Sartre. This reception effectively ignored Heidegger's claim that the main purpose of the exploration of human existence as Dasein was the illumination of the deeper question of Being in general. It is a matter of some controversy, whether *Being and Time* ultimately fails to fulfil this ambitious goal and relapses into something more like an existentialist exploration of subjective truth (of the 'existentiell' rather than the 'existential').[93] It is a matter of further controversy whether Heidegger's later writings represent the continuation of his earlier philosophy or a radical change of direction and 'turning' (*Kehre*) away from it.[94] Certainly, in the later work what many had taken to be an existentialist preoccupation with individual existence as anxious, caring, authentic or fallen Dasein, gives way to a more impersonal preoccupation with Being. Heidegger places increasing emphasis on the importance of diverting our 'thinking' from its individualistic concerns, from the concerns of the subject of consciousness, towards a greater 'attentiveness' to Being. Only by transcending the limited perspective of the Cartesian subject, 'who may deign to release the beingness of beings into an all too loudly bruited "objectivity"', can 'thinking' 'realize the proper dignity of man' as 'the shepherd of Being'.[95] The 'subjectivism' exemplified in Enlightenment epistemology is still the counterpart of that 'forgetfulness of Being', for which the world is simply a collection of things present-at-hand.

Accompanying what is at least a change of emphasis, there is in Heidegger's later writings an overriding preoccupation with language as 'the house of Being'.[96] With this idea Heidegger comes close to restating the themes of philosophical idealism. The world is inseparable from our conceiving of a world: there is only the indivisible being-in-the-world. But our conception of the world is inextricably tied to our language. This train of thought leads Heidegger to a distinctive account of truth. He suggests an alternative and more literal translation of '*aletheia*', the Greek word normally translated as 'truth', namely 'unconcealment'.[97] In these terms language is clearly inseparable from truth, because it is language which 'discloses' Being or 'brings it into the open': 'language alone brings beings as beings into the open for the first time. Where there is no language, as in the Being of stone, plant, and animal, there is also no openness of beings, and consequently no openness either of nonbeing and of the empty.'[98] Language is the 'clearing' of Being, the possibility of Being's unconcealment. Once again, Heidegger speaks of language rather than consciousness here, in order to avoid falling into the familiar metaphysical pitfalls of subject and object. Language unmistakably transcends the individual subject, transcends individual consciousness and existence. At the same time, Heidegger becomes increasingly preoccupied with the poetic or creative use of language. The true philosopher is the poet who, through a 'projective saying', allows new aspects of Being to reveal themselves: 'The essence of art is poetry. The essence of poetry, in turn, is the founding of truth.'[99] Needless to say, the truth of poetry is not to be confused with the merely factual truths of scientific discourse.

Gadamer and the Universality of Hermeneutics

Thus there is undoubtedly no understanding that is free of all prejudices, however much the will of our knowledge must be directed toward escaping their thrall. Throughout our investigation it has emerged that the certainty achieved by using scientific methods does not suffice to guarantee truth. This especially applies to the human sciences, but it does not mean that they are less scientific; on the contrary, it justifies the claim to special humane significance that they have always made. The fact that in such knowledge the knower's own being comes into play certainly shows the limits of method, but not of science. Rather, what the tool of method does not achieve must – and really can – be achieved by a discipline of questioning and inquiring, a discipline that guarantees truth.[100]

Gadamer's philosophical hermeneutics grows directly from the philosophy of Heidegger. Like the *later* Heidegger, however, Gadamer is more immediately concerned with language, interpretation and art than with the explicitly ontological question of the meaning of 'being'. On the other hand, although issues concerning the nature and possibility of interpreting or understanding works of art and texts clearly lie at the heart of his philosophy, Gadamer still develops an ontological rather than merely epistemological hermeneutics. In Palmer's words, understanding is 'not conceived as a subjective process of man over and against an object but the way of being of man himself'.[101] That is to say, Gadamer is concerned with hermeneutics not, like Dilthey, as the characteristic method of the human sciences, but as the key to the nature of truth in understanding and interpretation and, in his opinion relatedly, the nature of human, historical existence. In other words, he adopts from Heidegger the idea that understanding and interpretation, as these are practised in the so-called human sciences or *Geisteswissenschaften*, are simply a more explicit form of an activity which we are engaged in all the time. Understanding is the basic way in which self-conscious, historically existing beings relate to the world. Understanding has ontological significance. Thus Gadamer responds to the universalist pretension of natural scientific reason with an ontological hermeneutics whose claims are no less universal. Hermeneutic categories are regarded as fundamental, not merely to specific cognitive enterprises such as history, aesthetic appreciation and legal interpretation, but rather to the very nature of self-consciousness and of the world as our world.

Gadamer shares with the hermeneutic tradition as a whole the belief that understanding, this most fundamental dimension of human existence, cannot be made sense of within the categories of the 'methodical' natural sciences. It is particularly important, in this context, that the conjunction of the terms 'truth' and 'method' in the title of Gadamer's best-known work, *Truth and Method*, is not misunderstood. A method, in Gadamer's terms, is a set of explicit procedures or rules designed to purge knowledge of all distorting or idiosyncratic subjective influences. Bacon and Descartes proposed a method in just this sense as the only reliable means of securing objectivity in the natural sciences. But Gadamer does not seek to formulate an equivalent method for the human sciences in order to secure the objectivity of its interpretations in analogous fashion. This, in effect, is the project of Dilthey. On the contrary, Gadamer's aim is to demonstrate the limits of methodical science. While the idea of method plays a valid role in natural sciences such as physics or chemistry, it cannot account for the practice of interpretation or understanding within the human sciences. These 'non-methodical' sciences can achieve truth only by renouncing all claims to methodical objectivity and relying instead upon the fundamental human capacity for understanding. What is more (and as we shall see in more detail in what follows), according to Gadamer even the methodical natural sciences ultimately have their foundation in this hermeneutic capacity. As some commentators have suggested, therefore, truth *or* method might have been a less misleading title. In Bubner's words, Gadamer's project is 'a matter of explicating the *reciprocal relations between methodical science* and an *original truth* which transcends the methodical'; as such it is a 'reflection on . . . methodological dogmatism'.[102]

In order to overcome the dogmatism of method Gadamer, again like Heidegger, seeks to displace the subject from its pivotal position in the western metaphysical tradition. In particular, he denies the subject that radical epistemological autonomy, that freedom from conditionedness, which modern philosophy since Descartes has tended to accord to it. The Cartesian view of the subject, together with the associated conviction that the knowing subject is capable of, and ought to strive for, absolutely certain knowledge, goes hand in hand with the glorification of an objectifying scientific knowledge and a manipulative, instrumental stance towards nature.[103] The characteristically modern celebration of humanity, which is considered capable of a comprehensive and objective scientific knowledge of nature, ultimately involves the 'dominance of the human subject and its calculating techniques and methods over the world considered as a realm of things'.[104] The exaggerated role accorded to the subject ultimately explains modern philosophy's tendency to reify nature as a realm of mere objects. What is worse, the untrammelled expansion of this calculating reason threatens to reduce human beings to the same condition as well.

In fact, of course, Husserl too had recognized the interdependent objectivism and subjectivism of modern thought. But for Gadamer, Husserl remains under the spell of his Cartesian and Kantian heritage. Husserl's starting point within transcendental consciousness condemns him to an endless replaying of dilemmas familiar from foundationalist epistemology. Despite the subtlety of his analyses, he never really escapes the labyrinth. Husserl comes closest to overcoming the standpoint of subjective consciousness with his concept of the life-world. But he still refuses to relinquish the standpoint of transcendental consciousness, insisting instead on a phenomenological account of the essence 'life-world' from the point of view of transcendental consciousness.[105] It is clear to Gadamer, on the other hand, that properly understood 'the notion of the "life-world" has a revolutionary power that explodes the framework of Husserl's transcendental thinking.'[106] There can be no transcendental perspective on the life-world because all our thinking inevitably occurs within, and so is necessarily conditioned by, the life-world. Philosophy must follow Heidegger's lead and turn, without either metaphysical preconceptions or transcendental pretensions, to the exploration of the life-world itself as the historical and intersubjective horizon of all human experience.

The recognition of the life-world as the unsurpassable horizon of all human experience and activity has radical implications for hermeneutics as well as for philosophy. According to Gadamer previous theorists of hermeneutics had, despite their valuable contributions, failed to recognize the universality of its claims. Certainly with Schleiermacher hermeneutics, which had previously been no more than a collection of disparate techniques for the interpretation of obscure or broken passages in ancient texts, was turned into a more organized procedure for securing the objectivity of interpretations. Schleiermacher recognized that hermeneutics was needed even when we experience no difficulty of understanding. We often merely think that we understand when in fact we do not, because we often fail to recognize changes in the meaning of terms that we have come to use in different ways. Dilthey systematically developed this conception of hermeneutics as a methodical procedure for overcoming the subjective limitations of understanding in the historical and human sciences.

But for Gadamer, Dilthey remains too close to the dogmatism of method. He remains wedded to the traditional model of method as a reliable instrument capable of generating objective truth, because he fails to recognize the full implications of acknowledging the subjective pole of understanding. The subjective and historically located point of view of the interpreter is simply an obstacle to be overcome on the path to objective knowledge. Dilthey, on Gadamer's reading, believes that 'scientific knowledge obliges one to sever one's bond with life, to attain distance from one's own history, which alone makes it possible for that history to become an object.'[107]

For Gadamer, by contrast, the subjective and historical foundation of understanding is not something to be eliminated or overcome in this way. Understanding is always inevitably *for* a subject as much as it is *of* some object; and it is inevitable that 'in such knowledge the knower's own being comes into play.'[108] Recognizing this subjective pole of understanding means acknowledging that even mutual understanding *within* a particular cultural horizon can never be taken for granted. Even the interpretation of a historical text has itself to be understood by the interpreter's contemporaries. The interpretation is, strictly speaking, no more self-evident than the text whose meaning the interpretation claims to capture. Linge elucidates this 'reflexive dimension' of understanding as follows: 'The familiar horizons of the interpreter's world, though perhaps more difficult to grasp thematically, are as integral a part of the event of understanding as are the explicit procedures by which he assimilates the alien object.'[109] The interpreter's subjectivity occurs within a present horizon of meanings and prejudgements or what Gadamer calls 'prejudices', which is as much a part of history – and as vulnerable to the vicissitudes of misunderstanding – as the historical texts studied by interpreters working within that horizon. In other words, historicity characterizes not just the object but also the subject of acts of understanding. There is no fixed, 'transcendental' pole of subjectivity capable of sustaining the possible objectivity of interpretation in the way that methodical dogmatism requires. Understanding always inevitably occurs within a historically situated, intersubjective lifeworld which itself depends on the achievement of understanding.

One corollary of this recognition of the essentially historical character of subjectivity is the unattainability of the Enlightenment's conception of science as a reliable method leading to an objective knowledge purified of all presupposition and prejudice. As Gadamer provocatively asserts, 'there is undoubtedly no understanding that is free of all prejudices.'[110] Every interpretation is liable not only to the difficulties of understanding an object obscured by distance and time, but also to the limitations implied by the historical situation of the subject of understanding. The interpreter's point of view is not something which can ever be escaped, however much we must also diligently try to do so. We are products of a particular history and tradition just as much as we are interpreters of other historical traditions. History is not simply an object to be known; history is also what has made us into the particular 'subjects' who attempt to understand it. Accordingly, there can be no such thing as a hermeneutic method, only what Gadamer describes as 'a discipline of questioning and inquiring'.[111] But by the same token, the fundamental importance of the discipline of interpretation must also be recognized. Even the cognitive activities of natural scientists must occur within the horizon of a particular conceptual structure, a particular conception of knowledge, truth and scientific practice. The usefulness of the methods employed by the specialized sciences is not disputed here, only their claim to stand outside a linguistically constituted and hermeneutically grounded intersubjectivity. The specialized sciences presuppose the life-world and the hermeneutic capacities on which it depends. So these sciences cannot, as philosophical naturalism would have it, either ground the hermeneutic categories of the life-world or replace them with scientifically 'purified' categories of their own. On the contrary, hermeneutics must be acknowledged to give access to truth in its own right, even though, in fact only if, it does not aspire to the status of an objective method.

Gadamer's ontological construal of understanding also corresponds to a revised account of the *practice* of interpretation, albeit an account that is as important for its illumination of human being-in-the-world as for any light cast on our more specifically hermeneutic activities. In the first place, there can be no uniquely true interpretation for any particular text – though there can certainly be better and worse or incorrect interpretations. Because it is always a question of understanding some meaning from the perspective of a particular historically situated interpretive horizon, understanding is irreducibly relational. At best there can be the correct interpretation from that perspective, which can coexist with different interpretations from other perspectives. Hermeneutics is always the link between two horizons rather than, as Schleiermacher and Dilthey thought, something which can in principle restore a forgotten text to the pristine clarity of an original meaning. We can only avoid distorting truth for the sake of such unattainable ideals of scientific objectivity if we recognize that we always seek understanding *from* as well as *of* a particular situation and horizon. Significantly, here, the complementary concepts of situation and horizon are to be understood positively as well as negatively. The possibility of vision, too, is insep-arable from the idea of a particular perspective or situation which also limits vision. A situation is 'a standpoint that limits the possibility of vision', but situation also implies a 'range of vision that includes everything that can be seen from a particular vantage point'.[112]

A further aspect of the practice of interpretation derives from the fact that the questions and concerns that we bring to the study of historical texts (and which make up our horizon of understanding) must themselves be seen as, at least in part, the product of the tradition which these texts helped to form. History 'determines in advance both what seems to us worth inquiring about and what will appear as an object of investigation'.[113] If we deny the effect of our history, we risk once again falling into a false objectivism which, like statistics, is such good propaganda, because it appears to 'let the "facts" speak' at the same time as it organizes them in terms of a particular set of questions and concerns. Instead 'we should learn to understand ourselves better and recognize that in all understanding, whether we are expressly aware of it or not, the efficacy of history is at work.'[114] Interpretation serves the interests and concerns of the present as much as it is directed towards the past, but we must also recognize that these concerns have themselves been shaped by the past and by tradition. It is in this sense that Gadamer speaks of the importance of the 'history of effect' (*Wirkungsgeschichte*) of the text, or in other words the way the text has taken effect in history and helped to shape the present.[115]

It is also important for Gadamer that this 'history of effect' should be regarded positively. The act of interpretation should not be seen, in the way Dilthey and historicism tended to do, as simply the more or less successful recovery of a meaning lost or obscured by time. Rather we should 'recognize temporal distance as a positive and productive condition enabling understanding'.[116] Gadamer illustrates this with reference to the understanding of both events and works of art. He points out that it is more difficult to understand the historical significance or the aesthetic value of a contemporary work of art than a work from the past. This is because the temporal distance between a work of art or historical event and its contemporary interpreter is a distance filled by the labours of past interpreters, whose insights (and even mistakes) may help the interpreter in the present to make sense of the work or event in the past. Temporal distance filters out certain misunderstandings which, for contemporaries, are difficult or even impossible to avoid, and 'new sources of understanding are continu-ally emerging that reveal unsuspected elements of meaning.'[117] Through the continuity of a tradition of interpretation the meaning of events, texts or works of art continues to unfold. Through interpretation the past continues to be effective in the present, and so interpretation is inseparable from the continuity and productivity of tradition. History is not an inert object which needs to be reconstituted, but something which, through understanding, continues to be active and to have effects in the present.

The productivity which is inseparable from texts and traditions has the further implication that meaning is strictly 'inexhaustible'. A single interpretation can never recover the meaning of a work fully and definitively for all times, for all interpretive horizons. The interpreter can never aspire to a final, unique and timelessly valid interpretation. It is in this sense that the meaning of the work is inexhaustible. On the other hand, this does not mean that all interpretations are equally valid. In fact, Gadamer assumes that every text or work has some definite meaning. Otherwise there would be no constraints on the process of interpretation at all: hermeneutically, everything would be permitted. In that case, too, it would not be obvious why what might be very different interpretations should nevertheless be regarded as interpretations of the same work. Rather, for Gadamer the meaning of a work is analogous to the 'thing-in-itself' in Kant's philosophy. Though strictly unknowable, the 'thing-in-itself' is what must be presumed to underlie and ultimately account for the orderly succession of appearances or 'phenomena', which makes up our experience of an external world of objects.[118] Similarly, a text's meaning is what both underlies and accounts for the succession of possible interpretations which the work inspires – interpretations which, according to Gadamer, the work can even be said to produce. All valid interpretations must bear some relationship to this meaning. But the meaning of the work, like the Kantian thing-in-itself, is never itself directly encountered in the succession of interpretations. So we can never test the accuracy of an interpretation simply by comparing it directly with the meaning of the work. There can be no correspondence theory of interpretation. All that we can ever do is to investigate the series of different interpretations in the same way as, in our experience of the external or physical world, we never escape from the 'manifold of appearances'.[119]

It is important to realize, though, that Gadamer's conviction that the work has some definite meaning does not support any authorial veto (whether actual or posthumously alleged) over possible interpretations. The author cannot be assumed to have an absolutely privileged relationship to the meaning of the work. The productivity of the work, manifest in the endless proliferation of possible interpretations, is not circumscribed by the supposed intentions of the author.

Although we might expect the author's intentions to bear an important relation to contemporary or later interpretations, their authority
is far from absolute. On the one hand, since understanding is relational, the text may support as many interpretations as there are historically distinct horizons of interpretation. But equally, the meaning
created by the author of a work itself depends on the horizon of
meanings, within which it was produced. This hermeneutic context is
always much richer than the author can ever comprehend. It is this
all-encompassing horizon of language and meaning, rather than the
author's intentions, which ultimately determines meaning. Language
speaks through individual subjects as much as they speak through
language. Gadamer is drawn to the image of play which, properly
understood, is not reducible to the intentions of the individual play-
ers. Those playing the game are absorbed into the activity in such a
way that 'play is not to be understood as something a person
does . . . the actual subject of play is obviously not the subjectivity of
an individual, who among other activities, also plays but is instead the
play itself.'[120] This 'primacy of play over the consciousness of the
player' provides a suggestive analogy both for the relationship of
the individual speaker to language and for the way the process of
interpretation has a life and a direction of its own. Language and so
also interpretation transcend the intentions of individual subjects.

Gadamer's account of hermeneutics very closely aligns the practice of interpretation with 'application'. Application, in the specific
sense that interests Gadamer, is involved whenever a general principle or rule is applied to a particular case. Application has traditionally played an important role in both legal judgement and biblical
exegesis. How should some law, always necessarily at least partially
abstract, be applied in particular, concrete situations? What is the
moral or spiritual lesson for people today of a particular biblical
parable or saying? In answering such questions, application, like
interpretation, involves mediating between past and present, between what is taken to be the meaning of the text or law and what
might be the very different conditions and concerns of the present.
The correct application of law, in Gadamer's terms, must be faithful
to the 'original meaning' or spirit of the law in question, but it must
also 'take account of the change in circumstances and hence define
afresh the normative function of the law'.[121] Analogously interpretation attempts to grasp the original meaning of a text but always from
within a present horizon of meanings. Interpretation 'applies' the
original text within a tradition which has, in the meantime, moved on.
But it is also important to realize that in both application and interpretation it is not a question of first recovering the uniquely true

meaning of a sacred or legal text and then applying that meaning in the present. Rather, it is only through the conscientious application of law or interpretation of text that genuine understanding takes place at all: 'Application does not mean first understanding a given universal in itself and then afterward applying it to a concrete case. It is the very understanding of the universal – the text – itself. Understanding proves to be a kind of effect and knows itself as such.'[122] Both application and interpretation, then, are productive activities or, in other words, examples of 'historically effected consciousness'. They do not simply make use of the resources (meanings or judgements) of a particular tradition, they also continually produce and reproduce those resources.

Application is such a significant model of hermeneutics, because it entrenches Gadamer's view of understanding as a creative, productive and yet highly disciplined activity. But in what ways can the practices of application and interpretation be described as disciplined? Certainly, the valid application of law in a particular case is never just 'arbitrary revision'.[123] The judges who apply the law do not *make* the law, at least not in the same sense that legislators do. Rather application is intended to preserve the law's 'normative content' or 'function' in a different context.[124] But clearly, like interpretation application can be no exact or methodical science either.[125] Rather (and here Gadamer emphasizes the connection between his own account of hermeneutics and an older tradition of European humanism) application is an important instance of that distinct human capacity, identified by Aristotle as 'practical knowledge' or *phronesis* – a capacity most directly involved in moral and aesthetic judgement. Unlike theoretical knowledge, exemplified in the methodical natural sciences, which seeks universal truths, practical knowledge is 'directed towards the concrete situation'; it includes (though is not equivalent to) 'the capacity to subsume the individual case under a universal category – what we call "judgment"'.[126] Application thus involves the kind of 'just weighing up of the whole' typified in moral and aesthetic judgement.[127] Like interpretation or understanding, it is unmethodical but certainly not, for that reason, merely arbitrary. It is essential to Gadamer's view, then, that interpretation, like application, can be disciplined without being methodical. Neither practice can be subsumed under the categories of technical or methodical knowledge. Both rely on the less mechanical but, for Gadamer, no less rigorous human capacity of judgement or practical knowledge.

The upshot of Gadamer's account of understanding is an emphasis on the importance of tradition as an ongoing dialogue or 'dialectic' between past and present.[128] Understanding works as a dialectic between the horizon of the present and the horizon of the past or tradition. This relationship is genuinely dialectical, because the past is not a simply inert or passive object of the hermeneutic process but more like a partner in dialogue. The interpreter only distorts the past, if she or he reduces the works of the past to the status of mere objects. Rather, the interpreter who seeks genuine understanding is engaged in a common pursuit with an interlocutor from the past, approaching the truth through a series of questions and answers. What is more, this dialogue not only serves to improve our understanding of the past and its texts, it may also unsettle some of our own convictions and lead to revisions in our present horizon of meanings. Understanding is always a productive fusion of horizons, through which the past continues to be active and 'effective' or productive in the present.

Gadamer's positive evaluation of the past and of tradition has led some to see his philosophy as essentially conservative. Certainly, he maintains that our understanding is always 'prejudged' by the horizon of meanings within which we act and think: 'Our being-in-the-world conditions us to certain structures of anticipated meanings. We pre-understand, or anticipate meaning in the very process of coming to understand.'[129] And in this sense, 'there is undoubtedly no understanding that is free of all prejudices.'[130] But Gadamer also emphasizes that horizons of meaning are always open to the possibility of critique and revision, including revisions deriving from a more adequate understanding of the past. Our prejudices are only obstacles to critical reason if they are dogmatically insulated from criticism. If anything, alert to the role that prejudices inevitably play, we are in a better position to challenge them. Thus Gadamer does not so much reject the Enlightenment's commitment to critical rationality as question its favoured view of reason as something absolutely other than and opposed to both tradition and authority:

> The Enlightenment's distinction between faith in authority and using one's own reason is, in itself, legitimate. If the prestige of authority displaces one's own judgment, then authority is in fact a source of prejudices . . . But this is not the essence of authority . . . authority has to do not with obedience but rather with knowledge.[131]

Authority is rational, if it is based on superior knowledge or genuine wisdom. Nor is obedience to authority blind, if it is based on the free and informed acknowledgement of the knowledge of that authority. On such grounds we usually accept the authority of doctors, lawyers, nuclear physicists and ecological scientists – though it is obviously decisive when, how long and in which areas we accept their authority.

It is Gadamer's claim that even the most ambitious rationalism cannot hope to escape from a similar dependence on authority. Reason can never achieve and should not even aspire to the independence from tradition and prejudices claimed on its behalf by Enlightenment philosophers. But Gadamer is equally convinced that a more modest rationalism need not be any less radically critical. Although 'there is undoubtedly no understanding that is free of all prejudices', still 'the will of our knowledge must be directed toward escaping their thrall.'[132]

Gadamer's philosophical hermeneutics thus holds out the possibility of a distinctive solution to one of the central dilemmas of post-Enlightenment rationalism. He claims to be able to navigate the difficult course between on the one side a reductive objectivism, with its universalist pretensions on behalf of calculating, methodical reason, and on the other side the relativist or historicist abdication of truth implicit in subjectivism. Like Hegel, Husserl and Heidegger, Gadamer regards the various manifestations of both objectivism and subjectivism as antithetical symptoms of the same underlying disorder of the western philosophical tradition. The disembodied subject of post-Cartesian philosophy is the logical counterpart of a reductive objectivism, for which reality is no more than a mechanical system of matter extended in space. Gadamer, on the other hand, rejects the standpoint of a transcendental subject outside both history and life-world and with it both the timeless truths of reason and the universalist claims made on behalf of an all-encompassing methodical science. Ultimately both truth and subjectivity are founded historically and hermeneutically in the life-world, always dependent on the precarious and always-to-be-recreated achievement of mutual understanding.[133] Both subjectivist and objectivist pathologies derive from a neglect of this foundation.

However, Gadamer's insistence on the universality of hermeneutics has led less sympathetic critics to see his approach as no more than a species of relativism.[134] Gadamer's hermeneutic ontology certainly implies that criticism of one horizon of meanings or prejudices can only come from within some other horizon. We can never escape from our life-world altogether, even if we may come to revise some of its fundamental assumptions. But Gadamer nevertheless rejects accusations of relativism or subjectivism. For him the fact that understanding always presupposes the standpoint of particular historical contexts or horizons need not imply that genuine critique and mutual understanding between them is impossible. In this sense Gadamer's position has, at least for his defenders, a clear advantage over the later philosophy of Wittgenstein, which presents a picture of language as comprising disparate 'language games' – in Linge's words, as 'a multitude of hermetically sealed usages and corresponding life forms', a 'monadic isolation of language games'. This picture implicitly denies the 'assimilative power of language as a constant mediation and translation' between horizons or language games.[135] According to Gadamer we can indeed, through our diligent efforts at understanding, escape the 'monadic isolation' of our particular horizons of understanding, albeit never absolutely or once for all. The dialogue between cultures and times is productive. It always brings fresh insights. In the end, Gadamer is confident that 'what the tool of method does not achieve must – and really can – be achieved by a discipline of questioning and inquiring, a discipline that guarantees truth.'[136]

5. Beyond Theory: Kierkegaard, Nietzsche, Existentialism

Søren Kierkegaard

The Enlightenment espoused a conception of knowledge and rationality closely modelled on the natural sciences. Enlightenment rationalism was correspondingly hostile to what many took to be the truths of traditional morality and religion. In these terms, Hegel's philosophy has been understood as an attempt to save these truths from an overhasty critique and place them on more secure philosophical foundations. His dialectical system is designed to express moral and religious truths in a more fully rational form. The limited insights of both scientific reason and dogmatic religion are transcended with the higher synthesis of Absolute knowledge. The antagonistic relationship between reason and faith can be overcome with the help of a more adequate understanding of them both. Hegel still believed, in Rohde's words, that 'it was possible to unite faith and thought and create an all-comprehending synthesis in which all oppositions could be reconciled.'[1] On this interpretation, Hegel is close to the tradition of humanist theology, which seeks to harmonize human reason and faith by making faith acceptable to reason. If faith does not survive in its original form, then this is the price that dogmatic religion has to pay for its rescue from a sceptical rationalism. Hegel was, of course, criticized by protagonists of Enlightenment rationalism, who saw his philosophy as a straightforward relapse into mysticism. Others, like Marx, though sympathetic with his dialectical and historical method, were still inclined to reject Hegel's philosophy as simply religion in another guise. In their different ways, these thinkers criticize Hegel from the point of view of rationalism and humanism, whether simple or more sophisticated.[2]

By contrast, Søren Kierkegaard (1813–55) proposes a radical defence of religious faith which, far from attempting to reconcile reason with faith, emphasizes the gulf between them. In effect, he renews the theological tradition of 'fideism', for which religious faith is diminished rather than strengthened by its reduction to merely human reason.[3] In retrospect Kierkegaard has, for reasons which will become clear, been identified as the first 'existentialist'. For the fideist tradition, which includes such thinkers as St Augustine, Meister Eckhart, Pascal and Luther, faith surpasses human understanding. Human reason is the limited capacity of an imperfect and sinful being, who is not surprisingly unable to comprehend an omnipotent, omniscient and perfectly benevolent God. The high point of reason in these terms is the recognition of its own limits. In the words of Pascal: 'Reason's last step is the recognition that there are an infinite number of things which are beyond it.'[4] The attempt to formulate a rational religion is really an expression of arrogance, which can never hope to do justice to the spiritual meaning of faith. This claim makes obvious sense in relation to the lifeless abstraction of Enlightenment deism which, though it preserved a metaphysical role for God as creator or 'first cause' of the universe, evidently failed to satisfy the specifically religious needs of humanity. For Kierkegaard, what is more, even the baroque edifice of Hegelian idealism concedes too much to humanism and rationalism and, as a result, neglects or distorts the meaning of faith.[5] In response, Kierkegaard develops a radical version of the fideist position, maintaining that religious faith not only does not require the support of reason but is essentially at odds with it. Religion has no particular significance, if it simply expresses in different terms truths which can be stated without it. The significance of religion is inseparable from its violation of merely human rationality and even morality. In Tertullian's phrase, *credo quia impossibile* – I believe because it is impossible to believe. It is as if Kierkegaard takes seriously the ironic taunt of David Hume who, after demolishing to his own satisfaction all rational grounds for belief in miracles as evidence of the truth of religion, remarks that anyone who still has faith 'is conscious of a continued miracle in his own person, which subverts all the principles of his understanding, and gives him a determination to believe what is most contrary to custom and experience'.[6]

A crucial part of Kierkegaard's strategy is to reject the rationalist conception of objective knowledge or contemplative theory, which plays a central role in the western philosophical tradition. The idea of

theory (*theoria*) as the disinterested and essentially unpractical contemplation of the world or cosmos is first clearly expounded in classical Greek philosophy. Aristotle describes theoretical knowledge as
contemplation of the eternal and unchanging: 'the object of scientific
knowledge necessarily exists. Consequently it is also eternal; for
things that are of necessity in the unqualified sense are eternal; and
things that are eternal are ungenerated and imperishable.'[7] With the
Enlightenment this conception of theory is transformed into an understanding of scientific knowledge as fundamentally instrumental.
Scientific knowledge is inseparable from the 'technological' capacity
to manipulate and control the external world.[8] Still, objectivity remains an essential characteristic of theory, surviving the originally
contemplative ideal. Theory must avoid all subjective bias, it must
transcend all purely subjective points of view, in order to attain an
intersubjective and eternal truth. Much of the western tradition of
epistemology sees its task as establishing with certainty that this goal
has been or can be achieved. Truth, on this view, is only attained
when theory has expunged all connection with the merely subjective
life of knowing subjects.

But according to Kierkegaard, this ideal of objective knowledge,
which was championed by the Enlightenment and then deployed
against it with such ingenuity and persistence by Hegel, is constitu-
tionally blind to the inner life or subjective existence of the human
individual. Objective theoretical knowledge makes no useful contribution to understanding human life. We are, however, easily misled,
because the intellectual approach to life (the attempt to understand
life in theoretical terms) gives a deceptive impression of complete-
ness. It seems that it can tell us something about everything, when it
does not even begin to tell us that we need to know in order to live.
In fact, we can understand life intellectually, without really existing at
all. Thus Kierkegaard can say of someone (a character he has invented in order to present a view he rejects) that 'he has thought everything possible, and yet he has not existed at all.'[9] As a result, any
attempt to weave the truths of religion into a theoretical account of
the world, however sophisticated or dialectical, inevitably distorts or
falsifies them. The truths of religion belong to the sphere of subjective existence and cannot be grasped by the abstract categories of
theoretical knowledge. Existence can only be known or understood
subjectively or from within. The problem of existence must, in Rohde's words, be thought 'not dispassionately and objectively, but with
the whole of our personality'.[10]

The fundamental move from objective theory to 'subjective truth'
is reflected in a number of aspects of Kierkegaard's work.[11] In the first

place he adopts a method radically different from the theoretical approach of mainstream western philosophy. Subjective truth cannot be expressed with the categories of abstract reason or a detached and impersonal philosophical discourse. Rather it must be expressed through 'indirect communication'. Like the Zen master, philosophy can only express the truth indirectly. It can only be the catalyst for an active process of subjective understanding, which must be performed by individuals for themselves. In this spirit, Kierkegaard accords an important role to the concept of irony as an important means of indirect communication. In his doctoral thesis he claims that 'the concept of irony makes its entry into the world through Socrates.'[12] The Socratic dialogue represents the ideal method for the philosophical exploration of human existence. Socrates leads his interlocutors to revise their limited, common-sense conceptions of justice or truth through irony and humour as much as through demonstrative argument. Irony can provoke subjective insights beyond the grasp of theoretical reason, leading to genuine understanding rather than merely intellectual knowledge. It can achieve what Hollander aptly describes as the 'negative liberation of subjectivity'.[13]

In pursuit of indirect communication Kierkegaard has recourse to an impressive array of discursive styles and registers in addition to more conventional styles of philosophical discourse. More dramatist than theorist, Kierkegaard often presents ideas which are not his own. His writings as a whole, mostly written at a frenetic pace between 1841 and 1849, exploit an impressive range of discursive forms. He explores a variety of subjective perspectives and, to this end, employs a number of pseudonyms and complex framing devices in order to place more or less distance between himself and a particular attitude to life. For example, one of Kierkegaard's best-known works is ostensibly a miscellaneous collection of essays, aphorisms, a diary, letters and a sermon, written by two unknown authors and accidentally discovered and published by a somewhat mysterious scholar, one Victor Eremita.[14] Kierkegaard also wrote a series of 'edifying discourses', which are more akin to religious sermons. A related aspect of Kierkegaard's approach is the autobiographical reference of much of his work.[15] His writings reflect important periods or decisive events in his life. Their pessimism recalls the stern atmosphere of his early childhood, his father's severe religiosity and the guilty secret of his father's illegitimate child. Kierkegaard's youthful life as a rich dandy, whose outward wit and bohemian excess concealed profound inner melancholy, is rehearsed in the despairing hedonism of the 'aesthetic' existence. His prolonged and ultimately abortive engagement with Regine Olsen, apparently broken off because of his feelings of inadequacy and sexual disgust, provoked the emotional crisis which sparked Kierkegaard's most productive creative period and also figures indirectly in the discussion of the ethical significance of marriage in the second volume of *Either/Or*. In the last few years of his life, most of his energies were absorbed in a bitter quarrel with Bishop Mynster and the state Church in Denmark, and as a result he wrote very little.

A further consequence of Kierkegaard's concentration on subjective truth is a revised understanding of the central element of Enlightenment accounts of theoretical knowledge, the demand for certainty. This demand is classically expressed in Descartes's method of radical doubt.[16] Subjective truth does not aspire to the certainty of objective theoretical knowledge, based on indubitable foundations and logical argument. Kierkegaard shares with the sceptic the belief that there can be no rationally certified moral system or religion. There are no irrefutable rational arguments, within either ethics or theology, in favour of living life in a particular way. In any case, theoretical certainty about moral or religious truth would abolish freedom at the same time as it relieved us of uncertainty. Again, even if rational argument could assure us intellectually that we were living correctly, it could never convince us subjectively or actually put us in a position to live in that way. For Kierkegaard, then, uncertainty is not so much a defect of subjective truth as its essence. Uncertainty is a consequence of what is most essential to human life, namely our freedom to choose or decide.[17]

At the same time, freedom implies responsibility. Even if we cannot aspire to theoretical or intellectual certainty, we nevertheless have a responsibility to strive for truth. We have no choice but to choose, because we must live life in one way or another, and live with the consequences of that choice. And, of course, not to choose is also to make a choice of a certain kind, albeit a less conscious one.[18] It is an important principle for Kierkegaard (and it will become axiomatic for later 'existentialists'), that we are responsible even when we appear to be unaware of our freedom. Ambivalence about human freedom is thus at the heart of Kierkegaard's philosophy and is part of his legacy to the subsequent existentialist tradition. Human beings are uniquely free in their ability to choose, uniquely burdened by the necessity to choose. Our responsibility to choose and to strive for subjective truth means that freedom is something which human beings endure as well as enjoy. Freedom is inextricably associated with a state of 'anxiety' or 'dread', which shares the ambivalence of freedom. Dread is both attractive and repulsive to 'man': 'He cannot flee from dread, for he loves it; really he does not love it, for he flees from

it.'[19] Dread is often described in terms which convey this ambivalence: 'One speaks of a sweet dread, a sweet feeling of apprehension,
one speaks of a strange dread, a shrinking dread.'[20] Anxiety is experienced as 'a feeling of fear which does not apply to anything definite
and which both frightens and fascinates at the same time'; it is the
counterpart of the enormous weight of responsibility carried by each
individual. But it is also 'the state of mind which precedes the act of
freedom'; it points 'towards the possibility of freedom and spiritual
realization'.[21]

The ambivalence of Kierkegaard's interrelated concepts of freedom and dread reflects a dualist metaphysics. Human beings are
understood as an uneasy mixture of the animal and the divine,
finite and infinite: 'A human being is a synthesis of the infinite and
the finite, of the temporal and the eternal, of freedom and necessity.'[22] This opposition has a long history in western and Christian
thought. It is prominent in both the philosophy of Plato and St Paul's
account of Christianity, in which spirit or soul and the possibility of
salvation is opposed to the body, nature and perdition. The rational
will of Kant's moral philosophy depends on the existence of a 'noumenal' self transcending the causally determined order of nature. For
Kierkegaard, too, the possibility of freedom depends on our spiritual
nature. But human beings are also animals. As pure souls, human
beings would, like angels, experience freedom as an unalloyed good,
but the human individual straddles two mutually antagonistic realms.
Still imprisoned in the body, still subject to the causal nexus of physical nature, the individual is weighed down by more earthly inclinations and drives. So freedom is experienced as conflict and dread.
'Dread is the point of intersection between two worlds inside man,
that of spirit and that of nature, that of God and that of animal.'[23]

The most basic choice faced by human beings is whether to
acknowledge their freedom or attempt to evade it. The evasion
of freedom is something Kierkegaard strongly associates with
nineteenth-century mass society. As Hannay puts it, 'Kierkegaard
detects in contemporary life-styles, in the kinds of goals people set for
themselves, in their ideals of fulfilment, a fundamental fear of conscious selfhood. He calls it "despair"'[24]. People conform to conventional standards of behaviour. They are satisfied with the mediocre or
the average. Rather than face up to the inevitability of death, they
seek distraction in transient pleasures. Kierkegaard castigates 'petty
bourgeois vulgarity' with as much vehemence as Marx:

> Devoid of imagination, as the petty bourgeois always is, he lives within a
> certain orbit of trivial experience as to how things come about, what is

possible, what usually happens, no matter whether he is a tapster or a prime minister. This is the way in which the petty bourgeois has lost himself and God.[25]

Despair 'is exactly man's unconsciousness of being characterized as spirit'.[26] Consequently, despair is at its most extreme when it is not even recognized as such: 'In his ignorance of his own despair a person is furthest from being conscious of himself as spirit.'[27] The sickness which characterizes the human condition in the absence of God is therefore a sickness which gets better only by getting worse.

Kierkegaard's chosen mission is to make the individual aware of its despair and so bring it to recognize itself as free spirit. In *The Sickness unto Death* Kierkegaard describes the various ways in which human beings can either passively ignore or actively deny their selfhood. Only the self which comes to a self-conscious decision to accept God overcomes despair. The progression of selfhood through a series of ascending stages (which in some ways recalls Hegel's phenomenology of spirit, particularly the dialectic of master and bondsman) culminates in the 'infinite self' which stands directly before God: 'the self is intensified in proportion to the standard by which the self measures itself, and infinitely so when God is the standard . . . Only when a self, as this particular individual, is conscious of being before God, only then is it the infinite self; and that self then sins before God.'[28] As the last remark implies, despair is exchanged for a condition which is no less arduous and painful. Full self-awareness before God presents the individual with the clearest possible choice between sin and faith, for 'the opposite of sin is faith.'[29] Significantly, *The Sickness unto Death* was published under one of Kierkegaard's pseudonyms, the convinced Christian Anti-Climacus, and is subtitled 'A Christian Psychological Exposition for Edification and Awakening'. But why should the agnostic be persuaded by Anti-Climacus' vigorous assertion of the Christian faith? Kierkegaard is adamant that even if choice is free, it is certainly not arbitrary. The fully self-conscious individual can only choose between faith and sin.

But what can persuade the sceptic or agnostic to come to the same conclusion, if there can be no intellectually irresistible proofs in questions of religion or morality? Kierkegaard's response is to elucidate a series of distinct 'spheres of existence' or 'stages on life's way'. Our most important decision can be informed by a subjective understanding of the alternative approaches to life from which we must choose. In the first place, he describes what is essentially a life lived in the absence of resolute decision. The 'aesthetic existence' is empty and drifting, a life of disconnected and ultimately meaningless pleasures and moods. The aesthetic individual is prey to 'the soul's momentary passion' and his ultimate fate is melancholy and boredom:[30]

> My soul is so heavy that thought can no more sustain it, no wingbeat lift it up into the ether. If it moves, it sweeps along the ground like the low flight of birds when a thunderstorm is approaching. Over my inmost being there broods a depression, an anxiety, that presages an earthquake.[31]

In what has sometimes been taken to be a description of Kierkegaard's own rather dissipated youth, the anonymous author of the first part of *Either/Or* dwells somewhat tediously (and so, perhaps, all the more effectively) on the ultimate futility of his existence.

The second volume of *Either/Or* gives expression to a different sphere of 'ethical' existence where, in contrast to the shifting and aimless drifting of the aesthetic sphere, 'The thinker gives himself stable ethical reality by forming and renewing himself in critical decisions which are a total inward commitment (decisions, for example, as to vocation, marriage, faith).'[32] The first part of the second volume consists of a long letter on the 'aesthetic validity of marriage', supposedly written by a certain Judge William to the wayward author of the aesthetic reflections of the first volume. The romantic love celebrated from the aesthetic point of view is merely transient. Its claim to be eternal is deception, since 'the eternity it claims' is 'built upon the temporal'.[33] Only Christian marriage can unite love with duty and so render love both reflective and eternal. Although the aesthete regards duty as 'the enemy of love', it is in fact love's friend. Marriage embeds love in a context of social responsibility, giving it permanence. Less attractively, perhaps, dutiful love also involves a degree of resignation, a relinquishing of the endless possibilities of passion and desire.[34] If the ethical life, as exemplified by the commitment of marriage, ultimately appears unappealing, this is because it only represents a transitional stage on the way to a fully adequate, religious existence. The ethical sphere corresponds to the social dimension of existence. It harbours dangers of mere conformity to social convention, and the 'despairing' abdication of freedom that this implies.

Only religion offers the possibility of a fully satisfactory existence, though the choice of faith is once again emphatically not an easy one. Only religion answers to the fully self-conscious individuality of authentic existence. Here it is crucial for Kierkegaard's account that the religious sphere is not simply an alternative manifestation of the ethical. In fact, the demands of religion may even be incompatible with the demands of morality. God's will may go against not only our strongest human feelings but also our deepest moral convictions.

Kierkegaard makes this point in terms of an extended discussion of God's command to Abraham, that he should kill his son Isaac. Issued without apparent justification or reason, this command goes against both the natural emotional ties of parental love and the basic moral principles of any conceivable human society. In its absoluteness and unconditionality God's command marks the strict separation of the religious from the ethical sphere. Abraham has faith and acts to obey God's will, but in the end he is not required to sacrifice his son:

> All along he had faith, he believed that God would not demand Isaac of him, while still he was willing to offer him if that was indeed what was demanded. He believed on the strength of the absurd, for there could be no question of human calculation, and it was indeed absurd that God who demanded this of him should in the next instant withdraw the demand. He climbed the mountain, even in that moment when the knife gleamed he believed – that God would not demand Isaac.[35]

The story of Abraham reveals faith as 'monstrous paradox', 'a paradox capable of making a murder into a holy act well pleasing to God, a paradox which gives Isaac back to Abraham, which no thought can grasp because faith begins precisely where thinking leaves off'.[36]

For Kierkegaard, then, we must believe even though, or perhaps even because, faith violates human rationality, nature and morality. A faith which was humanly reasonable, a faith conforming to human moral intuition, would have no distinctive significance. It is the absurdity of religion which proves its unique value, its irreducibility. But why, then, should human beings believe in what they must find irrational, unnatural and immoral? Kierkegaard's fideist reading of Christianity presents the transition to faith as an ungroundable 'leap of faith' or *saltus mortale*.[37] He supposes that once the fundamental choice in favour of faith has been made, then the overwhelming value of the religious life will be apparent. His varied and ingenious writings can be seen as heroic attempts to give both the non-believer and the merely conventional Christian some idea of what that life involves. He hopes to awaken his contemporaries to the urgency of self-conscious and authentic decision, to counteract the soporific effect of a conformist society. At the same time Kierkegaard presents a powerful and passionate case for the essential inwardness of religious life and the emptiness of merely external observances within the established Church. What he calls 'objective Christianity', which includes the historical evidence, the established Church and practising Christians, is totally inadequate. It obscures the full and severe demands of true Christianity. The Christian should admit that these demands are unfulfillable but nevertheless resolve to fulfil them and be prepared to live in a state of permanent tension. Like the revivalist preacher, Kierkegaard calls for inward renewal, a return to the original purity and ferocity of Christianity. In that sense Kierkegaard is certainly an important figure in the development of Protestantism.

However, Kierkegaard is also important for philosophy more generally. In his attempts to illuminate the nature of faith, he also sheds light on the subjective or, in later terms, 'existential' truth of the human condition. If his solution to the problem of existence has not always been persuasive, his diagnosis of the problem is powerful. In his intense preoccupation with the choice between faith and unbelief he uncovers the significance of freedom and responsibility. He leaves us in little doubt that the theoretical reason of the Enlightenment cannot help much with either. The emphasis on individual existence and decision is complemented by a critique of the inauthenticity of modern, urban life. The worldly superficiality of the careerist and materialist is castigated. Kierkegaard's central concepts of anxiety or dread, despair, freedom and authenticity, his exploration of basic dimensions of human existence, are now seen as the origin of existentialism. But it is crucial to this later tradition, that Kierkegaard's explorations are not intended simply as descriptions of contingent psychological states to which particular individuals may be more or less susceptible, let alone as the autobiographical reflections of someone who was, by all accounts, a fairly eccentric individual. Rather, they must be seen as a powerful attempt to chart the distinctive space of human subjectivity. Ironically, Kierkegaard's advocacy of religion has not always persuaded subsequent existentialists.[38]

Friedrich Nietzsche[39]

Friedrich Nietzsche (1844–1900) did not come across Kierkegaard's writings until about 1888, shortly before he became insane, and at first sight seems to have little in common with him. Nietzsche was suspicious of religion and is notorious for his announcement of the 'death of God', his absolute conviction that religious faith is no longer tenable and that this has fateful implications for western culture and civilization. At times his suspicion of religion turns into outright hostility. He describes the faith of Pascal and the early Christians, similar in many ways to Kierkegaard's, as a 'protracted suicide of reason', which involves 'sacrifice of all freedom, all pride, all self-confidence of the spirit, at the same time enslavement and self-mockery, self-mutilation'.[40] Nevertheless, there are significant affini-

ties between them. Like Kierkegaard, Nietzsche is as contemptuous
of the thin-blooded abstractions of Enlightenment deism as he is of
attempts to ground religious belief on rational principles.[41] He also
sees little value in secular moral philosophies, such as utilitarianism,
which gained ground in the nineteenth century as religious values
gradually lost their appeal. He sees both religious and secular versions as complacent and half-hearted attempts to avoid the nihilistic
implications of Enlightenment rationalism, as unprincipled compromises with conventional bourgeois morality. Nietzsche is equally
hostile to the historical dialectic of Hegel.[42] Nietzsche shares Kierkegaard's scepticism that any systematic philosophy can fill the moral
vacuum within Enlightenment thought and, like him, values the individual and the present moment rather than either historical process
or collective social agents. On the other hand, Nietzsche does not
believe that nihilism can be outwitted by sophisticated manoeuvres of
a Kierkegaardian kind either. He is determined to avoid the characteristic weakness of systematic philosophers and 'metaphysicians' of
all kinds, who wish 'to solve all with one stroke, with one word' and
so become 'unriddlers of the universe'.[43] Kierkegaard falls victim to a
parallel temptation, albeit practical rather than intellectual, when he
founds everything on the single decision to accept God. Nietzsche's
response is very different. Rather than evade the logic of Enlightenment rationalism, he sets out to apply the critical force of reason with
even greater ruthlessness.

Thus, although Nietzsche shares his hostility to religion with many
Enlightenment free thinkers, he is much more acutely aware of the
drastic implications of the widespread loss of faith associated with
modernity. Recognition of these implications was, in effect, delayed
by the intervention of humanism, which at its most extreme simply
replaces belief in God with something akin to worship of humanity.
After all, scientists had demonstrated the ability of unaided human
reason to discover the laws of the natural universe. The Renaissance
expressed a similarly self-confident celebration of the beauty of the
human form and of human accomplishments, in its art and architecture, its poetry and philosophy. Humanist theology interpreted religion to conform more closely to human conceptions of value and
reason. More radically still, some arrived at the conclusion that humanity need no longer subject itself to divine law at all. Feuerbach
argued that alienated human capacities, magnified and projected self-
abasingly on to a non-existent God, should be reappropriated. Morality should be based directly on the value of human life and its
achievements.[44] But the rush of self-confidence that came with the
thought that there is no greater being than 'man' had delayed the

consequent realization that without God, humanity's claim to metaphysical primacy no longer has any absolute basis. The self-abasement of humanity before God had always harboured the less modest presumption of a special relationship with the Creator. With the 'death of God', then, humanism finds itself in the precarious position of the cartoon character poised over the precipice, suspended only by its ignorance of the drop. A philosophy still permeated by essentially religious conceptions fails to realize the devastating blow inflicted upon it by the demise of religion. Humanism, like metaphysics, remains a species of faith.[45] Related scientific developments had implications for the status of humanity. Copernican astronomy implied that the earth, and with it humanity, was not at the centre of the universe as had been assumed. The earth moves and its inhabitants are little more than specks of dust upon its surface: 'Since Copernicus man has been rolling from the centre toward "x".'[46] In the nineteenth century Darwin's theory of evolution confirmed our familial ties with the beasts and brutes. Human beings are simply animals with a number of distinctive attributes, who have evolved by a process of natural selection.[47]

Nietzsche recognizes, perhaps more clearly than any previous thinker, the fragility of the pretensions of humanism. His critique of humanism can be approached through his attitude to the ideals of truth, reason, beauty and goodness. For humanism it is our access to these ideals which confirms the almost godlike status of humanity, our transcendence of merely animal existence. As a philologist and classicist, Nietzsche's demystification of these ideals first emerges in his discussion of the origins, in ancient Greece, of tragedy as a distinctive art form. For humanism the artistic achievements of ancient Greece were the inspiring embodiment of the ideals of beauty, harmony and perfection. But in his first book, Nietzsche accounts for the origins of Greek tragedy in terms quite unsettling to the humanist consciousness. Thus, art owes its continuous development to the interaction of two fundamentally opposed forces, the Apolline and the Dionysiac. The god Apollo is associated with the order and harmony of Greek poetry, sculpture and visual art, and the 'principle of individuation' (*principium individuationis*), which sustains the identity of 'the individual man' 'in the midst of a world full of suffering'.[48] As Kaufmann explains,

> Apollo represents the aspect of the classical Greek genius extolled by Winckelmann and Goethe: the power to create harmonious and measured beauty; the strength to shape one's own character no less than works of art; the 'principle of individuation'; the form-giving force, which reached its consummation in Greek sculpture.[49]

But for Nietzsche, still impressed by Schopenhauer, the world of orderly appearances and secure individuality is essentially an illusion. Apollo is also associated with dreams, with the 'beautiful illusion of the inner fantasy world', through which 'life is made both possible and worth living.'[50]

The Apolline is constantly struggling against the underlying chaos and oneness of reality, the impersonal 'will' of Schopenhauer's metaphysics, which is expressed in the Dionysiac.[51] Dionysus is the god of music, intoxication and the collective oneness of Bacchanalian revelry and dance. Intoxication induces 'complete forgetting of the self' and access to a deeper wisdom, an overcoming of the illusory bonds which separate us from other men and from nature.[52] As Kaufmann puts it, 'Dionysus . . . is the symbol of that drunken frenzy which threatens to destroy all forms and codes; the ceaseless striving which apparently defies all limitations; the ultimate abandonment we sometimes sense in music.'[53] Nietzsche's account implies that the serenity and harmony of Greek culture is not so much the expression of serene and harmonious minds in contact with an eternal world of Platonic Forms as the product of a hard-won victory over the creative but disruptive forces of the Dionysiac. Art is valuable not as the reflection of a harmonious cosmos but as the productive overcoming of disorder.[54] The sublime in classical art is 'the artistic conquest of the horrible'.[55] The tragedies of Aeschylus and Sophocles, in particular, represent the ideal fusion of the two conflicting principles. However, at this formative moment of western culture the precarious balance of Apolline and Dionysiac is squandered under the combined influence of Euripides and 'aesthetic Socratism'. It is Socrates who imposes an extraneous moral purpose on art, seeing morality in the exclusively Apolline terms of intelligibility, consciousness and individuality. The result is the 'excision of the primitive and powerful Dionysiac element from tragedy, and the rebuilding of tragedy on non-Dionysiac art, morality and philosophy'.[56] Evidently, Nietzsche's account is a significant challenge to the humanist conception of art and beauty. Far from being proof of the near-divine abilities of human beings, art can only be understood as a modified expression of the chaotic, frenzied and destructive force of the Dionysiac. This does not mean that Nietzsche sees art as anything less than essential. On the contrary, he inherits from Schopenhauer the conviction that art can give meaning to existence. Art alone can turn 'thoughts of repulsion at the horror and absurdity of existence into ideas compatible with life'.[57]

The humanist conception of truth fares even worse at Nietzsche's hands than the ideal of beauty. Socrates' subjection of art and the aesthetic to moral and intellectual goals is linked to a further illusion, 'The unshakeable belief that rational thought, guided by causality, can penetrate to the depths of beings, and that it is capable not only of knowing but even of *correcting* being. This sublime metaphysical illusion is an instinctual accompaniment to science . . .' Nietzsche sees the western metaphysical tradition, at least since Socrates, as engaged in a sophisticated but futile attempt to distort reality. Metaphysics is 'the science that treats of the fundamental errors of mankind – but does so as though they were fundamental truths'.[58] ' "Reason" is the cause of our falsification of the evidence of the senses'; 'It is what we *make* of their evidence that first introduces a lie into it, for example the lie of unity, the lie of materiality, of substance, of duration . . .' In what seems like a direct reply to Kant, one which accepts his basic view of experience but with a quite different emphasis, Nietzsche claims that the phenomenal world of appearances is 'the only one: the "real" world has only been *lyingly added* . . .'[59] What Kant sees as the constitution of objective experience by the transcendental self, Nietzsche calls lie and deception. There is still truth, but only in the chaotic flux of subjective appearances, the evidence of the senses.[60] Nietzsche's radicalization of the critical reason of the Enlightenment leads him to a position not too distant from positivism. Nietzsche adds a further twist to Kant's Copernican revolution in philosophy:

> it is high time to replace the Kantian question 'how are synthetic judgements *a priori* possible?' with another question: 'why is belief in such judgements *necessary*?' – that is to say, it is time to grasp that, for the purpose of preserving beings such as ourselves, such judgements must be *believed* to be true . . .[61]

Rather than engage in the futile task of supplying our beliefs with metaphysical foundations, we should look for the actual origins of our beliefs, their reasons for existing. Once we pursue this 'genealogical' approach, we will come to recognize that these origins are much more lowly than humanists suppose. We will discover the origins of truth in error, deception and even the covetousness behind the 'pure radiant gaze' of the sage. It is just another prejudice of the philosophers to insist that 'the higher must not be *allowed* to grow out of the lower, must not be *allowed* to have grown at all.'[62]

Nietzsche applies his genealogical method to the demystification of other areas of human experience. Morality in particular is an object of concern. When Enlightenment thinkers had doubted the religious basis of morality, they tended to substitute a corresponding faith in the natural dispositions of 'man'. Rid of the corrupting effects of civilization (with Rousseau) or the state (with Godwin), man is naturally good or at least capable of improvement.[63] Even a hard-headed sceptic like Hume supposes that 'where interest or revenge or envy perverts not our disposition, we are always inclined, from our natural philanthropy, to give the preference to the happiness of society, and consequently to virtue above its opposite.'[64] Nietzsche's genealogy of morals is far less reassuring. Since we can no longer take them for granted, Nietzsche sets out to trace the 'origin of our moral prejudices' and traces them to Christianity. The result is not simply a challenge to the truth of Christian belief, which after all was a common object of Enlightenment scepticism, but rather a challenge to Christian values, which even most atheists wished to preserve more or less intact.[65] According to Nietzsche, these values represent the historic and highly regrettable victory of the mediocre masses over an earlier aristocratic morality. Pity, humility and self-sacrifice are values which serve the interests of envious slaves, seeking to abolish the superior position of their betters. This 'slave morality' of good and evil is contrasted with the more aristocratic opposition of good and bad. Values such as courage, generosity and magnanimity or greatness of spirit reflect the strength and vitality of 'the noble, powerful, high-stationed and high-minded, who felt and established themselves and their actions as good, that is, of the first rank, in contradistinction to all the low, low-minded, common and plebeian.'[66] Nietzsche's genealogy raises a disturbing possibility: 'What if a symptom of regression were inherent in the "good", likewise a danger, a seduction, a poison, a narcotic, through which the present was possibly living at the expense of the future? Perhaps more comfortably, less dangerously, but at the same time in a meaner style, more basely?'[67] To the extent that conventional secular morality embodies Christian values, it may be not so much the highest expression of human civilization as an obstacle to man's 'highest power and splendour'.

Nietzsche's genealogy of morality is reinforced by a series of acute psychological analyses, which foreshadow the psychoanalytic theories of Sigmund Freud.[68] Nietzsche's observations are in the tradition of satirists such as Dean Swift and French 'moralistes' like La Rochefoucauld, whose concise maxims uncover the selfish motivation at the root of apparently moral or altruistic behaviour. Selfishness outwits even the best intentions: 'Selfishness is cleverer than the cleverest man.'[69] In a similar way, the moral and psychological analyses of *Human, All Too Human* point to the real motivations behind conventionally lauded human emotions and attitudes. Nietzsche refers to La

Rochefoucauld in his well-known discussion of pity, which he sees as the characteristic virtue of Christianity. Live among 'invalids and the mentally afflicted', he suggests,

> and ask yourself whether their eloquent moaning and complaining, their displaying of misfortune, does not fundamentally have the objective of *hurting* those who are with them: the pity which these then express is a consolation for the weak and suffering, inasmuch as it shows them that, all their weakness notwithstanding, they possess at any rate *one power*: the *power to hurt*.[70]

The strategies of weak or 'reactive' individuals underlie the valuations of slave morality. Aristocratic values, on the other hand, are treated more approvingly as manifestations of strength or power. Thus gratitude is an expression of the strong or 'active' individual, who demonstrates his power: 'It is a milder form of revenge. If he did not have the compensation of gratitude, the man of power would have appeared unpowerful and thenceforth counted as such. That is why every community of the good, that is to say originally the powerful, places gratitude among its first duties.'[71] Justice is not so much a selfless expression of natural benevolence as 'requital and exchange under the presupposition of an approximately equal power position', when 'a contest would result in mutual injury producing no decisive outcome'.[72] Evil acts are 'motivated by the drive to preservation or, more exactly, by the individual's intention of procuring pleasure and avoiding displeasure'. They only become evil when the individual is subjugated by a more powerful individual or collective.[73] Overall, values are evaluated in terms of their source in the perspective of either 'active' or 'reactive', strong or weak individuals, and approved or disapproved of accordingly. Values are the varied manifestations of an underlying and universal 'will to power':

> What is good? – All that heightens the feeling of power, the will to power, power itself in man.
> What is bad? – All that proceeds from weakness.[74]

In this sense Nietzsche is really closer to Spinoza than to the French *moralistes*. Indeed on his first encounter with Spinoza's philosophy, Nietzsche remarked, 'my lonesomeness [*Einsamkeit*] . . . is now at least a twosomeness [*Zweisamkeit*].'[75] The difference lies in the fact that for La Rochefoucauld the detection of egoism immediately implies moral condemnation: in Pascal's words, 'the self is detestable.'[76] Altruism is desirable even if unattainable. La Rochefoucauld's stance is still recognizably Christian in its disapproval of the devious stratagems of the self from a vantage point which, by his own analysis, no human can ever attain. Spinoza, on the other hand, who is similarly sceptical of claims to act altruistically, sees self-interest as the legitimate basis for our evaluations. Ethics is based on the *conatus* or 'will', the desire to 'persist in its own being', which constitutes the essence of every individual. He condemns hypocrisy and self-delusion rather than self-interest which, if adequately understood, is the proper basis of ethics. Spinoza also distinguishes 'active' from 'passive' emotions, active emotions corresponding to the increased perfection and pleasure of the organism. In a parallel way, Nietzsche's moral and psychological studies lead him to posit a universal will to power, which both explains existing varieties of reactive morality and provides the basis for a 'transvaluation of all values', the discovery of more active values 'beyond good and evil'.[77]

The notion of will to power has often been misunderstood as implying a universal will to dominate or subjugate others. But for Nietzsche, the will to power is not equivalent to the desire for worldly power. On the contrary, Nietzsche's psychological investigations are designed to show that it is the weak who need to hurt others in their frustrated lust for power. The powerful have no need to do so. The powerful individual is quite the opposite of the petty tyrant or the scheming neurotic. His actions and virtues are manifestations of independence and strength rather than a desire to dominate. Thus although a worldly ruler like Julius Caesar is one of Nietzsche's examples of a powerful individual, more often artists or philosophers such as Goethe and Schopenhauer are held up as models. In fact power is expressed most clearly in all forms of 'self-overcoming'. It is even manifest in the apparent self-denial of asceticism, because 'ascetic self-torture is the source of the greatest possible feeling of power.'[78] Self-control, the disciplining of inclinations and ruthless self-criticism may all be motivated by the will to power, if they lead to the greater power and perfection of the individual.[79]

In this respect, too, there is ambivalence in Nietzsche's attitude both to religion generally and to Christianity in particular. He has considerable respect both for Jesus Christ as a historical individual and for 'Christianness', in the sense of that which the founder of Christianity 'did and desired'. Christ is praised as a rare individual, who was willing to accept the evil done to him by others.[80] On the other hand, faith in Christ is an evasion of responsibility and the expression of a reactive or weak will. Particularly in its Lutheran form, faith is the resort of the individual who feels otherwise incapable of doing what is right. Nor is self-overcoming equivalent to the elimination of animal instinct or selfish inclination. That is the practice of the Church, which 'combats the passions with excision in every sense of the word: its practice, its "cure" is *castration*.' Rather power is evident in the continuing tension of an always fragile mastery of passion, the attempt to 'spiritualize, beautify, deify a desire', just as the highest art involves a difficult balance between the Apolline and the Dionysiac, between order and chaos.[81] Finally, for Nietzsche as for Spinoza, the powerful individual is also the rational individual. One of his most frequent charges against Christianity is its hostility to reason, its 'sacrifice of the intellect': 'Christianity also stands in opposition to all *intellectual* well-constitutedness – it *can* use only the morbid mind as the Christian mind, it takes the side of everything idiotic . . .'[82] According to Kaufmann's plausible interpretation, Nietzsche takes rationality to be the mark of great power: 'Rationality . . . gives man mastery over himself; and as the will to power is essentially the "instinct of freedom", it can find fulfilment only through rationality.' Power is measured in terms of 'man's willingness to subject even his most cherished beliefs to the rigour of rationality'.[83] The will to power is the opposite of the sacrifice of the intellect perpetrated by Pascal or Kierkegaard.

However, religion is not the only way in which the rigorous demands of the will to power are evaded. Nietzsche is equally vehemently opposed to any faith in the process and ultimate meaning of history. Hegel's ambitious dialectical system is seen as little more than the pursuit of religion by other means, the substitution of history for divine providence.[84] The problem of life is deferred rather than resolved by a philosophy of history which values present existence only as a stage on the way to the foreordained reconciliation of Absolute spirit. Marx's materialist theory of history is similarly eschatological in structure. The sufferings undergone during the prehistory of class struggle have meaning only in so far as they are necessary for the attainment of communism. Nietzsche is radically opposed to philosophy of history in either sense. Against the prevailing historicism of nineteenth-century thought, he maintains that there is no inevitability of progress, however dialectically mediated. By the same token, he resists the absorption of individual existence by the collective agencies of the world-historical process. It is not the historical fate of the collective which is significant or valuable but individuals, particularly exceptional individuals: 'No, the *goal of humanity* cannot lie in its end but only *in its highest exemplars*.'[85] Whether history is understood in terms of Hegelian spirit or the social classes of Marxism, the meaning of individual existence is lost rather than confirmed by any philosophy of history.

If the meaning of existence cannot be found in the final stage or ultimate goal of history, then it must be sought in the intensity of the present moment. The point of existence lies in the immediacy of present experience: 'Enough of becoming, let me be.'[86] Nietzsche is drawn to the ideal of the 'supra-historical man', 'who does not envisage salvation in the process but for whom the world is finished in every single moment and its end attained'.[87] His famous doctrine of 'eternal recurrence' (or 'eternal return'), 'this highest formula of affirmation that is at all attainable', is an affirmation of the value of present existence in this sense.[88] The meaning of eternity here lies not in the infinite expanse of time but in the intensive quality of the moment. The joy of the powerful, life-affirming individual is expressed in that 'love of fate' (*amor fati*) which is willing to affirm the eternal recurrence of the present moment: 'All joy wants the eternity of all things . . .'[89] For this reason Nietzsche also values 'supra-historical' powers, which 'lead the eye away from becoming towards that which bestows upon existence the character of the eternal and stable, towards art and religion'.[90] In other words, ultimate value lies in the cultural, intellectual or personal achievements of exceptional individuals, in whatever time they exist. Socrates or Plato, Christ or Julius Caesar, Goethe or Spinoza were individuals who might never, probably would never be surpassed.

Nietzsche's emphasis on individual life and the present moment also implies a relatively distanced relationship to conventional politics. As Kaufmann puts it, Nietzsche develops 'the theme of the antipolitical individual who seeks self-perfection far from the modern world'.[91] Certainly, only an overhasty reading could blame Nietzsche for the rise of fascism, even though some of his favourite terms, such as 'master race' and 'will to power', would later be adopted by Nazi philosophers.[92] There is also little justification for seeing him as a racist or a nationalist. He was openly hostile to both nationalism and the nation-state, which he saw as one of the principal forces of mediocrity and conformity. He was particularly contemptuous of German nationalism and the new Reich. Nietzsche advocates race mixture as a stimulus to the development of culture and conceives the 'master race' as 'a future, internationally mixed race of philosophers and artists who cultivate iron self-control' – not exactly the self-indulgent gangsters of the national socialist leadership.[93] Partly responsible for this misreading of Nietzsche was his eventual collapse into insanity. For the last decade of his life he was under the control of his sister, Elisabeth Förster-Nietzsche. She was a self-confessed anti-Semite and German nationalist who spent several years in Paraguay, attempting to set up an Aryan colony of pure race. During her brother's insanity and after his death she used her control of his papers and manuscripts to further her own ideological beliefs. For their part, the

Nazis had a pressing need for intellectual credentials and these were willingly provided by Förster-Nietzsche. Misunderstanding is all the easier, since Nietzsche's style is aphoristic, deliberately unsystematic and often ironic. His sense of humour, which is not always easily distinguished from later episodes of megalomania, further adds to difficulties of interpretation. On the other hand, it is difficult to deny that Nietzsche was elitist, anti-democratic and anti-liberal. He was convinced that the value of humanity resided in its outstanding individuals rather than in the ordinary masses of nineteenth-century European society.[94]

In effect, then, Nietzsche reacts to the loss of religious faith and signs of the hollowness of humanism, such as Darwin's scientific demolition of the special status of *homo sapiens*, as devastating but also liberating blows to the values underpinning nineteenth-century morality and society. Once the supernatural aura of Christian morality has disappeared, we should recognize it for what it is, a slave morality incompatible with the full development of human powers. Nietzsche is contemptuous of the hypocritical other-worldliness of Christianity and of conventional bourgeois morality. Nietzsche self-consciously confronts the stark possibility of nihilism. Can human life have value in a world without God? In the words of a character of Dostoyevsky, he considers the possibility that, 'were mankind's belief in its immortality to be destroyed . . . nothing would be immoral any longer, everything would be permitted.'[95] Nietzsche's vivisection of conventional morality is designed to lay bare a thinking capable of resisting the descent into nihilism. And following at least one line of intellectual descent, Nietzsche's emphasis on the individual, creativity and the present moment is echoed in the 'existentialism' of Jaspers, Marcel, Sartre and Camus. Authenticity and the individual's unconditional responsibility for his or her life become pre-eminent (if not always unambiguous) values.

However, more recent waves of interpretation, particularly in France, have placed greater emphasis on Nietzsche's anti-humanism and less on his apparent celebration of exceptional and heroic individuals. On this view – one substantially inspired by Heidegger – Nietzsche proclaims a far more radical break with the western philosophical tradition and its 'ontotheological' quest for truth, pursuing instead a relentless onslaught on all metaphysics.[96] This Nietzsche is a practitioner of what Gilles Deleuze calls 'counter-philosophy' or 'nomad thought', whose 'statements can be conceived as the products of a mobile war machine and not the utterances of a rational, administrative machinery, whose philosophers would be bureaucrats of pure reason'.[97] This discourse does not aim for any kind of ultimate truth or knowledge of reality. No univocal meaning is intended, for 'The "signifier" is really the last philosophical metamorphosis of the despot.'[98] Meanings are allowed to proliferate, freed from the proprietorial grasp of either author or reader. The ambiguities of Nietzsche's aphoristic, metaphorical and playful style, his humour and irony, are thus more than merely formal characteristics, they are the essence of a discourse subversive of all codes and conventions. For nomadic thought both language and the world display, in Allison's words, a 'kind of fertility or richness that refuses to be systematized, discretely categorized, and, ultimately, calcified by some ruse or device of language, some simple definition, or essence, or form'.[99] Will to power and affirmation of life are as thoroughly beyond subject and object, meaning and truth, as they are beyond good and evil. For truth and philosophy are substituted 'woman', who is 'one name for this non-truth of truth'. Woman and 'writing', on Derrida's reading, subvert the 'phallogocentric' categories of philosophy driven, Heathcliff-like, to destruction: 'From the endless, bottomless depths, she submerges all essentiality, all identity, all propriety, and every property. Blinded in such a way, philosophical discourse founders, and is left to dash headlong to its ruin.'[100] And 'from that moment on, it becomes the question of style as the question of writing.'[101]

Jean-Paul Sartre and French Existentialism

Jean-Paul Sartre (1905–80) is perhaps the best-known philosopher of existentialism and a complex and intriguing figure. His philosophical preoccupations were at first mainly metaphysical. An important point of departure, in common with much modern philosophy and most French philosophy, is the methodical doubt and *cogito* of Descartes. But it is from the phenomenological method of Husserl and Heidegger that Sartre adapts his philosophical method. Still, Sartre's main influence has been as an existentialist philosopher of freedom, a politically engaged intellectual and, later in his life, theorist of Marxism. As an existentialist philosopher he reiterates themes already encountered with Kierkegaard and Nietzsche – themes which also figure, albeit in more ontological guise, in Heidegger's earlier philosophy. His works contain nuanced explorations of a variety of human situations and emotional states. Like Kierkegaard, too, he exploits a range of discursive forms from short stories, plays and philosophical novels to political essays and biography as well as more conventional philosophical exposition. Sartre differs from both

Kierkegaard and Nietzsche, however, in the privileged status he accords to social existence as opposed to the religious or aesthetic and cultural experience of the individual. In contrast to most earlier existentialists Sartre is concerned from the beginning with embodiment, sexuality and intersubjectivity. His more social and embodied approach is complemented by a strong emphasis on political experience and action and the 'engagement' of the intellectual.

Sartre's major philosophical work, *Being and Nothingness* (1943), develops Heidegger's ontological-hermeneutic analysis of the meaning of 'being' from the perspective of human existence or 'being-in-the-world'. From the beginning, though, Sartre's philosophical interests are different. According to Heidegger, this leads Sartre to misunderstand *Being and Time* as an existentialist tract.[102] Sartre's ontological odyssey can be understood as an attempt to respond to the problem, clearly formulated but less convincingly resolved by Kant, of how to account for freedom and responsibility in a world which we experience as a causally determined order of things. Sartre steers a difficult path between realism and idealism, rethinking the relationship between mind or consciousness and the world in order to preserve the possibility of freedom without falling into the trap of idealism. It is evident to Sartre that idealism cannot tell us anything about the world in its brute materiality and contingency – about the 'being' or existence of the world as opposed to its formal or essential or ideal structure.[103] At the heart of idealism is a deceptive view of consciousness as a kind of receptacle, which contains sensations (impressions or ideas) within itself. Sartre absolutely rejects this 'alimentary' view of consciousness, though he admits that it exerts a certain attraction: 'we have all believed that the spider-mind attracted things into its web, covered them with a white foam and slowly digested them, reduced them to its own substance. What is a table, a rock, a house? A certain assemblage of "contents of consciousness", an order to these contents.'[104] He finds the clue to overcoming this view of consciousness in phenomenology and, in particular, the insight that the distinguishing feature of mind or consciousness is its 'intentionality' or 'directedness toward an object'. Sartre takes the intentionality of consciousness to imply a radical break with any reifying view of consciousness – any way of conceiving either the mind or its 'contents' as things or thing-like. In characteristically flamboyant style Sartre describes consciousness as an active 'explosion' towards objects in the world. Aronson's explanation here is helpful:

> consciousness was 'a connected series of explosions which tear us away from ourselves, which do not even allow a "myself" the leisure to form

behind them.' This totally active consciousness was totally spontaneous, and such a consciousness was nothing at all. It existed only as it moved out of itself, towards objects.[105]

And of course, a consciousness which is not a thing is nothing (the point alluded to in the title of *Being and Nothingness*).

Sartre's resistance to any kind of reification of consciousness leads him to criticize Husserl for reverting to the epistemological project of Kant. Both Kant and Husserl describe experience in terms of a transcendental ego, something supposedly 'behind' consciousness. But once the self is conceived as a thing in this way (whether as a Cartesian self or soul or as that transcendental agency which makes experience of a world possible), any explanation of the relationship between self and world becomes highly problematic. Having misunderstood the implications of his own insight, Husserl, according to Sartre, falls victim to those perennial traps of western philosophy, solipsism and idealism. Sartre's attempt to make a radical break with the assumptions of modern epistemology owes a great deal to Heidegger's revival of fundamental ontology. Heidegger too criticized Husserl for relapsing into transcendentalism and overemphasizing the subject at the expense of the world. For Heidegger the fundamental ontological entity is the unanalysable unity 'being-in-the-world': conscious existence or '*Dasein*' and the objective world are aspects of an inseparable unity. Sartre proceeds to explore the being-in-the-world of consciousness, though his path diverges from Heidegger's in its greater preoccupation with the body, emotions and relations with other people. Sartre also arrives at an unashamedly existentialist position.

Sartre nevertheless attempts to define consciousness, albeit in a non-reifying way, independently of its situation in the world and so, in effect, he analyses the unanalysable unity of 'being-in-the-world' after all.[106] Even in his early Husserlian works on the 'image' and 'imagination', Sartre identifies the distinctive nature of consciousness as a kind of nothingness.[107] In this respect, perception is not the best guide to the nature of consciousness, because it is essentially passive or receptive and contains, as it were, too much of what is not pure consciousness. An exclusive focus on perception encourages a view of consciousness as the merely passive receptacle for external sensations. The phenomenological analysis of imagination, where no such element of receptivity is involved, is more likely to cast light on the creative spontaneity of mind. According to Sartre's analysis imagination is both more certain and less rich than perception. An object which is perceived has an infinity of potential aspects or 'profiles' (*Abschattungen*), corresponding to the infinity of possible perspectives we can adopt in relation to it. Perception is, in that sense, inexhaustible. The relative poverty of the image stems from the fact that there is no more to it than we are aware of. The existence of an image is simply its being 'perceived' by consciousness (its *esse est percipi*). As a result, imagination is also more certain. It does not involve any surprises. The image 'teaches nothing, never produces an impression of novelty, and never reveals any new aspect of the subject. It delivers it in a lump. No risk, no anticipation: only a certainty.'[108] There is also a clear phenomenological difference – a difference for consciousness – between the mental contents involved in imagining and perceiving. The image presents itself to conscious-ness as *only* an image and, in this sense, is more 'negative' than a perception: 'The image presented its object as *absent*, and itself, therefore, as *only* an image. At the heart of the experience of imag-ining was negativity, known and accepted as such from the outset.'[109] For Sartre imagination and consciousness are essentially negative in character and at their most pure when they are most negative. Al-ready in these early works the dualism of Sartre's basic ontology is apparent in outline:

> Never could my consciousness be a thing, because its way of being in itself is precisely to be *for* itself; for consciousness, to exist is to be conscious of its existence. It appears as a pure spontaneity, confronting a world of things which is sheer inertness. From the start, therefore, we may posit two types of existence. For it is indeed just insofar as things are inert that they escape the sway of consciousness; their inertness is their safeguard, the preserver of their autonomy.[110]

The negative spontaneity of consciousness is set against an inert and positive realm of existence.

In *Being and Nothingness* these two orders of existence are pre-sented more explicitly and extensively as 'being-in-itself' (*l'être-en-soi*) and 'being-for-itself' (*l'être-pour-soi*). The being of the 'for-itself' is presented in terms of a critique of Descartes for his neglect of the intentionality or 'positionality' of consciousness, a neglect which ultimately leads to the positing of a substantial soul. Sartre hopes to avoid the problems associated with such a reifying view of conscious-ness by insisting on a rigorously ontological definition of conscious-ness as 'positional consciousness':

> The first procedure of a philosophy ought to be to expel things from consciousness and to reestablish its true connection with the world, to know that consciousness is a positional consciousness of the world. All consciousness is positional in that it transcends itself in order to reach an object, and it exhausts itself in this same positing.[111]

The essence of consciousness is its intentional relation to the objects of an objective world. The corollary of this view is rejection of Descartes's epistemological or cognitive reading of consciousness as a 'reflective' or knowing consciousness. Reflective consciousness always involves self-consciousness, in the sense that 'To know is to know that one knows.' On the Cartesian view, consciousness must be accompanied by self-consciousness for it to be genuinely consciousness. It is only on this assumption that Descartes's 'I think therefore I am' is actually valid, or in other words that the existence of a thought implies knowledge of the existence of a thinker of that thought. But if my consciousness of some object must involve knowing that I am conscious of it, then *self*-consciousness must involve my knowing that I am conscious of myself. Thus, by introducing the epistemological dualism of subject and object into our understanding of consciousness the Cartesian view inevitably leads to an infinite regress. Self-consciousness, understood as knowledge of consciousness, is only possible if we have knowledge of that knowledge of consciousness, and so on *ad infinitum*.[112]

It follows, according to Sartre, that we must understand consciousness ontologically rather than epistemologically as an 'immediate, non-cognitive relation of the self to itself', as 'non-reflective consciousness':

> Thus reflection has no kind of primacy over the consciousness reflected-on. It is not reflection which reveals the consciousness reflected-on to itself. Quite the contrary, it is the non-reflective consciousness which renders the reflection possible; there is a pre-reflective cogito which is the condition of the Cartesian cogito.[113]

Reflection, understood as a kind of knowledge of self, is secondary to non- or pre-reflective consciousness. Consciousness is always accompanied by an awareness which makes self-reflection possible, but consciousness does not depend on self-reflection in a way which would require it to be the intentional or positional object of another consciousness. To regard consciousness in this way leads, as we saw in the previous paragraph, to an infinite regress.[114] Sartre's notion of pre-reflective consciousness can avoid the regress, because consciousness is no longer regarded as an object standing in a particular relationship to other objects. Pre-reflective consciousness is a 'consciousness (of) objects', where the 'of' is parenthesized in order to make the point that no duality of subject and object is involved. Descartes's cognitive or 'reflective' cogito is thus preceded by a more fundamental 'pre-reflective cogito', which is therefore ontological rather than epistemological.

Because consciousness does not presuppose the existence of a substantial ego or 'I' which sustains or carries particular mental states, there is nothing to the existence of consciousness other than its occurrence – the '*esse*' or existence of consciousness is its '*percipi*' or 'being perceived'. This contrasts with the case of real objects in the world, whose 'being perceived' does not exhaust what it is for them to exist – except for idealists such as Bishop Berkeley.[115] Being perceived is a sufficient but not a necessary condition for the existence of material objects: if we genuinely perceive an object then it exists, but we also suppose that objects continue to exist when they are not being perceived. By contrast, it is of the essence of consciousness, that it is a sufficient condition of its own existence: 'The existence of consciousness comes from consciousness itself.'[116] More strongly, Sartre claims that existence is the *only* essence that consciousness has. He illustrates this with the point that pleasure and the consciousness of pleasure are inseparable. Not only can there be no such thing as an unconscious pleasure, but there cannot be a conscious pleasure which is not a pleasure and, to that extent, consciousness is also infallible:

> There is an indivisible, indissoluble being – definitely not a substance supporting its qualities like particles of being, but a being which is existence through and through. Pleasure is the being of self-consciousness and this self-consciousness is the law of being of pleasure. This is what Heidegger expressed very well when he wrote (though speaking of *Dasein*, not of consciousness): 'The "how" (*essentia*) of this being, so far as it is possible to speak of it generally, must be conceived in terms of its existence (*existentia*).'[117]

Consciousness can have no other essence, because that would require it to have substance as well: 'Consciousness has nothing substantial, it is pure "appearance" in the sense that it exists only to the degree to which it appears.'[118] And, of course, consciousness can only appear to itself. Consciousness is being 'for-itself' rather than being 'in-itself'. More provocatively put, consciousness is not a thing in the world, it is nothing.

Sartre's account of being 'in-itself' is equally economical in onto-logical terms. He rejects the positing of any Kantian 'noumenon' or thing-in-itself behind appearances, 'For the being of an existent is exactly what it appears.'[119] On the other hand, as we have seen, there is more to the being of real things in the world than their appearing to consciousness or being perceived. The objective existence of a world outside consciousness is implied by the intentionality of con-sciousness: 'Consciousness is consciousness of something. This means that transcendence is the constitutive structure of consciousness; that is, that consciousness is born *supported* by a being which is not itself.'[120] Sartre accepts here something very close to the phenomenological account of the constitution of the objective world. The reality of an object is to be sought, not in some underlying substance, which would inevitably be inaccessible and unknowable, but in the 'inexhaustibility' or 'infinity' of the series of appearances. The difference between images and sense perceptions is that the latter occur in a particular order, which is not dependent on consciousness. As we move around an object, for example, we experience a series of perceptions, corresponding to the different perspectives we assume in relation to the object. Although, as embodied beings, we can choose the series of perspectives – we can move around the object in a clockwise or anti-clockwise direction, for example – we cannot choose the series of perceptions which then occur. Equally, it is a characteristic of real existents, that there is an inexhaustible infinity of possible perceptions: we can never see something from every possible perspective. The essence of 'existents' in the world, then, is the principle of this series of perceptions: 'The essence of an existent is no longer a property sunk in the cavity of this existent; it is the manifest law which presides over the succession of its appearances, it is the principle of the series.'[121]

If the essence of existents is defined in terms of the series of appearances, then prior to the 'negating' activity of consciousness, on which depends the conceptual content of these appearances, the in-itself must be conceived as undifferentiated and featureless positivity, as brute existence. It is timeless and therefore changeless; it is 'neither passivity nor activity'; it is neither necessary nor possible but simply is, it is pure contingency; it is 'equally beyond negation as beyond affirmation'. All that can be said is that 'being is what it is'.[122] Roquentin, the hero of Sartre's philosophical novel *Nausea*, has a disturbing experience of the absurdity of brute, nameless existence whilst sitting in the park looking at the root of a tree:

> And then, all of a sudden, there it was, as clear as day: existence had suddenly unveiled itself. It had lost its harmless appearance as an abstract category: it was the very stuff of things, that root was steeped in existence. Or rather the root, the park gates, the bench, the sparse grass on the lawn, all that had vanished; the diversity of things, their individuality, was only an appearance, a veneer. This veneer had melted, leaving soft, monstrous masses, in disorder – naked, with a frightening, obscene nakedness.[123]

The familiar world of differentiated existents in space and time, on the other hand, depends on the negating activity or 'nihilation' of consciousness: 'nothingness is given as that by which the world receives its outlines as the world.'[124] Sartre, like Heidegger, takes the stance of someone posing a question about being as the basis for his account of consciousness as nihilation. Because any question may be answered by either 'yes' or 'no', either affirmatively or negatively, Sartre can say that, with the first question, being is supplemented by non-being or negation: 'a glance cast on the question itself has revealed to us suddenly that we are encompassed with nothingness.'[125] The in-itself can only be ascribed specific properties in relation to the negating activity or nihilation of consciousness. To characterize being in a particular way is to negate it, in the sense that to ascribe a particular property or quality to being is to exclude a range of other properties.[126] The world as differentiated, objective reality depends on the particular projections of consciousness: 'non-being always appears within the limits of a human expectation . . . The world does not disclose its non-beings to one who has not first posited them as possibilities.'[127] In other words, the conceptual structure, in terms of which our experiences or appearances are organized, is a projection of consciousness. Different conceptual schemes are conceivable. Beyond that consciousness itself is not any thing, it remains nothing.[128]

The nothingness which comes into the world with human existence also goes by another name: 'it is *freedom*.' With consciousness and negation comes the possibility of human freedom, the possibility to escape the circuit of being – the determinism of the world of things – whereas, by itself, 'Being can generate only being.'[129] The negativity of consciousness is, for Sartre, the essential foundation of the possibility of human freedom. It is only because we can imagine alternative futures, conceive of possibilities, which we may or may not ultimately realize, and project those possibilities on to the world, that human reality can be detached from the world and we can be free. In fact, freedom is equivalent to consciousness and defines the human essence: 'What we call freedom is impossible to distinguish from the *being* of "human reality". Man does not exist *first* in order to be free *subsequently*; there is no difference between the being of man and his *being-free*.'[130] Rather, the fundamental existentialist principle that for human beings 'existence comes before essence', implies the absolute freedom of individuals from any pre-given essence and consequently their absolute responsibility for their own lives. Our existence defines our essence, in the sense that we are free to create our own lives and values. To allow oneself to be constrained by custom, ideas of human nature or divine will, or any other notion of human essence, is to deny one's freedom and to live inauthentically or in 'bad faith'. Bad faith is to lie to oneself. It is the equivalent of despair in Kierkegaard's account of the 'sickness unto death'. As with Kierkegaard, too, freedom is something to be endured rather than enjoyed: we are 'condemned to liberty'. We experience our freedom as anxiety – the 'reflective consciousness of freedom' is anxiety.[131] Because the practice of freedom is exceedingly difficult, we are always tempted to claim that our actions were caused rather than freely chosen, and so disclaim responsibility. Sartre sees the unconscious mind postulated by Freudian psychoanalysis as a useful accomplice in bad faith. We can attribute our actions or emotions to unconscious impulses or complexes acquired in early childhood, presumed beyond our control.[132]

Sartre provides a number of illuminating examples of the self-deception involved in bad faith: 'a woman who has consented to go out with a particular man for the first time' who denies to herself that she 'knows very well the intentions' which he 'cherishes regarding her'; a waiter who is acting as if he were a waiter and nothing more; being sad as a deliberate 'conduct' which we are really free to abandon.[133] Perhaps most interesting is the example of a homosexual, who denies that he is essentially or 'by nature' a 'paederast', a denial which Sartre commends as the recognition of his freedom. But the same homosexual falls into bad faith when he claims that he is essentially *not* a paederast 'in the sense in which this table *is not* an inkwell'.[134] Significantly the 'sympathetic' friend, who insists on a sincere admission from the homosexual of his homosexual nature, is equally in bad faith. Sincerity is equally likely to be a stratagem of bad faith. The sincere man 'constitutes himself as a thing' by claiming to be essentially what he in fact has freely chosen to do.[135] But at the same time, he seeks advantage by distancing himself from the evil, thing-like self, which he has guiltily confessed himself to be:

> He derives a *merit* from his sincerity, and the deserving man is not the evil man as he is evil but as he is beyond his evilness. At the same time the evil is disarmed since it is nothing, save on the plane of determinism, and since in confessing it, I posit my freedom in respect of it; my future is virgin; everything is allowed to me.[136]

Not only, however, is freedom an extremely arduous responsibility always likely to be evaded, it is also inevitably unrewarding. Sartre describes the condition of 'human reality' as a 'useless passion' (*passion inutile*). The for-itself of consciousness is constantly striving to realize its projects, to actually become whatever it posits as a goal for itself, and so become a for-itself-in-itself. But it can never achieve this state of fulfilment without ceasing to be what it is as negativity or 'nothingness' – as the projection of further unrealized possibilities. As Aronson explains,

> Consciousness can exist only as it sees the world as lacking, only as it rejects and surpasses it in order to give it meaning, only as it projects its possibilities as goals to be realized. Hence, consciousness is doomed to frustration. By nature consciousness is that which detaches itself from the world because the world is not enough; by its very nature the world is that which lacks.[137]

In effect, Sartre incorporates something very like the pessimism of the Schopenhauerian worldview. Human beings are doomed to the frustration of ceaseless striving, because once a particular goal has been achieved consciousness inevitably posits further goals or ceases to be a for-itself. Fulfilment exists as future promise or fond memory, but never as present reality. Once consciousness has achieved a particular goal, it ceases to have value for it, and consciousness ceases to experience satisfaction: 'But pleasure is the death and the failure of desire. It is the death of desire because it is not only its fulfillment but its limit and its end.'[138]

The inevitable frustration of human existence is particularly evident in sexual love for another person, which aims at the possession of the other as free selfhood through his or her body, but which can succeed only in possessing the body:

> It is certain that I want to *possess* the Other's body, but I want to possess it in so far as it is itself a 'possessed', that is, in so far as the Other's consciousness is identified with his body. Such is the impossible ideal of desire: to possess the Other's transcendence as pure transcendence and at the same time as *body*, to reduce the Other to his simple *facticity* because he is then in the midst of my world but to bring it about that this facticity is a perpetual appresentation of his nihilating transcendence.[139]

For Schopenhauer the obvious implication is that human fulfilment can only be fully and finally realised in death, an idea which finds expression in the famous '*Liebestod*' (or 'attainment of love in death') of Wagner's *Tristan and Isolde*. There are also resonances here with Freud's notion of the 'death wish' as an essential counterpart of 'eros', or the pleasure principle. For Sartre, the futility of human striving is an immediate reflection of the ontological commitment of consciousness to become a for-itself-in-itself. In fact, it reflects humanity's wish to be God, the only entity which could correspond to the concept of a for-itself-in-itself. This idea can perhaps be understood in a Feuerbachian sense: the idea of God is a projection of human aspirations.

On the other hand, it would be wrong to give the impression that Sartre understands human reality as abstract and disembodied consciousness. He also provides an acute phenomenological description of the human situation as both embodied and essentially related to the 'Other'. We must also recognize the 'facticity' of consciousness, the fact that 'the for-itself *is*' both 'in so far as it appears in a condition which it has not chosen' and 'in so far as it is thrown into a world and abandoned in a "situation"': 'It *is* in so far as there is in it something of which it is not the foundation – its *presence to the world*.'[140] An important aspect of the facticity of the for-itself is its embodiment. With his account of embodiment Sartre seeks, above all, to escape the 'reef of solipsism', which is implicit in any dualist account of body and mind as separate entities – entities which must somehow, mysteriously, be brought into relation with each other. The for-itself must not be conceived as simply located within a body or connected to a body: 'Being-for-itself must be wholly body and it must be wholly consciousness; it can not be *united* with a body.'[141] The body as 'being-for-itself' is 'a point of view and a point of departure': it is the perspective from which the world as an 'instrumental complex' unfolds and the centre from which consciousness projects its possibilities.[142]

The essentially embodied state of consciousness also implies and is implied by a 'primary relation between my consciousness and the Other's'. The Other appears to the for-itself as embodied also. The perception of another person creates an absence or 'hole' at the heart of my world, which follows from the recognition of a different 'point of view and point of departure' from my own. The perception of the Other 'unfolds a spatiality which is not my spatiality'. The situation is dramatically transformed, once again, with the 'look'. When the Other looks at me, I come to recognize myself as object and, reciprocally, the Other as subject: 'It is in and through the revelation of my being-as-object for the Other that I must be able to apprehend the presence of his being-as-subject.'[143] Subjected to the gaze of the Other, I become an object for his freedom. I live 'my being as it is written in and by the Other's freedom' and apprehend myself as nature.[144] Relationships with others are, as a result, characterized by the inevitability of conflict, which follows from the reciprocal interdependence of subject and object, freedom and thinghood, for-itself and in-itself. Subjects are condemned to an ultimately futile struggle for mutual recognition. Accordingly, sadism and masochism are not so much pathologies as fundamental modalities of human relations.[145]

Of course, Sartre's claim that we are always free to act or to feel in any way whatsoever, that it is never true to say that we 'had no choice', has been regarded as highly implausible. A concern more internal to Sartre's philosophical interests – and one to which he directs considerable attention – is the difficulty of deriving a concrete morality or ethics from his philosophical position. The freedom of consciousness implies its absolute ability to project any values whatever. Sartre attacks any view which assumes the objective existence of values independently of human choice as a symptom of the 'spirit of seriousness' (*l'esprit de sérieux*) typical of bourgeois morality.[146] The archetypal expression of human freedom is the apparently unmotivated 'arbitrary act' (*acte gratuit*). It even seems as if the more meaningless or irrational the act is, the more safely we can regard it as free. This impression is supported by an example from one of Sartre's novels, when, for no apparent reason, the hero Mathieu stabs his own hand with a knife.[147] Subsequently Sartre attempted to derive a more concrete moral position from his philosophy. In the popular essay, *Existentialism and Humanism*, he defends existentialism from the reproach, that it represents no more than a morbid and individualistic celebration of despair and anxiety, leading inevitably either to political quietism or to nihilism.[148] He maintains there that our choices have social and political implications as well. Individuals must regard their free decisions as proposals for the adoption of corresponding values by humanity in general. However, this existentialist reformulation of Kant's categorical imperative faces similar problems to the original.[149] It is unclear, in particular, why or how the seemingly arbitrary choices of an individual, unconstrained by convention or pre-existing moral norms, carry such universal moral weight. How does the individual distinguish between an evil action and one which might be recommended to humanity? It is not obvious, in other words, how it is possible to avoid bad faith without complete arbitrariness.

In fact, Sartre draws quite radical ethical and political conclusions from his philosophy, whether or not he is strictly entitled to do so. Throughout his life he argued for the political and social responsibility of both the artist and the intellectual. In *What is Literature?* (1948) he argues that literature can help to dissolve bad faith by encouraging us to act more reflectively, with greater self-awareness. His Japanese lectures in the 1960s are less confident of the role of the artist, but still confront intellectuals with activist political demands.[150] Sartre himself was involved with the French resistance to the German occupation during the Second World War. After the war he embarked on a long and tortuous relationship with Marxism and the French communist party. In 1948 there was a short-lived attempt, with Merleau-Ponty and others, to set up an alternative and more democratically revolutionary party of the left, the Revolutionary People's Assembly. He was a prominent figure in the opposition both to American 'imperialism and genocide' in Vietnam and to France's rearguard colonialism in Algeria, culminating in 1961 with a terrorist attack on Sartre's apartment.[151] Sartre's political commitments were expressed through a long-standing involvement, starting in 1945, with the political review, *Les Temps Modernes*. He wrote a large number of political articles, pamphlets and tracts. On the other hand, as the autobiographical sketch *Words* makes clear, he always stood in a close relationship with the 'unreal' (*irréel*) world of art and literature. Even in his philosophical works he sometimes represents art as the only reliable context for the expression of freedom. In fact, much of Sartre's literary output is also political. In a series of novels and plays he explores various aspects of political practice and experience, from the complex existential and political concerns of *The Roads to Freedom* to the moral dilemmas of the political terrorist in *Les Mains sales* and a portrayal of the formation of a fascist sympathizer in the short story, 'Childhood of a Leader'.[152] This politically engaged literature supplements the more metaphysical concerns of his earlier novel, *Nausea* (1938).[153]

In later theoretical works Sartre attempts to combine the insights of existentialism and Marxism, but at the level of social action rather than individual engagement. His suggestive but problematic *Critique of Dialectical Reason* theorizes human society and history according to the principle that human beings make history under conditions of scarcity.[154] He describes a series of social forms mediating between individual and society, including the group, the organization and class. Here, in contrast to his earlier ontological pessimism, he holds out the optimistic promise that, in Poster's words, 'human beings can attain freedom through the recognition of freedom in the other and in the consequent action of solidary groups pursuing this freedom.'[155] Particularly interesting is his analysis of different kinds of collective or 'ensemble': the alienated, 'serial' interaction between individuals relating to one another as things, as for example in a bus queue; the 'indirect gathering' of the passive and isolated listeners to the radio broadcast; and the 'impotent bond' of individuals buying and selling in a free market.[156] This analysis is designed to pose the problem of genuinely collective action in a novel way. How can we explain the occasional and often unexpected eruption of solidary action in the 'fused group', that sudden 'upsurge of mutual recognition in the context of daily life' which is the precondition of freedom?[157] Much of the *Critique* describes the way revolutionary collective action, once achieved, typically degenerates as, for reasons which seem inescapable, revolutionary spontaneity is subjected to the constraints of formal organization and centralized leadership. By what is presented as an almost unavoidable dialectical logic of social forms,

revolutionary organizations either suppress or purge internal difference and opposition and then impose a new order, which is not
necessarily less oppressive than the order they replace. The second,
unfinished volume of the *Critique* applies the analytical categories of
the first volume to an exhaustive – and sometimes exhausting –
description of the experience of the Soviet Union under communism
and Stalinism.

In another significant contribution to existentialism, Simone de
Beauvoir (1908–86), beginning from the assumptions of Sartrian existentialism, in particular his conception of freedom, addresses the
question of woman as the 'perpetual Other' of man – woman as
'second sex'. The peculiar situation of woman is that,

> she – a free and autonomous being like all human creatures – nevertheless
> finds herself living in a world where men compel her to assume the status
> of Other. They propose to stabilize her as object and to doom her to
> immanence since her transcendence is to be overshadowed and for ever
> transcended by another ego [*conscience*] which is essential and
> sovereign.[158]

She emphasizes throughout that the factors distinguishing women
from men, even biological differences, do not necessitate the oppression of women: 'Woman is the victim of no mysterious fatality; the
peculiarities that identify her as specifically a woman get their importance from the significance placed upon them.'[159] In fact, her account
of woman's 'situation and character' makes quite a radical departure
from the tenets of Sartrian existentialism. In particular, it implies that
the freedom of the individual can indeed be limited by social conditions, that it is not necessarily an instance of bad faith for woman's
consciousness to be affected by these conditions. Woman's oppression denies her access to the consciousness of freedom expressed in
existentialist philosophy, which is necessary in order to overcome a
genuinely involuntary servitude. In effect, de Beauvoir attempts to
mediate between the radical freedom and individualism of Sartre's
existentialism on the one hand and the evidently social and psychological oppression of women on the other.[160] An analogous intellectual role is played by Frantz Fanon's analysis of racism, which applies
Sartrian philosophy to the condition of the colonized.[161] On the other
hand, it is not clear that Sartre's existentialism can be consistently
socialized and politicized in this way. If the individual's actions are
constrained by a socio-cultural complex such as patriarchy, what
other causal complexes are to be admitted as factors mitigating *prima
facie* instances of bad faith? It is difficult to draw the boundary
between unconditioned ontological freedom and a social condition of

oppression. Still, de Beauvoir's reworking of existentialism exerted a significant impact on feminism. It also helped to inspire the later, more political writings of Sartre as well as his biography of Jean Genet.[162]

However, de Beauvoir's feminism has also been criticized for being unduly influenced by Sartre's misogynist view of femininity and the female body. In *Being and Nothingness* Sartre associates woman with the 'sliminess' of the in-itself, the self reduced to the status of a thing, with its tendency to engulf the transcendent subjectivity and untrammelled freedom of the for-itself: 'Slime is the revenge of the in-itself. A sickly-sweet, feminine revenge . . . a soft yielding action, a moist and feminine sucking . . .'[163] Femininity threatens to reduce a presumably masculine for-itself to the inertness and passivity of 'sticky existence'. What is worse, de Beauvoir 'shares this view of femininity as "the Other" that threatens the free consciousness with its cloying and "appealing" nature'. Women are biologically weaker than men, they suffer 'instability', 'lack of control' and are 'fragile'; they are condemned by their biology to motherhood and by their socialization to an emotionally dependent and narcissistic femininity.[164] Accordingly women's fuller participation in social and intellectual life is thought to require the sacrifice of their feminine otherness or difference as women – in order to be free, women must become more like men: 'women's participation in (the) fraternity is predicated on her repudiation of the female body and femininity. A symmetrical repudiation of the male body and masculinity is not in evidence in the case of men's participation.'[165] If this interpretation is correct, then clearly de Beauvoir's feminism contrasts with more recent (including postmodernist) feminisms, which value woman and femininity as unconditional and irreducible 'difference'.[166] It is not, as de Beauvoir implies, that women are oppressed by being made feminine, as the slave is oppressed by being made servile. Rather, patriarchal oppression devalues and disempowers female biology and feminine qualities.

Albert Camus (1913–60) gives a quite different account of the philosophy and politics of existentialism.[167] He differs most strikingly from Sartre in his conception of the absurd. For Sartre absurdity belongs to the world prior to the conceptual projections or nihilating activity of consciousness. Camus's idea of the absurd is more self-consciously located within the existentialist tradition of Kierkegaard and Nietzsche. The absurd is a direct consequence of the absence of God. Without religion the discrepancy between human aspirations and the world is acute. The human condition is characterized by the probability of suffering and the certainty of death, a fate which human reason cannot accept as reasonable. In the face of this absurdity the 'universal reason, practical or ethical' of the Enlightenment has nothing to say: 'At this point of his effort man stands face to face with the irrational. He feels within him his longing for happiness and for reason. The absurd is born of this confrontation between the human need and the unreasonable silence of the world.'[168] In his novel *The Plague* (1947) this confrontation is epitomized in the painful death of a young and unquestionably innocent child from an unexplained outbreak of pestilence. The arbitrariness of the plague parallels the absurdity of existence. At the end of the novel one of the characters remarks: 'But what does it mean, the plague? It's life and that's all.'[169] The absurdity of existence raises the question of suicide and the meaning of life as 'the one truly serious philosophical problem.'[170] The myth of Sisyphus gives Camus a potent image of the futility of existence. Sisyphus is condemned to roll a heavy stone up a great hill, only to see the stone roll down again and face the prospect of the repetition of the same task for all eternity. Camus's response is that only the 'lucid' recognition of the absurdity of existence liberates us from belief in another life and permits us to live for the instant, for beauty, pleasure and the 'implacable grandeur' of existence. Lucidity is that clarity and courage of mind which refuses all comforting illusions and self-deception. Lucidity, in other words, is the counterpart of the notion, common to both Kierkegaard and Sartre, of anguish as the self-conscious and unflinching apprehension of freedom. But in the end Camus is more positive than either Kierkegaard or Sartre. Though living with absurdity is 'a confrontation and a struggle without rest', Camus concludes his account of the mythical Sisyphus with defiance: 'One must imagine Sisyphus happy.'[171]

Camus draws a political moral from the absurdity of existence in *The Rebel* (1951), a series of essays on a variety of topics from the French and Russian Revolutions, de Sade, Marx, Nietzsche and nihilism to anarchism. In a move similar to Sartre's existential modulation of the categorical imperative, Camus makes a dramatic, and for French philosophers seemingly obligatory, allusion to Descartes. Camus attempts to derive collective solidarity from individual defiance or 'revolt' in the face of the absurdity of existence: 'I rebel – therefore we exist.'[172] His ethic of uncompromising honesty and lucid revolt against absurdity encounters its most obvious enemies in the stifling atmosphere of conventional bourgeois morality and, more horrifyingly, in totalitarianism and the concentration camp of either fascist or Stalinist varieties. Though briefly a member of the communist party in his youth, Camus is openly hostile to communism. Above all, he rejects both the idea that the ends can justify the means and the arrogance of philosophies of history, which claim to know the end of history in advance. Both ideas were, of course, resorted to in defence of revolutionary expediency and even the Stalinist terror. Camus was attacked by Sartre for keeping clean hands at the expense of political engagement on the side of the exploited. Camus's political reputation also suffered when he supported his former compatriots, the French colonists, in the Algerian war of independence.[173]

Overall the contribution of French existentialism is complex and sometimes paradoxical. Camus has been more influential as a novelist and stylist than for either his philosophy of the absurd or his more overtly political writings. Sartre increasingly distanced himself from exstentialism to work on Marxist social theory. If *Being and Nothingness* is undoubtedly an impressive contribution to philosophy, it must be admitted that it bequeaths a problematic legacy. At the heart of this legacy is Sartre's concept of freedom. This has been criticized most vehemently for its detachment from social and political conditions, for example by theorists associated with the Frankfurt School. Because freedom is grounded in a basic ontological lack, a tendency to frustration is intrinsic to consciousness rather than something socially or politically conditioned. The uselessness of existence is unavoidable and so, from a political point of view, irrelevant. Marcuse sees existentialism as an apolitical and ultimately futile attempt to resolve, by philosophical means, problems of 'concrete existence' which demand a political solution, a critical theory of society. Like the Stoic, who withdraws to a subjective world beyond the reach of social and political realities, the underlying tendency of Sartrian existentialism seems conservative or, at best, apolitical.[174] Although de Beauvoir and Fanon develop existentialism in a social and political direction, it is not clear that their reconciliation of radical freedom and social oppression can ultimately be sustained. On the other hand, there are a number of similarities between Sartre's Marxism and that of the Frankfurt School. Both include a 'humanist' commitment to the freedom of the individual subject, both reject the determinism of orthodox historical materialism and both envisage an important role for art and creativity in the transcendence of existing social conditions. Not surprisingly, then, both are prime targets for the proponents of a further distinctive constellation of ideas within continental philosophy. Both the philosophy of Nietzsche and the later writings of Heidegger play a significant role in the 'anti-humanist critique of the subject'. This critique is inseparable from the interrelated intellectual tendencies of structuralism and poststructuralism.

6. Beyond the Subject: Structuralism and Poststructuralism

Decentring the Subject

Structuralism and poststructuralism can be understood as the culmination of a number of more sceptical strains of post-Enlightenment thought. These philosophical positions emerge clearly in the twentieth century, as a reaction to Hegelianism and Marxism on the one hand and Sartrian existentialism and phenomenology on the other. The associated critiques of humanism and the 'subject' develop tendencies apparent for some time both in philosophy and in the human and social sciences.[1] In this development Nietzsche, the later writings of Heidegger and the linguistics of Saussure play an important role. The major outcome of these changes is a radical questioning of the privileged philosophical and political status of the subject within humanism and rationalism. Both what we have termed the dominant tradition of Enlightenment thought and some of its most influential continental critics rely on views of the philosophical subject which, according to structuralists and poststructuralists, cannot be sustained. But in what sense does Enlightenment rationalism tend to accord a privileged status to the subject?

In effect, the philosophical rationalism of the modern period holds human reason, or subjectivity, responsible for the validity of its own beliefs, values and decisions. Human reason is regarded as the sole and sufficient arbiter of truth, goodness and justice. Rationalism also challenges the authority of inherited tradition, whether in the form of the received wisdom of classical antiquity or the supernatural claims of religion and the Church. Knowledge, values and even political power are to be placed on new and more secure, because more rational, foundations. In support of these ambitious claims for the power of human reason, rationalist philosophers make certain assumptions about both the cognitive and the practical subject, that is the subject both as site of knowledge and as source of values. Both epistemology, or the theory of knowledge, and the attempt to provide rational foundations for morality become central preoccupations. Descartes's founding of knowledge on the certainty of self-consciousness is an influential instance. Kant transposes epistemological inquiry to a transcendental level, depersonalizing the subject or ego in the process. The subject of knowledge becomes abstract mind or reason, a reconstruction of the cognitive capacities of human or rational beings in general, or in other words capacities which every sane individual can be presumed to possess. The cognitive subject in this sense remains central to much subsequent philosophy in both continental and analytical traditions.

Emerging alongside philosophical rationalism were a variety of forms of moral and political individualism. From the sixteenth century, the Protestant Reformation expressed this tendency within the religious sphere, pointing to individual conscience rather than the authority of priests as the criterion of right action and salvation. Taking this tendency to its extreme, in the nineteenth century Kierkegaard would assert the 'subjective truth' of existence against the institutionalized Protestant Church.[2] The ultimate moral authority of the individual is also implicit in such philosophical doctrines as utilitarianism, intuitionism and subjectivism, which account for morality in terms of the pleasure or pain (happiness or unhappiness), the considered moral intuitions or the attitudes and emotions of individuals respectively. Liberalism asserts the right of the individual to a 'private sphere' free from all external interference. The ideal of democracy claims the right of individuals to take part in or to determine the actions of their own government.[3] The bounds of legitimate political agency are also extended beyond the restricted sphere of rulers or princes, typically to include 'responsible' individuals or 'men of property' and their parties and factions. Rulers are expected to justify their actions in the face of a largely bourgeois public opinion. Politics in the modern sense, as opposed to mere rule, begins to assume a historically novel importance. Overall, a similar position of authority is claimed for the subject in the practical sphere as epistemology implies in the theory of knowledge.

However, both in philosophy and in the human or social sciences a series of developments soon threatens the newly acquired status of the subject. The intellectual 'decentring' of the subject can be traced even to Kant's transcendental philosophy, despite the fact that Kant promotes the subject to a position of the highest epistemological and moral importance. The subject is made responsible both for the essential structure of reality and, as self-legislating rational will, for the moral law as well. Kant claims to identify the necessary and eternal or 'transcendental' features of any subject of knowledge or action. But precisely the transcendental status of Kant's conclusions – the necessity of exactly those structural characteristics of the subject identified by Kant – proved difficult to sustain. Unconvinced by Kant's transcendental deduction, Hegel historicizes and collectivizes the Kantian subject. The bearer of knowledge and ethical life becomes a particular, concrete manifestation of 'mind' or 'spirit' (*Geist*), embodied in the life of a particular historical community. Ultimate truth, or the 'Absolute', is only guaranteed in the historical culmination of a dialectically unfolding series of forms of life and worldviews. By implication, the site of rational assessment is no longer located within the sphere of competence of ordinary historical individuals. The dialectic takes place behind the backs of individual subjects. History manifests the 'cunning of reason', which realizes the aims of the world spirit as the unintended by-product of the actions of individual agents. The site of rational assessment is removed to the final stage of the dialectic (whether already achieved or yet to be realized) or, perhaps, the authority of Hegel himself as self-proclaimed herald and philosophical guarantor of the Absolute.[4]

With Marx a parallel narrative of humanity's historical self-constitution materializes the already historicized subject of Hegelian idealism. The dialectical development of the subject is explained in terms of the relationship between humanity and nature through work or production. The historical process is driven by contradictions within the mode of production rather than by intellectual or conceptual oppositions within worldviews.[5] The Marxist theory of ideology makes plain the implications of this view for the subject. Consciousness, whether as knowledge or as will, depends on the achievements and limitations of a collective subject which, in turn, corresponds to the society's level of social and economic development. More pointedly, consciousness depends on class. Our beliefs and attitudes, even our most deeply held moral values, reflect our position in society rather than absolute truth.[6] Thus, the characteristically Enlightenment commitment to universal values of liberty, fraternity and equality is really a reflection of bourgeois conscience and, what is worse, self-interest. These values are no more than projections of the interests of the capitalist class, ideological weapons which could be used to undermine feudalism without endangering capitalist exploitation.

The Marxist theory of ideology represents a further blow to the self-confidence of the cognitive and practical subject. Individual subjects can no longer be presumed to have reliable access to rational criteria of theoretical or moral truth. But as with Hegelian idealism, Marxism does not so much abolish as displace the privileges of the individual subject. These privileges are transferred to a collective historical subject, namely the proletariat which, in virtue of its position within the capitalist mode of production, is destined to overthrow capitalism and achieve true consciousness. Individuals can only achieve true consciousness, as it were vicariously, by subordinating their alienated self to the collective will of the class. In the Leninist tradition the centre of cognitive and practical privilege is further removed to the leadership and policies of the revolutionary party. With the abolition of capitalism and the arrival of communism, the ideological distortions of class society will come to an end. Social relations will become transparent and individuals will attain their true 'species being', the full and undistorted flowering of all their human capacities.

A further major decentring of the subject, this time more psychological than sociological, occurs with the 'psychoanalysis' of Sigmund Freud (1856–1939). Nineteenth-century psychology took a variety of forms, but two of its most influential currents correspond to the predominant mind–body dualism of post-Cartesian metaphysics. Experimental psychologists investigated the physiology of the brain and nervous system as the causally explanatory reality underlying the mind. Introspectionist psychologists described the distinctive character of mental or psychic states 'from within' or, in other words, through their own subjective experience. In the main, studies of mental disorder or 'pathology' were restricted to the exhaustive description and classification of the sometimes startling phenomena of nervous disease, dementia, hysteria and sexual 'perversion'.[7] Much more unsettling to the assumptions of nineteenth-century thought were Freud's theories of the unconscious mind. Freudian psychoanalysis challenges the status of the conscious subject of experience, because it suggests that individual consciousness and behaviour can only be understood in terms of the less than rational or transparent workings of the unconscious mind. But again, like Marx, psychoanalysis does not so much cancel as transfer the privileges of the subject.

Freud's distinctive approach can be traced to his early work with Breuer and Charcot on the causes of 'hysteria'. Freud originally qualified as a physiologist and, in fact, throughout his career retained a preference for mechanistic models of explanation and neurophysiological hypotheses. Like Charcot, then, he was struck by the curious physical symptoms involved in cases of hysteria, a nervous disorder suffered mainly by women and traditionally blamed on the erratic behaviour of the womb.[8] Hysterical symptoms often made little sense in physiological terms. For example, in the case of a patient complaining of paralysis of the hand, the paralysis would correspond to the patient's common-sense ideas about physiology rather than the actual workings of the body, which do not allow such limited paralysis.[9] There also seemed to be a relationship between hysterical symptoms and hypnosis. Symptoms could be induced by suggestion, when someone was in a hypnoid state. Later Freud used hypnosis in both diagnosis and cure. These and other observations led Freud to postulate an 'ideogenic' – psychological or mental – rather than physiological aetiology for hysteria. On the other hand, Freud was convinced that the symptoms of the hysteric were not simply voluntary or consciously faked. At least some patients genuinely suffered from an extremely unpleasant mental disorder, which made anything like an ordinary life impossible. If such disorders were involuntary, but nevertheless caused by mental rather than physiological factors, then only *unconscious* mental states could provide an explanation.

Freud went on to elaborate a series of related concepts describing the relationship between conscious and unconscious mind. Concepts such as trauma, repression, resistance, ego, id and superego have become part of our everyday vocabulary. He also developed a number of techniques for gaining access to the unconscious mind. Most famously, word association and the analysis of dreams are two significant tools in what he began to call 'psychoanalysis'. In his case studies Freud claimed a number of impressive cures with the help of these techniques.[10] But the implications of his theories extend far beyond the realm of mental pathology. In fact Freud is concerned with a much wider range of mental phenomena. The impact of the unconscious mind can be recognized in a wide range of apparently normal behaviour. Jokes and slips of the tongue, the forgetting of names or appointments, dreams and fantasies, religion and culture, all can only be properly understood in terms of the unconscious mind.[11]

Freud's concept of the unconscious mind has far-reaching implications.[12] Consciousness never gives us more than a partial and distorted view of our mental life, so the Cartesian principle that the mind or subject is simply equivalent to a fully transparent consciousness is undermined. On the contrary, for Freud the reasons we give for our actions may be no more than rationalizations, obscuring the real origin of our behaviour in the trauma or unresolved emotional conflicts of early childhood. The conscious mind, even when it enjoys 'healthy' or 'normal' functioning, is ultimately the plaything of the unconscious, the creature of its whims and fancies – subject, in the final instance, to its repressive veto.[13] In this sense, clearly, Freudian psychoanalysis betokens a further decentring of the subject. The individual subject has no guarantee of 'knowing its own mind'. We may be dupes of our unconscious, just as for Marx we are, for the most part, dupes of history and class. On the other hand, and again with parallels to Marx, psychoanalysis holds out for the conscious self at least some prospect of recovering its sovereignty. A protracted dialogue of analyst and patient promises eventual relief from neurotic and even psychotic symptoms – what has been described as a 'talking cure'.[14] The self can, in principle at least, come to understand the unconscious springs of its conscious states and impulses. In the terms of Lorenzer and Habermas, analysis can help to remove the barriers to a free 'internal communication', a transparent subjectivity.[15] Through the 'depth hermeneutics' of psychoanalysis individuals can hope to approach, if perhaps never to attain – analysis may turn out to be 'interminable' and repression and neurosis may be the inevitable accompaniments of 'civilization' – something like the ideal of transparent selfhood held out by the Cartesian tradition.[16] The subject, as site of cognitive or practical rationality, is dethroned only provisionally.[17]

The Break with Humanism

Thus, though in different ways, Hegelian idealism, Marxism and Freudian psychoanalysis displace the subject from its privileged position, yet they do not break irrevocably with humanism. Each of these theoretical approaches retains a qualified or conditional role for the subject and so remains within the pale of humanist assumptions. A more decisive break with humanism occurs with further developments in two areas of intellectual activity, namely hermeneutics and linguistics. Both areas are closely concerned with language and, as a result, are of obvious significance for both philosophy and the human sciences. In fact, traditional hermeneutics involves only a provisional decentring of the subject analogous to the decentring of the subject implicit in Marxism and psychoanalysis. The development of the hermeneutic approach within the human sciences, which are concerned in a major way with the interpretation or criticism of texts and the historical reconstruction of past events, reflects increased awareness of the difficulties of mutual understanding. Hermeneutic principles are called upon, not only where texts present obvious difficulties of interpretation, but all the time, since mutual understanding between subjects can never be taken for granted. To understand any text or utterance involves knowledge of the social and linguistic context in which it was produced – understanding of the part depends upon understanding of the whole. This realization further undermines the position of the subject of discourse, since meaning can no longer be regarded as completely under the control of the individual speaker or writer. However, traditional hermeneutics regards this dependency as remediable. Thus for Dilthey, the recovery of the original intentions or meaning of the author can be achieved through knowledge of the broader cultural and linguistic context. The practice of hermeneutics promises an always improving, though in some versions never perfect, interpretation of meaning – an always improving degree of mutual understanding between subjects.[18]

From this point of view, the radical hermeneutics of both Heidegger and Gadamer represents a more decisive break with humanist assumptions. Although it is particularly in his later writings that Heidegger explicitly distances himself from humanism, his abandonment of epistemology for ontology directly implies a rejection of the exaggerated role accorded to the subject in modern western philosophy. The overemphasis of the subject within epistemology corresponds to a reductive 'objectification' of the world in metaphysics. Heidegger associates this objectification with the destructive reign of instrumental thinking and technology. The fundamental starting point of Heidegger's philosophy is, hence, the indivisible unity of 'being-in-the-world' (in effect, the unity of subject and object). Heidegger's position is evident in his reaction to Sartre. Although he claims to follow Heidegger in rejecting the assumptions of modern metaphysics and epistemology, according to Heidegger Sartre still falls into subjectivism. Thus in the 'Letter on Humanism' (1947) Heidegger explicitly responds to Sartre's claim that existentialism is also a humanism, taking issue in particular with the Cartesian assumption that 'one must take subjectivity as his point of departure.'[19] *Being and Nothingness* applies Heidegger's 'hermeneutic of Being' in an explicitly existentialist direction and so misunderstands its basic point. Heidegger's anti-humanist critique of the subject–object dichotomy of western thought leads instead to advocacy of 'thinking' as the 'letting-be' of a transcendent Being. Thinking is to be understood not as the directed activity of a conscious subject but rather as an impersonal openness or receptiveness to the world. Heidegger advocates something close to a religious attitude of humility, a deferential attentiveness to Being. Indeed, the almost mystical status accorded to Being has led some to see it as a cipher for God, despite the fact that, according to Heidegger, this attitude 'can be theistic as little as atheistic'.[20] Still, it can hardly be denied that 'thinking' takes us a long way from the humanist assumptions of Enlightenment rationalism.

Of course, anti-humanism in Heidegger's sense is not equivalent to the assertion of the worthlessness of human life. There is a clear distinction between anti-humanism and the 'affirmation of inhumanity'.[21] Rather the objection is to any philosophy of 'values', which reduces the worth of things to their status as 'valued by some subject'. There are clearly affinities with the anti-humanism of Nietzsche, who provides an incisive diagnosis of humanism's arrogant premise:

> The whole attitude of 'man *versus* the world,' man as world-denying principle, man as the standard of the value of things, as judge of the world, who in the end puts existence itself on his scales and finds it too light – the monstrous impertinence of this attitude has dawned upon us as such, and has disgusted us – we now laugh when we find 'Man *and* World' placed beside one another, separated by the sublime presumption of the little word 'and'![22]

Indeed, humanism is held responsible for many of the characteristic vices of modern society, including its not infrequent inhumanity. For the technological attitude, which is one significant expression of humanism, all beings, whether human or non-human, are manipulable objects available for exploitation. Nature too is 'set-upon' as a mere object, as nothing more than a 'standing-reserve' or resource for human use. Even with what would now be called ecological tourism, nature is treated as 'an object on call for inspection by a tour group ordered there by the vacation industry'. Even 'man', as the supposed subject of this instrumental relationship with nature, is reduced to an object in the same way: 'If man is challenged, ordered, to do this, then does not man himself belong even more originally than nature within the standing-reserve?'[23] Indeed, the historical guilt of humanist philosophy may extend even further than this. Humanist arrogance is held responsible for colonialism, genocide and even the holocaust. The technological and bureaucratic sophistication of the Nazi genocide is a striking instance of modernity and, for some, also humanism, despite its evident inhumanity.

Certainly, then, although Heidegger's philosophical anti-humanism may explain his less than robust commitment to Enlightenment values such as equality and liberty, it does not so obviously account for his association with Hitler's national socialism or his subsequent tardiness in disowning this involvement.[24] The injunction to be 'attentive to Being', like the call to obey the will of God, is in principle compatible with almost any political stance. On the other hand, the evident difficulty of 'thinking' in its full Heideggerian sense, with the suggestion that only the philosophically adept are capable of achieving the appropriate relationship with Being, provides a possible foothold for authoritarian claims. It may be true that when Heidegger spoke in 1935 of 'the internal truth and the greatness of the movement', he was not speaking of the Nazis. As Lyotard interprets it, Heidegger's position is that,

> 'those people [who] were far too limited in their thinking' . . . could only mask and mislead the authentic anxiety that Heidegger thinks he recognises in the desperate search (the 1930s) which, at that time, projects the Volk towards a decision, a resolution that may be in accord with what is 'peculiar' to it. The movement that derives from the unbearable anxiety of being thrown before nothingness, Heidegger believes, needs 'knowledge' in order to guide and resolve itself to a decision.[25]

But a philosophy which shelves so steeply into obscurity and mysticism offers little apparent resistance to the charismatic despot.

Gadamer's ontological hermeneutics surely represents a less questionable development of Heidegger's anti-humanist approach. In a clear departure from Cartesian assumptions, which ground the existence of both an objective world and other minds on a self-founding and transparent consciousness, for Gadamer it is the subject which is ontologically derivative. The subject exists only within the irreducibly intersubjective medium of understanding and language. Understanding is not only and not primarily one dimension of the knowledge of a subject, as it was for Dilthey, but rather the medium in which the subject has its existence. In other words, Gadamer repeats Heidegger's move from epistemology to ontology. Understanding is conceived not 'as a subjective process of man over and against an object but the way of being of man himself'.[26] Accordingly, hermeneutics is not simply the characteristic method of the human sciences, but the key to truth in general. By the same token, the close relationship between understanding and historicity, already identified by Dilthey, characterizes not just the objects but also the subject of acts of interpretation. It is not only the historical text which is inseparable from a concrete historical, cultural and linguistic context. The subject is situated not only, as it were, horizontally in the dimension of language or understanding but also vertically in the dimension of history and tradition. Understanding always as much derives from a particular perspective as it aims at a historical context. A corollary of this view of the subject is that the author of a historical text can no longer be regarded as the ultimate authority on its meaning. The work is understood not solely or, perhaps, even principally as the product of an individual subject. From the perspective of Gadamer's hermeneutics the subject – whether as author or as interpreter – is much less important than the surrounding medium of understanding or language itself.

An even more radical challenge to the subject is evident in the thought of Emmanuel Levinas (1906–), who blames the humanist focus on identity, sameness and the subject for a deep-seated neglect of the 'other' in western thought – a neglect which finds its most horrifying expression in the death camps and killing fields of the twentieth century. Levinas's 'genetic phenomenology' is clearly influenced by Hegel, Husserl and Heidegger but diverges from them in crucial respects. Unlike Hegel, Levinas's dialectic leads not to the comprehensive totality of the 'absolute' but toward 'alterity' or otherness. To this end Levinas also dissociates phenomenology from any remaining, Husserlian infatuation with the transcendental subject. Even Heidegger's ontological overcoming of subjective consciousness for the sake of a greater 'attentiveness to Being' is left behind. It is western philosophy's very insistence on the primacy of epistemology and ontology, on 'knowledge and understanding' or on 'being and truth', which must be abandoned in the face of the fundamental primacy of the ethical. In Richard Cohen's words, 'alterity must be acknowledged in terms of what *surpasses* understanding absolutely, what is *superior* to the horizons of being and the truth of being, what exceeds or precedes the beginning of philosophy: the *surplus* or *excellence* of ethical command and the infinite responsibilities it calls forth.'[27]

In the process the 'existent' or subject must be radically decentred: 'the *I* is *first* for-the-other *before* the very firstness of its being for-itself.'[28] The 'radical passivity' of the good will is referred to a 'Desire' which 'has its center outside of itself'.[29] The subject only comes into existence as always already responsible to otherness. As Bauman puts it, 'I become responsible while I constitute myself into a subject. Becoming responsible *is* the constitution of me as a subject.'[30] Levinas also draws deeply on religious texts, particularly those of Judaism, in order to develop his views. In a phrase derived from the Old Testament – and in obvious contrast to Descartes's privileging of consciousness with his 'I think, therefore I am' – the 'Here I am!' founds the self as '*subjectum*, subjectivity as substitution and expiation for the other'.[31] The active, heroic will favoured by existentialism and even the earlier Heidegger is replaced by a passive will, which declares its availability for the ethical demands of the other. Although, like both Heidegger and Gadamer, Levinas's later work attends increasingly to the nature of language, it is the ambiguous, open expression of the 'saying' rather than the 'coherent language' and 'contaminated' logic of the 'said' that is celebrated.[32] Saying speaks 'the hyperbolic passivity of giving, which is prior to all willing and thematization'.[33] It allows a responsibility for the other, which is lost once the 'logocentric' certainties of the 'said' take over: 'Saying opens me to the other before saying what is said, before the said uttered in this sincerity forms a screen between me and the other.'[34]

Language, albeit in a very different sense, is at the heart of another important source of anti-humanist thought. The 'structural linguistics' of Ferdinand de Saussure (1857–1913) has been the main inspiration for the approach known as structuralism.[35] Like Gadamer, Saussure focuses on language rather than the speaking or interpreting subject. The challenge to the conventional view of the relationship between subject and language is already evident in Saussure's primary distinction between 'language' (*langue*) and 'speech' (*parole*). It seems obvious to Saussure that language exists as a system of signs (words and meanings) independently of the particular 'speech acts' of individual speaking subjects. The latter are instances of *parole* in the sense of the 'actual speech, the speech acts which are made possible by the language'.[36] Speakers can only say or mean something with the help of a language, which already exists before they speak. By implication, the meaning of language cannot be accounted for in the subjective terms of either phenomenology or psychology. Meaning cannot depend on the subject's conscious acts of intending or meaning, as phenomenology suggests, any more than it can be understood as the product of some kind of psychological or mental association between sign and meaning.

A second important step towards structuralism results from Saussure's argument for a 'synchronic' rather than a 'diachronic' approach to language.[37] The study of language must break radically with diachronic approaches, which study the changes undergone by language over time. Thus classical philology traces the meaning and phonetic character of words in contemporary languages to their roots in earlier ones. But diachronic accounts can never really explain how a language works. After all, even if the etymological roots of a word can be traced, nothing guarantees that the word has not radically changed meaning in the meantime. In any case, we need to establish the meaning of the root word itself, and we cannot refer this to *its* etymology without falling into a vicious regress. However interesting may be the findings of philology, language must ultimately be explained synchronically. In other words, the meaning and functioning of language depend on facts about an existing system of signs and meanings rather than on any genetic or developmental story about the origins of this system.

But if meanings are neither inherited from the past nor the creation of intending subjects, how are they to be explained? In Saussure's terms, an explanation of the meaning of a sign must provide an account of the relationship between the 'signifier' – the word or sign considered as a particular sound or set of written characters – and its 'signified' – the meaning or concept the signifier represents. Crucially for Saussure, this relationship does not reflect any intrinsic or essential quality of the signifier, as if meaning were the property of an underlying linguistic substance. The mere existence of different languages proves that the relationship between signifier and signified must be an arbitrary one. Only onomatopoeic words such as 'splash' or 'quack', which sound like the thing to which they refer, are not clearly arbitrary in this way.[38] According to Saussure, what gives particular words their meaning is the language as a whole, considered as a structured system of elements. Meaning depends on the differential relations or contrasts between elements, which in the case of language are signs: 'Since the sign has no necessary core which must persist, it must be defined as a relational entity, in its relations to other signs.'[39] The meaning of a term like 'blue', for example, depends on the particular colour contrasts which the language allows: blue is whatever is not green or red or yellow and so on. Significantly, different languages embody different conceptual distinctions, which may involve more or less refined gradations of meaning and may even draw conceptual boundaries in different places.

One obvious result of this account of language is that translation between languages is always imperfect, as there can be no guarantee of a one-to-one correlation between their elements. It also implies that the acquisition of language essentially involves mastery of the particular system of distinctions and contrasts which it comprises. A child first learns to speak not by learning the meanings of more and more words as discrete entities, but rather by making basic distinctions between words for mother and father, self and other, good and bad, proceeding to ever more refined distinctions. From this structuralist perspective the only essential feature of any language or code (the only thing which is not arbitrary from the point of view of the linguist) is the fact that it consists of a number of distinguishable and differentially related elements. In principle, there is no difference or priority between spoken and written languages or between these and the 'signed' languages used mainly by deaf people. A structuralist account of meaning also helps to explain how an apparently abstract medium such as music can have meaning, since music can also be understood as a system of differentially related elements. Overall the structural analysis of meaning reinforces the anti-humanist implications of Saussurean linguistics, because meaning can no longer be attributed to individual speaking subjects. Speakers are only able to mean something with their words thanks to the pre-existing system of linguistic and semantic oppositions embodied in language.

Structuralism is, in effect, the result of extending Saussure's structural method and the associated critique of the subject and humanism to the entire field of the human sciences. With his project of a general semiotics or theory of the sign Saussure had himself anticipated an extension of that kind. Developments in mathematics, logic, biology and psychology – associated with the group of mathematicians known as Bourbaki, Claude Bernard and Waddington in biology and *Gestalt* psychologists – lent support to structuralism.[40] By the 1960s an array of approaches in the social and human sciences argued that social and cultural phenomena should be treated neither as the intentional products of human subjects nor as the unintentional by-products of history, but rather as structured systems of elements with specific and irreducible rules of combination and transformation. By abstracting from everything subjective (from the conscious self and its intentions or acts of meaning), structuralists also hoped to demonstrate the strictly scientific nature of their enterprise. As Dreyfus and Rabinow put it: 'Structuralists attempt to treat human activity scientifically by finding basic elements (concepts, actions, classes of words) and the rules or laws by which they are combined.'[41] On the other hand, structuralists distanced themselves from the reductively atomistic, analytical approach of the dominant tradition of science, emphasizing instead the distinctive properties of systems as wholes, which are more than the sum of their parts. Structuralism is also a species of holism.[42]

Perhaps most famously the structural anthropology of Claude Lévi-Strauss (1908–), probably the most persistent, austere and unashamed advocate of structuralism, influenced a generation of social scientists. Lévi-Strauss certainly acknowledged his debt to Saussure as well as to Roman Jakobson.[43] Lévi-Strauss also suggests a link with Freud, when he claims that 'anthropology draws its originality from the unconscious nature of collective phenomena.'[44] Like the rules of a language, patterns of social organization are typically reproduced from one generation to another without being either consciously understood or deliberately chosen. Accordingly society, like language, cannot be understood by simply examining the intentions or actions of individual social agents. Again like Saussure, Lévi-

Strauss's approach is synchronic rather than diachronic. Social and cultural forms are not explained in terms of their origin or genesis, a method which only pushes the problem of explanation one step further back. Rather, each element is explained in terms of its position within the overall system of society as it exists at any one time. The various dimensions of social life (including kinship systems, mythology and rituals) are understood as structured systems of elements with their own distinctive and irreducible rules of combination and transformation. Lévi-Strauss adapts Jakobson's phonological model of binary oppositions between discrete sounds or 'phonemes', analysing mythology as a structured system of 'mythemes'. Similarly, totemism is understood as a sophisticated set of isomorphisms between the structures of the natural and the human world, whereby classifications of animal or plant life correspond to a parallel ordering of human kinship relations.[45] More dubiously, Lévi-Strauss combines his structuralist methodology with the universalist claim that there is a 'fundamental unity of all cultures'. In other words, he supposes that the diversity of structures found in human societies and cultures can be shown to derive from a single underlying structure (or structure of structures) common to humanity as a whole. Implicitly, such an underlying structure must depend on a conception of shared human nature, albeit a nature that determines how rather than what people think.[46]

Another influential example of structuralist and anti-humanist theory was the Marxism of Louis Althusser (1918–90).[47] Structuralist Marxism was exciting to many, because it promised to apply the apparently ahistorical, synchronic categories of structuralism, which has often been accused of eliding the dimension of history altogether, to an explicitly and irreducibly historical body of theory. It also seemed to offer a more scientific alternative to historicism and idealism, which had dominated French intellectual life since the revival of interest in Hegel from the 1930s.[48] Certainly, contemporary capitalist society was readily susceptible to structuralist analysis. After all, Marxism was always an explicitly holistic theoretical approach. Society cannot be understood in the reductive atomistic terms of bourgeois social science, but only according to the dialectical categories of historical materialism, for which society is, in Lukács's terms, a 'totality'.[49] Althusser's account of the structural relations between relatively autonomous state and non-state 'apparatuses', therefore, is compatible with the spirit of Marx's original theory (though some would claim that it does not add very much either). More radically, Althusser argues that the historical dimension of Marx's theory can be subjected to a similarly structuralist analysis. All that is required are 'diachronic' rules of transformation to supplement the 'synchronic' rules of combination that govern the structural elements of society at any one time. Once applied, these rules of transformation reveal history as a series of 'ruptures' or discontinuous transformations from one structured whole to the next. In similar terms Althusser provides an account of Marx's own intellectual development, identifying a fundamental break between his earlier 'pre-scientific' writings, which are still infected with essentialism and humanism, and the mature and fully scientific achievement of *Capital*.

Although his immediate adversaries were uncritical followers of the French communist party's line such as Garaudy, Althusser's interpretation of Marx is also directed against Sartre's attempt to combine the insights of existentialism and Marxism. Equally clearly it is diametrically opposed to the Marxism of the Frankfurt School too. For those unashamed 'humanists' it is precisely the scientific pretensions of the later economic writings, which prepare the ground for the positivist and Stalinist degeneration of Marxism. By contrast, Althusser sees Stalinism as a kind of humanism. He describes socialist humanism as an ideological formation that reflects problems unresolved during the Stalinist period in the Soviet Union, just as eighteenth-century bourgeois humanism 'was the visible counterpart to a shadowy inhumanity' or, in other words, to capitalism.[50] On the other hand, Althusser's anti-humanist Marxism raises a problem often attributed to structuralist analyses, namely how to account for political practice without resorting to some notion of the subject. Revolutionary political practice apparently depends on the deliberate choices of actual historical agents. But an account of history as the rule-governed transformation of impersonal social structures seems hostile to, or at least uninformative about, deliberate human practice of that kind. In other words, it is not clear in the end whether structuralism leaves much room for politics.[51] This problem becomes even more pressing when the strictly determined (indeed, overdetermined) transformations of the capitalist system do not point towards communism. As we shall see, the problem of accounting for political agency will recur in the later incarnations of structuralism and poststructuralism.

Foucault's Genealogy of the Subject

Michel Foucault (1926–84) is responsible for one of the most provocative recent contributions to the anti-humanist critique of the subject.[52] Such has been his influence in the areas of social and political theory and philosophy that it has even been suggested that we are living in the century of Foucault.[53] His critique of the subject is particularly radical for a number of reasons. In the first place, Foucault accepts the critical implications of the decentring of the subject effected by both the Marxist theory of ideology and Freudian psychoanalysis, which unmask the subject as the formed and deformed product of social and psychological conditions. But secondly, like theorists of both radical hermeneutics and structuralism, Foucault does not entertain any hopes of eventually recovering the lost transparency of the subject at a higher level or a later stage, in the way that both psychoanalysis and Marxism appear to do. It is necessary to break irrevocably with the humanist conception of the subject. Furthermore, like Althusser, one of Foucault's teachers at the École Normale in Paris, Foucault's anti-humanism is explicitly political. According to one of his many programmatic statements the objective of his work 'has been to create a history of the different modes by which, in our culture, human beings are made subjects'.[54] The play on the ambiguity of 'subject' here reflects his concern, influenced by Althusser's Marxist critique of the bourgeois subject of humanism, to explore the links between the philosophical subject of modern epistemology and political individualism on the one hand and 'subjection' to authority or power on the other. Humanist faith in the subject is no longer merely a sign of philosophical credulity or epistemological laxity, but rather a politically suspect manifestation of modernity. Finally, though, as Foucault's statement also implies, he proposes not so much to dispense altogether with the subject as to provide a historical account of its emergence. His anti-humanist critique denies the subject its privileged moral and epistemological status only to place it near the centre of his thought – even if it is sometimes an absent centre. The subject is no longer a premise but still a prime object of analysis.

Foucault regards the subject as a kind of umbilical cord, entangling modern philosophy and the human sciences from their inception. In *The Order of Things* (1966) Foucault discusses the problematic relationship of modern epistemology and the human sciences after Descartes. He is particularly interested in the intellectual transformation that sets the scene for their subsequent symbiotic development. It is most clearly expressed in Kant's transcendental philosophy which, in order to secure the subject as the absolute condition of all knowledge and action, extracts it from the contingencies of nature and history. The failure of this ruse, the recognition that the subject is a finite historical entity, leaves epistemology with a seemingly insoluble problem. If knowledge is based on a finite or contingent subject, then the conditions of knowledge are neither timeless nor universal, and anything like absolute truth is unattainable. This predicament, what Foucault calls Kant's 'analytic of finitude', also has serious implications for the 'human sciences', which are implicated in the epistemological conundrum of modern philosophy from the beginning. To ground knowledge in humanity, as the subject of knowledge, makes 'man' an object of his own knowledge. In Dreyfus and Rabinow's words,

> Man, who was once himself a being among others, now is a subject among objects. But Man is not only a subject among objects, he soon realizes that what he is seeking to understand is not only the objects of the world but himself. Man becomes the subject and the object of his own understanding.[55]

Foucault describes the contorted responses of modern philosophy to this problem (some of which should by now be familiar, albeit in slightly different terms). The reductive naturalism of positivism brazenly refuses to be troubled by the fact that knowledge is founded on a contingent being, and simply adds the empirical study of 'man' to its agenda. For the historical eschatologies of Hegel and Marx absolute truth eventually arrives with the closure of the dialectic or the arrival of communism. But Foucault is dissatisfied with all of these solutions.

Foucault was, however, variously attracted to structuralism, hermeneutics and phenomenology as promising attempts to evade the interrelated problems of the modern philosophy of the subject and the human sciences. But he soon rejects both phenomenology and structuralism as unwitting accomplices in the subjection of the modern subject. We have already touched upon the basic ambiguity in the notion of subject. Foucault identifies both senses with subjugation and power: 'There are two meanings of the word subject: subject to someone else by control and dependence, and ties to his own identity by a conscience or self-knowledge. Both meanings suggest a form of power which subjugates and makes subject to.'[56] The two meanings of subject correspond to complementary processes of 'objectification' and 'subjectification'. In the end structuralism, like positivism, avoids the Kantian dilemma only by treating human beings as mere objects; it is a symptom of the objectifying tendencies of rationalism and modernity, which have constructed modern individuals as objects amenable to power and authority. But hermeneutic practices are implicated in the construction of the modern subject in a complementary way. Both the Catholic confessional and Freudian psychoanalysis are significant examples of the role played by practices of interpretation in the emergence of contemporary subjects prepared to take responsibility for their own subjection to authority and order.[57] Where structuralism is involved in the constitution of the subject as object, phenomenology and hermeneutics are involved in its constitution as subject.

Foucault's eventual 'overcoming' of both phenomenology and structuralism only becomes clear with his return to something like a political perspective on modern society and with it the centrality of the concept of power. After brief membership of the French communist party in the 1950s, Foucault's work had, after *Madness and Civilization* and *The Birth of the Clinic*, seemed almost idealist in its exclusive concern with discourse and in the virtual absence of any concept of power.[58] When Foucault returns to a more 'materialist' approach, it is, however, in terms of Nietzsche rather than Marx. In fact, Marxist philosophies of history become one of the main targets. Foucault is Nietzschean above all in his conviction that power and knowledge are really two sides of the same coin. '[P]ower and knowledge directly imply one another' and, as a result, Foucault sometimes even speaks of 'power/knowledge' as an indivisible amalgam.[59] On the one hand, as with Nietzsche, the will to truth is just one manifestation of an underlying will to power. Our claims to objective knowledge or absolute truth are at best illusions. Knowledge is always the relative and questionable expression of a particular constellation of relations of power or force. On the other hand, 'the exercise of power is accompanied or paralleled by the production of apparatuses of knowledge.'[60] The exercise of power requires knowledge. In Smart's words, 'knowledge is not neutral or objective but rather is a product of power relations. In other words knowledge is political in the sense that its conditions of existence or possibility include power relations.'[61] The symbiotic relationship between power and knowledge is, as we shall see, at the heart of Foucault's account of the parallel emergence in modern societies of the human sciences as 'disciplines' with scientific pretensions and what he calls 'disciplinary power'.

The challenge to the Enlightenment's faith in the emancipatory potential of reason is reinforced by a similarly sceptical understanding of history. Foucault is inspired by Nietzsche's project of 'genealogy', which renounces the credulous faith in history as progress and traces specific institutions and forms of discourse to 'naked struggles of power' instead. History should not be understood teleologically as humanity's progress towards some overall purpose or goal, whether this is conceived as freedom and happiness or the classless society. Genealogy is also hostile to any attribution of historical continuity, an attitude that helps to explain Foucault's early attraction to structuralism. Already in the *Archaeology of Knowledge* Foucault conceives history according to 'categories of discontinuity and difference, the notions of threshold, rupture and transformation, the description of series and limits' as against notions of continuity, tradition, influence, development or evolution.[62] Genealogical history should 'record the singularity of events outside of any monotonous finality'; it must 'maintain passing events in their proper dispersion'.[63] It is Nietzschean will to power rather than any ultimate purpose which lies behind the confusion of historical change. This confusion is not to be wished away or outwitted by a philosophy of history.

With Foucault's return to Nietzsche the concept of power is placed at the centre of his analysis, and it is important for him to avoid any misunderstanding of its nature. Foucault contests a number of common assumptions that, in his view, tend to blind us to the multifarious manifestations and devious stratagems of power. In the first place, we should not be limited by a 'juridical' view, which sees power only in the negative, prohibitive functions of a repressive state apparatus, law and the police. This view is rendered obsolete by the increasingly positive and productive deployment of power in modern society. Other aspects of the juridical view obscure the nature of this deployment. Power is seen as something that is possessed and consciously exercised by an agent or group of agents over others in order to further its own interests. But power is not a thing that can be possessed or owned in the way such models require. Foucault is unwilling to reify power in this way, preferring to speak of 'power relation' rather than 'power' in order to emphasize that power is not a thing but a mode of interaction: 'Power exists only when it is put into action.'[64] Nor can power relations be traced to a single underlying mechanism or source such as capitalism or the ruling class. Power constitutes a much broader and more diffuse field than such theories imply. Nor, finally, is it correct to assume that power always involves straightforwardly 'binary' or 'top-down' relations. Power is not 'a property located at the summit of the social order employed in a descending direction over and throughout the entire social domain'.[65] Relationships of domination exercised by one group over another (for example, by the bourgeoisie over the proletariat or by men over women) are predicated on more finely grained and multi-directional relations of power and resistance at the 'micro-level' of society. Accordingly, social explanation should give priority to this micro-level. In Alan Sheridan's words, 'It is a matter of examining how the techniques and procedures of power operating routinely at the level of everyday life have been appropriated or engaged by more general power or economic interests rather than the converse.'[66]

Foucault's more constructive remarks about the emergence of novel forms of power in western societies illuminate these rather abstract critical points. He is particularly interested in what he calls the 'threshold of modernity': the transition from the 'classical age' of the seventeenth century to the 'modern world' inaugurated with the French Revolution of 1789.[67] Characteristic of this period is a double operation of power, by which the 'repressive hypothesis' implicit in the juridical conception of power as exclusively prohibitive diverts attention from power's more productive activities, and to the extent that we are unaware of these activities, we are less able to resist them: 'Power as a pure limit set on freedom, is, at least in our society, the general form of its acceptability.'[68] The repressive hypothesis becomes all the more functional to the operations of power, as power becomes more positive and productive with the passing of the threshold of modernity. This period witnesses the decline of the more exclusively repressive, 'classical' mode of government, symbolized in the sovereign's 'power of life and death' over the subject. The classical mode of government is gradually replaced by a more productive management of individuals and peoples, which Foucault calls 'biopower'. Regimes becomes 'managers of life and survival, of bodies and the race': 'what might be called a society's "threshold of modernity" has been reached when the life of the species is wagered on its own political strategies.'[69] The rise of bio-power is also associated with the spread of racist theories in the nineteenth century.[70]

The deployment of bio-power involves a series of transformations in the nature of what Foucault calls 'governmentality'. This term refers to an increasingly autonomous 'governmental rationality', developed since the Renaissance alongside the narrower *raison d'état* first clearly expressed in Machiavelli's *The Prince*.[71] An important contribution to the emergence of distinctively modern forms of governmentality is made by a number of discourses on the 'science of police' or 'policy', written from the seventeenth century onwards. Although 'police' and 'policing' are now words normally associated with the straightforwardly repressive functions of the state, Foucault reminds us of their originally much broader meaning. Early discussions of policing concerned a lot more than law and order in the contemporary sense. They dealt with nothing less than the welfare of the population as a whole, and so helped to formulate a distinctively 'pastoral' conception of power. The centralizing and bureaucratizing tendencies of modern societies have often been highlighted, for example by Weber and theorists associated with the Frankfurt School. However, for Foucault what is particularly novel about pastoral power is its attention not just to the state of the community as a whole, but to each individual in particular and in detail throughout the course of his or her life.[72] Pastoral power's 'individualizing' attention is inspired by the example of the Catholic Church, which through the confessional and other techniques develops 'a knowledge of the conscience and an ability to direct it'.[73] Adapting such techniques, modern states apply a similarly pastoral, and similarly intrusive, attention to the health, wealth and welfare of their populations.[74]

As Foucault's conception of 'power/knowledge' would lead us to expect, the rise of pastoral power fosters a new knowledge of 'man'. It is no surprise, then, that the threshold of modernity also sees the emergence of a number of new disciplines within the humanities and social sciences. These 'human sciences' are essentially of two kinds, corresponding to the dual focus of the pastoral state on the population as a whole and on the individuals who make it up. They involve 'the development of knowledge of man around two poles: one globalizing and quantitative, concerning the population; the other analytical, concerning the individual.'[75] In the first place, there are the globalizing, statistical disciplines of economics, demography, epidemiology and eventually sociology.[76] Typically these describe general laws governing the normal behaviour of the population as a whole; in fact, they give rise to the notions of population and normality as we understand them. These disciplines enhance the state's ability to control and care for the health of its population, to ensure adequate human resources for its military activities, to promote economic growth and so on. But pastoral power also requires detailed and systematic knowledge of individuals and, consequently, a radical break with the Aristotelian view of knowledge as exclusively concerned with the generalities of *genus* and *species*. The more individualizing disciplines of medicine, psychiatry, psychoanalysis and education study individuals in all their potential eccentricity. Thus, in *Discipline and Punish*, Foucault describes how with the emergence of the modern prison 'a specific mode of subjection was able to give birth to man as an object of knowledge for a discourse with a "scientific" status.'[77] Similarly, the clinic and the asylum were sites for the development of modern medicine and psychiatry.[78]

As these examples suggest, though, pastoral power is not purely a matter of knowledge but involves a range of unmistakably material practices and interventions. These again take two principal forms: the global 'regulatory controls' of a 'bio-politics of the population' and an individualizing 'discipline' or 'anatomo-politics of the body'. Again, it is the latter modality of pastoral power, which is perhaps most interesting and distinctively modern. Alongside the emergence of the human sciences there is an unprecedented expansion of disciplinary practices, deployed by both state and non-state institutions (in some cases initiated variously by 'do-gooders', reformers, helpful doctors or concerned aristocrats). Disciplinary power is directed primarily at the body; it is designed to produce 'subjected and practised bodies, "docile" bodies'.[79] But at the same time it aims for psychological effects. In Smart's words, 'discipline is a power which infiltrates the very body and psyche of the individual, which . . . transforms the life and time of the individual into labour-power, that property essential to the capitalist mode of production.'[80] A variety of techniques are developed to this end, including detailed schedules and timetables, exercises and training, examinations, report-keeping, isolation of inmates and so on. Emblematic of such practices is Bentham's 'panopticon', which Foucault describes as an 'architectural figure' of disciplinary power. Jeremy Bentham (1748–1832) designed a prison building with individual cells radiating from a central observation point, ensuring the permanent visibility of the inmates to the warder but their complete invisibility to one another. In Foucault's words, the panopticon is a way of 'arranging spatial unities' in order 'to induce in the inmate a state of conscious and permanent visibility that assures the automatic functioning of power'.[81] As this example also makes clear, in the modern period there is a 'reversal of visibility' between sovereign and subject. It is no longer the sovereign who is the focus of attention, but the humble individual, who becomes the not-always-willing object of pastoral care. According to Foucault, similar disciplinary techniques are developed in a range of 'carceral' institutions modelled on the prison (in schools, hospitals, asylums, factories and barracks), all concerned with 'increasing the utility of individuals'.[82] These characteristically modern institutions are not so much humane products of a more enlightened and rational age as more efficient and more intrusive instruments of an expansive power.

However, the constitution of the subject as an object of disciplinary practices and objectifying disciplines is only half the story. Of equal significance in the genealogy of modern subjectivity is a parallel series of processes, constituting the individual subject *as subject*. Thus Foucault's history of sexuality traces the emergence of a series of discourses and practices that are designed to make the subject more reliably and extensively responsible for itself. The explosion of discourses on sexuality in the nineteenth century, with their minute attention to the details of 'perverse' sexual variations from the norm, is related to the emergent bio-politics of population, but it also contributes to the more intimate constitution of the subject as subject.

Important episodes in this story are the Catholic Confessional, Freudian psychoanalysis and the promotion of 'sexuality' from a relatively unimportant fact about bodies to something decisive for the individual's sense of identity. Foucault's analysis implies a critique of the 'depth hermeneutics' practised in different ways in both psychoanalysis and the confession. The deep truths about the mind or the soul, which these practices of patient interrogation are supposed to uncover, really function as instances of power. Far from uncovering some deeper meaning or truth, their interpretations inscribe in the subject truths that are essentially of their own making. The subject is enticed into assuming responsibility for more and more regions of its life.

Foucault's account of power has radical implications for political theory and practice. In particular, it undermines any 'totalizing theory' which, like Marxism, seeks to unify the diversity of social and historical events within a single explanatory framework. To theorize the complex field of relations of power as an organized totality is a strategy which, even in the hands of critical intellectuals or socialist militants, inevitably contributes to the reproduction of domination. As the experience of bureaucratic state socialism demonstrates, rulers can appeal to totalizing theories in order to legitimate their authority or to exercise power more effectively. Foucault, in conversation with his colleague Gilles Deleuze, suggests a less authoritarian role for theory.[83] Just as relations of power are complex and dispersed, so resistance should be multi-centred and diverse. The multiplicity of power relations incites a multifarious resistance to instances of power, which can nonetheless be conceived as interconnected or as a network. In Sheridan's words,

> Because 'power' is multiple and ubiquitous, the struggle against it must be localized. Equally, however, because it is a network and not a collection of isolated points, each localized struggle induces effects on the entire network. Struggle cannot be totalized – a single, centralized, hierarchized organisation setting out to seize a single, centralized, hierarchized power; but it can be *serial*, that is, in terms of *horizontal* links between one point of struggle and another.[84]

Similarly, social and political theory should be a 'local and regional practice'. Rather than a single 'master' theory, there should be a plurality of theories engaging with power at different points and to different ends. The role of the intellectual is also different:

> The intellectual's role is no longer to place himself 'somewhat ahead and to the side' in order to express the stifled truth of the collectivity; rather it is to struggle against the forms of power that transform him into its object

and instrument in the sphere of 'knowledge', 'truth', 'consciousness', and 'discourse'.[85]

Intellectuals should not put themselves forward as representatives of the people or vanguard of the proletariat. They should avoid 'the indignity of speaking for others'.[86] Foucault's recasting of the relationship between theory and practice finds considerable resonance in the politics of contemporary (or sometimes 'new') social movements, with their emphasis on difference, diversity and autonomous organization.[87]

In fact, Foucault's account of the emergence of modern forms of power and governmental rationality has analogies both with Weber's account of the irreversible rationalization of society and with the Frankfurt School's pessimistic narrative of the fateful 'dialectic of Enlightenment'. Although Foucault has acknowledged these similarities, his overriding aim is not so much to invoke 'the progress of rationalization in general' as 'to analyze such a process in several fields'.[88] His concentration on the actual mechanisms and techniques of power, his emphasis on the individualizing manifestations of pastoral power and suspicion of hermeneutics as complicit in the constitution of subjugated subjects *as* subjects are all distinctive features of his analysis. Foucault's Nietzschean anti-humanism also makes him much more consistently sceptical of the value of rationality than Frankfurt School theorists (particularly, of course, Habermas). As a result Foucault is often accused of promoting a disabling moral relativism or even nihilism. His account of power has been taken to imply 'the equivalence of power with sociality itself', a view that would render resistance to power impossible and, since no alternative to power is imaginable, unnecessary.[89] On the other hand, Foucault also appeals to the normative force of something close to Habermas's model of idealized dialogue. The distinction between dialogue and polemic, for example, is one on which 'a whole morality is at stake, the morality that concerns the search for the truth and the relation to the other'. In dialogue 'the rights of each person are in some sense immanent in the discussion.' The polemicist, on the other hand, 'proceeds encased in privileges that he possesses in advance and will never agree to question'.[90] Certainly, Foucault's Nietzschean suspicion of transcendental guarantees for morality and truth does not mean that he regards all values as redundant or simply equivalent. Undoubtedly, both in theory and in life, Foucault was politically engaged; he was not without moral convictions. Whether Foucault's sceptical assumptions entitled him to those convictions remains controversial.

Derrida's Deconstruction of Western Metaphysics

And philosophy is perhaps the reassurance given against the anguish of being mad at the point of greatest proximity to madness.

Derrida, *Writing and Difference*

Jacques Derrida (1930–), following the structuralist path from meaning to sign, from the subject of speech to the anonymous system of language and beyond, carries anti-humanism to the heart of philosophy and metaphysics. His considerable influence on the philosophical scene dates from the publication of three of his major works in 1967.[91] His work is more exclusively philosophical than Foucault's, although ironically he has had most influence in the field of literary studies, and of all contemporary continental philosophers he is the most reviled within the analytical tradition. This reception is ironic for the further reason that Derrida's deconstruction of western metaphysics is far from being an easy or flippant dismissal. He is unhappy with the humanism of the western philosophical tradition but sees no easy escape from this unhappy condition either.[92] Derrida can be described as 'poststructuralist', in the sense that 'Post-Structuralism is a critique of Structuralism conducted from within.'[93] In effect, Derrida draws out the philosophical implications of a structuralist account of language and meaning, overturning the framework of structuralist assumptions in the process. Where Saussure still regards language and meaning as a relatively stable system of oppositions, Derrida believes that Saussure's account of meaning as a differential system of contrasts fatally undermines any account of representation as simple 'presence' and, as a result, removes all fixity and stability from both language and thought. In other words, the contrast between structuralism and poststructuralism is not one of outright opposition or antagonism.[94] Poststructuralism develops the implications of structuralist premises about meaning, in order to develop a position which, though recognizably distinct, does not discard those premises altogether.

Derrida's position can be approached initially in terms of his reaction to Husserl. Although he approves of Husserl's philosophical response to the universal pretensions of positivism, he believes that the phenomenological search for essences is mired in the 'logocentrism' of the western philosophical tradition. Logocentrism is the pervasive tendency of western thought to associate truth with the voice or 'the word' (*logos*), which is conceived as the immediate expression of the self-presence of consciousness. Logocentrism, in Grosz's words, 'seeks beyond signs and representation, the real and the true, the presence of being, of knowing and reality, to the mind – an access to concepts and things in their pure, unmediated form'.[95] Logocentrism thus also involves a prejudice in favour of 'presence', or what Derrida calls the 'metaphysics of presence'. Husserl's logo-centrism is evident in his insistence on the independence of experi-ence, of meanings and the contents of consciousness, from their expression in language. Language is seen simply as a medium for the expression or communication of meanings that are ultimately to be explained in terms of the meaning-giving acts of a subject of con-sciousness. In other words, pure meanings or 'essences', which corre-spond to the 'signified' in Saussure's terms, are primary; the sign as 'signifier', as sound or as written inscription, is secondary, the merely derivative and contingent vehicle of thought. Husserl's logocentrism also leads him to privilege the immediacy and presence of the voice or speech as opposed to writing. In other words, it leads him to reproduce another deep prejudice of western thought, which Derrida terms 'phonocentrism'. Phonocentrism regards speech as a more transparent medium of thought or meaning than writing. The voice is closer to the immediacy and self-presence of consciousness. As Hab-ermas puts it, the 'fleeting transparency of the voice promotes the assimilation of the word to the expressed meaning'.[96] In speech we are not as aware of the gap between the word-as-sound and its meaning, between signifier and signified.

Husserl falls victim to the metaphysics of presence, because he ignores the fundamental and ineliminable role of the signifier in thought. By the same token, Derrida's recognition of the 'quasi-transcendental' role of the signifier is at the heart of his critique and radicalization of Saussure. Derrida's position involves a significant shift in the understanding of the concept of difference, which plays such a central role in Saussure's account of language as a differential system of oppositions. This shift is encapsulated in one of Derrida's best-known neologisms, *différance*, a term subtly but significantly unlike *différence*, the normal French word for difference. In accord-ance with Derrida's stress on writing as opposed to speech, it is also appropriate that, though the two words are written differently, they are pronounced identically in French. The notion of *différance* is specifically designed to disrupt the metaphysics of presence. It does so by reminding us that the recognition of sameness and difference involved in all acts of representation cannot itself be temporally present. Representation is never sheer presence or immediacy, since it always involves both the recognition of 'difference' and a temporal 'deferral'. Here Derrida relies on the fact that in French '*différer*' means both 'to differ' and 'to defer'. On this point at least, Habermas's reading is helpful:

> The experience that is present 'at the moment' is indebted to an act of representation, perception is indebted to a reproducing recognition, such that the difference of a temporal interval and thus also an element of otherness is inherent in the spontaneity of the living moment . . .
> . . . at the very source of this apparently absolute presence, a temporal difference and otherness looms on the horizon, which Derrida characterizes both as a *passive difference* and as a *deferral that produces difference.*[97]

Derrida's argument here is a direct consequence of the structuralist account of meaning as difference. As Sturrock puts it, 'Every sign contains . . . a "trace" of signs other than itself', and this implies that 'there can be no escape from time in the process of signification.'[98]

Derrida sees the difference and deferral of *différance* as fundamental to all thought and representation. It is in this sense that it has a 'quasi-transcendental' role, since it 'refers' to the condition of conceptual thought as such. *Différance* produces the differences, without which neither thought nor language would be conceivable. Still, Derrida is at pains to deny *différance* any substantial existence as metaphysical 'origin':

> What is written as *différance*, then, will be the playing movement that 'produces' – by means of something that is not simply an activity – these differences, these effects of difference. This does not mean that the *différance* that produces differences is somehow before them, in a simply and unmodified – in-different – present. *Différance* is the non-full, non-simple, structured and differentiating origin of differences. Thus, the name 'origin' no longer suits it.[99]

In contrast to Saussure's apparently static system of differential oppositions, *différance* is therefore intrinsically temporal and dynamic. This feature of *différance* reflects a more general contrast between the dynamic categories of Derrida's poststructuralism and the static oppositions of structuralism: 'Post-Structuralism differs from Structuralism in being a philosophy of Becoming rather than of Being: it is endlessly dynamic, allowing us no escape or apparent respite from the shifting play of meanings.'[100] Derrida's account of representation also helps to show more clearly, what is wrong with the metaphysics of presence. Sturrock's explanation here is worth quoting at some length:

> The 'metaphysics of presence' presumes that whatever is present to us is wholly and immediately so, grasped in an act of pure intuition which has no

recourse to signs. Presence precedes signification. If this were the case, however, it is hard to see how we could be conscious of it, since consciousness *does* have recourse to signs. Presence, according to Derrida, can never be immediate therefore, only mediated by language. We are conscious of what is present to us as *being* present; and the concept of presence, like all concepts, is not a self-enclosed unity, but one inhabited by its contrary. There can be no meaning to asserting that something is 'present' if there is no possibility of its being 'not-present': the concept of presence entails that of non-presence or absence, for such is the fundamentally differential nature of language.[101]

In other words, Derrida insists on 'the indissoluble interweave of the intelligible with the sign-substrate of its expression', the 'transcendental primacy of the sign as against the meaning'.[102] But in order to provide an even stronger intellectual bulwark against the metaphysics of presence, Derrida seeks to establish writing rather than speech as the best model for an understanding of language and meaning. In contrast to phonocentrism, which privileges the voice and the spoken word, writing makes it obvious that meaning need not, indeed cannot, be guaranteed by the 'living presence' of the subject. Writing makes manifest the fact that meaning is only generated by *différance* or, in other words, the temporally extended system of oppositions between signifiers. This is because, in comparison with the deceptive immediacy of speech, 'the written form detaches any given text from the context in which it arose.'[103] We are not tempted to attribute meaning to presence, because in the case of writing the author is normally absent. The exemplary status that Derrida assigns to writing as opposed to speech also reinforces the contrast between his own approach and that of Saussure. Derrida locates the symptom of Saussure's failure to recognize the implications of his own theories in his tendency, despite his structuralist account of meaning as a differential system of signs, to lapse into the phonocentric prejudice of western metaphysics. Saussure still assumes that there is a 'natural bond', 'the only true bond', between sound and sense and refers to writing as a secondary and potentially dangerous activity.[104] The evidence that Saussure's phonocentric prejudices represent a lapse from the logic of his own argument is provided by the fact that he nevertheless frequently resorts to metaphors of writing in order to explain his views of language.

Once we recognize that the meaning of written texts has a life of its own in this way, we are more likely to realize that the same applies to meaning and language as such. Derrida makes this point by describing every use of language, including speech, as an instance of 'writing' in his own more general sense. Significantly, Derrida does not advocate a reverse prioritizing of writing over speech, but rather a revised account of both as the basis for a more adequate account of language, meaning and representation. Language must be understood as a form of 'writing'. In this spirit Derrida assigns transcendental significance to an originary writing or 'arche-writing' (*arché-écriture*): 'writing is not only an auxiliary means in the service of science – and possibly its object – but first . . . the condition of the possibility of ideal objects and therefore of scientific objectivity.'[105] 'Grammatology' is Derrida's term for a general theory of writing in this special sense. He believes such a theory can provide a less misleading basis for both philosophy and the human sciences. Grammatology is thus Derrida's equivalent for what Saussure envisioned as a general theory of the sign or 'semiology'.[106]

In a further series of excursions into the history of philosophy Derrida grapples with a number of earlier incarnations of the logocentric and phonocentric prejudices of the western philosophical tradition. Plato, not surprisingly, is identified as a major source of the 'idea of a pure self-authenticating knowledge'.[107] In Platonic terms knowledge is conceived as something ideal and eternal, something radically opposed to the changeable, corrupted world of everyday reality. Ordinary human experience of the world represents at best a confused reflection of underlying 'Forms' or 'essences', in effect the concepts instantiated in particular experiences. Platonic Forms are eternal, unchanging and ideal. Our nearest approach to pure and absolute truth is through our knowledge of the deductive truths of logic and mathematics. These are truths which, once we have been led to 'remember' them, are self-evident to consciousness and patently independent of the corruptible evidence of the senses. The privileged path to genuine philosophical knowledge is the Socratic dialogue. Only through the 'dialectical' exploration of questions about the nature of justice, truth or beauty, only through the to-and-fro of question and answer which Plato learned from Socrates and set down in his dialogues, can we come to know the ideal Form of these concepts and so make appropriate judgements about the truth, justice or beauty of things.

According to Derrida this association of truth with the ideal, with mind or consciousness rather than the body of the 'material', pervades western philosophical and religious traditions.[108] That Plato's philosophy is an example of the metaphysics of presence becomes clear if we consider more closely his conception of the Socratic dialogue. For Plato, significantly, only those who actually attend the Socratic debates are assured of the appropriate relationship to truth. This is because the power of reason and the word, the power of *logos*, must be relived by each in turn, by each for herself. The dialogue can only point towards truth; it works as a kind of intellectual midwifery or 'maieutic'.[109] There is no evidence for the truth superior to the conviction and certainty of one's own immediate consciousness, and anything less than the immediate self-presence of truth represents a falling away from its purity and certainty. Thus even the memory of a recent proof or a demonstration is potentially unreliable. For the same reason, Plato is suspicious of writing. In the *Phaedrus* writing is condemned, because it removes the need for the 'active reanimation of knowledge . . . its reproduction in the present' and so encourages loss of memory.[110] Writing only appears to be good for memory: 'writing is only apparently good for memory, seemingly able to help it from within, through its own motion, to know what is true. But in truth, writing is essentially bad, external to memory, productive not of science but of belief, not of truth but of appearances.'[111] Writing is the surrogate science of the sophist. As such, writing threatens the legitimate authority of the teacher, who is the only one qualified to reanimate the truth in the appropriate way. There is thus a parallelism between the relationships of 'father to son, speech to writing'.[112] As Norris puts it, 'It is through writing that the *logos* is deflected from its proper, truth-seeking aim and abandoned to a state of hazardous dependence on the vagaries of *unauthorized* transmission.'[113] Writing is a less secure means for the transmission of knowledge, because it releases the truth from the control and supervision of the teacher and so permits misunderstanding and distortion.

But as Derrida's exegesis makes clear, Plato is caught in a seemingly inescapable paradox. Although he denounces writing as a source of error, writing is nevertheless an essential means for the transmission not only of truth in general but even of Plato's particular claims about the dangers of writing. After all, it is Plato who would preserve the dialogues of Socrates in written form. And like Saussure, Plato's arguments for the superiority of speech constantly appeal to metaphors drawn from writing. As Norris puts it:

> So speech is represented, not only as the opposite of writing, but as a 'good' kind of writing that is inscribed in the soul by revealed or self-authorized truth. Living memory is that which avoids the bad detour through writing (mere marks on a page), but which is still very often defined by metaphors of engraving, deciphering, inscription and other such textual figures.[114]

Plato's philosophical discourse (and, Derrida suggests, western philosophical discourse generally) is forced to affirm, albeit indirectly and metaphorically, the indispensability of writing at the same time as it overtly accords to it a secondary, derivative status. For Derrida this paradox is epitomized in the ambiguity of the Greek word '*pharmakon*', which can mean either 'poison' or 'cure'. The word captures perfectly philosophy's ambiguous relationship to writing, which it is forced to see both as poison and as cure.

Derrida's reading of Plato is one of the clearest examples of what he calls 'deconstruction'. The critical practice of deconstruction relates to the notion of *différance* and is also partly modelled on Heidegger's projected 'destruction' (*Destruktion*) of western metaphysics. A deconstructive reading of a philosophical text is designed to bring into the open the tensions between its logical and rhetorical construction, tensions which reflect the problematic relationship between philosophy and writing. Derrida pays particular attention to the unregarded 'margins' of texts, their images and metaphors, the rhetorical resources they find themselves compelled to exploit – even words that are only 'present in their absence'. Thus although the word '*pharmakos*' (wizard, magician, poisoner), a cognate of *pharmakon*, never actually appears in the dialogue of Plato we have been discussing (and for many, of course, this might be thought a significant objection), for Derrida this word belongs to a 'chain of significations' which 'for all its hiddenness, for all that it might escape Plato's notice, is nevertheless something that passes through certain discoverable *points of presence* that can be seen in the text'.[115] The word is present in the sense that its absence is felt. Norris's description of deconstruction is helpful at this point:

> deconstruction is the vigilant seeking-out of those 'aporias', blindspots or moments of self-contradiction where a text involuntarily betrays the tension between rhetoric and logic, between what it manifestly *means to say* and what it is nonetheless *constrained to mean*. To 'deconstruct' a piece of writing is therefore to operate a kind of strategic reversal, seizing on precisely those unregarded details (casual metaphors, footnotes, incidental turns of argument) which are always, and necessarily, passed over by interpreters of more orthodox persuasion.[116]

It is also important to emphasize that deconstruction is not as fixed or predictable as a method. Deconstruction 'in its technical sense refers to a series of tactics and devices rather than a method: strategies to reveal the unarticulated presuppositions on which metaphysical and logocentric texts are based'.[117] The overriding aim of deconstruction is to disrupt the metaphysics of presence. Deconstruction is 'a means of carrying out this going beyond being, beyond being as presence, at least'.[118]

The practice of deconstruction also reflects Derrida's distinctive hermeneutic. His poststructuralist account of the nature of representation and meaning implies that writing (in all its forms) cannot be referred to the intentions of an author. In fact, texts cannot be tied to any single or univocal source of meaning of any kind. The interpretation of texts depends on a potentially infinite array of possible contexts and interpreters, and so leads to what Derrida describes as 'dissemination', an endless dispersion and multiplication of meanings. Dissemination 'marks an irreducible and *generative* multiplicity'.[119] It undermines all fixities of interpretation, proliferates rather than reduces instances of ambiguity. As McCarthy puts it: 'our meaning always escapes any unitary conscious grasp we may have of it, for language, as "writing", inevitably harbors the possibility of an endless "dissemination" of sense, an indefinite multiplicity of recontextualisations and reinterpretations.'[120] Or as Rorty says, Derrida maintains 'that meaning is a function of context, and that there is no theoretical barrier to an endless sequence of recontextualizations'.[121]

However, as Norris is at pains to point out, and despite what some of the literary theorists influenced by Derrida have thought (and despite, too, it must be said, some of Derrida's own less careful statements), this is not equivalent to complete interpretive licence. Derrida's own deconstructive readings of philosophical and literary texts might at times be thought wilfully obscure or even perverse, but they unquestionably also demonstrate considerable rigour and a minute attention to detail. Furthermore, in contrast to those like Foucault and Barthes who have enthusiastically proclaimed the 'death of the author', a deconstructive reading aims to go beyond the author's intentions without leaving them behind altogether. As Derrida remarks in the context of a deconstructive reading of Rousseau, 'His declared intention is not annulled by this but rather inscribed within a system which it no longer dominates.'[122] Deconstruction cannot simply ignore the apparent meaning of a text: 'When one attempts . . . to pass from an obvious to a latent language, one must first be rigorously sure of the obvious meaning.'[123]

The difficult practice of deconstruction exemplifies Derrida's refusal to accept any easy solution. He refuses to deny what he sees as the ineradicable tensions inherent in the basic conceptual oppositions of western thought, which always remain 'violent hierarchies'. Typical are the oppositions between mind and body, masculine and feminine, reason and emotion, sameness and difference, self and other, where in each case the first of the pair dominates or is thought superior to the second. Deconstruction targets these hierarchies, but without assuming that the tensions they embody can easily be resolved or the hierarchies easily reversed. There can be no easy or absolute break with the fundamental dichotomies of western metaphysics. This explains Derrida's hostility to the Hegelian dialectic, which makes the futile attempt to absorb and neutralize these contradictions in a stable synthesis. In these terms, the interrelated concepts of deconstruction and *différance* embody Derrida's distance from Hegel: 'If there were a definition of *différance*, it would be precisely the limit, the interruption, the destruction of the Hegelian *relève* wherever it operates.'[124] Instead deconstruction must embark on an 'interminable analysis', if it is 'to avoid both simply *neutralizing* the binary oppositions of metaphysics and simply *residing* within the closed field of those oppositions, thereby confirming it'.[125] It is also Derrida's insistence on the irresolvable tension of deconstruction that distinguishes his position most clearly from the more Hegelian hermeneutics of Gadamer. Where Gadamer describes a fruitful productivity of interpretation through dialogue, Derrida proposes something more like the unhappy lot of Sisyphus. We are condemned to an endless labour of conceptual disruption without guarantees.[126]

Derrida also associates his projected disruption of the violent hierarchies of western metaphysics with a distinctive political stance. In the end, the refusal of the 'longing for an impossible truth' is politically radical.[127] Violent conceptual hierarchies correspond to oppressive social relations, and to challenge the former is inevitably to undermine the latter. In McCarthy's words,

> deconstruction counteracts the 'politics of language' which conceals practices of exclusion, repression, marginalisation, and assimilation behind the apparent neutrality of 'purely theoretical' discourses. Its effects, however, are not confined to language, but 'touch all the social institutions . . . More generally, it touches everything, quite simply everything.'

Deconstruction bears witness 'to the other of western rationalism'. It counteracts the associated 'repression of the other in nature, in ourselves, in other persons and other peoples . . . (it) speaks on behalf of what does not fit into our schemes and patiently advocates letting the other be in its otherness.'[128] Certainly, Derrida has espoused a number of radical political causes. He has been involved in the reform of the teaching of philosophy in France. He has written admiringly of Nelson Mandela's role in resisting apartheid. He makes plain both his opposition to neo-colonialism and his support for feminism.[129]

Again, Derrida's approach has influenced a wide range of other theorists. Michael Ryan has recruited the critical resources of deconstruction for an anti-authoritarian socialism, which is 'worked out, as a texture and not as a punctual instance of power', and for which socialist unity need not imply an organized and potentially authoritarian movement but 'the articulation of a diverse, differentiated plurality'.[130] But Derrida himself does little to develop a constructive political stance. Indeed, it is difficult to see how he could do so, without abandoning his entrenched resistance to systematic theorizing. His bold claim, that 'all of our political codes and terminologies still remain fundamentally metaphysical', seems to leave little space for anything but the most abstractly intellectual political engagement, or alternatively, political commitments without intellectual motivation.[131] Even Derrida's overtly political comments tend to be undercut by irony. On McCarthy's analysis at least, Derrida prefers to avoid the perspective of the participant in social life, who is forced to adopt a position and assume certain values, ending up instead with a stance that is ultimately conservative.[132]

Overall, Derrida does not abandon the Enlightenment project altogether (something he regards as impossible anyway), but rather seeks to occupy a critical and, by all accounts, difficult position within and against it:

> Derrida . . . insists that there is no opting out of that post-Kantian enlightenment tradition, and certainly no question of our now having emerged into a post-modern era where its concepts and categories lack all critical force. On the contrary: it is only by working persistently *within* that tradition, but *against* some of its ruling ideas, that thought can muster the resistance required for an effective critique of existing institutions.[133]

In fact, Derrida's nuanced relationship to western metaphysics and rationality is already signalled in his early reaction to Foucault's *Madness and Civilization*. Derrida sees Foucault's attempt to express a truth beyond a divisive and exclusionary western reason as precisely the 'maddest aspect' of his project. In Norris's words, 'thought is self-deluded if it tries to achieve a standpoint "outside" or "above" the very discourse of philosophical reason.'[134] This view of Derrida, as at heart a 'transcendental philosopher' with an unhappy conscience, is consistent both with his explicitly philosophical interests and the strong influence of Nietzsche and the later Heidegger.[135] Certainly, if Derrida retains a commitment to western rationality, it is by no means an easy or complacent one, involving endless critical labour, an interminable work of deconstructive analysis. In the end, the difficulty of Derrida's position reflects his view of philosophy as a series of impossible attempts to say the unsayable. Philosophers grapple with a truth that cannot be expressed within the received order of reason, only to fall back into forgetfulness and complacency, as they develop a newly authoritative truth, itself destined to become the focus of subsequent philosophical revolt. For 'philosophy is perhaps the reassurance given against the anguish of being mad at the point of greatest proximity to madness.'[136]

7. Postmodernism

Varieties of Postmodernism

With postmodernism it is as if we pass through the looking-glass of western reason. As we do so, apparently reliable conceptual distinctions are inverted or abolished altogether, and what was previously most solid 'melts into air'.[1] Postmodernism attempts a radical break with all of the major strands of post-Enlightenment thought. For postmodernists both the orthodox Enlightenment 'meta-narrative' of progress and emancipation and the 'speculative' narrative of Hegelianism and Marxism have lost their spell.[2] Phenomenology and existentialism are condemned as varieties of humanism or nostalgic philosophies of the subject. Even Derrida's acrobatic manoeuvres on the margins of metaphysics fail to convince. Perhaps not surprisingly, then, it is impossible to provide a straightforward definition of postmodernism. Not only are there conflicting views about what postmodernism is, but postmodernist positions are also adopted within a variety of disciplinary settings. There is a wide range of contexts for what are nevertheless related discourses of modernity and postmodernity. These include history and sociology, philosophy, art and art theory as well as literature and literary criticism. As a result, too, 'postmodern', 'postmodernity' and 'postmodernism' are not always straightforwardly cognate terms either. They have different connotations, depending whether a historical period, a form of society, a philosophical stance or an artistic movement is in question. In other words, postmodernism cannot be regarded as a purely philosophical development. It is just as much a response to the calamitous history of the West.

The genealogy of postmodernist thought involves at least four distinct but interrelated contexts of formation. In the first place, postmodernism draws radical conclusions from a number of developments in philosophy. Certainly, postmodernism reiterates themes that have frequently been explored within the previous continental tradition. Postmodernists are critical of all of the most characteristic assumptions of the orthodox Enlightenment. They reject the universal pretensions of natural science and the 'instrumental', 'objectifying' or 'reductive' (sometimes also 'male' or 'masculinist') rationality it embodies. They also reject universal claims made on behalf of moralities founded on pure reason or an essential human nature. Again like some earlier critics, they speak up for traditions, cultures, values and peoples who fared badly at the hands of the 'civilizing mission' of Enlightenment rationalism. However, typically these earlier critics of Enlightenment still argued for the role of rationality, albeit a rationality differently constituted and articulated, in the advance and emancipation of humanity. In this sense, they were still committed to a version of the 'Enlightenment project' as a key factor in the momentum of western modernity. This is most clear in the case of Hegel and Marx, whose dialectical accounts of the advance of reason through history presuppose the advanced state of European culture and society. Both retain a clear commitment to modernity, if only as the necessary precursor to a more thoroughgoing social and intellectual revolution.

By contrast, postmodernism defines itself, on one level at least, by its rejection of any commitment to modernity or Enlightenment, including the more nuanced commitment of Hegel and Marx. It is here that anti-humanism and the critique of the subject, from Nietzsche and Heidegger to structuralism and poststructuralism, plays a decisive role in preparing the ground for a more radical break with the Enlightenment project. In its most radical form, the anti-humanist critique of the subject problematizes all the fundamental categories of modern western philosophy. Not only the universalist rationalism of the Enlightenment, but also Hegelian and Marxist narratives of the dialectical self-constitution of humanity are challenged. Even more recent phenomenological and existentialist inheritors of the project of modern philosophy are undermined. Foucault's Nietzschean genealogy traces knowledge, truth and the modern subject to constellations of power that are seemingly beyond the reach of a divisive and exclusionary reason. Derrida's deconstruction of the 'metaphysics of presence' applies a similarly corrosive scepticism to the most basic conceptual oppositions of western thought. But these poststructuralists remain unwilling to make the final break with the Enlightenment project. Thus at the same time as Derrida demonstrates the impossibility of inhabiting the conceptual framework of western metaphysics, he also asserts the impossibility of simply leaving it behind. For him, to adapt Samuel Beckett's phrase, western philosophy 'can't go on, must go on'.[3] Foucault too refuses to describe himself as a postmodernist. But equally clearly, the ideas of both thinkers prepare the ground for postmodernism. It is a relatively small step from the uncomfortably sceptical positions they both adopt to a more whole-hearted rejection of modernity and Enlightenment. Though not postmodernists themselves, Derrida and Foucault provide the most immediate point of entry into that mode of thought.

A second important context for the formation of postmodernist thought is provided by the history of Europe and the West (and the world in so far as it has been a victim of this history) in the twentieth century. This history includes two unprecedentedly destructive world wars, the rise of fascism in Germany, Italy and Spain and a protracted 'Cold War', maintained by the balanced nuclear terror of 'mutually assured destruction'. In the meantime, the colonial mission of modern and 'enlightened' European nations to civilize their 'barbarian' neighbours has lost conviction. Former colonies have been abandoned to movements of national liberation and the atrocities of former colonial regimes have been widely recognized. Most shockingly of all, though, the Nazi genocide of more than six million Jews, communists, homosexuals, gypsies and disabled people (and many others) dealt a fatal blow to any complacent reading of western history as the privileged site of civilization. The holocaust refutes in the starkest possible way that combination of ethnocentrism and optimism which has allowed the West to see itself as the embodiment of progress and the very antithesis of barbarism. In Germany, one of Europe's most economically developed, artistically cultured and philosophically creative nations, emerged a regime of the most refined brutality. But the holocaust is shocking not, or not simply, as an atavistic lapse from the path of progress and Enlightenment, but also as a demonstration of dangers intrinsic to modernity itself. The holocaust was a very modern affair. The genocide of six million people was carefully planned, administered with bureaucratic thoroughness and carried out with considerable technological sophistication. In Bauman's words, 'The Holocaust was a unique encounter between the old tensions which modernity ignored, slighted or failed to resolve – and the powerful instruments of rational and effective action that modern development itself brought into being.'[4] The combined effect of these catastrophic events of recent European history, from imperialist slaughter to Nazi genocide, is thus a dual challenge to the West's self-consciousness as modernity. Is modernity a secure achievement of the West? Is modernity really an achievement at all?

Another important episode from this history provides a third context for the formation of postmodernism, but one this time that is both historical and intellectual in nature. This is the fate of Marxism. It is also in the twentieth century, after all, that Marxism completed its evolution from theory to practice, becoming the official ideology of a number of 'actually existing' socialist regimes.[5] It is, of course, possible to argue that these self-styled Marxist or Marxist-Leninist regimes have been anything but faithful to the more attractive ideals of Marx and Engels or even Lenin. Still, the bureaucratization of the socialist idea and, even more starkly, the Stalinization of both the Soviet Union and major cohorts of the communist movement could hardly fail to have a profound impact on the fate of Marxist theory and philosophy.[6] Less dramatic, but in the long run equally corrosive, has been the stubborn failure of revolution to occur in the more developed capitalist societies of the West. A situation in which there is relatively widespread affluence and a working class apparently loyal to social democracy has offered scant basis for revolutionary optimism.

Against this fairly discouraging background a series of traumatic historical events has triggered repeated waves of intellectual exile from communist parties, from Marxism and ultimately from any remaining faith in socialist revolution. These events have ranged from revelations about party purges, 'show-trials', massacres and the 'gulag' of prison camps under Stalin, to the Soviet invasions of Hungary in 1956 and Czechoslovakia in 1968. The French communist party's failure to anticipate and its subsequent attempts to manipulate and co-opt the Paris 'May Events' of 1968 brought further disillusionment. In the mid-1970s came further revelations, this time concerning the excesses of China's 'cultural revolution' under Mao Tse-tung, with the implication that all was far from well under the Maoist model of socialism as well. Nor, finally, have the fortunes of Marxism and communism improved notably in recent years. Chinese communism survives only by dint of a combination of market reforms and repression. The collapse of communist regimes in the Soviet Union and eastern Europe since 1989 has eroded much of the remaining confidence in anything like the Marxist project.

The historical fate of Marxism has had considerable intellectual repercussions. 'Western Marxism', which includes the work of the Frankfurt School and Habermas but also such figures as Gramsci and

Althusser, has responded to the double disappointment of failed revolution and revolutionary failure with theoretical innovations of considerable ingenuity. Despite the recalcitrance of the 'problem of practice', these remain for many fertile currents of thought.[7] But the same historical fate has produced a number of more radical departures. For a variety of reasons intellectual disillusionment has been particularly marked in France. In post-war France Marxism was not only a powerful political force, it also dominated the intellectual scene in a way unparalleled in most other western countries.[8] Althusser's structuralist Marxism exerted considerable influence for a number of years. Even within existentialism and phenomenology Marxist theory was influential. Merleau-Ponty, Sartre and de Beauvoir were aligned with the revolutionary left for much of their careers. They were, at various times, all members of the French communist party. Their socialist commitment was expressed not only in extensive journalistic activities and political articles but also in much of their philosophical work, including Merleau-Ponty's writings on history and communism, and Sartre's lengthy *Critique of Dialectical Reason*. Even many of those now associated with poststructuralism and postmodernism were previously Marxists. Lyotard and Baudrillard belonged to a variety of Marxist groupings. Foucault was a member of the French communist party, albeit only for a short time.

This background is important, because Marxism is arguably the most frequent, if not always the explicit, target of postmodernist critics of modernism. Warnings about the dangers of 'totalizing' theory, and scepticism about the unfounded pretensions of the philosophy of history are most plausibly read as references to Marxism. Attacks on the totalitarian tendencies of modernism make more sense in relation to the Stalinist degeneration of communism than they do when applied to liberal or pluralist strands of post-Enlightenment thought. And for intellectuals who regarded Marxism as the best available response to this more liberal Enlightenment, it is not surprising that Marxism's apparent failure is taken as final proof of the bankruptcy of the Enlightenment project and modernism. From this perspective, then, it is not just the prevailing forms of power and rationality, the capitalist rationalization of production or the bureaucratic rationalization of the state, which exemplify the baneful condition of modernity. Marxism too is a part of the problem. East and West are the two faces of modernity. By the same token, only an even more radical intellectual critique promises release from an Enlightenment project with nowhere to hide. Only by enthusiastically embracing the 'other' of western reason can we avoid forever reliving the totalitarian nightmares of modernism.

Developments in art and art theory provide a further context for the formation of postmodernist thought, one which, in terminological terms at least, proves decisive. 'Modern' and its cognates have been used to describe western society and philosophy at least since the Renaissance quarrel of 'ancients and moderns'. In historical periodizations the 'modern period' or 'modernity' usually refers to the period of European history from the Renaissance or about 1500 onwards.[9] However the term 'modernism' has been restricted to a number of more specialized contexts and, until recently, was largely associated with artistic or literary modernism.[10] Modernism in this sense refers to the self-conscious pursuit of formal innovation and the consequent overturning of artistic convention by a self-conscious 'avant-garde'. Although artistic modernism has clear roots in the nineteenth century, it is usually regarded as being at its height in the early years of the twentieth. In Gaggi's words, 'modernism' is used 'to apply to those major movements and techniques in the various arts that developed early in the century: Cubism, Fauvism, Futurism, Expressionism, Surrealism, Functionalism, atonality, serialization, and stream-of-consciousness'.[11] Modernism is thus associated with figures such as Marcel Proust and James Joyce in literature, Arnold Schoenberg in music and Le Corbusier and the Bauhaus School in architecture and design. Among these movements Gaggi also usefully distinguishes between a modernism of 'classicist order', for example with Corbusier and Mondrian, and the 'romantic assertion of the self' in primitivism, expressionism, fauvism and cubism.

In theory at least artistic modernism might seem a potentially limitless project, renewable as each successive avant-garde rebels against the conventions established by a previous generation of innovators. However by around the middle of the twentieth century modernism was betraying clear signs of mortality. In the first place, the pursuit of formal or artistic innovation for its own sake seemed more and more futile, resulting in novelty without genuine artistic or creative significance. By this time, too, the political hopes associated with artistic modernism had dissipated. The revolutionary ambitions of dadaists and surrealists remained unfulfilled; the futurists were discredited by their association with fascism.[12] Artistic modernism belonged increasingly to the establishment. Modernist works adorned the corporate temples of capitalism as well as the private collections of millionaires. As David Harvey puts it, modernism was more readily associated with the worship of 'corporate bureaucratic power and rationality' than with any kind of political radicalism.[13] The emancipatory role which Frankfurt School theorists such as Adorno and Benjamin, in their different ways, assigned to modern art could no longer be sustained either.[14] By the late 1950s more and more artists and critics regarded modernism as aesthetically barren and politically compromised, a prestigious and profitable branch of the artistic establishment it had originally set out to shock.

The point of emergence of postmodernism as an artistic movement in reaction to modernism is usually located in the 1960s (though Barry Smart mentions the use, in the 1930s, by Federico de Onis of *postmodernismo* to refer to a 'kind of exhausted and mildly conservative modernism').[15] Architecture was the first medium to exhibit clear postmodernist tendencies. These include eclecticism, ambiguity, wit and a playful allusion to earlier styles in the form of pastiche. As Jameson explains, pastiche is devoid of the serious ulterior motivation of parody; it does not deviate in order to assert a norm. Rather it is 'a neutral practice of such mimicry, without any of parody's ulterior motives, amputated of the satiric impulse, devoid of laughter and of any conviction that alongside the abnormal tongue you have momentarily borrowed, some healthy linguistic normality still exists. Pastiche is thus blank parody, a statue with blind eyeballs.'[16] What are more sympathetically described as the playful aspects of postmodernism reflect one of its most important characteristics, namely its challenge to the privileged status of 'high' art and culture. In contrast to artistic modernism, which affirms the quasi-religious significance of art, postmodernism rejects any absolute distinction between high and low culture, between art and entertainment. Walter Benjamin's germinal essay on 'The Work of Art in the Age of Mechanical Reproduction' is thus an important clue to the understanding of artistic postmodernity. Benjamin discusses the disruption of the 'aura' of the great work of art as a result of the easy availability of copies, produced by techniques of mechanical reproduction such as printing, photography and sound recording.[17] Artistic postmodernism can be seen as the outcome of the tendency Benjamin identifies (even though he foresaw a different outcome), reinforced by the extensive role of communications and information technology in contemporary societies.

Gaggi also identifies 'self-referentiality' and 'epistemological scepticism' as key features of artistic postmodernism, along with a corresponding 'interest in great works from the past that turn in on themselves or otherwise make art itself the subject of art'.[18] Self-referentiality is also apparent in postmodernist art's playful mixing of previous styles in pastiche. There are clear connections between this interest in self-referentiality and poststructuralist critical theory, which diverts attention from the author and the figurative or representational role of the work of art, focusing instead on language or the work itself as the subject of artistic production.[19] Style is the message as well as the medium of art. There is in this context also an interesting interaction between artistic and scientific developments. Einstein's relativity theory and quantum mechanics, notably in the form of Heisenberg's 'uncertainty principle', undermine both notions of absolute space and time and deterministic interpretations of causality. At the same time, realist interpretations of science have come under attack even from analytical philosophers of science such as Kuhn and Feyerabend.[20] In art, chance and uncertainty are the basis of 'aleatoric music', whose completion depends on the unscripted, random choices of the performer, as well as of some aspects of dadaism. Artistic and scientific tendencies contribute to both the mood of uncertainty and flux and the greater openness to non-western cultures and worldviews, which are characteristic of postmodernism.

At roughly the same time as the emergence of artistic postmodernism, historical and sociological uses of the term were being canvassed. Smart refers to Toynbee's discussion in 1954 of a 'postmodern age', associated with the decline of the middle classes from around the turn of the century after their long period of hegemony. At about the same time Wright Mills identifies a 'post-modern period', characterized by loss of faith in both of the major ideologies of modernity, liberalism and socialism. There is also 'an increasingly pervasive sense that modern assumptions about the intrinsic relation of reason and freedom can no longer be sustained'.[21] However, it is not until after 1968 that postmodernism emerges clearly, first as a recognizable intellectual current linking a broader range of philosophical and cultural themes, then as a self-conscious and distinct philosophical position. The Events of 1968 symbolize an important point of transition. The last years of the sixties saw the defeat of the new Left, accelerating disillusionment with Marxism and the frustration, or perhaps diversion, of the utopian aspirations of a generation. These events were also the prelude to the emergence of the multi-centred politics of new social movements. This political context, finally, helps to explain a basic ambivalence running through postmodernism. There is a disjunction between 'a postmodernism of resistance and a postmodernism of reaction', a postmodernism of revolutionary disappointment and a postmodernism of defiant radicalism.[22] The critical evaluation of postmodernism is correspondingly ambivalent. Postmodernism is seen either as the last resort of critical intelligence or as a thinly disguised form of neo-conservatism.

In the further development of postmodernism along both of these paths, two separate regions must be distinguished (discussed in the following two sections). In the first place, there is a radically sceptical, philosophical critique of the intellectual universe of modernism. This tendency targets both the Enlightenment project and some of its most influential continental critics. Postmodernism in this guise rejects all philosophies of history and provides a radical challenge to the most basic categories of western philosophy and metaphysics. But secondly, and of course not unrelatedly, a number of theorists make a connection between postmodern tendencies in art and culture and the state of contemporary, sometimes 'postindustrial', sometimes 'late' or 'advanced capitalist', sometimes 'postmodern' societies. This is primarily a postmodernism of social and cultural theory, identifying postmodernity as a stage of western society. Evidently there are significant tensions between the two approaches. Philosophical postmodernism seems to deny what postmodern social and cultural thought seems to require – a philosophy or, at least, an overall account of history.

The Philosophical Critique of Enlightenment and Modernity

The philosophical critique of modernism and the Enlightenment project has emerged most clearly in France in the aftermath of structuralism and poststructuralism. It is largely the product of a number of intellectuals who, whilst rejecting or at least significantly distancing themselves from Marxism, do not follow the simple return to liberalism of some 'new philosophers' (*nouveaux philosophes*) in the early 1970s.[23] One of the clearest expositions of the philosophical critique of modernity is provided by Jean-François Lyotard (1924–) in his 'report on knowledge', entitled *The Postmodern Condition*. During his career Lyotard has occupied a variety of political positions from Marxism and 'spontaneist' anarchism to his present identification with the 'mood' of postmodernity. In fact, as we shall see, despite its espousal of postmodernist themes his position retains a tangential allegiance to Marxism in the sense that capitalism remains a problem.

Lyotard describes postmodernity as a 'condition' or 'mood' that corresponds to the present stage of 'post-industrial' society. Postmodernity is, therefore, a sign of the obsolescence of modernity. Lyotard defines modernity in terms of the role played in western societies since the Enlightenment by 'metanarratives' for the legitimation of both science and the state. A metanarrative in Lyotard's sense is equivalent to a philosophy of history. The contingent events of history are understood in terms of an all-inclusive narrative, which is supposed to encapsulate 'the' meaning of history. The reliance on legitimating metanarratives is intrinsic to 'the choice called the Occident'.[24] Lyotard proceeds to list a number of forms which metanarratives can take, for example 'the dialectics of Spirit, the hermeneutics of meaning, the emancipation of the rational or working subject, or the creation of wealth'.[25] Clearly these narratives correspond to some of the major currents of post-Enlightenment thought considered so far, including Hegelian idealism, hermeneutics, Marxism and theories of economic progress and modernization. But Lyotard isolates two major types, representing what he sees as the two dominant strands of post-Enlightenment thought. These are what we have identified as the mainstream of the Enlightenment and its most influential critique, firstly the 'narrative of emancipation' demonstrated both in modern science and in the politics of the French Revolution and, secondly, the 'speculative narrative' of Hegelianism and Marxism.[26] Both narratives imply that progress is guaranteed, either through the application of reason to production, politics and morality or as a result of the motor force of the dialectic. Both narratives have played an important role not only in modern philosophy but also in the West's self-consciousness as the embodiment of modernity.

The onset of a postmodern mood or condition, then, is marked by a gradual erosion of faith in meta-metanarratives, provoked by far-reaching developments in both society and culture. Lyotard refers to the onset of 'postindustrial society', a notion associated in France mainly with the work of Alain Touraine.[27] Postindustrial society depends on a mode of production in which, by contrast with earlier forms of society, knowledge and information technology play the central role. In particular, they are involved in 'the technological production of symbolic goods which shape or transform our representation of human nature and of the external world'.[28] Technical knowledge is applied to the production of new commodities, fostering new needs and even cultural values. According to Lyotard postindustrial society is dominated by the 'spirit of performativity', the attempt to reduce society to an efficient system, which guarantees 'the best possible input/output equation'.[29] The cultural and intellectual counterpart of this social form is a postmodern culture characterized by 'incredulity toward metanarratives'.[30] There is scepticism about all philosophies of history, all claims to foresee the inevitable goal of history and all political ideologies which promise to lead us to that goal. There is even scepticism about the universal validity of the values that define a particular historical future as good or bad. The 'death of God' announced by Nietzsche is closely followed by the death of history and progress. There is even a loss of faith in anything other than the instrumental effectiveness of western rationality. Paradoxically, this loss of faith is the ultimate outcome of the Enlightenment's own historically novel demand for the rational justification of every claim to truth, rightness and authority. In other words, the Enlightenment project has fallen victim to its own sceptical onslaught against religious dogma, tradition and authority.

If the mood of postmodernity is defined in terms of incredulity towards metanarratives, the politics of postmodernity is radically anti-authoritarian. The sceptical mood of postmodernity is also intolerant of grand projects and ambitious political programmes, which are a prominent feature of modern states and ideologies. Attempts to unify society artificially according to some grand, 'totalizing' theory or ideology are no longer convincing. Even more clearly, the consequences of such attempts have often been disastrous.[31] The twentieth century has witnessed unlimited global wars, bureaucratically organized genocide and fascist and Stalinist totalitarianism. Totalitarianism, for Lyotard and other postmodernists, is perhaps the quintessential expression of the modernist search for unity and order. Instead, society should be recognized as a 'heterogeneity of language games' or 'institutions in patches'. Far from being susceptible to theorizing in the unifying style of Newtonian mechanics, society consists of 'clouds of sociality' more amenable to a 'pragmatics of language particles'.[32] With the demise of totalizing theories of society, the value or even viability of centralized state politics is also brought in doubt. As Hoy puts it, Lyotard questions 'the idea of holding state power rationally accountable for a complex modern society'.[33] The state cannot deal with the irreducible complexity of contemporary society except by resorting to the totalitarian imposition of unity and order.

Lyotard's enthusiasm for diversity even makes him suspect Habermas's 'discourse ethics' of potentially authoritarian implications. Habermas's consensus theory of truth ignores the diversity of language games and seeks to reduce heterogeneity to an oppressive unity. For the mood of postmodernity, 'Consensus has become an outmoded and suspect value.'[34] Only the diversity and heterogeneity of social and cultural forms can resist the invasive modernist spirit of performativity. It follows that only temporary and local consensus is desirable, only provisional contracts should be sought. The price to be paid for any residue of nostalgia for totalizing theory is 'terror', which is 'the efficiency gained by eliminating, or threatening to eliminate, a player from the language game one shares with him'.[35] *Artistic modernism*, on the other hand, is an ally in Lyotard's 'war on totality', but only if it is understood as a constantly renewed challenge to the rules of image and narration, even those rules instituted by earlier modernisms: 'Postmodernism thus understood is not modernism at its end but in the nascent state, and this state is constant.'[36] The challenge facing each new avant-garde is how to express through the medium of art something previously inexpressible. At the heart of this conception of art, in other words, is the notion of the sublime as something beyond representation, something 'unpresentable'. Although by definition art cannot represent the unpresentable, modern art can at least 'present the fact that the unpresentable exists'.[37] In this way, art should constantly remind us of the limitations of both representational language and calculating reason.

Despite the radical scepticism of these arguments, Lyotard does not endorse ethical or political nihilism. He claims that 'justice as a value is neither outmoded nor suspect.'[38] Far from undermining the value of democracy or justice, which are after all central values of modernity, Lyotard's postmodernism is, on John Keane's reading, a 'vigorous agent of the renewal and deepening of modernity's democratic potential', 'a dialectical intensification of its democratic impulses'.[39] The emphasis on the irreducible plurality of language games reinforces the commitment to a diversity of viewpoints and their right to a voice. At the same time, it discourages 'ideological' language games, or in other words 'those which demand their general adoption' and the suppression of all rivals. The sceptical mood of postmodernity makes it more difficult to launch totalizing projects on the basis of claims to universal moral or theoretical truths. Postmodernist principles provide strong arguments for democratic institutions, including 'mechanisms capable of preventing absolute state power' and 'civil associations' beyond the state.[40] Nor can Lyotard be convicted of producing a universalizing ideology of his own – a universal veto against universalist ideologies – because democracy is founded on the denial of universal reason in a spirit which welcomes 'indeterminacy, controversy and uncertainty'.[41]

Not everyone, though, is so sympathetic to the mood of postmodernity. Habermas, for his part, has attacked postmodernism as a new form of conservatism, which has prematurely abandoned the uncompleted project of the Enlightenment. Habermas, in common with other theorists associated with the Frankfurt School, is well aware of the problematic legacy of the Enlightenment project, but he is unwilling to give up its commitment to bring about human emancipation through the application of reason. According to Habermas, postmodernists, like Nietzsche, too easily bid 'farewell to the dialectic of enlightenment', resorting instead to a messianism of art, poetry and myth beyond reason.[42] They respond to the one-sided, 'subject-centred' reason of the Enlightenment with an equally one-sided and reductive irrationalism, 'reason's absolute other'.[43] Again Heidegger, like Nietzsche an important source of the postmodernist stance, gestures towards 'a thinking more rigorous than the conceptual', but his views are easily reconciled with conservatism and prejudice. Heidegger's 'propositionally contentless speech about Being has, nevertheless, the illocutionary sense of demanding resignation to fate'.[44] Habermas deals with poststructuralist sources of postmodernism just as harshly. Derrida's deconstructionism falsely universalizes the 'poetic use of language specialized in world-disclosure' and so aestheticizes both language and philosophy.[45] Foucault's political stance is the 'arbitrary *partisanship* of a criticism that cannot account for its normative foundations'. The critical practice of genealogy is no more than 'the vertical projection of its position', similarly ungrounded.[46]

Habermas proposes instead his own universal pragmatics and discourse ethics as a way of pursuing the Enlightenment project without falling into the problems of the 'philosophy of the subject'. In effect, Habermas thinks that the anti-humanist critique of the philosophy of the subject implies only the abandonment of its 'monological' or individualistic versions. Where a subject-centred reason is based on the monological perspective of the observer it implies, in Rasmussen's words, 'the concept of a completely isolated subject whose relationship to the world can be only instrumentally conceived and not intersubjectively established'.[47] It is this perspective which underlies both the instrumental, calculating reason of the orthodox Enlightenment and the unattractive face of modernity. By developing the *inter*subjective 'paradigm of mutual understanding' through the theory of communication, Habermas hopes to avoid the impasse of the 'philosophy of consciousness'. It will then be possible to advance further the incomplete project of modernity without falling into the relativist, apolitical and, at least by default, conservative morass of postmodernism.[48] Habermas is also unconvinced that Lyotard's fears about anything beyond local and provisional consensus are really justified. For Habermas, truth is the outcome of an idealized discourse free from the distortions of power but, as he acknowledges, we can never be certain that the ideal has been fully realized. Genuine consensus is a state that can always only be anticipated. Actual consensus is always provisional and subject to challenge or revision. What is more, without a concept of truth it is not clear how we can challenge an imposed or 'ideological' consensus as something less than truth, and so provoke a renewal of discussion and inquiry.[49]

Jean Baudrillard (1929–), like Lyotard, is a former Marxist who, in his attempts to provide an account of western society, has moved increasingly in the direction of postmodernism. He emphasizes not only novel features of contemporary culture but, more particularly, the transformed role of the cultural sphere in society. His position has analogies both with the Frankfurt School's analyses of the culture industry and the 'situationist' diagnosis of the 'society of the spectacle'.[50] The transformed state of capitalist society still provides the spur for his theoretical approach, though it is a society no longer amenable to Marxist categories.[51] For Baudrillard, the unprecedented saturation of both economy and society by the 'image' is definitive of contemporary society. In his earlier (still Marxist) works Baudrillard identifies an important shift in the role of commodities in 'consumer society', which he sees not simply as a superstructural outgrowth of capitalism but as 'a fundamental mutation in the ecology of the human species'.[52] In this new form of society individuals are indoctrinated into consumption, where previously they were merely made to work: 'Modern man spends less and less of life in production, and more and more in the continuous production and creation of personal needs and of personal well-being. He must constantly be ready to actualize all of his potential, all of his capacity for consumption.'[53] To earn pleasure through consumption rather than work is the pre-eminent duty according to the 'fun morality' of consumer society. Advertising, market research, television and other media of communication are designed to produce willing and pliable consumers.

But a fundamental shift in the meaning of consumption is also involved. Within liberal capitalism the production of objects was already determined by monetary profit rather than human need. In Marx's terms, production was determined by the 'exchange value' rather than the 'use value' of things. But in consumer society the object is even more radically detached from use or need, even more radically alienated. The consumption of objects is now determined by their position within a differential system of meanings or 'signs', corresponding to gradations of social status and so on, which are expressed in and reinforced by advertising. According to Baudrillard's evidently structuralist account, 'commodities and objects, like words and once like women, constitute a global, arbitrary, and coherent system of signs, a *cultural* system which substitutes a social order of values and classifications for a contingent world of needs and pleasures, the natural and biological order.'[54] Marxian political economy is no longer appropriate for the new socio-economic formation, which must henceforth be understood in terms of a 'political economy of the sign'. Because of the interpenetration of meaningful commodities and the capitalist system of production, culture and economy must henceforth be understood as an indivisible amalgam. In Connor's words, 'it is no longer possible to separate the economic or productive realm from the realms of ideology or culture, since cultural artefacts, images, representation, even feelings and psychic structures have become part of the world of the economic'.[55]

In Baudrillard's later, more apocalyptic writings the image or sign displaces reality altogether. In effect, the arguments of poststructuralism are taken to (or even beyond) their logical conclusion. If, as he takes poststructuralism to imply, there is nothing outside the text, any duality of image and reality, sign and referent, must be superseded. Images can no longer be tied to an external referent or reality. The map, to take Baudrillard's example, no longer corresponds to some real territory but rather precedes and even engenders it: 'Simulation is no longer that of a territory, a referential being of a substance. It is the generation by models of a real without origin or reality: a hyperreal. The territory no longer precedes the map, nor survives it. Henceforth, it is the map that precedes the territory . . . it is the map that engenders the territory . . .'[56] In Baudrillard's somewhat hyperbolic terms, there is no longer any truth or reality, only universal and inescapable simulations. Soap operas and theme parks are the only reality. Disneyland embodies the 'truth' of America and the American way.[57] By implication ideology too has become a thing of the past, because ideology is defined as something falling short of undistorted truth, and no such standard is available in hyperreality. The only remaining ideology is the belief in reality or truth itself, the belief that the social spectacle is more than mere performance: 'It is no longer a question of a false representation of reality (ideology), but of concealing the fact that the real is no longer real.'[58]

In 'The Ecstasy of Communication' Baudrillard provides an evocative, if somewhat impressionistic, account of the contemporary world of simulation. It is a world of information and communication, where 'screen and network' are the only ontological essentials and culture is just 'the smooth operational surface of communication'. Television is 'the ultimate and perfect object' for an era, in which everything is invaded by advertising.[59] We have already seen the essential role played by consumption in this world. But the regime of mass media and isolated consumption does not leave the rest of society unchanged. The very sociality of social life is threatened, to the extent that that depends on meeting and talking with other people: 'we have come to live in less proximity to other human beings, in their presence and discourse, and more under the silent gaze of deceptive and obedient objects which continuously repeat the same discourse, that of our stupefied (*médusée*) power, of our potential affluence and of our absence from one another.'[60] And not only do we lose access to a genuine public sphere, there is no longer any secrecy either. The distinction between public and private spheres collapses under the weight of information and communication. Because communication makes 'public' what was once secret, it is obscene: 'we live in the ecstasy of communication. And this ecstasy is obscene ... All secrets, spaces and scenes abolished in a single dimension of information. That's obscenity.'[61] There is henceforth only the 'promiscuity' of unrestricted connections. Drawing on Deleuze and Guattari's *Anti-Oedipus*, Baudrillard identifies the characteristic pathology of this universe as schizophrenia. Lost amidst 'the immanent promiscuity of all these networks, with their continual connections', the 'schizo' is 'bereft of every scene, open to everything in spite of himself, living in the greatest confusion', dominated by 'the feeling of no defence, no retreat', 'a pure screen, a switching centre for all networks of influence'.[62]

Nor, in this 'cold universe', is there much space for either the 'theatre of the social' or the 'theatre of politics'.[63] Society and politics, those two children of modernity, are both either dead or dying. Both society, as the object of conventional sociology, and the collective class agents of socialist ideology are disappearing and, along with them, the relevance of existing models of social analysis and political action. But what are we left with after society, after politics, after the individual? Baudrillard announces the arrival of the 'masses' as counterparts to a world of mass media, isolated consumption and public opinion. This is an 'ensemble', to use Sartre's term, which is collective only in the statistical sense. The masses are the apotheosis of 'seriality'. Like listeners to a radio broadcast or viewers of television, the masses no longer meet or discuss but simply coexist as a dispersed, passive and otherwise unconnected audience.[64] In a postmodern world dominated by information and communications media, therefore, the masses cannot generate the self-conscious, organized groups required for collective political action. In contrast to the militant collective struggle traditionally expected of the proletariat by Marxism, the resistance of the masses assumes the form of passivity, a stubborn refusal of all incitements to speak, to act or to participate: 'the present argument of the system is to maximize speech, to maximize the production of meaning, of participation. And so the strategic resistance is that of the refusal of meaning and the refusal of speech.'[65] On Bauman's reading, 'We are now being told that the bovine immobility of the masses is the best form of activity we have, and that their doing nothing is the most excellent form of resistance.'[66] More sympathetically, Baudrillard's position can be seen as symptomatic of a society in which, as Foucault's writings suggest, human beings are the product of relations of power constituting them not only as objects but also as subjects.[67] Foucault's diagnosis at least casts doubt on those characteristic ideologies of modernity, liberalism and socialism, which demand 'the liberating rights of the subject'.[68] Do these demands simply play into the hands of power? Nor, to be fair, does Baudrillard rule out altogether the more active resistance advocated by modern political ideologies. But in the end, Baudrillard's prognosis for traditional politics is not encouraging.

Postmodernity as a Stage of Western Society

Marxism is the dark matter of the postmodernist universe. It exerts greater and more complex effects on postmodernist thought and discourse than are at first apparent. The exit from Marxism by French intellectuals, especially after 1968, is one of the major contributing factors in the emergence of postmodernism, and postmodernists typically see Marxism as a significant manifestation of modernism. Lyotard and Baudrillard both belong to a growing diaspora of formerly Marxist intellectuals in exile from their previous theoretical convictions. However, a number of other theorists attempt to accommodate what they see as the insights of postmodernism within a still recognizably Marxist or, at least, materialist framework. In effect, for theorists like Jameson, Laclau, Mouffe, Lash and Urry, postmodern culture and social relations correspond to contemporary capitalism, just as bourgeois ideology and values were the 'ruling ideas' of nineteenth-century liberal capitalism.[69] For these theorists, the postmodern is an inescapable feature of contemporary society, which any relevant social theory must deal with. In effect, they are revisionists who agree with other western Marxists, that a substantial rewriting of Marxist theory is necessary. And in fact, although these theorists emphasize different aspects of the transformation of capitalist society, and a number of other important theoretical shifts occur, there are significant analogies with the approach of the Frankfurt School. By the same token, postmodernist Marxism of the kind discussed here is very different from the position of more orthodox Marxists like Callinicos. For him, though postmodern thought and culture do reflect objective features of contemporary capitalism, in the end they must be demystified as ideological diversions and not allowed to distort unduly either theoretical analysis or class struggle.[70]

For a variety of revisionist perspectives, then, capitalism has been fundamentally transformed on a number of dimensions since the nineteenth century. In the first place, the working class is a less homogeneous, less united and seemingly less willing bearer, at least in any foreseeable future, of the revolutionary task allotted to it by orthodox Marxism. Reformist social democracy and trade unionism have remained the favoured avenues of working-class activism and can no longer be dismissed as the 'infantile disorders' of an immature class consciousness. The proletariat's retreat from its allotted role reflects a number of other changes to the capitalist economy. Manufacturing industry has declined relative to the more dispersed and less unionized service sector. Finance and production are increasingly globalized, removing power from national labour movements and even national governments. Ownership has been dispersed through joint stock companies. The 'managerial revolution' has led to a growing gap between ownership and control of the production process. A further set of changes have resulted from technological innovations made possible by the earlier stages of capitalism. Perhaps most important are the rise of mechanized and later electronic mass media and the information and communications revolutions brought about by computerization. These technological changes have had a profound impact in a number of areas. The work process has been transformed, demanding new kinds of technical expertise from the workforce whilst deskilling many traditional occupations. Leisure and consumption have been progressively revolutionized by newspapers, film, television, sound reproduction, computers, multimedia technology and the 'information superhighway'.[71]

The rapid development of electronic technologies of information processing and communications is inseparable from other important cultural shifts. The expansion of electronic mass media has allowed an unprecedented saturation of everyday life with the imagery of advertising. This, in conjunction with the development of more flexible, 'post-Fordist' processes of production, has encouraged new patterns of consumption.[72] Consumption is increasingly an opportunity to assert difference rather than equal social status. Consumers purchase a 'lifestyle', 'image' or 'identity', which has been conceived by product designers, promoted by advertising consultants and supplied by a flexible production process. The fragmentation of production, class membership and consumption is confirmed in the area of politics. In contrast to the monolithic collective agents and norms of solidarity characteristic of socialist politics, there has emerged a multiplicity of struggles, regions of conflict, issues and modes of political action. A plurality of 'new social movements' or 'subject positions' contribute to an irreducibly pluralist politics of resistance.[73] The movements in question include women, peace activists, environmentalists and 'greens', lesbians and gays, anti-racists, ethnic minorities and indigenous peoples, urban civil rights and citizenship campaigns.

Marxist theorists have discussed these social and cultural transformations in terms of theories of 'advanced' or 'late' capitalism.[74] Alain Touraine describes basically similar features of contemporary society as signs of a transition from 'industrial' to 'postindustrial' society. By choosing this terminology Touraine both signals his distance from Marxism, as appropriate only to the industrial stage of capitalism, and points to what he regards as the substantial similarities between capitalism and communism as variants of industrial society.[75] Frederic Jameson (1934–) is closer to the first group of theorists. Although he takes very seriously the various ways in which western society has been transformed, he continues to understand it as a variant of capitalism and so maintains his allegiance to Marxism. Postmodernism is 'the cultural logic of late capitalism': 'postmodernism is not the cultural dominant of a wholly new social order (the rumor about which, under the name of "postindustrial society", ran through the media a few years ago), but only the reflex and the concomitant of yet another systemic modification of capitalism itself.'[76] Jameson adapts Ernest Mandel's three-stage model of capitalist development, which relates each stage of capitalism to the dominance of a particular technology. Market capitalism (analysed by Marx) is the stage of steam-driven mechanization and, in the cultural realm, artistic realism. Monopoly or imperialist capitalism (described by Lenin and Luxemburg) is the stage of electrical power, the internal combustion engine and artistic modernism. Finally comes the gradual emergence, from the 1950s in the area of technology and from the 1960s in the area of culture, of 'consumer', 'late' or 'multinational capitalism'. The dominant technologies of this stage are electronics and nuclear power. But this stage of capitalism also has its own 'dominant cultural logic', reflected in the prominence of both cultural and intellectual currents of postmodernism.[77]

The cultural logic of late capitalism has two aspects. In the first place, the cultural forms corresponding to this stage of society have familiar postmodern features. Postmodernism in the artistic sphere involves the 'effacement . . . of the older (essentially high-modernist) frontier between high culture and the so-called mass or commercial culture' and the integration of 'aesthetic production' into commodity production.[78] Jameson also notes a declining ability to think historically and 'the disappearance of master narratives'.[79] We are increasingly isolated from our own histories, 'condemned to seek History by way of our own pop images and simulacra of that history, which itself remains forever out of reach'.[80] We experience history through theme parks and TV 'mini-series' rather than the historic projects of political movements or ideologies. But the distinctiveness of the contemporary phase of capitalism does not consist only in the prevalence of postmodern cultural themes. A second aspect of the cultural logic of late capitalism is a new relationship between culture and the rest of the social totality. Postmodernism is not just a new cultural form but a 'cultural dominant', which stands in a novel relationship to the economic system. Culture is both less separate and more pervasive. Postmodern culture invades society. Not only is consumption increasingly defined in cultural terms, but culture itself has also been commodified to an unprecedented extent. In the age of mechanical reproduction works of art are more and more subject to market forces. At the same time, commodities in general are advertised as works of art. The consumer is encouraged to fashion for himself a unique identity through individualized acts of consumption, which are made to resemble the creative activity of the artist. The interpenetration of society and culture means both the 'dissolution of an autonomous sphere of culture' and the 'prodigious expansion of culture throughout the social realm'.[81]

An important consequence of the distinctive cultural logic of late capitalism is the impossibility of maintaining an effective 'critical distance' from its institutions and values. In effect, here, Jameson incorporates the sceptical conclusions of poststructuralist and postmodernist philosophy, which disqualify Enlightenment attempts to provide objective rational foundations for moral and political values. The universal validity once claimed by such moralizing discourses as Marxism and liberalism is no longer sustainable. Jameson wishes to defend Marxist theory as a critical discourse without pretensions to absolute truth. Marxism remains a 'master discourse', but on terms that remove its absolute status. Marxism is a 'single great collective story' and 'untranscendable horizon', which subsumes other approaches; but its 'imperative to totalise' may not be feasible. Marxism is not the 'affirmation of some place of truth' but 'a perspective and a method whereby the "false" and the ideological can be unmasked and made visible'.[82] The role of the Marxist literary critic is 'to engage in a symptomatic analysis that reveals and dismantles the covert ideological content of literary texts'.[83] However, Jameson is less clear about the practical politics of such a project. He is sceptical of an unmediated pluralism of social movements or subject positions which, he claims, reflects not the disappearance of classes but merely the illusion thereof.[84] We still need a 'genuine' or 'totalising' politics that takes in the economic or systemic level, and Jameson is still prepared to name multinational capital and its agents as 'enemy'. But his more constructive remarks are unfortunately vague. Possible strategies would involve 'turning the image against itself' and a 'cognitive mapping' of the space of contemporary capitalism, revealing the need for a 'multilevel strategy'.[85]

Somewhat closer to the anti- or post-Marxist assumptions of philosophical postmodernism are a number of sociologists who see postmodernity as an identifiable stage of society that either has or is destined to succeed modernity, but who see no particular connection between postmodernity and Marx's vision of communism. The sociological critique of modernity and modernization is closer to the philosophical critique of the Enlightenment project than it is to Marxism. According to Zygmunt Bauman (1925–) Marxism and communism are modernity in its purest form. Communism takes even further the limited conception of rationality manifest in the modernization of the West. In comparison to capitalism (for Weber already the 'rationally calculated pursuit of profit'), communism promises to abolish disruptive economic cycles of boom and recession. It promises to replace the chaos of market forces and ruthless competition with planning, to replace politics and class conflict with routine administration in the interests of the needs of the whole community. As Bauman puts it, 'Communism was modernity in its most determined mood and most decisive posture; modernity streamlined, purified of the last shred of the chaotic, the irrational, the spontaneous, the unpredictable.'[86] The Soviet Union, China, Cuba and other communist countries were initially successful in their 'modernizing' programmes of primary industrialization, electrification, education and health care.[87]

By contrast, Bauman describes an emergent *postmodernity* in positive terms, as a 'fully-fledged comprehensive and viable type of social system' in which consumer satisfaction plays a particularly important role.[88] Anthony Giddens too regards postmodernity less as a condition to be endured than as a political ideal. Giddens's perspective has affinities with other theories influenced by the Frankfurt School tradition of social theory. Like John Keane and Claus Offe, for example, he identifies basic contradictions at the heart of the systems of rationality which structure contemporary societies. These contradictions are the by-product of what Barry Smart calls 'the modern quest for order': 'The idea of order as a task, as a practice, as a condition to be reflected upon, preserved and nurtured is intrinsic to modernity.' But 'ordering interventions seem to promote disorders.'[89] The attempt to impose order on society inevitably generates resistance or, at the extreme, the irruption of disorder. Giddens emphasizes the close interdependence between the ordering impulse of modernity and academic sociology. Sociology emerges as a distinct discipline along-side the characteristic institutions of modern society and is, in Giddens's terms, a medium for the reflexivity of society in the service of its quest for order. Sociology contributes to the self-knowledge of society and hence furthers its potential for self-control and transformation.[90]

Logically, then, the crisis of modernity implies both a potential crisis for 'modern' sociology and the possibility of a postmodern approach to the study of society. Giddens argues for a number of changes. For example, as a result of the globalization of finance, production and consumption, communications, culture and so on, the nation-state is no longer an adequate focus for sociological research. Both global and 'micro-social' levels of analysis have been unduly neglected. The prominence of social movements, with the character-istic motto of 'think globally, act locally', is again relevant here. Sociology and theories of development have traditionally been based on the Eurocentric assumption, that western society is the most mod-ern or advanced and that other societies must gradually evolve along the same path. This assumption also needs to be rethought. Develop-ing a similar perspective, Barry Smart argues for a less exclusionary and more imaginative sociology. The perspectives of a diversity of cultures, including those of traditional and religious societies, should be incorporated into a sociology based less on 'modern reason' and more on '*post*modern imagination'.[91] In other words, the disrup-tion of the philosophical assumptions of modernity implies a funda-mental recasting of its social scientific self-image as well, if not, as with Baudrillard, the complete abandonment of both sociology and 'society'.

Politics of Difference and Ethics of the Other

Postmodernism, then, involves a number of divergent currents of thought and a number of disciplinary regions. Its political and intel-lectual postures range from defiant radicalism to an ironic and, some would say, complacent detachment. Postmodernists provide a number of provocative (if occasionally hyperbolic) descriptions of contemporary western culture and society, which serve to undermine conventional styles of political action. They are most frequently criti-cized for their relentless negativism and scepticism, their refusal to offer more positive moral or political recommendations. However, even at the level of scepticism, the value of the postmodernist critique should not be underestimated. The suspicion that this critique touches sensitive spots is confirmed, in the aftermath of the Cold War, by postmodernism's recent 'elevation', in place of communism, to the 'other' of western rationality and freedom, the target of ritualized and unthinking abuse as often as serious engagement. At the very least, the postmodern diagnosis is a salutary reminder of the darker episodes of western history. Twentieth-century totalitarianisms are only the most striking proof of the dangers inherent in modernity. The postmodern mood also reflects a pervasive anxiety, a sense of 'ontological insecurity' (in Giddens's phrase), and widespread dissatisfaction with bureaucratized capitalist society, even if bureaucratic socialism is not regarded as an alternative either. The aftershocks of colonialism and decolonization as well as the resurgence of powerful religious fundamentalisms also tug at the philosophical roots of western self-assurance. Postmodernity may be a useful concept for an understanding of contemporary society and culture, even if the associated philosophical position is not adopted.

In fact, the negative, sceptical stance of postmodernism is most frequently taken to have anti-authoritarian implications. Postmodernists disrupt all forms of discourse (and, of course, not only political discourse) which, however secretly, promote the terroristic suppression of diversity or difference. Derridean deconstruction challenges the 'violent hierarchies' of western reason, and postmodernists, too, oppose any denial of the 'other', any reduction of difference to a devalued otherness for the sake of the security of our own identity. Far from producing some new and grandly unifying theory or inciting organized struggle against the 'system', postmodernists seek to entrench the multiplicity of discourses, knowledges, cultures, struggles and voices. They challenge the claims of all leaders, particularly leaders who claim to be experts or intellectuals, even those who claim to be experts in resistance or Marxist revolution. They even impugn intellectuals like Habermas for claiming authority on the conditions of democratic will formation or 'undistorted communication'. In this respect postmodernists are closer to earlier members of the Frankfurt School such as Adorno, whose 'negative dialectics' resisted the temptations of positive thinking as tenaciously as anyone could.

The critical impetus of postmodernist ideas has found particular resonance in a number of discourses or perspectives previously marginalized within (albeit, of course, not only within) western thought. Especially productive has been an interaction between postmodernism and feminism, in which the writings of Lacan and Derrida have probably been most influential. The deconstructive challenge to all 'hierarchized dichotomies' is applied to the opposition between woman and man, masculine and feminine. Where Simone de Beauvoir remains at least partially under the spell of this dichotomy, retaining traces of a negative view of woman as 'lack' or as the 'other' of man, postmodern feminism celebrates unreservedly the specificity and difference of woman. But the challenge is even more radical than that. Postmodernist doubts about the status of philosophy as an autonomous, self-contained and rigorously rational enterprise provide an opening for feminist critique at the most fundamental level. A number of postmodernist feminists suggest, that the 'malestream' of western philosophy depends on an originary exclusion of woman or the feminine. Crucially, then, it is not only the status of women that is in question. The feminist concern with the position of women interacts with a philosophical critique which, if it can be sustained, demands a far-reaching recasting of western reason.

Grosz expresses the radical nature of the postmodern feminist challenge with some force: 'Destabilising existing forms of writing and knowing is a precondition for the positive assertion of femininity. Without the fissuring of existing intellectual categories and textual norms, there is simply no conceptual space available for women's positive self-representations.'[92] Grosz discusses three French feminists who, in their different ways, contribute to the destabilizing of existing discursive categories and norms. Perhaps most approachably, Michèle Le Doeuff (1948–) deconstructs the 'imaginary' of western philosophy.[93] Although this imaginary turns out to be male or masculine in significant ways, Le Doeuff's interests are wideranging. In particular, she points to the way that the institutionalization of philosophy has always involved a certain relationship between power and knowledge. The actual dependence of philosophical argument on officially excluded subjects and forms of discourse is shown in its reliance on metaphors, images or literary figures drawn from these marginalized domains. These elements of a philosophical imaginary 'both reveal and conceal philosophy's conditions of production and self-justification'.[94] Crucially for the deconstructive case, the philosophical text's imaginary is not just an incidental accompaniment, a lapse from a more rigorous train of argument. Rather the philosophical imaginary is inseparable from the discursive strategies officially recognized within the tradition. In terms of feminist strategy, 'Le Doeuff affirms the position of images, models and metaphors of femininity in masculinist philosophies, seeing them as points of tension and contradiction, points which can illuminate what is at stake in various philosophical positions.'[95] A persuasive example of this strategy is Le Doeuff's discussion of Bacon's early formulation of the project of modern science in terms of the relationship between a masterful science and womanly nature.[96]

More exclusively feminist in their concerns, Julia Kristeva (1941–) and Luce Irigaray (1930–) pursue a parallel deconstruction of knowledges and discourses revealed to be covertly male or masculinist in their deepest assumptions and constitution. Both theorists attempt to conceive women in their irreducible difference. They theorize woman from a woman's point of view in order to discover a 'feminine feminine', and so overcome a long tradition of regarding woman as lack, as the deficient and subordinate other of man.[97] Although Kristeva's early work was influenced by Althusser, the influence of Derrida is apparent in her deconstructive reading of texts. These readings seek to uncover the repressed desires of the 'maternal', to recover the repressed sex of woman: 'She asserts the play of sexual differentiation running within and between all texts, and overflowing their intentions, which always leaves ineradicable, traceable residues in texts which make these texts amenable to different readings and to the play of sexual pleasures they contain.'[98] In terms derived from Lacan's reading of Freud, Kristeva explores the interplay between the 'pre-symbolic' or 'semiotic' disorder of the unconscious and the 'symbolic' realm of order, which is aligned with consciousness and explicit meaning. The symbolic order incorporates the law of the father, male power and phallocentrism and is 'founded on the repression of the imaginary'.[99] On the other hand, the semiotic realm, which is repressed when the subject enters the order of language at the Oedipal stage, is associated with the mother and woman as well as with the chaotic psychic pleasures and energies of the pre-Oedipal child.

The subject is normally constituted within the dynamic of a repressive hierarchy of symbolic and semiotic, male order and systematically repressed female imaginary. For Kristeva, on the other hand, 'a liberated person is someone able to acknowledge "the play of semiotic and Symbolic" – the continual vacillation between disorder and order.'[100] This interplay reflects the actual but denied interdependence of symbolic and semiotic: 'The symbolic provides the semiotic with its only possibilities of expression; in turn, the semiotic provides the symbolic with its raw materials and its energetic impetus.' The semiotic is creatively disruptive when it 'erupts and overflows its symbolic boundaries in certain "privileged" moments of "rupture, renovation and revolution"', which Kristeva associates with 'madness, holiness and poetry'.[101] In parallel terms, Hélène Cixous (1937–) contrasts masculine 'literature' with a feminine 'writing' of movement, subversion and transformation. Feminine writing is more closely aligned with desire than with reason, and 'desire, not reason, is the means to escape the limiting concepts of traditional western thought.'[102]

Luce Irigaray works as a psychoanalyst and philosopher who seeks to liberate 'the feminine from male philosophical thought'.[103] Irigaray is critical of the ways in which psychoanalysis and philosophy universalize an essentially male representation of humanity. Because language, society and culture are all constituted on the basis of this false universalization of male perspectives, interests and desires, women can only gain full representation by means of thoroughgoing social reconstruction. In Grosz's words:

> The feminine has thus far functioned in muted, suppressed or unheard ways, obscured by the domination and pseudo-representation of the masculine . . . For women to be accorded autonomy as women, the entire social fabric requires major reorganisation: only *half* the possibilities, the alternatives, world-views, interests (at best) gain social expression or recognition.[104]

In particular, society and culture must recognize their debt to the 'mother'. Like the child who forgets what it owes to its mother, language and society have repressed the feminine in their original constitution as an essentially masculine order. Important strategies for Irigaray's contestation of this order are interrelated explorations of language and the specific and plural sexualities of women.[105] Woman should be understood not in Freud's negative terms of 'penis envy' or the absence of the phallus, but more positively as the presence of the 'two lips' of the vulva. The suppression of woman as an irreducibly distinct sex has meant that sexual relationships have existed not as the 'meeting of sexually different subjects', but as the insipid encounter between a male subject and his reflection in woman. The recognition of genuine sexual difference, on the other hand, would inaugurate a completely different kind of sexual relationship: 'When each sex acknowledges the radical otherness of the other, then mutually rewarding exchanges between them become possible.'[106] Similarly productive exchanges would become possible in other non-sexual forms of sociality, for example in intellectual or ethical relationships.

Other currents of contemporary political thought address identifiably postmodern themes. Iris Marion Young challenges the ideal of community in socialist and some feminist thought. The communitarian desire for 'mutual identification in social relations' is a desire she connects with sectarianism, chauvinism and even racism. The desire for unity, wholeness and identity, here as elsewhere in the postmodernist universe, 'generates borders, dichotomies, and exclusions'.[107]

The celebration of otherness and difference, on the other hand, is a potential antidote to these effects of closure and, indeed, an important theme for many contemporary feminists.[108] In analogous terms, Edward Said describes how colonialism devalues other cultures as inferior reflections of western civilization. Subordinated or marginalized groups and cultures can be represented within the discursive regime of colonialism only in relation to western norms. Discourses of resistance against this regime must appeal to a common 'ethico-discursive principle', namely 'the right of formerly un- or misrepresented human groups to speak for and represent themselves in domains defined, politically and intellectually, as normally excluding them, usurping their signifying and representing functions, overriding their historical reality'.[109]

Taking the deconstructionist strategy one step further, Gayatri Spivak and Homi Bhabha question even the characteristically postmodern opposition between excluding subject or identity and marginalized other. They argue 'the need for the careful deconstruction of the very structures of dominant and marginal', in the belief that 'such oppositional models themselves may derive from and reproduce colonial structures of thought – so that to proclaim oneself as a marginalized or silenced people is implicitly to accept and to internalize the condition of marginality.' In fact, Said too aims to focus 'not on the exterior, countervailing strength of a marginal position, but on the internal contradictions within dominant western forms of knowledge'.[110] Resistance to a particular order of power and discourse struggles, possibly in vain, to avoid defining itself in terms which derive from and so perhaps reinforce that order. Movements of homosexuals (gays or lesbians), indigenous and Black people all struggle on the basis of identities originating in the discourse of an oppressor. The work of Kristeva and Irigaray confirms the similar position of women. By implication, we should be suspicious of any 'politics of identity' which seeks to contain the 'flux' or 'flight' of resistance within a fixed and almost certainly compromised identity.[111]

For some critics, though, postmodernism is too inclined to identify with the pure intention rather than the unavoidably compromised reality of resistance. Like anarchism, postmodernism is accused of celebrating the pure moment of rebellion or critique at the expense of the necessarily untidy task of constructing a new political order – an order which, perhaps inevitably, will institute an exclusionary regime of its own. This accusation is reinforced by the fact that the positive political agenda of postmodernism remain unclear. How can postmodernists provide an account of justice without violating their own

austere critical principles? In the absence of some account of justice
we are left with few options. We may be politically engaged on behalf
of our friends, but then we forget our commitment to the 'other', to
what is not friendly or familiar or like us. In any case, the postmodernist critique seems to depend on an unarticulated normative framework of its own. As Connor remarks, 'when inspected closely, it
becomes apparent that the postmodern critique of unjust and oppressive systems of universality implicitly depends for its force upon the
assumption of the universal right of all not to be treated unjustly and
oppressively.'[112] If some equivalent assumption is not made, then how
can universalism or, for that matter, the exclusion and domination of
others be condemned? In the absence of some such principle obvious
difficulties face an unqualified politics of difference. A viable politics
cannot be deduced from the simple denial of universality or an unqualified respect for difference.[113] Not all cultures, religions and
worldviews can be respected simultaneously, when they make absolute and incompatible political demands of their own. It is not only
Enlightenment universalism that devalues other perspectives. Religious, national and ethnic identities may be just as exclusive and
oppressive. Surely fundamentalists (of whatever variety) have more
in common with one another than with postmodern advocates of
plurality and difference. Postmodernism may not be as far from a
conventionally liberal pluralism as some postmodernists suggest. Of
course, Rorty for one is happy to admit the connection.[114]

Silvio Gaggi even sees dangers in the rigorously negative stance of
postmodernism – what Allan Megill calls its 'perpetual holding
operation'.[115] On the one hand, 'the fact that it can *only* be subversive
and provides no grounds for arguing in favor of any ethical, social, or
political system, progressive, reactionary, or otherwise, is a severe
limitation on its potential for aiding in social change.'[116] Postmodernism bars itself from systematic and constructive involvement in emancipatory politics and so, in effect, helps to disarm opponents of
existing regimes of power. This supports Eagleton's view that postmodernism and poststructuralism encourage an escape from politics
and amount to 'conservatism by default'.[117] To see no good reason for
active political engagement leads to acceptance of the status quo.
After all, the self-styled (though by no means conventional) conservative Michael Oakeshott also directs his attack on 'rationalism in
politics' against both of the main parties of modernity. He berates not
only 'doctrinaire liberal' advocates of universal human rights and
liberties but also 'left Hegelian' Marxist protagonists of the 'upstart'
classes.[118] Even worse, Gaggi suggests, postmodernist scepticism effectively erases the distinction between power and justice and so

offers intellectual solace to fascism. Mussolini was aware of the connection: 'From the fact that all ideologies are of equal value, that all ideologies are merely fictions, the modern relativist infers that everybody has the right to create for himself his own ideology and to attempt to enforce it with all the energy of which he is capable.'[119]

Connor, too, is inclined to question the motives behind the postmodernist stance, seeing it as a last-ditch effort by intellectuals to hold on to their positions of privilege in the face of the sceptical onslaught of poststructuralism. The postmodernist bar on explicit criteria of normative critique is just one last desperate ploy by predominantly male critical intellectuals who, in the face of the increasing influence of feminist, anti-racist, anti-homophobic and other forms of critique, seek to retain their traditional monopoly on intellectual opposition. As Hebdige puts it:

> Rather than surrender mastery of the field, the critics who promulgate the line that we are living at the end of everything (and are *all* these critics men?) make one last leap and resolve to take it all – judgement, history, politics, aesthetics, value – out of the window with them . . . The implication seems to be that if they cannot sit at the top of Plato's pyramid, then there shall be no pyramid at all.[120]

Postmodernism is part of 'an intellectual-discursive process which simultaneously multiplies critical options and binds them into recognizable and disseminable forms'.[121] Connor's hostile reading is supported by an intellectual sociology of postmodernist culture. Why has postmodernism recently become so popular among intellectuals and academics and why particularly in certain fields? On this view, postmodernism's recognition of difference and the sublime in fact belongs to a strategy of recuperation, which names the unnameable only to bring it more effectively under control.

Said's discussion of the relationship between postmodernism and interdisciplinarity intimates a more sympathetic intellectual sociology of postmodernism. He argues that the present academic organization of disciplinary specializations has deeply conservative implications in the 'era of Reagan'. Postmodernism can be understood as a new way of conceiving the relationship between intellectual disciplines, challenging conventional academic boundaries, for example between literature and philosophy. Postmodernism has also become a topic of discussion within a number of different disciplines: in art, art theory and criticism, cultural studies, communication theory, philosophy, history, sociology, anthropology and geography among others. What Habermas sees as regression behind modernity's necessary differentiation of scientific, moral and aesthet-

ic judgement, Said evaluates more positively. By reproblematizing
the divisions between faculties of judgement postmodernism reinte-
grates the aesthetic dimension into life and, perhaps, fulfils Schiller's
earlier hopes for a playfully creative resolution of the conflict and
alienation characteristic of modern subjectivity.[122]

Evidently, postmodernism is now one protagonist in an intellectual scene dominated by radically opposed positions, which do not
always pay close attention to the arguments of the other side. In a
different spirit, Stephen K. White has recently proposed a suggestive
synthesis of postmodernism with something more like a continuation
of the Enlightenment project. He seeks to reconcile central ideas of
Heidegger, who is an important source of postmodernist themes, with
those of Habermas, who is the most influential continental proponent
of the 'incomplete project' of modernity. According to White, an
adequate political response to the postmodern problematic requires
both an ethic of 'responsibility to act' and an ethic of 'responsibility to
otherness'. Responsibility to act relates to pragmatic concerns of
practical or political effectiveness. It has been the predominant concern of western reason. But as a number of critics of Enlightenment
and modernity, from Nietzsche and Heidegger to Horkheimer and
Adorno, have emphasized, 'This modern orientation toward a reason
aimed at enhancing human will and control has no limits.'[123] Although it has delivered great power over nature and has permitted a
dramatic increase in the complexity of human societies, it is vitiated
by a systematic inability to recognize or respect otherness. By contrast, both poststructuralism and postmodernism point stubbornly to
what is suppressed or neglected as a result of modern reason's 'will to
mastery'. Foucault's genealogies 'incite the experience of discord or
discrepancy between the social construction of self, truth and rationality and that which does not fit neatly within their folds'. Postmodernist strategies 'bear witness' to the dissonance at the heart of
western reason and so show 'responsibility to otherness'.[124]

According to White, Heidegger is the thinker who shows greatest
insight into responsibility to otherness and the 'world-disclosing' as
opposed to 'action-coordinating' dimension of language to which it
corresponds.[125] He understands that genuine community depends on
a 'radical willingness to hear and experience the difference of the
other'. Above all Heidegger's concept of 'nearness' (*Nähe*) embodies
recognition of the other in its otherness.[126] Nearness involves a 'playing back and forth in relation to the other', which brings it closer at
the same time as it lets it be in its otherness: 'Attentive concern for
otherness means that the gesture of nearing, bringing into one's
presence, into one's world, must always be complemented by a letting

go, an allowance of distance, a letting be in absence, thus bearing witness to our own limits, our own finitude.'[127] Our creative 'bringing into presence' or 'disclosure' of the world through language must not displace that sense of otherness or absence, from which presence emerges and to which it must finally be allowed to return.[128] However, though Heidegger shows a strong sense of responsibility to otherness, his sense of 'responsibility to act' is sadly undeveloped. He is unable to conceptualize 'the normative tension and interconnection between actors in social and political life'.[129] He is contemptuous of the everyday conflicts and compromises of politics. His critique of modernity is 'totalistic', because it provides no guidelines for its transcendence, only a vague and potentially authoritarian longing for what is to come (*das Kommende*). Postmodernism's understanding of responsibility to act remains undeveloped because of a prevailing mood of 'impertinence', a deep-seated tendency to prefer deconstructive critique to constructive engagement. According to White's diagnosis, 'an *over*emphasis on disruption and impertinence creates for postmodern thinking a momentum that threatens to enervate the sense of responsibility to otherness, subtly substituting for it an implicit celebration of the impertinent subject who shows his or her virtuosity in deconstructing whatever unity comes along.'[130]

White's proposed synthesis in effect combines Habermas's discourse ethics with a suitably refreshed Heideggerianism. Discourse ethics provides, for White, a persuasive account of our responsibility to act. But Habermas is still too complacent about our responsibility to otherness, persisting – unjustifiably, according to White – 'in the belief that the problem of otherness can be adequately settled' within his own theoretical framework.[131] White garners from a variety of poststructuralist and postmodernist thinkers a number of clues for the required reconstruction of moral and political thought. Derrida usefully distinguishes a responsibility 'to' the particular other from the more generalized responsibility 'before' others, which is conventionally embodied in law and morality. Close to Heidegger's conception of 'closeness' (*Nähe*) is the importance Derrida accords to friendship, conceived in Kantian terms as an 'unstable equilibrium' of love and respect, attraction and repulsion.[132] Lyotard's 'sublime of everyday life' and Foucault and Rorty's approval of an uncontrolling 'curiosity' point similarly to an attitude of unpossessive care towards others. Feminism, finally, is an important source of insights. Carol Gilligan's discussion of a feminine 'ethic of care', Sara Ruddick's notion of a non-possessive attitude of 'holding' rather than 'grasping' and Seyla Benhabib's emphasis on the 'concrete' rather than 'generalised other' all provide clues.[133] Overall, according to White, we should positively delight in difference without tolerating those who would suppress otherness. The state should actively foster a diversity of communities or associations without succumbing to paternalism. The norms required for contemporary society can be derived from a Habermasian discourse ethic reinforced by more whole-hearted commitment to otherness.

Whatever might be thought of White's attempt to reconcile Habermas's nuanced version of Enlightenment rationalism with postmodern sensibility, responsibility to act with responsibility to otherness, it serves to highlight the point that postmodernism can only be understood as an episode within the post-Enlightenment tradition of western philosophy it is so eager to criticize and deconstruct. The debate between Habermasian critical theory and postmodernism is characteristic of the current state of this tradition. It may not be the most important debate, and it may turn out to have suggested false directions for future work. Certainly, to hope for an eventual reconciliation of the critical insights of postmodernism with other major currents of post-Enlightenment thought is to conceive the quarrel of modernity and postmodernity in terms closer to Habermas's incomplete project of Enlightenment. It can hardly be denied, too, that postmodernism presents a serious challenge to any remaining faith that some combination of reason and politics can be welded into a reliable instrument for the mastery of history in the interest of humanity. Postmodernists may be right in thinking that this faith is no longer plausible. The benefits of this kind of politics have been too meagre and the disasters too calamitous to inspire much confidence. We are left with an uncomfortable dilemma. It is hard to deny that there is continuing need for effective principles of political engagement and critique, if only for the sake of those who have scarcely begun to benefit from the achievements of modernity. On the other hand, this is to assume that modernity does convey some benefit, and one that is not cancelled by a greater loss. Political engagement is unavoidable, its value inevitably in doubt.

Notes

——

Chapter 1 Introduction: What is Continental Philosophy?

1 If reference is nevertheless made to 'a' continental tradition, this term should always be understood as an abbreviation for a more complex constellation of thinkers and ideas.
2 Thus although the eighteenth-century Scottish philosopher David Hume casts doubt even on our knowledge of relations of cause and effect, which underpins all scientific knowledge concerning matters of fact, at the same time he defines his whole project as an attempt to apply the methods of natural science to the 'sciences of man': D. Hume, *A Treatise of Human Nature*, p. xx.
3 The main themes of modern European philosophy, the Enlightenment and its continental critics will be discussed in the following chapter.
4 At this point some readers may wish to proceed directly to ch. 2.
5 See Willis Kirk, 'The Introduction and Critical Reception of Hegelian Thought in Britain, 1830–1900' and P. M. Kennedy, 'Idealists and Realists: British Views of Germany, 1864–1939'.
6 A. N. Whitehead and B. Russell, *Principia Mathematica*. For a classic history of recent analytical and continental philosophy, see J. Passmore, *A Hundred Years of Philosophy*. The second edition contains useful additional material on continental philosophy.
7 David Hume, *Enquiry Concerning Human Understanding*, Book IV, part I, sections 20–1, pp. 25–6.
8 Michael Dummett quoted in David E. Cooper, 'The Presidential Address: Analytical and Continental Philosophy', p. 11.
9 A. J. Ayer, *Language, Truth and Logic*, pp. 59–61.
10 See ch. 4.
11 Of course, Wittgenstein's philosophy was also significantly influenced by continental currents of thought. Members of the Vienna Circle included Moritz Schlick and Rudolf Carnap.
12 Gilbert Ryle, *The Concept of Mind*.

13 On developments in France and Germany see V. Descombes, *Modern French Philosophy* and R. Bubner, *Modern German Philosophy*.

14 J. Derrida, 'The Ends of Man', in *Margins of Philosophy*, p. 114.

15 A recent attempt from an analytical point of view is Cooper, 'Analytical and Continental Philosophy', who also mentions John Passmore, *Recent Philosophers*, P. F. Strawson, *Analysis and Metaphysics* and Michael Dummett, 'Can Analytical Philosophy be Systematic, and Ought it to be?'

Chapter 2 Modernity, Enlightenment and their Continental Critics

1 See M. Weber, *Economy and Society*, vol. 1, pp. 85–6 and passim. For an accessible account of Weber see J. Keane, *Public Life and Late Capitalism*, ch. 2 or D. G. MacRae, *Weber*. See also S. Lash and S. Whimster, eds, *Max Weber, Rationality and Modernity*.

2 Weber, *Economy and Society*, vol. 2, pp. 882–9. On Roman law see also, for example, Myron P. Gilmore, *Arguments from Roman Law in Political Thought 1200–1600* and Paul Sigmund, *Natural Law in Political Thought*, or A. D. E. Lewis and D. J. Ibbetson, eds, *The Roman Law Tradition*.

3 In fact, Harold Berman argues that the popes of the eleventh and twelfth centuries were responsible for the spread of Roman law, when they adapted it for the reform of canon law. See H. J. Berman, *Law and Revolution*.

4 Even when religious belief is retained, it tends to be reinterpreted so as to be compatible with more rational procedures.

5 See N. Machiavelli, *The Prince*.

6 See, for example, Marc Bloch, *Feudal Society*. On some of the developments occurring during the medieval period see M. Oakeshott, 'The Masses in Representative Democracy', in *Rationalism in Politics, and Other Essays*, Richard Tuck, *Natural Rights Theories* and Quentin Skinner, *The Foundations of Modern Political Thought*.

7 See Jürgen Habermas, *Philosophical Discourse of Modernity*.

8 Ibid., p. 5.

9 Ibid. Here Habermas also draws on the work of Kossellek. Compare Skinner, Tuck and Oakeshott (see note 6) who locate this transition somewhat earlier, from around the thirteenth century.

10 See for example Daniel Defoe's novel *Robinson Crusoe* (1719) or some of the *contes* or stories of Voltaire.

11 On these developments in art see E. H. Gombrich, *Symbolic Images: Studies in the Art of the Renaissance*.

12 F. Bacon, *The Advancement of Learning*, p. 8; and see the third essay in M. Oakeshott, *On Human Conduct*, esp. p. 288.

13 Bacon, quoted by M. Oakeshott, 'Rationalism in Politics', in *Rationalism in Politics*, p. 15.

14 Ironically Nicolaus Copernicus (1473–1543) was inspired to propose heliocentrism by his enthusiasm for sun-worship. It was Johannes Kepler (1571–1630) who, in his *Astronomia Nova* of 1609, was able to simplify calculations of these movements with his assumption that the motion of planets is elliptical rather than circular.

15 See B. Brecht, *Life of Galileo* and G. Galilei, *Dialogue on Two World Systems* (1632).

16 This view of the world supports the 'argument from design' for the existence of God. See, for example, Aquinas' arguments for the existence of God, which relied heavily on newly discovered texts of Aristotle: Mary T. Clark, ed., *An Aquinas Reader*, pp. 115–27. Contemporary ecology manifests a rather different appreciation of the order in nature.

17 Charles Taylor, *Hegel*, p. 4.

18 On Descartes see, for example, Bernard Williams, *Descartes* or Jonathan Rée, *Descartes*.

19 R. Descartes, 'Meditations on First Philosophy', pp. 151–2. Of course, even the claim that the occurrence of a thought implies the existence of an 'I' which thinks would be doubted, most notably by Hume (see below, p. 89, note 38) and see Rée, *Descartes*, ch. 6.

20 Taylor, *Hegel*, pp. 8ff.

21 Bacon, *The Advancement of Learning*, p. 35.

22 It is also worth noting that Newton spent a considerable portion of his later life studying alchemy, astrology and theology.

23 See Marlowe's play *Doctor Faustus* (1592), Goethe's *Faust* (1808, 1832) and Mary Shelley's *Frankenstein* (1818).

24 Descartes, 'Meditations', VI, esp. pp. 172ff.

25 Bacon, *Advancement of Learning*; J. Locke, *Essay concerning Human Understanding*, pp. 6ff, 296.

26 I. Kant, 'An Answer to the Question: What is Enlightenment?', p. 41.

27 In fact, similar views had already been advanced, though in cautious or veiled terms, by earlier modern philosophers such as Thomas Hobbes. See Hobbes, *Leviathan* and cf. the Introduction to this edition by K. R. Minogue, esp. pp. xxi ff.

28 For Hume's analysis of causality see *Treatise of Human Nature*, Book I, part III or *Enquiry Concerning Human Understanding*, section VII.

29 Hume, *Treatise of Human Nature*, pp. xix ff.

30 Hume, *Enquiry Concerning Human Understanding*, section X, and *Dialogues concerning Natural Religion*.

31 Hume, *Treatise of Human Nature*, p. 470.

32 Ibid., p. 299.

33 Ibid., p. 471. Significantly, this view allows no clear distinction between aesthetic and ethical experience. For Hume the distinction rests only on the kinds of object valued – objects or things in the world may be beautiful; virtues, characters and actions are good or bad.

34 On Kant's moral philosophy see the following section.

35 For a concise account of Kant's philosophy see R. Scruton, *Kant*. An important recent study is Henry E. Allison, *Kant's Transcendental Idealism*. See also C. D. Broad, *Kant: An Introduction* or S. Körner, *Kant*.

36 Kant, *Critique of Pure Reason*, p. 7.

37 On the debate between rationalism and empiricism see R. Scruton, *A Short History of Modern Philosophy*, parts I–II or B. Aune, *Rationalism, Empiricism, and Pragmatism*.

38 Plato, *Phaedo*, 72B, pp. 120ff.

39 See Plato, *Meno*, 82, pp. 130ff.

40 Kant, *Critique of Pure Reason*, p. 93.

41 Kant, *Critique of Pure Reason*, pp. 22–3. On Copernicus and Galileo, see above pp. 11–12. Ironically, the effect of Kant's revolution is, in a sense, to reinstate the human subject at the centre of its world.

42 Allison, *Kant's Transcendental Idealism*, p. 7.

43 Ibid., p. 8. A fuller account is provided by Allison, *Kant's Transcendental Idealism*, chs 1–3.
44 Ibid., p. 7.
45 Allison, *Kant's Transcendental Idealism*, ch. 2, section B.
46 Ibid., p. 38. See Allison, *Kant's Transcendental Idealism*, ch. 3, for a useful discussion of the cosmological argument.
47 For a detailed discussion of the transcendental deduction see Allison, *Kant's Transcendental Idealism*, ch. 7.
48 The latter seems to be the strategy of P. F. Strawson, *The Bounds of Sense* and cf. his more recent 'Sensibility, Understanding, and the Doctrine of Synthesis'.
49 Kant, *Critique of Pure Reason*, quoted above p. 17.
50 Dieter Henrich, 'Kant's Notion of a Transcendental Deduction and the Methodological Background of the First *Critique*', p. 41.
51 Kant, 'What is Enlightenment?' p. 41.
52 Ibid., pp. 41 & 46.
53 See Julien Offray de La Mettrie, *Man a Machine*.
54 See above p. 16.
55 Kant, *Critique of Pure Reason*, p. 29 and cf. Scruton, *Kant*, ch. 2.
56 I. Kant, *Groundwork of the Metaphysic of Morals*, pp. 88, 95.
57 S. Hampshire, 'The Social Spirit of Mankind', p. 145.
58 Ibid., p. 152.
59 Reinhard Brandt, 'The Deductions in the *Critique of Judgment*', p. 186.
60 F. Schiller, *Über die ästhetische Erziehung des Menschen*, pp. 56–7.
61 Indeed, the terms 'conservative' (earlier 'conservatory') and 'reaction' only capture distinct political positions on the assumption of an established direction of history as 'progress' or 'improvement'. The notion of progress as an 'evident or discoverable general movement of history' was first apparent in the 'Universal histories of the Enlightenment': see R. Williams, *Keywords*, p. 206. 'Reactionary' was first used in its modern political sense in contemporary French reactions to the Revolution of 1789, to describe those 'wishing to re-establish a pre-revolutionary state of affairs': ibid., p. 215.
62 J.-J. Rousseau, 'Discourse on the Origin of Inequality', p. 104.
63 Ibid., p. 64.
64 Ibid., p. 66n.
65 Ibid.
66 Ibid., p. 81.
67 This is despite his famous intention of 'laying all facts aside', a pledge which in context refers to the 'facts' of religion: ibid., p. 45.
68 Ibid., pp. 112–13.
69 This is not to deny that some of Rousseau's remarks lend support to such an interpretation, for example the first sentence of Rousseau's *Émile*, according to which 'God makes all things good; man meddles with them and they become evil': p. 35.
70 Rousseau, 'Discourse on the Origin of Inequality', p. 45.
71 See T. Hobbes, *Leviathan*, ch. 17, pp. 87ff. 'Leviathan', in Hebrew a kind of monster, is Hobbes's term for the sovereign collective entity created by the social contract or, in effect, the state.
72 Rousseau, 'Discourse on the Origin of Inequality', p. 45.
73 Ibid., pp. 177–8.

74 See above, pp. 24–6.
75 Rousseau, *Social Contract*, Book I, ch. VII, p. 177.
76 In John Keane's words, Rousseau describes 'an individualism of coopera-
    tion and uniqueness (*Einzigkeit*) compared with that of mere singleness
    (*Einzelheit*)': J. Keane, *Public Life and Late Capitalism*, p. 254.
77 J. G. Herder, *Discourse on the Origin of Language*.
78 See I. Berlin, *The Crooked Timber of Humanity*, p. 39.
79 Ibid., p. 210.
80 Ibid., p. 37.
81 R. C. Solomon, *Continental Philosophy since 1750*, p. 13.
82 Sentiment figures prominently in novels like Henry Fielding's *Tom Jones*
    (1749).
83 Berlin, *The Crooked Timber of Humanity*, p. 215.
84 Taylor, *Hegel*, pp. 15–16.
85 Ibid., p. 17. See also C. Taylor, *Sources of the Self*, ch. 21.
86 This remains, of course, a disputed claim. Some Kantians argue that the
    universalization principle is capable of supporting a determinate moral con-
    clusion, for example, Lucien Goldman, *Immanuel Kant*. More conventional-
    ly, T. C. Williams, *The Concept of the Categorical Imperative*, defends the
    assumption that 'reason can be "practical" and can, of itself alone, be the
    motive of actions' (p. 4) and see esp. ch. 9.
87 Kant, *Groundwork of the Metaphysic of Morals*, pp. 57–8.
88 G. W. F. Hegel, *The Phenomenology of Mind*, pp. 601–2. The translation of
    this work by A. V. Miller, *Hegel's Phenomenology of Spirit*, is generally
    clearer than J. B. Baillie's translation, cited here.
89 Ibid., p. 604.
90 G. W. F. Hegel, *The Philosophy of Right*, para. 139, p. 92.
91 In the terms of a later tradition, the Kantian reconstruction is based on a
    process which is purely 'monological' rather than 'dialogical'. Although
    universalization involves considering what would happen if all subjects were
    to adopt a particular maxim, the process of deliberation can in principle be
    carried out by a single subject in isolation. There is no genuine recognition
    of the other. On this distinction in relation to Habermas, see T. McCarthy,
    The Critical Theory of Jürgen Habermas, pp. 326ff. As we shall see, this
    requirement also implies the importance of history. If individuals must
    always be understood as members of a concrete community and culture,
    then they must also be understood historically.
92 Hegel, *The Philosophy of Right*, p. 23.
93 In terms more often used by Fichte and subsequent commentators than by
    Hegel himself, the contradictions within a particular 'thesis' lead to an
    opposing thesis or 'antithesis'. The antithesis in turn gives way to a new
    position, which preserves the 'truth' of both thesis and antithesis and so
    represents a higher 'synthesis'. Hegel speaks rather of the 'negation' of
    a 'truth' leading to its 'sublation' or 'transcendence' (*Aufheben*). In fact,
    Hegel's use of the dialectic is far less mechanical than some descriptions
    suggest.
94 G. W. F. Hegel, *The Philosophy of History*, p. 19.
95 See Hegel, *The Philosophy of History*. For a succinct account of Hegel's
    philosophy of history see P. Singer, *Hegel*, ch. 2 or Taylor, *Hegel*, part IV.
96 Singer, *Hegel*, p. 51. See also the Preface to Hegel's *The Phenomenology of
    Mind*.

97 Richard Norman, *Hegel's Phenomenology*, p. 14. See also Taylor, *Hegel*, part II.
98 Hegel, quoted by Norman, *Hegel's Phenomenology*, p. 17.
99 Taylor, *Hegel*, pp. 109–10.
100 J. N. Findlay, *Hegel: A Re-examination*, p. 23.
101 Other aspects of Hegel's many-sided philosophy will be introduced in the context of these responses.

Chapter 3 Dialectics of Emancipation: Marx, the Frankfurt School and Habermas

1 Hegel saw America as a new moment in the unfolding of history. See W. Kaufmann, 'The Hegel Myth and its Method'.
2 See above, ch. 1, n. 7 and ch. 2, pp. 40–1.
3 On the Frankfurt School and Habermas see the second and third sections of this chapter, pp. 55–78. On the relationship of Marxism and postmodernism, see ch. 7, pp. 190–3.
4 David McLellan, *Karl Marx: His Life and Thought*, p. 128.
5 Some, such as Michael Oakeshott, have argued that Marx fundamentally misunderstands Hegel as a result. See M. Oakeshott, 'Michael Oakeshott on Marx on Hegel'.
6 Compare the atheist conservatism of David Hume with the defiant immorality of the Marquis de Sade (1740–1814).
7 Voltaire, *Épîtres*, no. 96, 'À l'Auteur du livre des trois imposteurs', in *Oxford Dictionary of Quotations*, p. 716.
8 L. Feuerbach, *Essence of Christianity*, p. 14.
9 Ibid., p. 26.
10 Ibid., p. 13.
11 Ibid., p. 13.
12 E. Kamenka, *The Philosophy of Ludwig Feuerbach*, p. 39. The allusion to psychoanalysis here is appropriate, since Feuerbach, who also describes religion as 'the dream of the human mind', provides a model for Freud's subsequent 'demystification' of dreams and other aberrations from the self-transparency of the conscious mind (see below, ch. 6, pp. 157–9).
13 L. Feuerbach, *Principles of the Philosophy of the Future* (1843).
14 Feuerbach quoted by Kamenka, *The Philosophy of Ludwig Feuerbach*, pp. 78, 80.
15 Ibid., p. 76.
16 K. Marx, 'Critique of Hegel's Doctrine of the State' (1843) and 'On the Jewish Question' (1843).
17 See K. Marx, *The Civil War in France* and *Critique of the Gotha Programme*. Cf. Bob Jessop, *The Capitalist State* and *State Theory*.
18 Marx, 'On the Jewish Question', pp. 218, 217.
19 D. McLellan, *Marx*, p. 29.
20 Marx, 'On the Jewish Question', pp. 227, 229.
21 Marx, 'Hegel's Doctrine of the State', p. 191.
22 Adam Smith, *The Wealth of Nations* (1776), vol. 1, IV, ii, 9, p. 456. There were of course also substantial disagreements between the classical political

economists, e.g. over the degree of compatibility of the interests of landowners, wage-labourers and capitalists. See for example, M. Blaug, *Economic Theory in Retrospect*, B. Burkitt, *Radical Political Economy* and M. C. Howard and J. E. King, *The History of Marxian Economics*.

23 Engels famously described the miserable conditions endured by the working classes at the height of the industrial revolution in England in *The Condition of the Working Class in England in 1844*.

24 Marx, 'On the Jewish Question', p. 233.

25 Marx, 'Economic and Philosophical Manuscripts', p. 333.

26 Ibid., pp. 328–9. For some, this notion reflects an early 'essentialist' or 'humanist' Marx, superseded in the writings of the mature Marx.

27 Ibid., pp. 325–31.

28 McLellan, *Marx*, p. 39.

29 Karl Marx and Friedrich Engels, *The German Ideology*, p. 62.

30 Marx, 'Theses on Feuerbach', p. 423.

31 Marx and Engels, *The German Ideology*, p. 48.

32 Hegel sees the struggle by one subject for recognition by another as an essential stage in the development of consciousness. But in seeking recognition, consciousness enters into a dialectical struggle, in which the dominated subject is reduced to the status of object, and so becomes incapable of delivering true recognition as opposed to the mere obedience of a slave. Hegel's dialectic culminates in a stage of harmonious mutual recognition and equality. The stage of mutual recognition and harmony corresponds to the classless society of communism. The dialectic of lordship and bondage is discussed in Hegel, *Phenomenology of Mind*, pp. 228–40, and see R. Norman, *Hegel's Phenomenology*, ch. 3 and A. Kojève, *Introduction to the Reading of Hegel*.

33 Marx and Engels, *The German Ideology*, p. 58.

34 Ibid., p. 64.

35 Ibid., p. 57.

36 K. Marx, *Critique of the Gotha Programme*, p. 16.

37 See K. Marx and F. Engels, *The Communist Manifesto*, p. 16.

38 Marx, *Critique of the Gotha Programme*, p. 17.

39 Marx and Engels, *The Communist Manifesto*, p. 17.

40 See in particular K. Marx, *Grundrisse* and *Capital*. I discuss the economic and sociological theory here only in so far as it helps to clarify, both what Marx and Engels understood by 'scientific' as opposed to 'utopian' socialism, and what Frankfurt School theorists would later mean by a 'critical theory' of society.

41 Marx, 'Theses on Feuerbach', pp. 421–3.

42 This view is in fact much closer to Feuerbach than to Marx.

43 McLellan, *Marx*, p. 75.

44 An early use of this term was in Engels's article 'On Historical Materialism'. See T. Carver, *Engels*, p. 38. Bertell Ollman, *Alienation*, offers a rather different interpretation of Engels's role.

45 On Comte and positivism see below, pp. 58–9.

46 T. Carver, *Friedrich Engels: His Life and Thought*, p. 238. The text referred to is F. Engels, 'The Part Played by Labour in the Transition from Ape to Man' (1896).

47 F. Engels, letter to J. Bloch, 21 September 1890, quoted in *Fontana Dictionary of Modern Thought*, p. 285.

48 It is worth noting, however, that Marx himself did not have a fixed opinion on this question, recognizing the possibility of revolutionary transformations in the less developed regions of Europe including Russia. See McLellan, *Marx*, pp. 62ff.
49 See F. Fukuyama, *The End of History* and cf. E. J. Hobsbawm et al., *The Forward March of Labour Halted*.
50 On Althusser see Gregory Elliott, *Althusser*, T. Benton, *The Rise and Fall of Structural Marxism*, and see below, ch. 6, pp. 167–8. On Sartre's Marxism see M. Poster, *Sartre's Marxism* and below, ch. 5, pp. 149–50. In contrasting style the 'analytical Marxism' of Jon Elster and G. Cohen is closely related to the analytical tradition in philosophy. See for example, J. Elster, *An Introduction to Karl Marx* and G. A. Cohen, *Karl Marx's Theory of History: A Defence*.
51 Marx's *Economic and Philosophical Manuscripts* was first published in 1932. Nor was the *German Ideology*, written in 1846, published in the lifetime of Marx and Engels either.
52 T. Adorno and M. Horkheimer, *Dialectic of Enlightenment*, p. x.
53 For the definitive history of the Frankfurt School see Rolf Wiggershaus, *The Frankfurt School*. For the period 1923–50 see Martin Jay, *The Dialectical Imagination*. For an account which also discusses Jürgen Habermas see David Held, *Introduction to Critical Theory*.
54 See Held, *Introduction to Critical Theory*, ch. 2. On some interpretations, though, these developments are not really incompatible with Marx's theory of crisis: see for example Simon Clarke, *Marx's Theory of Crisis*.
55 M. Horkheimer, *Critical Theory*, p. vi.
56 See H. Marcuse, *Soviet Marxism*.
57 Marx, 'Theses on Feuerbach', p. 423 (quoted above).
58 G. Lukács, *History and Class Consciousness*, p. 1.
59 For an alternative account see P. Dunne, *Quantitative Marxism* and Clarke, *Marx's Theory of Crisis*.
60 For a critique of this conception from a Trotskyist point of view see C. Harman and A. Callinicos, *The Changing Working Class*.
61 The inability of the working class to get beyond merely 'trade union consciousness' without the leadership of the 'vanguard party' is alleged in V. I. Lenin, *What is to be Done?*, esp. parts II–IV.
62 R. Williams, *Keywords*, p. 200.
63 Hume, *Treatise*, p. xx.
64 Raymond Geuss, *The Idea of a Critical Theory*, p. 2.
65 M. Horkheimer 'Traditional and Critical Theory' (1937), in *Critical Theory* and see T. Adorno et al., *The Positivist Dispute in German Sociology*.
66 Marcuse, *Soviet Marxism*.
67 Compare the similar analysis of C. Castoriadis in *The Imaginary Institution of Society*, part I.
68 See S. Lukes, *Marxism and Morality*, ch. 6.
69 Marcuse quoted by Held, *Introduction to Critical Theory*, p. 85.
70 H. Marcuse, *Counterrevolution and Revolt*, p. 107.
71 See T. W. Adorno, *Aesthetic Theory* and *The Culture Industry*. See also L. Zuidervaart, *Adorno's Aesthetic Theory*.
72 H. Marcuse, *One-Dimensional Man*, p. 155.
73 In their more favourable evaluation of 'bourgeois' art and philosophy, Frankfurt theorists were again closer to the Marx of the *Economic and*

Philosophical Manuscripts, with its extensive quotation from Shakespeare for example, than to the 'socialist realism' and 'agitprop' of Soviet communism. Their relationship to contemporary artistic movements that attempted to combine politics and art was a complex one. See Jay, *The Dialectical Imagination*, ch. 6.

74 Horkheimer, *Critical Theory*, p. 218.
75 Ibid., p. 213.
76 See Held, *Introduction to Critical Theory*, p. 178.
77 Ibid., pp. 205, 181–2. In this respect, Adorno and Horkheimer anticipate the warnings about 'totalizing theories' made more recently by theorists like Foucault and Deleuze (see below, ch. 6).
78 T. W. Adorno, *Negative Dialectics*. See Held, *Introduction to Critical Theory*, ch. 7 and Gillian Rose, *The Melancholy Science*.
79 At the same time, Frankfurt theorists were critical of what they saw as Nietzsche's elitist, anti-democratic and even anti-political philosophy. For a fuller account of Nietzsche see below, ch. 5.
80 Habermas, *Philosophical Discourse of Modernity*, p. 108. See Adorno and Horkheimer, *Dialectic of Enlightenment*.
81 Adorno and Horkheimer, *Dialectic of Enlightenment*, p. 5.
82 Held, *Introduction to Critical Theory*, p. 151.
83 Adorno and Horkheimer, *Dialectic of Enlightenment*, p. 12.
84 Ibid., pp. 4, 9.
85 Ibid., pp. 25 and ff.
86 Habermas, *Philosophical Discourse of Modernity*, p. 110.
87 Adorno and Horkheimer, *Dialectic of Enlightenment*, p. 86.
88 On Weber's account of the rationalization of society see above, ch. 2, pp. 8–9.
89 On the distinction between formal and substantive rationality see M. Weber, *Economy and Society*, vol. 1, pp. 85–6.
90 S. Freud, *Civilization and its Discontents*.
91 H. Marcuse, *Eros and Civilization*. Compare the theories of Wilhelm Reich's *The Invasion of Compulsory Sex-Morality*.
92 W. Benjamin, 'The Work of Art in the Age of Mechanical Reproduction' in *Illuminations*, p. 223.
93 Ibid., p. 225.
94 Ibid., p. 236.
95 Ibid., pp. 243–4. Walter Benjamin committed suicide in 1940 whilst attempting to escape Nazi rule.
96 On Benjamin's aesthetics see Susan Buck-Morss, *The Origin of Negative Dialectics*. 'Agitprop' was originally the Department of Agitation and Propaganda of the Communist Party of the Soviet Union, set up in 1920.
97 T. W. Adorno, 'Culture industry reconsidered', in *The Culture Industry*, p. 85.
98 Held, *Introduction to Critical Theory*, pp. 94–6 and cf. T. W. Adorno, 'How to Look at Television', in *The Culture Industry*.
99 P. Connerton, *Tragedy of Enlightenment*, ch. 3 esp. pp. 55ff.
100 Adorno quoted by J. M. Bernstein, Introduction to Adorno, *The Culture Industry*, p. 13.
101 Adorno, *The Culture Industry*, p. 43.
102 Ibid., p. 52.
103 Ibid., p. 85.

104 See Marcuse, *One-Dimensional Man*.
105 Connerton, *Tragedy of Enlightenment*, pp. 58–9 and cf. J. Habermas, *The Structural Transformation of the Public Sphere*.
106 Marcuse, *One-Dimensional Man*, pp. 199–200.
107 Connerton, *Tragedy of Enlightenment*, p. 102.
108 The phrase derives originally from Romain Rolland. See A. Gramsci, *Selections from the Prison Notebooks*, p. 175 and note.
109 Habermas diverges from the earlier Frankfurt School in ways which reflect, among other things, his less sympathetic attitude to Nietzsche. For useful introductions to the ideas of Habermas see William Outhwaite, *Habermas*, Held, *Introduction to Critical Theory*, part II and McCarthy, *The Critical Theory of Jürgen Habermas*.
110 Labour is the equivalent of the Weberian notion of rationalization and the concept of instrumental rationality as used by earlier members of the Frankfurt School.
111 J. Habermas, 'Technology and Science as "Ideology"' in *Toward a Rational Society*, p. 92.
112 Ibid., p. 87.
113 Ibid., p. 92.
114 See above, p. 49ff.
115 Habermas, *The Structural Transformation of the Public Sphere*, pp. 25–6.
116 Decisionism is the view that, in the absence of objective criteria, moral values can be nothing more than the product of arbitrary decisions.
117 Habermas, *Toward a Rational Society*, p. 90 and cf. *The Structural Transformation of the Public Sphere*, parts V–VI.
118 On the distinction between forces and relations of production see above, pp. 49, 69.
119 Held, *Introduction to Critical Theory*, ch. 10. See also J. Habermas, *Zur Rekonstruktion des historischen Materialismus*.
120 J. Habermas, *Knowledge and Human Interests*, p. 309.
121 A classic exposition of the hypothetico-deductive account of science is provided by C. G. Hempel, *Aspects of Scientific Explanation*.
122 Habermas, *Knowledge and Human Interests*, p. 91 and see below ch. 5 passim.
123 Ibid., p. 93.
124 Habermas quoted by Held, *Introduction to Critical Theory*, p. 303.
125 Habermas, *Knowledge and Human Interests*, ch. 7.
126 Ibid., p. 313.
127 Ibid., p. 175. On Dilthey and hermeneutics see below, ch. 4.
128 Habermas, *Knowledge and Human Interests*, p. 310.
129 Habermas, *Zur Rekonstruktion des historischen Materialismus*, pp. 10–11.
130 Habermas, *Knowledge and Human Interests*, p. 314.
131 McCarthy, *The Critical Theory of Jürgen Habermas*, p. 7. In fact, this 'linguistic turn' is paralleled in much of the century's analytical and continental philosophy.
132 Habermas quoted by McCarthy, *The Critical Theory of Jürgen Habermas*, p. 288.
133 J. Habermas, *Über Sprachtheorie*, p. 17, my translation.
134 J. Habermas, 'Wahrheitstheorien', p. 226, my translation. The American pragmatist C. S. Peirce is an important source of Habermas's consensus theory of truth.

135 See below, ch. 7, pp. 199–201. See the discussion in McCarthy, *The Critical Theory of Jürgen Habermas*, ch. 4 and S. Benhabib and F. Dallmayr, *The Communicative Ethics Controversy* or J. Thompson and D. Held, *Habermas: Critical Debates*.

136 J. Habermas, 'Discourse ethics' and 'Morality and ethical life' in his *Moral Consciousness and Communicative Action* and P. Dews, Introduction to J. Habermas, *Autonomy and Solidarity*, pp. 18ff.

137 Habermas, *Philosophical Discourse of Modernity*, p. 312.

Chapter 4 Historicism, Hermeneutics and Phenomenology

1 Historicism in the sense discussed here should not be confused with Karl Popper's somewhat eccentric use of the term to refer to philosophies of history which are committed to a belief in overall laws of historical development: see *The Poverty of Historicism*. The Enlightenment was also associated with significant contributions to the writing of history, notably Edward Gibbon's (1737–94), *The History of the Decline and Fall of the Roman Empire* (1776–88), as well as works of Herder, Fichte and the Grimm brothers.

2 See ch. 2, pp. 36–38.

3 See Hegel, *Philosophy of Right*, para. 348, p. 218 and cf. para. 344, p. 217. Related assumptions are made by the 'Whig interpretation of history', classically expressed in Herbert Butterfield, *The Whig Interpretation of History*.

4 This development is associated with the German nineteenth-century 'critical historians' Leopold von Ranke (1795–1886) and Theodor Mommsen (1817–1903) among others.

5 See Taylor, *Hegel*, pp. 34ff. On romanticism see above, pp. 33–34.

6 On Kierkegaard and the development of existentialism see below, ch. 5.

7 Bollnow, quoted in Richard E. Palmer, *Hermeneutics*, p. 101.

8 Thus, for historians like Ranke and Droysen the category of life plays a similar role to the concept of spirit in Hegelianism.

9 On the meaning of speculative idealism see above, p. 34.

10 This possibility finds some confirmation in the writings of Schopenhauer.

11 The German word *Geisteswissenschaften*, literally the systematic study of spirit or mind (*Geist*), signals the connection with the ideas of both Herder and Hegel.

12 Dilthey in *W. Dilthey: Selected Writings*, from 'Introduction to the Human Studies', pp. 161–2. Dilthey uses the word *Erlebnis* as opposed to *Erfahrung* to refer to experience which is not merely intellectual or cognitive but also affective, a part of life in the fullest sense. This emphasis, characteristic of life philosophy, is reflected in the etymological relationship between *Erlebnis* and *Leben* (life).

13 Rickman in Introduction to *W. Dilthey: Selected Writings*, p. 17.

14 This phrase is the subtitle of W. Dilthey, *Introduction to the Human Sciences*.

15 Dilthey, from 'Ideas about a Descriptive and Analytical Psychology', in *W. Dilthey: Selected Writings*, p. 88.

16 Dilthey, 'The Development of Hermeneutics', in *W. Dilthey: Selected Writings*, p. 248.

17 Ibid., p. 248.
18 Quoted by Palmer, *Hermeneutics*, p. 115.
19 Rickman, Introduction, *W. Dilthey: Selected Writings*, p. 20.
20 Dilthey, 'The Rise of Hermeneutics', in H. A. Hodges, *Wilhelm Dilthey*, pp. 125–6.
21 As Foucault helpfully remarks, Hermes is also reputed to have taught human beings how to masturbate – through the good offices of Pan . . . 'And the shepherds seem to have learned it subsequently from Pan': M. Foucault, *The Care of the Self*, p. 140.
22 Foucault, *The Care of the Self*, p. 6.
23 Palmer, *Hermeneutics*, pp. 35ff.
24 There was a related growth at this time in the comparative and historical study of languages or philology. For an account of the development of philology in the nineteenth century see H. Pedersen, *The Discovery of Language*.
25 D. E. Linge, Introduction to H.-G. Gadamer, *Philosophical Hermeneutics*, p. xiii.
26 Dilthey, 'Development of Hermeneutics', p. 259.
27 For example, see David Wootton's scholarly Introduction to Locke's *Political Writings* on their relationship to the 'Glorious Revolution' of 1688.
28 David Boucher, *Texts in Context*, p. 21.
29 Dilthey, 'Development of Hermeneutics', p. 258.
30 Rickman, Introduction, *W. Dilthey: Selected Writings*, p. 15.
31 Habermas, *Knowledge and Human Interests*, p. 147.
32 H. A. Hodges, *The Philosophy of Wilhelm Dilthey*, pp. 141–2.
33 E. Husserl, 'Philosophy as Rigorous Science', p. 81.
34 Dilthey quoted by Husserl, 'Philosophy as Rigorous Science', p. 124. Incidentally Dilthey returns the favour, describing Husserl as 'A true Plato, who first of all fixes in concepts things that become and flow and then supplements the fixed concept with a concept of flowing' (ibid., p. 124, editor's note 62).
35 P. Dews, *Logics of Disintegration*, p. 6.
36 Husserl, 'Philosophy as Rigorous Science', p. 72.
37 Ibid., pp. 145–6. One of Husserl's major works is entitled *Cartesian Meditations*.
38 See above, ch. 2. For Descartes it is at least certain that I exist as a thing which thinks and perceives. For the even more persistent scepticism of Hume we can be certain only that there are sensations – and then only at the time of their occurrence. What we cannot be sure of is that these sensations provide us with indubitable knowledge of an external reality or even that 'I' exist as an enduring subject of experience.
39 For a more detailed account of Kant's philosophy, see above, ch. 2.
40 See E. Husserl, *Ideas*, para. 62, p. 166.
41 E. Husserl, *Logical Investigations*, vol. 1, p. 42.
42 Cited by Edo Pivcevic, *Husserl and Phenomenology*, p. 149.
43 While much of Frege's critique is arguably based on misunderstanding, he rightly points out that in this work Husserl fails to distinguish between describing what number is and describing what it is for us to understand number concepts. This is something which Husserl himself had begun to appreciate by the time the *Philosophy of Arithmetic* appeared. On Husserl's

early work see J. Mohanty, *Edmund Husserl's Theory of Meaning* and D. Willard, *Logic and the Objectivity of Knowledge*. For a contrasting view see, D. Føllesdal, *Husserl und Frege* or H. L. Dreyfus and H. Hall, *Husserl, Intentionality and Cognitive Science*. It was Frege's criticism of Husserl which helped to inspire Russell and Whitehead's account of the foundations of mathematics and so contributed to the birth of contemporary analytical philosophy (see above, ch. 1).

44 Husserl, 'Philosophy as Rigorous Science', p. 86.
45 Pivcevic, *Husserl and Phenomenology*, p. 42.
46 Passmore, *A Hundred Years of Philosophy*, p. 176.
47 Husserl, 'Philosophy as Rigorous Science', p. 104.
48 Passmore, *A Hundred Years of Philosophy*, p. 178. See also H.-G. Gadamer, 'The Phenomenological Movement', in *Philosophical Hermeneutics*, pp. 155–6.
49 Franz Brentano, *Psychology from an Empirical Standpoint*, pp. 88–9. Husserl acknowledges the importance of Brentano's criterion of the mental in *Ideas*, para. 85, p. 229.
50 Brentano, *Psychology from an Empirical Standpoint*, pp. 93ff. Within the analytical tradition in philosophy the relation between intentionality in Brentano's sense and the 'intensionality' of certain kinds of sentence, including those describing mental states (e.g. 'I believe that . . .', 'I imagine that . . .' in contrast to 'I stroked (the dog)' etc.) has been shown to be a complex one. See D. Carr, 'Intentionality' and J. L. Mackie, 'Problems of Intentionality', in E. Pivcevic, ed., *Phenomenology and Philosophical Understanding*.
51 This concern also preoccupied another of Brentano's students, Alexius von Meinong (1853–1928).
52 Pivcevic, *Husserl and Phenomenology*, p. 76.
53 The term has been used in German philosophy in a variety of different senses, for example by J. H. Lambert (in 1764), Herder, Kant, Fichte, Hegel and others. See J. Hoffmeister, *Wörterbuch der philosophischen Begriffe*, pp. 463ff.
54 Husserl, *Ideas*, para. 32, pp. 99–100.
55 Husserl, 'Philosophy as Rigorous Science', pp. 110, 112. Of course, the distinction between essence and existence also plays a crucial role both for Heidegger and for existentialism (see following section and below, ch. 5).
56 Husserl, *Ideas*, para. 53, pp. 150–1.
57 Husserl, 'Philosophy as Rigorous Science', p. 111.
58 Whether phenomenology can really *explain* this achievement is, of course, more controversial.
59 Husserl, 'Philosophy as Rigorous Science', p. 89.
60 See Husserl, *Ideas*, para. 62, p. 166 and *The Crisis of European Sciences*, pp. 87–8. Cf. Passmore, *A Hundred Years of Philosophy*, p. 189.
61 Husserl, *The Crisis of European Sciences*, pp. 5–6.
62 Pivcevic, *Husserl and Phenomenology*, p. 88, and compare the very similar concerns of members of the Frankfurt School (see above, ch. 3).
63 Husserl, *The Crisis of European Sciences*, pp. 104–5. Compare Habermas's notion of the 'life-world' in *Theory of Communicative Action*.
64 It also seems to be no coincidence that Husserl's language begins to show

signs of the influence of Heidegger, who provides something close to a phenomenological analysis of the life-world.

65 Bubner, *Modern German Philosophy*, p. 21. Indeed, in his predilection for technical terms as well as in many of his philosophical concerns Husserl has much in common with philosophical contemporaries and successors who, despite their 'continental' origins, are now regarded as securely within the analytical tradition – e.g. Frege, Carnap and Wittgenstein.

66 See for example M. Merleau-Ponty, *The Structure of Behaviour* and *The Phenomenology of Perception*.

67 See for example Alfred Schütz, *The Phenomenology of the Social World*.

68 Clear and readable introductions to Heidegger's philosophy are provided by J. Macquarrie, *Martin Heidegger* and G. Steiner, *Heidegger*.

69 But compare Gadamer's defence of philosophical etymology as necessary to provide a 'firm foundation' for the etymologies of linguistic science which are 'not proofs but achievements preparatory to conceptual analysis' in *Truth and Method*, p. 103 and n. 195.

70 This notion of substance is much stronger than the merely formal or logical notion of substance as that which has properties or that of which things can be predicated – the equivalent of the 'x' in 'x is green and made of glass.'

71 On Descartes see above, ch. 2, pp. 12–14.

72 For a fuller exposition of Kierkegaard and existentialism see below, ch. 5 and cf. Preface, p. viii.

73 M. Heidegger, *Being and Time*, p. 494, n. vi to Division Two, section 45 (my emphasis).

74 Heidegger, *Being and Time*, p. 33.

75 Ibid., pp. 454, 72.

76 Gadamer, 'On the problem of self-understanding' (1962), in *Philosophical Hermeneutics*, pp. 48–9.

77 Macquarrie, *Martin Heidegger*, p. 5.

78 Heidegger, *Being and Time*, p. 455.

79 Ibid., p. 455. Husserl too was concerned to explore the distinctive 'being' of mental or psychic phenomena as the clue to a general understanding of truth and being, including the being of nature, more adequate to human life and culture. See previous section.

80 Macquarrie, *Martin Heidegger*, p. 8. There are analogies (though clearly also important differences) between Heidegger's project and Descartes's method of radical doubt, which sets out from the perspective of the doubting subject. Heidegger's 'Dasein' is accordingly the equivalent of the Cartesian 'ego'.

81 See Heidegger, *Being and Time*, p. 27 and n. 1. In German *da* can mean both 'there' and 'here'. As 'Dasein' is so closely associated in English with Heidegger's philosophy, I leave it untranslated and treat it as an English word.

82 Kant uses this distinction to refute the 'ontological' argument for the existence of God. According to this argument, the concept of God is the concept of a perfect being. A perfect being cannot lack any attribute, otherwise it would not be perfect. Therefore God cannot lack existence. This argument does not work in the same way, if existence cannot be treated as a predicate. See Kant, *Critique of Pure Reason*, pp. 500–7.

83 Heidegger, *Being and Time*, pp. 83–4.

84 Ibid., pp. 96–8. For this reason Heidegger's views have been compared to

the philosophical pragmatism of Peirce and Habermas (see above, ch. 3, section on Habermas).

85 Heidegger, *Being and Time*, p. 225.

86 Ibid., pp. 153–5.

87 Ibid., p. 155.

88 Ibid., p. 164. In German '*man*' is the third person indefinite pronoun equivalent to 'one' or 'they' used in a non-specific sense. '*Das Man*' is a Heideggerian neologism.

89 Ibid., pp. 33–4.

90 Ibid., p. 220.

91 Ibid., p. 378.

92 Ibid., pp. 294, 298.

93 On this distinction see above, p. 99.

94 See H.-G. Gadamer, 'Heidegger's Later Philosophy', in *Philosophical Hermeneutics*. Gadamer sees the later philosophy as a continuous development of themes already present in the earlier work.

95 M. Heidegger, 'Letter on Humanism' (1947), in M. Heidegger, *Basic Writings*, p. 210. Compare M. Heidegger, *Discourse on Thinking*.

96 Heidegger, 'Letter on Humanism', p. 193.

97 Heidegger, 'On the Essence of Truth' (1961), in *Basic Writings*, p. 127.

98 Heidegger, 'The Origin of the Work of Art' (1936), in *Basic Writings*, p. 185.

99 Ibid., p. 186. The poetry of Hölderlin, also greatly admired by Hegel, 'still confronts the Germans as a test to be stood' (ibid., p. 187).

100 Gadamer, *Truth and Method*, pp. 490–1 – the concluding remarks. For an account of Gadamer see G. Warnke, *Gadamer*.

101 Palmer, *Hermeneutics*, p. 163.

102 Bubner, *Modern German Philosophy*, pp. 53, 54.

103 Cf. M. Heidegger, 'The Question Concerning Technology', in *Basic Writings*.

104 Linge, Introduction to Gadamer, *Philosophical Hermeneutics*, p. l.

105 Gadamer, 'The Phenomenological Movement' (1963), in *Philosophical Hermeneutics*, esp. pp. 163ff. On the concept of the life-world see above, pp. 95–6.

106 Gadamer, 'The Science of the Life-World' (1969), in *Philosophical Hermeneutics*, p. 196.

107 Ibid., p. 7.

108 Ibid., p. 491, quoted above.

109 Linge, Introduction to Gadamer, *Philosophical Hermeneutics*, p. xxii.

110 Gadamer, *Truth and Method*, p. 491, quoted above.

111 Ibid.

112 Ibid., p. 302.

113 Ibid., p. 300.

114 Ibid., p. 301.

115 Ibid., pp. 300–1.

116 Ibid., p. 297.

117 Ibid., p. 298.

118 On Kant's notion of the thing-in-itself or noumenon see above, pp. 20–1.

119 I am grateful to Bruin Christensen for this interpretation of Gadamer's account of meaning as well as for many other helpful suggestions.

120 Gadamer, *Truth and Method*, p. 104. Cf. Warnke, *Gadamer*, pp. 48ff.

121 Gadamer, *Truth and Method*, p. 327.

122 Ibid., pp. 340–1.
123 Ibid., p. 328.
124 Ibid., pp. 326–7.
125 Application in this sense is very different from the theoretical application of a scientific law to make a prediction or to test an hypothesis.
126 Gadamer, *Truth and Method*, p. 21. Beyond this, moral knowledge also presupposes a 'direction of the will – i.e., moral being (*hexis*)' (ibid., p. 22). Cf. R. Beiner, *Political Judgment*, esp. pp. 19ff.
127 Gadamer, *Truth and Method*, pp. 328–9.
128 'Dialectic' derives from the Greek '*dialektike*' meaning '(art) of debate': see *Concise Oxford English Dictionary*, p. 322.
129 Boucher, *Texts in Context*, p. 26.
130 Gadamer, *Truth and Method*, p. 491, quoted above.
131 Ibid., p. 279.
132 Ibid., p. 490, quoted above.
133 On the historicity of truth see R. Campbell, *Truth and Historicity*.
134 For the debate between Gadamer and Habermas see J. Habermas, 'On Systematically Distorted Communication', H.-G. Gadamer, 'On the Scope and Function of Hermeneutical Reflection' and J. Habermas, 'Summation and Response', and cf. above, ch. 3, pp. 73–4. The debate is discussed in Robert C. Holub, *Jürgen Habermas*, ch. 3.
135 Linge, Introduction to Gadamer, *Philosophical Hermeneutics*, pp. xxxvi–xxxvii. On the concept of language-game see L. Wittgenstein, *Philosophical Investigations*, para. 7, p. 5 and passim.
136 Gadamer, *Truth and Method*, p. 491, quoted above.

Chapter 5 Beyond Theory:
Kierkegaard, Nietzsche, Existentialism

1 P. Rohde, *Kierkegaard*, p. 31.
2 See above, ch. 2 on Hegel and ch. 3 on Feuerbach and Marx.
3 Fideism is 'the doctrine that all or some knowledge depends on faith or revelation': *Concise Oxford English Dictionary*, p. 434.
4 B. Pascal, *The Provincial Letters*, p. 85.
5 In retrospect humanist theology is risky in another way. By subordinating religious to scientific truth, it renders religion permanently vulnerable to future scientific developments. This possibility was confirmed later in the nineteenth century by developments such as Darwin's theory of evolution and new geological estimates of the age of the universe.
6 Hume, *Enquiries*, p. 131.
7 Aristotle, *Aristotle's Ethics*, p. 122. See also Habermas, *Knowledge and Human Interests*, p. 301.
8 By contrast, for Aristotle *techne*, as the 'workmanlike skill' required for the production of 'useful or beautiful artefacts', is associated with the distinct category of productive activity or *poiesis* – see T. McCarthy, *The Critical Theory of Jürgen Habermas*, p. 3.
9 Kierkegaard, quoted in Translators' Preface to S. Kierkegaard, *Either/Or*, vol. 1, p. xi.
10 Rohde, *Kierkegaard*, p. 149.

11 The notion of subjective truth is developed most extensively in S. Kierke-gaard, *Concluding Unscientific Postscript*, vol. 1, pp. 189ff.
12 S. Kierkegaard, *The Concept of Irony*, p. 9.
13 Lee M. Hollander, Introduction to Kierkegaard, *Selections from the Writings of Kierkegaard*, p. 7.
14 Kierkegaard, *Either/Or*.
15 For the relation of Kierkegaard's thought and life see Rohde, *Kierkegaard*.
16 On Descartes see above, ch. 2, pp. 13–14.
17 Not unconnectedly, in Christian theology goodness could not exist without the possibility of sin.
18 Cf. Sartre's notion of 'bad faith' as a prime object of moral condemnation, and see below, pp. 144–5.
19 S. Kierkegaard, *The Concept of Dread*, p. 40. It is, of course, this 'existential' sense of anxiety or dread which is now usually referred to as *angst*.
20 Ibid., p. 38.
21 Rohde, *Kierkegaard*, pp. 55, 102, 66.
22 S. Kierkegaard, *The Sickness unto Death*, p. 43.
23 Rohde, *Kierkegaard*, p. 66.
24 Hannay, Introduction to *The Sickness unto Death*, p. 4.
25 Kierkegaard, *The Sickness unto Death*, p. 71.
26 Ibid., p. 55.
27 Ibid., p. 75.
28 Ibid., p. 112.
29 Ibid., p. 115.
30 Kierkegaard, *Either/Or*, vol. 1, p. 26.
31 Ibid., p. 28.
32 H. J. Blackham, *Six Existentialist Thinkers*, p. 9.
33 Kierkegaard, *Either/Or*, vol. 2, p. 28.
34 Ibid., pp. 149, 37. These possibilities are personified, for the aesthete of the first volume, by Don Juan. Vol. 1 contains a lengthy discussion of 'the musical erotic' in relation to Mozart's opera *Don Giovanni*.
35 S. Kierkegaard, *Fear and Trembling*, p. 65. Sartre provides a rather different reading of the story of Isaac in *Existentialism and Humanism*.
36 Kierkegaard, *Fear and Trembling*, p. 82.
37 The phrase derives from Jacobi: see Hoffmeister, *Wörterbuch der philoso-phischen Begriffe*, p. 532. Kierkegaard takes the expression from Lessing: see Kierkegaard, *Philosophical Fragments* and cf. A. Hannay, *Kierkegaard*, pp. 97–9.
38 Of course, a significant tradition of existentialist theology, including Martin Buber and Gabriel Marcel, also draws inspiration from Kierke-gaard's writings. For a brief account of 'theistic existentialism', see F. Copleston, *Contemporary Philosophy*, ch. 10. A lucid introduction to existentialism more generally is provided by J. Macquarrie, *Existentialism*.
39 The following is a brief and confessedly systematic account of Nietzsche's thought. It should be said that there is another view of Nietzsche, in which the essayistic and aphoristic form and paradoxical style of his writing reflect the essentially unsystematic nature of his thought. This view of Nietzsche is emphasized, for example, by A. C. Danto, *Nietzsche as Philosopher*.
40 F. Nietzsche, *Beyond Good and Evil*, p. 57. In fact Nietzsche has a much

more nuanced attitude to both Christianity and Jesus Christ than this quotation might suggest.

41 See his extended polemic against the rational religion of 'David Strauss, the confessor and the writer', the first of Nietzsche's *Untimely Meditations*. There he remarks that 'the new religion is not a new faith, but precisely on a par with modern science, and thus not religion at all' (p. 41).

42 On Kaufmann's interpretation, Nietzsche is not as hostile to Hegel as others, such as Deleuze, suppose. See W. Kaufmann, *Nietzsche*, pp. 235–46 and G. Deleuze, *Nietzsche and Philosophy*, ch. 5.

43 Quoted by Kaufmann, *Nietzsche*, p. 204.

44 See above, ch. 3.

45 See Nietzsche, *Gay Science*, 347, pp. 287–90.

46 Nietzsche quoted by Kaufmann, *Nietzsche*, p. 122.

47 See C. Darwin, *The Origin of Species*, esp. ch. 14. Nietzsche, though, is critical of Darwin's 'incomprehensibly onesided doctrine of the "struggle for existence"' in *Gay Science*, 349, p. 292.

48 Nietzsche, quoting Schopenhauer, in *Birth of Tragedy*, p. 16 and see para. 1, pp. 14–16.

49 Kaufmann, *Nietzsche*, p. 128.

50 Nietzsche, *Birth of Tragedy*, p. 16.

51 See Schopenhauer, *The World as Will and Representation*.

52 Nietzsche, *Birth of Tragedy*, p. 17.

53 Kaufmann, *Nietzsche*, p. 128.

54 Compare Thomas Mann's novella *Death in Venice*, influenced by Nietzsche, in which artistic achievement is understood as the result of a fragile victory over disorder and disease.

55 Nietzsche quoted by Kaufmann, *Nietzsche*, p. 131. Nietzsche also admires the Greek obsession with the contest (or *agon*) and sees conflict as the crucible in which culture is formed.

56 Nietzsche, *Birth of Tragedy*, 12, pp. 59ff.

57 Ibid., 7, p. 40.

58 F. Nietzsche, *Human, All Too Human*, 18, p. 22.

59 Nietzsche, *Twilight of the Idols*, p. 36.

60 Ibid.

61 Nietzsche, *Beyond Good and Evil*, 11, p. 24. On Kant's Copernican revolution see above, pp. 18–19. For an interpretation of Nietzsche as something close to a positivist see H. Schnädelbach, *Philosophy in Germany 1831–1933* and M. Clark, *Nietzsche on Truth and Philosophy*.

62 Nietzsche, *Beyond Good and Evil*, 2, pp. 15ff and *Twilight of the Idols*, p. 37.

63 For Rousseau, as for many other Enlightenment thinkers, woman was not necessarily as naturally good as man. See J.-J. Rousseau, *Émile* and W. Godwin, *Enquiry concerning Political Justice*.

64 Hume, *Enquiry concerning the Principles of Morals*, para. 184, p. 227.

65 A notorious exception, of course, is the Marquis de Sade.

66 F. Nietzsche, *On the Genealogy of Morals* (1887), p. 26. For an account of Nietzsche's 'genealogical' method see M. Foucault, 'Nietzsche, Genealogy, History', pp. 149–64.

67 Nietzsche, *On the Genealogy of Morals*, p. 20.

68 On Freud see below, ch. 6, pp. 157–9.

69 'L'amour-propre est plus habile que le plus habile homme du monde',

maxim 4 in La Rochefoucauld (1613–80), *Maximes et réflexions diverses*, p. 25 (my translation).

70 Nietzsche, *Human, All Too Human*, vol. 1, 50, pp. 38–9 and cf. *The Anti-Christ*, 7, p. 118.

71 Nietzsche, *Human, All Too Human*, vol. 1, 44, p. 42.

72 *Ibid.*, vol. 1, 92, p. 49.

73 *Ibid.*, vol. 1, 99, p. 53.

74 Nietzsche, *The Anti-Christ*, 2, p. 115.

75 Nietzsche on a postcard to Overbeck quoted in Kaufmann, *Nietzsche*, p. 140.

76 'Le moi est haïssable', my translation, from B. Pascal, *Pensées*, para. 136, p. 82.

77 Compare Deleuze, *Nietzsche and Philosophy* and his account of Spinozist 'ethics' as opposed to Kantian 'morality' in *Spinoza: Practical Philosophy*, ch. 2.

78 Kaufmann, *Nietzsche*, p. 196 and cf. F. Nietzsche, *Thus Spake Zarathustra*, 'Of Self-Overcoming', p. 138.

79 Nietzsche also explicitly denies that sex is the most basic motive of human action, seeing it instead as a special case of the will to power. On the other hand, Nietzsche objects to Christianity's negative attitude toward sexuality. See Kaufmann, *Nietzsche*, p. 222.

80 See R. J. Hollingdale, *Nietzsche*, pp. 186ff.

81 Nietzsche, *Twilight of the Idols*, 'Morality as Anti-Nature', 1, p. 42.

82 Nietzsche, *The Anti-Christ*, 52, p. 169.

83 Kaufmann, *Nietzsche*, pp. 230, 232 and cf. Hollingdale, *Nietzsche*, ch. 4.

84 See Deleuze, *Nietzsche and Philosophy*, ch. 5.

85 Nietzsche, 'On the Uses and Disadvantages of History for Life', in *Untimely Meditations*, p. 111.

86 My translation of 'Genug des werdens, lass mich sein' from Wagner, *Five Songs by Mathilde Wesendonck*.

87 Kaufmann, *Nietzsche*, p. 147.

88 F. Nietzsche from 'Ecce Homo', in *On the Genealogy of Morals and Ecce Homo*, p. 295.

89 Nietzsche, *Thus Spake Zarathustra*, p. 332. Nietzsche's notion of eternal recurrence has parallels with Kierkegaard's notion of 'repetition'. See S. Kierkegaard, *Repetition* and cf. Hannay, *Kierkegaard*, pp. 66–72.

90 Nietzsche, *Untimely Meditations*, p. 120.

91 Kaufmann, *Nietzsche*, p. 418. This interpretation of Nietzsche has been challenged recently by K. Ansell-Pierson, *Nietzsche contra Rousseau* and M. Warren, *Nietzsche and Political Thought*.

92 See J. P. Stern, *Nietzsche* and J. A. Bernstein, *Nietzsche's Moral Philosophy*.

93 Kaufmann, *Nietzsche*, p. 303.

94 For Nietzsche's attitude to women see P. Patton, ed., *Nietzsche, Feminism and Political Theory*.

95 F. Dostoyevsky, *The Brothers Karamazov*, p. 69.

96 M. Heidegger, *Nietzsche*, and see above, pp. 97–8.

97 G. Deleuze, 'Nomad Thought', p. 149 and cf. G. Deleuze, *Nietzsche and Philosophy*.

98 Deleuze, 'Nomad Thought', p. 149.

99 David B. Allison in *The New Nietzsche*, p. xiv.

100 Jacques Derrida, 'The Question of Style', p. 179.

101 Ibid., p. 188. For the further development of these 'poststructuralist' themes, see below, ch. 6. For an account of Nietzsche as contributor to a postmodernist theory of agency see M. Warren, *Nietzsche and Political Thought*.
102 J.-P. Sartre, *Being and Nothingness*. Heidegger rejected Sartre's interpretation of his ideas: M. Heidegger, 'Letter on Humanism', in *Basic Writings*.
103 On the distinction between essence and existence see above p. 100.
104 Sartre, 'Une idée', quoted in Aronson, *Jean-Paul Sartre*, p. 97.
105 Aronson quoting Sartre in *Jean-Paul Sartre*, pp. 90–1.
106 Cf. Sartre, *Being and Nothingness*, pp. 3–4.
107 J.-P. Sartre, *Imagination: A Psychological Critique* (1936) and *L'Imaginaire* (1939).
108 Sartre quoted by Aronson, *Jean-Paul Sartre*, p. 41.
109 Aronson, *Jean-Paul Sartre*, p. 41. In fact, Sartre describes a range of mental states, which become increasingly negative ('creative' and 'spontaneous') as they approach the status of pure imagination.
110 Sartre quoted by Aronson, *Jean-Paul Sartre*, p. 42.
111 Sartre, *Being and Nothingness*, p. xxvii.
112 Ibid., p. xxviii.
113 Ibid., p. xxix.
114 Ibid., p. xxvii.
115 See Berkeley, *The Principles of Human Knowledge*.
116 Sartre, *Being and Nothingness*, p. xxxi.
117 Ibid., p. xxxi.
118 Ibid., p. xxxii.
119 Ibid., p. xxii.
120 Ibid., p. xxxvii.
121 Ibid., pp. xxii.
122 Ibid., pp. xlii, xl, xli.
123 J.-P. Sartre, *Nausea* (1938), p. 183.
124 Sartre, *Being and Nothingness*, p. 18.
125 Ibid., p. 5.
126 Compare Saussure's account of 'language' as a system of differential oppositions. See below, pp. 164–6.
127 Sartre, *Being and Nothingness*, p. 7.
128 Ibid., p. 8.
129 Ibid., pp. 24–5.
130 Ibid., p. 25.
131 A. C. Danto, *Sartre*, p. 74.
132 Sartre, *Being and Nothingness*, pp. 48ff and *Existentialism and Humanism*, pp. 28–9.
133 Sartre, *Being and Nothingness*, pp. 55–63. For a sceptical discussion of these examples see M. Le Doeuff, *Hipparchia's Choice*, pp. 70ff.
134 Sartre, *Being and Nothingness*, pp. 63–4.
135 Ibid., p. 64.
136 Sartre, *Being and Nothingness*, p. 65. Sartre's attitude to the emotions as a deliberate orientation to the world is developed in *Sketch for a Theory of the Emotions*.
137 Aronson, *Jean-Paul Sartre*, p. 81.
138 Sartre, *Being and Nothingness*, p. 397.
139 Ibid., p. 394.
140 Ibid., p. 79.

141 Ibid., p. 305.
142 Ibid., p. 326. The notion of the world as an instrumental complex is borrowed directly from Heidegger (see above, p. 101).
143 Sartre, *Being and Nothingness*, pp. 252–6.
144 Ibid., pp. 262–3.
145 Here Sartre expresses, albeit in rhetorically heightened terms, an insight similar to that of Hegel's dialectic of master and bondsman. See above, ch. 3, p. 50 and note 32.
146 Compare Heidegger's discussion of the 'everyday' and the 'they' and Kierkegaard's disdain for conformity to the masses: see pp. 102, 122.
147 J.-P. Sartre, *The Age of Reason*, p. 195. Paradoxically, as several commentators have noted, there is a parallel with Kant's very different view of moral duty, which also implies that only actions bearing no relation to the agent's desires or inclinations can safely be regarded as ones performed 'for the sake of duty alone'.
148 Sartre, *Existentialism and Humanism*. Sartre would later distance himself from the not very convincing arguments of this essay.
149 On Kant's categorical imperative and its problems see above, pp. 25f, 35f.
150 J.-P. Sartre, *What is Literature?* (1948) and 'A Plea for Intellectuals' in *Between Existentialism and Marxism*. See Aronson, *Jean-Paul Sartre*, pp. 142ff, 310.
151 Aronson, *Jean-Paul Sartre*, p. 157 and passim. See also Gregory Elliott, 'Further Adventures of the Dialectic' for a useful review of Sartre's political and intellectual context.
152 'Childhood of a Leader' is translated in J.-P. Sartre, *Intimacy*.
153 See Philip Thody, *Jean-Paul Sartre*.
154 J.-P. Sartre, *Critique of Dialectical Reason*, vol. 1, p. 113.
155 M. Poster, *Sartre's Marxism*, p. 43.
156 Sartre, *Critique of Dialectical Reason*, pp. 256–342.
157 Poster, *Sartre's Marxism*, p. 86.
158 Simone de Beauvoir, *The Second Sex*, p. 29.
159 Ibid., p. 736 and cf. p. 734.
160 On the philosophical relationship between Sartre and de Beauvoir see Le Doeuff, *Hipparchia's Choice*, pp. 135ff and passim.
161 F. Fanon, *The Wretched of the Earth* and see D. Caute, *Fanon*, pp. 34ff on Fanon's relationship to Sartrian philosophy.
162 See Sartre, *Critique of Dialectical Reason* and *Saint Genet*. On de Beauvoir see Deirdre Bair, *Simone de Beauvoir*.
163 Sartre quoted by M. Gatens, *Feminism and Philosophy*, p. 56.
164 Beauvoir, *The Second Sex*, p. 66.
165 Gatens, *Feminism and Philosophy*, p. 57.
166 See below, ch. 7, pp. 211–15.
167 See J. Cruickshank, *Albert Camus and the Literature of Revolt* and C. C. O'Brien, *Camus*.
168 A. Camus, *The Myth of Sisyphus*, pp. 26, 31–2.
169 My translation of 'Mais qu'est ce que ça veut dire, la peste? C'est la vie et voilà tout', in Camus, *La Peste* (1947), p. 246, translated as *The Plague*.
170 Camus, *The Myth of Sisyphus*, p. 11.
171 Ibid., p. 111.
172 A. Camus, *The Rebel*, p. 22.
173 Cf. Simone de Beauvoir, *The Ethics of Ambiguity*.

174 H. Marcuse, 'Sartre's Existentialism', p. 174. On the Frankfurt School see above, ch. 3.

Chapter 6 Beyond the Subject:
Structuralism and Poststructuralism

1 A useful discussion of humanism and anti-humanism is provided by Kate Soper, *Humanism and Anti-humanism.*
2 On Kierkegaard see above, ch. 5.
3 Of course, the notion of the individual has undergone significant transformations since the onset of the modern period. Women, servants and the propertyless were not, at first, regarded as individuals in their own right but as the property of particular men, who represented them. See C. Pateman, 'The Fraternal Social Contract' and her *The Sexual Contract*, esp. ch. 1.
4 See above, ch. 2.
5 See above, ch. 3.
6 K. Marx and F. Engels, *The German Ideology*, pp. 58–9, 64–5.
7 See R. Thompson, *The Pelican History of Psychology*, part I and ch. 14. On Freud see R. Wollheim, *Freud*, ch. 1 and P. Rieff, *The Triumph of the Therapeutic*, ch. 1. The assumptions of both experimental and introspectionist psychology were, as we have already seen, questioned by Brentano and Husserl (see above pp. 91ff). The description and classification of 'abnormal' sexual behaviour has a long history, including the eighteenth-century works of the Marquis de Sade, particularly his *The 120 Days of Sodom* (lost in 1789, first published in Berlin, 1904) and Richard von Krafft-Ebing (1840–1902), *Psychopathia Sexualis* (1893) as well as more recent works.
8 The word 'hysteria' derives from the Greek '*husterikos*' meaning 'of the womb': *Concise Oxford English Dictionary*, p. 582.
9 See Wollheim, *Freud*, p. 23.
10 See for example J. Breuer and S. Freud, *Studies on Hysteria*, esp. part II.
11 See S. Freud, *Psychopathology of Everyday Life* and *The Interpretation of Dreams.*
12 The notion of the unconscious was not itself new. It is implicit in the writings of La Rochefoucauld, Schopenhauer and Nietzsche among others.
13 Norris describes this demotion of the conscious ego in favour of the unconscious as Freud's 'Copernican revolution': C. Norris, *Derrida*, p. 207. On Deleuze's interpretation this particular Copernican revolution was already achieved by Spinoza in the seventeenth century: see G. Deleuze, *Spinoza: Practical Philosophy*, ch. 2.
14 See Colin MacCabe, ed., *The Talking Cure.*
15 Alfred Lorenzer, *Kritik des psychoanalytischen Symbolbegriffs* and J. Habermas, *Knowledge and Human Interests*, ch. 10.
16 In effect, Freud's interpretations of unconscious mental states and phenomena extend hermeneutic principles beyond their traditional concern with deliberate expressions of mental life. Beneath the surface meaning of text or utterance, mental categories of interpretation or understanding can be applied to unconscious, unintentional and hidden meanings.
17 See S. Freud, 'Analysis Terminable and Interminable' and 'Civilization and its Discontents' in *Civilization, Society and Religion*. In fact, some of Freud's

collaborators and successors came closer to breaking with his ultimately individualistic assumptions. Carl Gustav Jung (1875–1961) uses the notion of a '*collective unconscious*' to refer to the accumulated past experiences of humanity. These experiences are supposedly preserved as collective memories available, in ways never made entirely clear, to each individual. Dreams and myths are analysed in similar terms as manifestations of universal human 'archetypes', explaining symbols (phallic being only the most familiar) commonly encountered in Freud's case-histories. However, even with Jung the fundamental human striving is towards individual wholeness and fulfilment. See C. G. Jung, *The Integration of the Personality*, F. Fordham, *An Introduction to Jung's Psychology* and Rieff, *Triumph of the Therapeutic*, ch. 5.

18 On hermeneutics see above, ch. 4.
19 Sartre, *Existentialism and Humanism*, p. 17. Compare Heidegger, 'The Question concerning Technology' and 'Letter on Humanism', in *Basic Writings* and see above, ch. 4.
20 Heidegger, 'Letter on Humanism', p. 230.
21 Ibid., pp. 225, 228.
22 Nietzsche, *Gay Science*, para. 346, quoted in D. B. Allison, *The New Nietzsche*, p. xix.
23 Heidegger, 'The Question concerning Technology', pp. 297, 299 and passim. Compare the Frankfurt School's critique of instrumental rationality (above, ch. 3).
24 On Heidegger's associations with the Nazis see P. Lacoue-Labarthe, *Heidegger: Art and Politics* and J.-F. Lyotard, *Heidegger and the Jews*.
25 Lyotard, *Heidegger and the Jews*, p. 64.
26 R. E. Palmer, *Hermeneutics*, p. 163 and see above, ch. 4.
27 Richard A. Cohen, Introduction to Emmanuel Levinas, *Time and the Other*, pp. 14–15. Cohen's introduction provides a clear overview of the development of Levinas's thought. See E. Levinas, *The Levinas Reader*, for a useful collection of his writings. See also D. T. Awerkamp, *Emmanuel Levinas* and R. Bernasconi and S. Critchley, *Re-reading Levinas*.
28 Cohen, in Levinas, *Time and the Other*, p. 16.
29 Ibid., p. 15.
30 Z. Bauman, *Modernity and the Holocaust*, p. 183.
31 S. Hand, Introduction to Levinas, *The Levinas Reader*, p. 6.
32 Levinas, *The Levinas Reader*, p. 158.
33 Ibid., p. 183.
34 Ibid. There are obvious affinities between Levinas and Derrida. See for example J. Derrida, 'Violence and Metaphysics' in *Writing and Difference*; on logocentrism see below, pp. 178–9.
35 See F. de Saussure, *Course in General Linguistics*. Appropriately enough for someone who is credited with dislodging both subject and author from their pre-eminent positions, Saussure's major work was in fact compiled from lecture notes by his students and published only posthumously.
36 J. Culler, *Saussure*, p. 29. The term 'speech act' is associated with the work of J. L. Austin and John Searle.
37 In Piaget's terms, Saussure explains language in terms of 'equilibrium laws' rather than 'developmental laws'. See J. Piaget, *Structuralism*, ch. 5, section 14.
38 Even then, different languages have different (though recognizably similar)

onomatopes for the same thing, e.g. 'quack' in English, 'couin-couin' in French.

39 Culler, *Saussure*, p. 36.
40 See Piaget, *Structuralism*, chs 2–3.
41 H. L. Dreyfus and P. Rabinow, *Michel Foucault*, pp. xv–xvi. See also P. Pettit, *The Concept of Structuralism*.
42 Sociology in the collectivist style of Émile Durkheim (1858–1917) has similar implications for the position of the subject. See É. Durkheim, *The Rules of Sociological Method* and S. Lukes, *Émile Durkheim*.
43 Jakobson (1896–1982), a member of the Prague School of linguistics, applied a structural method similar to Saussure's to the phonological analysis of language. Jakobson analysed the sound systems of languages in terms of contrasting sets of 'phonemes', which are defined as 'the smallest unit in the sound-system capable of indicating contrasts in meaning': *Fontana Dictionary of Modern Thought*, p. 470.
44 C. Lévi-Strauss, *Structural Anthropology*, p. 18 and see C. Lévi-Strauss, *The Elementary Structures of Kinship*. On Lévi-Strauss's debt to Freud, Marx and Saussure see Ino Rossi, 'Intellectual Antecedents of Lévi-Strauss' Notion of Unconscious'.
45 C. Lévi-Strauss, *The Savage Mind* and cf. J. Sturrock, *Structuralism*, p. 48.
46 Sturrock, *Structuralism*, p. 41. In a similar way, Noam Chomsky posits a 'universal grammar' common to speakers of all languages. In psychology Piaget claims to identify invariant and universal sequences in the child's development of intellectual capacities. Lawrence Kohlberg has applied Piaget's approach to moral development: see Lawrence Kohlberg et al., *Moral Stages*.
47 See L. Althusser and E. Balibar, *Reading Capital*, and Althusser, *For Marx*. Cf. P. Anderson, *In the Tracks of Historical Materialism*, ch. 2 and G. Elliott, ed., *Althusser: A Critical Reader*.
48 The revival of Hegelianism in France has been attributed to Alexandre Kojève's lectures on Hegel, 1933–9. Some of these lectures are published as A. Kojève, *Introduction to the Reading of Hegel*. See also V. Descombes, *Modern French Philosophy*, ch. 1.
49 See I. Meszaros, *Lukács' Concept of Dialectic*.
50 L. Althusser, 'Marxism and Humanism', in *For Marx*, pp. 237–9.
51 See E. P. Thompson, *The Poverty of Theory* and the response by P. Anderson, *Considerations on Western Marxism*.
52 In order to avoid unnecessary confusion the following brief account of Foucault will not attempt to recount every stage in his intellectual development, but rather to present his most influential ideas in something like their final form.
53 This is Eribon's gloss on a tribute by Deleuze; Foucault had written in 1970 that 'Some day this will be a Deleuzian century.' See D. Eribon, *Michel Foucault*, p. 4.
54 M. Foucault, 'Afterword: The Subject and Power', p. 208.
55 Dreyfus and Rabinow, *Michel Foucault*, p. 28.
56 Foucault, 'Afterword', p. 212.
57 Other examples are judicial practices, the 'panopticon' and 'practices of the self': see Foucault, *Discipline and Punish* and *The Care of the Self*.
58 According to Eribon, Foucault had left the communist party by no later than 1955: see *Michel Foucault*, p. 57. In particular M. Foucault's *The Archaeol-*

ogy of Knowledge was criticized as idealist because of its apparently exclusive concern with 'discourse'.

59 M. Foucault, *Discipline and Punish*, p. 27. On the other hand, Foucault also rejects any easy identification of the two to the effect that 'power *is* knowledge.'
60 B. Smart, *Foucault, Marxism, Critique*, p. 84.
61 Ibid., p. 80.
62 See Foucault, 'Nietzsche, Genealogy, History' and Nietzsche, *On the Genealogy of Morals*. In *The Archaeology of Knowledge* Foucault refers approvingly to the model of Nietzsche's 'genealogy' of morality (pp. 13–14).
63 Foucault, 'Nietzsche, Genealogy, History', pp. 76, 81.
64 Foucault, 'Afterword', p. 219.
65 Smart, *Foucault, Marxism, Critique*, p. 83.
66 A. Sheridan, *Michel Foucault*, p. 83.
67 As some critics have pointed out, Foucault's periodizations follow the conventions of French historiography quite closely.
68 M. Foucault, *History of Sexuality*, vol. 1, *An Introduction*, p. 86.
69 Ibid., pp. 137, 143.
70 E.g. A. Gobineau, *The Inequality of the Human Races*.
71 See M. Foucault, 'Governmentality' and Colin Gordon, 'Governmental Rationality: An Introduction', both in G. Burchell et al., *The Foucault Effect*.
72 Foucault, 'Afterword', p. 214.
73 Ibid., p. 214.
74 Ibid., p. 215.
75 Ibid.
76 The term 'statistics' derives from the French, 'statistique', originally the 'doctrine of the state': Hoffmeister, *Wörterbuch der philosophischen Begriffe*, p. 579.
77 Foucault, *Discipline and Punish*, p. 24. The quotation marks around 'scientific' reflect a problem not explicitly thematized in Foucault's thought. Although he is clearly sceptical of the scientific pretensions of the human sciences, he apparently accepts the genuinely scientific status of such natural sciences as astronomy, physics and chemistry. This raises the question whether the mutual implication of knowledge and power is, as he usually presents it, a feature of knowledge generally or only within the human sciences. On this question see G. Gutting, *Michel Foucault's Archaeology of Scientific Reason*, esp. final chapter.
78 See M. Foucault, *The Birth of the Clinic* and *Madness and Civilization*.
79 Foucault, *Discipline and Punish*, p. 138.
80 Smart, *Foucault, Marxism, Critique*, p. 113.
81 Foucault, *Discipline and Punish*, pp. 200–1.
82 Smart, *Foucault, Marxism, Critique*, p. 111. Cf. E. Goffman, *Asylums*, for an alternative account of these 'closed institutions'.
83 See M. Foucault, 'Intellectuals and Power'.
84 Sheridan, *Michel Foucault*, pp. 139–40.
85 Foucault, 'Intellectuals and Power', p. 208.
86 G. Deleuze, in Foucault, 'Intellectuals and Power', p. 209.
87 Cf. Foucault, 'Afterword', p. 212. Note also the influence of Foucault on contemporary gay or 'queer' politics: see D. Halperin, *Saint Foucault*.
88 Foucault, 'Afterword', p. 210.

89 E.g. Smart, *Foucault, Marxism, Critique*, p. 87.

90 M. Foucault, 'Polemics, Politics, and Problematizations', pp. 381–2.

91 J. Derrida, *Speech and Phenomena, Of Grammatology* and *Writing and Difference*.

92 One result of this difficult stance is that in the case of Derrida the usual disclaimers regarding attempts to provide a brief and clear guide to a complex body of thought must be considerably amplified. It is not only that with Derrida the terrain is uncompromisingly difficult and unforgiving (explorers may be lost without trace or return strangely changed), it is also that normal map-making conventions no longer apply. In fact, like a hall of mirrors or the well-designed labyrinth, the environment has been designed to defy such simple representational devices. At best one can warn of obvious pitfalls, recommend some useful conceptual equipment and preach the virtues of independent exploration from a safe distance.

93 Sturrock, *Structuralism*, p. 137 and see above, pp. 164–8.

94 In that sense, it differs from the usual contrast between modernism and postmodernism.

95 E. Grosz, *Sexual Subversions*, p. xix. '*Logos*' is Greek for 'the word', 'discourse' or 'reason' and a cognate of '*legein*', 'to speak'. It is both the etymological root of our word 'logic' and a suffix of words denoting particular branches of knowledge, such as 'geology', 'theology' or 'physiology'. Good accounts of Derrida are provided by R. Gasché, *The Tain of the Mirror* and J. Culler, *On Deconstruction*.

96 Habermas, *Philosophical Discourse of Modernity*, p. 176.

97 Ibid., pp. 174–5.

98 Sturrock, *Structuralism*, pp. 139–40.

99 J. Derrida, '*Différance*' in *Margins of Philosophy*, p. 11. Peter Dews has pointed to the similarities between this Derridean term of art and a basic theme within German speculative idealism of the nineteenth century. Thus the fundamental notion within Schelling's 'philosophy of identity' is the 'absolute I', which precedes any distinction between subject and object. Both *différance* and the 'absolute I' affirm 'the identity of identity and non-identity' as the basis of a theory of representation: Dews, *Logics of Disintegration*, pp. 28, 159.

100 Sturrock, *Structuralism*, p. 159.

101 Ibid., p. 138.

102 Habermas, *Philosophical Discourse of Modernity*, p. 171.

103 Ibid., p. 165.

104 Derrida, *Of Grammatology*, pp. 30ff (esp. pp. 35, 41) and cf. Norris, *Derrida*, pp. 90–1.

105 Derrida quoted by Norris, *Derrida*, p. 95.

106 Derrida, *Of Grammatology*, p. 51.

107 Norris, *Derrida*, p. 23.

108 It is also a feature of those 'other-worldly' eastern religions which see wisdom or truth as something to be approached only to the extent that the material world, the body and its desires are left behind: see M. Weber, *Sociology of Religion*.

109 In Christianity this relationship can be seen in the role of the direct encounter with the truth of the 'word of God', for example in the conversion of the apostles after meeting Christ or in the convincing of 'doubting Thomas' after he has seen the wounds or in the power attributed to miracles.

110 Derrida quoted by Norris, *Derrida*, p. 33.

111 Derrida, 'Plato's Pharmacy' in *Dissemination*, p. 103.
112 Ibid., p. 146.
113 Norris, *Derrida*, p. 33.
114 Ibid., pp. 35–6.
115 Derrida, *Dissemination*, p. 129.
116 Norris, *Derrida*, p. 19.
117 Grosz, *Sexual Subversions*, p. xv.
118 Derrida in R. Mortley, *French Philosophers in Conversation*, p. 97.
119 J. Derrida, *Positions*, p. 45.
120 T. McCarthy, 'The Politics of the Ineffable', p. 148.
121 R. Rorty, 'Is Derrida a Transcendental Philosopher?', p. 240.
122 Derrida quoted by Norris, *Derrida*, p. 113.
123 Derrida, *Writing and Difference*, p. 32.
124 Derrida, *Positions*, pp. 40–1, where *'relève'* is Derrida's translation of Hegel's *'Aufhebung'* ('sublation' or 'transcendence').
125 Ibid., pp. 41–2.
126 On the comparison between Derrida and Gadamer see D. P. Michelfelder and R. E. Palmer, *Dialogue and Deconstruction*.
127 Dews, *Logics of Disintegration*, p. 34.
128 McCarthy, quoting Derrida in 'The Politics of the Ineffable', pp. 153–4.
129 See J. Derrida, 'The Laws of Reflection: Nelson Mandela, in Admiration'.
130 M. Ryan, *Marxism and Deconstruction*, pp. 219, 215.
131 Derrida, quoted by McCarthy, 'The Politics of the Ineffable', p. 157.
132 McCarthy, 'The Politics of the Ineffable', p. 156. See R. Boyne, *Foucault and Derrida*, for a more positive view of Derrida's influence on politics.
133 Boyne, *Foucault and Derrida*, p. 217.
134 Norris, *Derrida*, p. 214.
135 Rorty, on the other hand, sees Derrida as much closer to the postmodern and 'post-metaphysical' position he himself favours. Rorty sums up Derrida's complex 'notions as merely abbreviations for the familiar Peircean-Wittgensteinian anti-Cartesian thesis that meaning is a function of context, and that there is no theoretical barrier to an endless sequence of recontextualizations': R. Rorty, 'Is Derrida a Transcendental Philosopher?' p. 240.
136 J. Derrida, *Writing and Difference*, p. 59 (quoted at the head of this section).

Chapter 7 Postmodernism

1 See Marshall Berman, *All that is Solid Melts into Air*. This phrase is used by Marx to describe the 'bourgeois epoch' in K. Marx and F. Engels, *The Communist Manifesto*, p. 16 and derives from Shakespeare, *The Tempest*, IV, 1: 'Are melted into air, into thin air'.
2 See J.-F. Lyotard, *The Postmodern Condition*, discussed below. The definition of postmodernism is itself controversial. The term is used here to refer to currents of thought which acknowledge, in some way, the usefulness of the concepts of 'postmodernity' or 'postmodern' and their cognates.
3 '. . . you must go on, I can't go on, I'll go on', the last words of S. Beckett, *The Unnamable*, p. 414.
4 Zygmunt Bauman, *Modernity and the Holocaust*, p. xiv.
5 This phrase was coined by Rudolf Bahro as the subtitle of his book, *The*

Alternative in Eastern Europe, to mark the difference between these regimes and the ideal of socialism or communism.

6 The question whether Marxist theory should be held responsible for the defects of actually existing socialism has a long history within Marxism: see, for example, G. Lukács, 'What is Orthodox Marxism?' in *History and Class Consciousness* and C. Castoriadis, *The Imaginary Institution of Society*, part I, ch. 1.

7 Essentially the problem of practice concerns the realization of communism. It is a particularly acute problem for Marxist theory, which sets out to overcome the gap between theory and practice characteristic of 'bourgeois idealism'. See above, ch. 3.

8 See G. Elliott, 'Further Adventures of the Dialectic' and P. Dews, *Logics of Disintegration*, Introduction. The exceptions are Italy and Spain.

9 See Raymond Williams, *Keywords*, p. 174.

10 The term was also used to describe a late nineteenth-century movement of modernizing Roman Catholic theologians.

11 S. Gaggi, *Modern/Postmodern*, p. 18.

12 In retrospect, though, both surrealism and dadaism display recognizably postmodernist themes.

13 David Harvey, *The Condition of Postmodernity*, p. 36.

14 See Hal Foster, 'Introduction' in *Postmodern Culture*, p. xv.

15 Barry Smart quoting M. Calinescu in *Postmodernity*, p. 19. Smart's first chapter provides a useful account of the history and variety of uses of 'postmodernism' and its cognates.

16 F. Jameson, *Postmodernism, or, The Cultural Logic of Late Capitalism*, p. 17.

17 In W. Benjamin, *Illuminations*, and cf. above, p. 64.

18 In this context he cites such works as *Las Meninas* of Velasquez, Cervantes's *Don Quixote*, Sterne's *Tristram Shandy*, Shakespeare's *Hamlet* and *The Tempest*, Caldéron de la Barca's *Life is a Dream* and the theatrical works of Pirandello and Brecht: Gaggi, *Modern/Postmodern*, p. 13. Gaggi also suggests that scepticism contributes to the intellectual background of modernism too.

19 See for example R. Barthes, *S/Z*.

20 See T. Kuhn, *The Structure of Scientific Revolutions* and P. Feyerabend, *Against Method*.

21 Smart, *Postmodernity*, pp. 25–6.

22 Foster, *Postmodern Culture*, pp. xi–xii.

23 Still, despite these radical intentions, postmodernist ideas have been taken by some to lead fairly directly to conventionally liberal or even conservative conclusions. This interpretation finds support in the political and philosophical stance of Richard Rorty, who explicitly defends a version of 'postmodernist bourgeois liberalism'. See R. Rorty, 'Postmodernist Bourgeois Liberalism'.

24 Lyotard, *The Postmodern Condition*, p. 8.

25 Ibid., p. xxiii.

26 Ibid., p. 37.

27 Some critics suggest that Lyotard is entangled in his own metanarrative of modernity and postmodernity – an impression reinforced by his association of postmodernity with a stage of postindustrial society.

28 A. Touraine, 'Introduction to the Study of Social Movements', p. 781 and cf.

The Voice and the Eye. The term was used earlier by Daniel Bell in *The Coming of Post-industrial Society*.

29 Lyotard, *The Postmodern Condition*, pp. 45–6 and compare Marcuse's similar use of the term 'performance principle' in *Eros and Civilization*, pp. 50ff and passim.
30 Lyotard, *The Postmodern Condition*, p. xxiv.
31 On totalizing theory see above, pp. 176–7.
32 Lyotard, *The Postmodern Condition*, pp. xxiv–xxv. 'Language-game' is a term derived from L. Wittgenstein, *Philosophical Investigations*, para. 7, p. 5 and passim.
33 D. Hoy, 'Foucault – Modern or Postmodern?', p. 34.
34 Lyotard, *The Postmodern Condition*, p. 66 and see discussion of Habermas above, pp. 75–7.
35 Ibid., p. 64.
36 Ibid., p. 79.
37 Ibid., p. 78. Compare D. Hebdige on the notion of the aesthetic sublime in contemporary theory quoted by S. Connor, *Postmodernist Culture*, pp. 212ff. Cf. Heidegger's conception of the role of poetry, above, pp. 104–5.
38 Lyotard, *The Postmodern Condition*, p. 66.
39 J. Keane in A. Benjamin, *Judging Lyotard*, pp. 84, 91.
40 Ibid., pp. 89, 92, 94.
41 Ibid., pp. 96, 95.
42 Habermas, *Philosophical Discourse of Modernity*, p. 86.
43 Ibid., p. 94.
44 Ibid., pp. 136–40.
45 Ibid., p. 205.
46 Ibid., pp. 276, 278.
47 D. M. Rasmussen, *Reading Habermas*, p. 26.
48 Habermas, *Philosophical Discourse of Modernity*, p. 296 and cf. his 'Modernity – An Incomplete Project' in Foster, *Postmodern Culture*.
49 For discussion of Habermas's views on modernity see R. J. Bernstein, ed., *Habermas and Modernity*.
50 See D. Kellner, *Jean Baudrillard*. On situationism see C. Gray, ed., *Leaving the 20th Century* and G. Debord, *Society of the Spectacle*.
51 Baudrillard makes his final break with Marxism in *The Mirror of Production*.
52 J. Baudrillard, 'Consumer Society', in *Jean Baudrillard: Selected Writings*, p. 29.
53 Ibid., p. 48.
54 Ibid., p. 47.
55 Connor, *Postmodernist Culture*, p. 51.
56 'Simulacra and Simulations', in *Jean Baudrillard: Selected Writings*, p. 166.
57 Ibid., pp. 171ff.
58 Baudrillard, quoted by Z. Bauman, *Intimations of Postmodernity*, p. 151.
59 J. Baudrillard, 'The Ecstasy of Communication', p. 127.
60 'Consumer Society', in *Jean Baudrillard: Selected Writings*, p. 29.
61 Baudrillard, 'The Ecstasy of Communication', pp. 130–1.
62 Baudrillard, 'The Ecstasy of Communication', pp. 132–3.
63 Ibid., p. 129. The distinction between 'hot' and 'cold' universes recalls Marshall McLuhan's distinction in *The Gutenberg Galaxy*.
64 See above, pp. 149–50.

65 'The Masses', in *Jean Baudrillard: Selected Writings*, p. 219.
66 Bauman, *Intimations of Postmodernity*, p. 153.
67 See above, ch. 6.
68 *Jean Baudrillard: Selected Writings*, p. 219.
69 As we have already seen, Lyotard too assigns postmodern culture to the contemporary stage of 'postindustrial' society.
70 See A. Callinicos, *Against Postmodernism*.
71 For a parallel account of contemporary society see S. Lash and J. Urry, *The End of Organised Capitalism*.
72 'Fordism' is associated with the domination of industrial society by the assembly-line production of more or less identical commodities for a mass market. It is named after Henry Ford, the American car manufacturer, whose 'Model T Ford' transformed the industry after 1912.
73 See for example E. Laclau and C. Mouffe, *Hegemony and Socialist Strategy* and J. Habermas, 'New Social Movements'.
74 For example, Frankfurt School theorists, but also Ernest Mandel, *Late Capitalism*.
75 Cf above, note 28 on Touraine.
76 Jameson, *Postmodernism*, p. xii.
77 Jameson, *Postmodernism*, Introduction and ch. 1, section IV. Jameson also explicitly refers to Adorno and Horkheimer's account of late capitalism (Introduction, pp. xvii–xviii).
78 Jameson, *Postmodernism*, p. 2.
79 Ibid., p. xi.
80 Ibid., p. 25.
81 Ibid., p. 48.
82 Jameson, quoted by Gaggi, *Modern/Postmodern*, pp. 180–1.
83 Gaggi, *Modern/Postmodern*, p. 180.
84 Jameson, *Postmodernism*, p. 319.
85 Ibid., pp. 329ff, 408ff. For a rather different attempt to pursue the socialist project in the face of the sceptical prohibitions of postmodernism see M. Ryan, *Marxism and Deconstruction*.
86 Bauman, *Intimations of Postmodernity*, p. 167.
87 Ibid., p. 168.
88 Smart, *Postmodernity*, p. 63.
89 Ibid., pp. 41–2.
90 See Smart, *Postmodernity*, p. 41 and A. Giddens, *Social Theory and Modern Sociology*.
91 Smart, *Postmodernity*, p. 106.
92 Grosz, *Sexual Subversions*, p. 231.
93 See M. Le Doeuff, *The Philosophical Imaginary*. See also M. Morris, 'Operative Reasoning'.
94 Grosz, *Sexual Subversions*, p. 227.
95 Ibid., p. 233.
96 Le Doeuff, in R. Mortley, *French Philosophers in Conversation*, ch. 5, pp. 86ff.
97 R. Tong, *Feminist Thought*, p. 227. On Irigaray see M. Whitford, *Luce Irigaray: Philosophy in the Feminine*.
98 Grosz, *Sexual Subversions*, p. 231. See for example J. Kristeva, *The Kristeva Reader*.
99 Ibid., p. xxiii.

100 Tong, *Feminist Thought*, p. 231.
101 Grosz, *Sexual Subversions*, p. 97 and compare Nietzsche's notions of the Apolline and the Dionysiac, above, pp. 128–9.
102 Tong, *Feminist Thought*, p. 226.
103 Ibid., See for example L. Irigaray, *This Sex which is Not One* and *The Irigaray Reader*.
104 Grosz, *Sexual Subversions*, p. 179.
105 Tong, *Feminist Thought*, pp. 226–8.
106 Grosz, *Sexual Subversions*, pp. 179, 181.
107 I. M. Young, 'The Ideal of Community and the Politics of Difference' in L. J. Nicholson, ed. *Feminism/Postmodernism* p. 301 and cf. Young, *Justice and the Politics of Difference*.
108 See, for example, Jane Flax's and Anna Yeatman's contributions to L. J. Nicholson, ed., *Feminism/Postmodernism*.
109 Said, quoted by Connor, *Postmodernist Culture*, p. 233, and see E. Said, *Orientalism*.
110 Connor, *Postmodernist Culture*, pp. 233–4.
111 'Flight' is a term used by G. Deleuze and F. Guattari, *A Thousand Plateaus*, esp. Introduction.
112 Connor, *Postmodernist Culture*, p. 243.
113 Cf. S. White, *Political Theory and Postmodernism*, p. 122.
114 Rorty, 'Postmodernist Bourgeois Liberalism'.
115 Quoted by White, *Political Theory and Postmodernism*, p. 16.
116 Gaggi, *Modern/Postmodern*, p. 175.
117 Quoted by Gaggi, *Modern/Postmodern*, p. 174. Eagleton does recognize a limited role for deconstruction and poststructuralist critique as political tools to be deployed against the ideology of western societies. See T. Eagleton, *Literary Theory: An Introduction*, esp. pp. 143–5.
118 Oakeshott, *Rationalism in Politics*, esp. pp. 22ff.
119 Mussolini, quoted by Gaggi, *Modern/Postmodern*, p. 177. Mussolini's admirer Pirandello, whose plays are considered to have made an important contribution to the postmodern sensibility, was also apparently aware of the connection.
120 Hebdige, quoted by Connor, *Postmodernist Culture*, p. 213.
121 Connor, *Postmodernist Culture*, p. 18.
122 See F. Schiller, *On the Aesthetic Education of Man*.
123 White, *Political Theory and Postmodernism*, p. 3.
124 William Connolly, quoted by White, *Political Theory and Postmodernism*, pp. 19–20.
125 White, *Political Theory and Postmodernism*, p. 22. Another influential thinker who emphasizes recognition of otherness is Emmanuel Levinas – see above, ch. 6, pp. 163–4.
126 White, *Political Theory and Postmodernism*, pp. 60, 61, 66.
127 Ibid., p. 67.
128 Ibid., p. 68–9.
129 Ibid., p. 33.
130 Ibid., p. 72.
131 Ibid., p. 22.
132 Ibid., p. 83.
133 Ibid., ch. 6.

Bibliography

Adorno, T. W.: *Negative Dialectics* (1966), trans. E. B. Ashton (Routledge, London, 1973).

Adorno, T. W.: *Aesthetic Theory* (Routledge & Kegan Paul, London and Boston, 1984).

Adorno, T. W.: *The Culture Industry: Selected Essays on Mass Culture*, ed. J. M. Bernstein (Routledge, London, 1991).

Adorno, T. W. et al., eds: *The Positivist Dispute in German Sociology*, trans. G. Adey and D. Frisby (Heinemann Educational Books, London, 1976).

Adorno, T. W. and Horkheimer, M.: *Dialectic of Enlightenment* (1994), trans. John Cumming (Verso, London and New York, 1979).

Allison, D. B., ed.: *The New Nietzsche: Contemporary Styles of Interpretation* (Delta, New York, 1977).

Allison, H. E.: *Kant's Transcendental Idealism: An Interpretation and Defense* (Yale University Press, New Haven and London, 1983).

Althusser, L.: *For Marx*, trans. B. Brewster (Verso, London, 1977).

Althusser, L. and Balibar, E.: *Reading Capital*, trans. B. Brewster (New Left Books, London, 1970).

Anderson, P.: *Considerations on Western Marxism* (New Left Books, London, 1976).

Anderson, P.: *In the Tracks of Historical Materialism* (Verso, London, 1983).

Ansell-Pierson, K.: *Nietzsche contra Rousseau: A Study of Nietzsche's Moral and Political Thought* (Cambridge University Press, Cambridge and New York, 1991).

Aristotle: *Aristotle's Ethics*, trans. John Warrington (Dent & Dutton, London and New York, 1963).

Aronson, R.: *Jean-Paul Sartre: Philosophy in the World* (Verso, London 1980).

Aune, B.: *Rationalism, Empiricism, and Pragmatism: An Introduction* (Random House, New York, 1970).

Awerkamp, D. T.: *Emmanuel Levinas: Ethics and Politics* (Revisionist Press, New York, 1977).

Ayer, A. J.: *Language, Truth and Logic* (1936) (Penguin Books, Harmondsworth and New York, 1971).

Bacon, F.: *The Advancement of Learning* (1605), ed. G. W. Kitchen (Dent, London, 1973).

Bahro, R.: *The Alternative in Eastern Europe*, trans. D. Fernbach (New Left Books, London, 1978).

Bair, D.: *Simone de Beauvoir: A Biography* (Cape, London, 1990).

Bakunin, M. A.: *Marxism, Freedom and the State*, trans. and ed. K. J. Kenafick (Freedom Press, London, 1950).

Barthes, R.: *S/Z*, trans. R. Miller (Cape, London, 1975).

Baudrillard, J.: *The Mirror of Production*, trans. M. Poster (Telos Press, St Louis, 1975).

Baudrillard, J.: 'The Ecstasy of Communication', in H. Foster, ed., *Postmodern Culture* (Pluto Press, London, 1985).

Baudrillard, J.: *Jean Baudrillard: Selected Writings*, ed. M. Poster (Polity Press, Cambridge, 1988).

Bauman, Z.: *Modernity and the Holocaust* (Polity Press, Cambridge, 1989).

Bauman, Z.: *Intimations of Postmodernity* (Routledge, London and New York, 1992).

Beauvoir, S. de: *The Ethics of Ambiguity*, trans. B. Frechtman (Citadel Press, Secaucus, NJ, 1972).

Beauvoir, S. de: *The Second Sex* (1949), trans. H. M. Parshley (Penguin Books, Harmondsworth, 1972).

Beckett, S.: *The Unnamable*, in *Three Novels by Samuel Beckett: Molloy, Malone Dies, The Unnamable* (Grove Press, New York, 1965).

Beiner, R.: *Political Judgment* (Methuen, London, 1983).

Bell, D.: *The Coming of Post-industrial Society* (Basic Books, New York, 1978).

Benhabib, S. and Dallmayr, F.: *The Communicative Ethics Controversy* (MIT Press, Cambridge, Mass., and London, 1990).

Benjamin, A., ed.: *Judging Lyotard* (Routledge, London and New York, 1992).

Benjamin, W.: *Illuminations*, trans. H. Zohn (Fontana/Collins, London, 1968).

Benton, T.: *The Rise and Fall of Structural Marxism: Althusser and his Influence* (Macmillan, London, 1984).

Berkeley, G.: *The Principles of Human Knowledge*, ed. G. J. Warnock (Collins, London, 1962).

Berlin, I.: *The Crooked Timber of Humanity: Chapters in the History of Ideas*, ed. H. Hardy (John Murray, London, 1990).

Berman, H. J.: *Law and Revolution: The Formation of the Western Legal Tradition* (Harvard University Press, Cambridge, Mass., 1983).

Berman, M.: *All that is Solid Melts into Air* (Verso, London, 1982).

Bernasconi, R. and Critchley, S., eds: *Re-reading Levinas* (Athlone Press, London, 1991).

Bernstein, J. A.: *Nietzsche's Moral Philosophy* (Fairleigh Dickinson University Press, Rutherford, NJ, 1987).

Bernstein, R. J., ed.: *Habermas and Modernity* (Polity Press, Cambridge, 1985).

Blackham, H. J.: *Six Existentialist Thinkers* (Routledge & Kegan Paul, London, 1961).

Blaug, B.: *Economic Theory in Retrospect*, 4th edn (Cambridge University Press, Cambridge and New York, 1985).

Bloch, M.: *Feudal Society* (Routledge & Kegan Paul, London, 1961).

Bollnow, O. F.: *Die Lebensphilosophie* (Springer, Berlin, 1958).

Boucher, D.: *Texts in Context: Revisionist Methods for Studying the History of Ideas* (Nijhoff, Dordrecht and Boston, 1985).

Boyne, R.: *Foucault and Derrida* (Unwin Hyman, London, 1990).

Brandt, R.: 'The Deductions in the *Critique of Judgment*: Comments on Hampshire and Horstmann', in Eckart Förster, ed., *Kant's Transcendental Deductions: The Three* Critiques *and the* Opus postumum (Stanford University Press, Stanford, 1989), pp. 177–90.

Brecht, B.: *Life of Galileo*, trans. D. Vesey (Methuen, London, 1965).

Brentano, F.: *Psychology from an Empirical Standpoint* (1874), trans. A. C. Rancurello, D. B. Terrell and L. L. McAlister (Routledge & Kegan Paul, London, 1973).

Breuer, J. and Freud, S.: *Studies on Hysteria*, trans. J. and A. Strachey (Penguin Books, Harmondsworth, 1974).

Broad, C. D.: *Kant: An Introduction* (Cambridge University Press, Cambridge, 1978).

Bubner, R.: *Modern German Philosophy*, trans. E. Matthews (Cambridge University Press, Cambridge and New York, 1981).

Buck-Morss, S.: *The Origin of Negative Dialectics: Theodor W. Adorno, Walter Benjamin and the Frankfurt School* (Harvester, Brighton, 1977).

Burchell, G., Gordon, C. and Miller, P., eds: *The Foucault Effect: Studies in Governmentality* (Chicago University Press, Chicago, 1991).

Burkitt, B.: *Radical Political Economy: An Introduction to the Alternative Economics* (Wheatsheaf, Brighton, 1984).

Butterfield, H.: *The Whig Interpretation of History* (G. Bell, London, 1950).

Callinicos, A.: *Against Postmodernism: A Marxist Critique* (Polity Press, Cambridge, 1989).

Campbell, R.: *Truth and Historicity* (Clarendon Press, Oxford, 1992).

Camus, A.: *The Plague* (Alfred A. Knopf, New York, 1948).

Camus, A.: *La Peste* (1947) (Livre de Poche/Gallimard, Paris, 1962).

Camus, A.: *The Myth of Sisyphus* (1942) (Penguin Books, Harmondsworth, 1975).

Camus, A.: *The Rebel: An Essay on Man in Revolt*, trans. A. Bower (Alfred A. Knopf, New York, 1978).

Carver, T.: *Engels* (Oxford University Press, Oxford, 1981).

Carver, T.: *Friedrich Engels: His Life and Thought* (Macmillan, London, 1989).

Castoriadis, C.: *The Imaginary Institution of Society*, trans. K. Blamey (Polity Press, Cambridge, 1987).

Caute, D.: *Fanon* (Fontana/Collins, London, 1970).

Clark, M.: *Nietzsche on Truth and Philosophy* (Cambridge University Press, New York, 1990).

Clark, M. T., ed.: *An Aquinas Reader: Selections from the Writings of Thomas Aquinas* (Hodder & Stoughton, London, 1972).

Clarke, S.: *Marx's Theory of Crisis* (St Martin's Press, New York, 1993).

Cohen, G. A.: *Karl Marx's Theory of History: A Defence* (Clarendon Press, Oxford, 1978).

Concise Oxford English Dictionary, ed. R. E. Allen (Clarendon Press, Oxford, 1990).

Connerton, P.: *Tragedy of Enlightenment* (Cambridge University Press, Cambridge and New York, 1980).

Connor, S.: *Postmodernist Culture: An Introduction to Theories of the Contemporary* (Basil Blackwell, New York, 1989).

Cooper, D. E.: 'The Presidential Address: Analytical and Continental Philosophy', *Proceedings of the Aristotelian Society*, 94 (1994), pp. 1–18.

Copleston, F.: *Contemporary Philosophy: Studies of Logical Positivism and Existentialism* (Search Press, London, 1972).

Cruickshank, J.: *Albert Camus and the Literature of Revolt* (Oxford University Press, New York, 1960).

Culler, J.: *Saussure* (Fontana/Collins, London, 1976).

Culler, J.: *On Deconstruction: Theory and Criticism after Structuralism* (Cornell University Press, Ithaca, 1982).

Danto, A. C.: *Nietzsche as Philosopher* (Macmillan, New York, 1965).

Danto, A. C.: *Sartre* (Fontana/Collins, London, 1975).

Darwin, C.: *The Origin of Species by Means of Natural Selection* (1859), ed. J. W. Burrow (Penguin Books, Harmondsworth, 1968).

Debord, G.: *Society of the Spectacle* (Black and Red, Detroit, 1977).

Deleuze, G.: 'Nomad Thought', in D. B. Allison, ed., *The New Nietzsche: Contemporary Styles of Interpretation* (Delta, New York, 1977), pp. 142–9.

Deleuze, G.: *Nietzsche and Philosophy*, trans. H. Tomlinson (Athlone Press, London, 1983).

Deleuze, G.: *Spinoza: Practical Philosophy*, trans. R. Hurley (City Light Books, San Francisco, 1988).

Deleuze, G. and Guattari, F.: *A Thousand Plateaus: Capitalism and Schizophrenia*, trans. B. Massumi (Athlone Press, London, 1988).

Derrida, J.: *Speech and Phenomena* (Northwestern University Press, Evanston, 1973).

Derrida, J.: *Of Grammatology* (Johns Hopkins University Press, Baltimore, 1976).

Derrida, J.: 'The Question of Style', in D. B. Allison, ed., *The New Nietzsche: Contemporary Styles of Interpretation* (Delta, New York, 1977), pp. 176–89.

Derrida, J.: *Writing and Difference*, trans. A. Bass (Routledge & Kegan Paul, London, 1978).

Derrida, J.: *Dissemination* (1972), trans. B. Johnson (Chicago University Press, Chicago, 1981).

Derrida, J.: *Positions*, trans. A. Bass (Chicago University Press, Chicago, 1981).

Derrida, J.: *Margins of Philosophy* (1972), trans. A. Bass (Harvester Wheatsheaf, New York and London, 1982).

Derrida, J.: 'The Laws of Reflection: Nelson Mandela, in Admiration', in J. Derrida and M. Tlili, eds., *For Nelson Mandela* (Seaver, New York, 1987).

Descartes, R.: 'Meditations on First Philosophy', in *The Philosophical Works of Descartes*, vol. 1, trans. E. S. Haldane and G. R. T. Ross (Dover, London and New York, 1931).

Descombes, V.: *Modern French Philosophy*, trans. L. Scott-Fox and J. M. Harding (Cambridge University Press, Cambridge and New York, 1980).

Dews, P.: *Logics of Disintegration* (Verso, London and New York, 1987).

Dilthey, W.: *W. Dilthey: Selected Writings*, ed. H. P. Rickman (Cambridge University Press, Cambridge and New York, 1976).

Dilthey, W.: *Introduction to the Human Sciences*, trans. R. J. Betanzos (Wayne State University Press, Detroit, 1988).

Dostoyevsky, F.: *The Brothers Karamazov*, trans. R. Pevear and L. Volokhonsky (Vintage Books, London, 1990).

Dreyfus, H. L. and Hall, H.: *Husserl, Intentionality and Cognitive Science* (MIT Press, Cambridge, Mass., 1982).

Dreyfus, H. L. and Rabinow, P.: *Michel Foucault: Beyond Structuralism and Hermeneutics* (Harvester, Brighton, 1982).

Dummett, M.: 'Can Analytical Philosophy be Systematic, and Ought it to be?' in *Truth and Other Enigmas* (Duckworth, London, 1978).

Dunne, P.: *Quantitative Marxism* (Basil Blackwell, Cambridge, Mass., 1991).

Durkheim, E.: *The Rules of Sociological Method* (1895), trans. S. A. Solovaye and J. H. Mueller (Free Press, New York, 1965).

Eagleton, T.: *Literary Theory: An Introduction* (University of Minnesota Press, Minneapolis, 1983).

Elliott, G.: *Althusser: The Detour of Theory* (Verso, London and New York, 1987).

Elliott, G.: 'Further Adventures of the Dialectic', in A. Phillips Griffiths, ed., *Contemporary French Philosophy* (Cambridge University Press, Cambridge and New York, 1987).

Elliott, G., ed.: *Althusser: A Critical Reader* (Basil Blackwell, Oxford, 1994).

Elster, J.: *An Introduction to Karl Marx* (Cambridge University Press, Cambridge and New York, 1986).

Engels, F.: 'On Historical Materialism', in *Anti-Dühring* (Lawrence & Wishart, London, 1947).

Engels, F.: *The Condition of the Working Class in England in 1844* (1845), trans. F. K. Wischnewetzky (Allen & Unwin, London, 1950).

Eribon, D.: *Michel Foucault*, trans. B. Wing (Harvard University Press, Cambridge, Mass., 1991).

Fanon, F.: *The Wretched of the Earth*, trans. C. Farrington (Penguin Books, Harmondsworth, 1969).

Feuerbach, L.: *Essence of Christianity*, trans. G. Eliot (Harper & Row, New York and London, 1957).

Feuerbach, L.: *Principles of the Philosophy of the Future*, trans. Manfred U. Vogel (Bobbs-Merrill, Indianapolis, 1966).

Feyerabend, P.: *Against Method* (Verso, London and New York, 1988).

Findlay, J. N.: *Hegel: A Re-examination* (Allen & Unwin, London, and Macmillan, New York, 1958).

Føllesdal, D.: *Husserl und Frege* (I kommisjon hos Aschehoug, Oslo, 1958).

Fontana Dictionary of Modern Thought, ed. A. Bullock and O. Stallybrass (Fontana/Collins, London, 1977).

Fordham, F.: *An Introduction to Jung's Psychology* (Penguin Books, Harmondsworth, 1953).

Foster, H., ed.: *Postmodern Culture* (Pluto Press, London, 1985).

Foucault, M.: *The Archaeology of Knowledge* (1969), trans. A. M. Sheridan Smith (Tavistock Publications, London, 1972).

Foucault, M.: 'Intellectuals and Power', in *Language, Counter-memory, Practice*, trans. D. F. Bouchard and S. Simon (Basil Blackwell, Oxford, and Cornell University Press, Ithaca, 1977).

Foucault, M.: 'Nietzsche, Genealogy, History', in *Language, Counter-memory, Practice*, trans. D. F. Bouchard and S. Simon (Basil Blackwell, Oxford, and Cornell University Press, Ithaca, 1977).

Foucault, M.: *History of Sexuality,* vol. 1: *An Introduction*, trans. R. Hurley (Penguin Books, Harmondsworth, 1978).

Foucault, M.: *Discipline and Punish* (Penguin Books, Harmondsworth and New York, 1979).

Foucault, M.: 'Afterword: The Subject and Power' (1982) in H. L. Dreyfus and P. Rabinow, *Michel Foucault: Beyond Structuralism and Hermeneutics* (Harvester, Brighton, 1982).

Foucault, M.: 'Polemics, Politics, and Problematizations', in P. Rabinow, ed., *A Foucault Reader* (Penguin Books, Harmondsworth, 1984).

Foucault, M.: *The Care of the Self: The History of Sexuality*, vol. 3, trans. R. Hurley (Penguin Books, Harmondsworth and New York, 1986).

Foucault, M.: *Madness and Civilization: A History of Insanity in the Age of Reason* (Routlege, London, 1989).

Foucault, M.: *The Birth of the Clinic: An Archaeology of Medical Perception* (Vintage Books, New York, 1994).

Freud, S.: *Psychopathology of Everyday Life* (Penguin Books, Harmondsworth, 1975).

Freud, S.: *The Interpretation of Dreams*, trans. J. Strachey (Penguin Books, Harmondsworth, 1976).

Freud, S.: *Civilization, Society and Religion: Group Psychology, Civilization and its Discontents and Other Works* (Penguin Books, Harmondsworth, 1985).

Freud, S.: 'Analysis Terminable and Interminable', in S. Freud, *On Freud's 'Analysis Terminable and Interminable'* (Yale University Press, New Haven, 1991).

Fukuyama, F.: *The End of History* (Free Press, New York, 1992).

Gadamer, H.-G.: 'On the Scope and Function of Hermeneutical Reflection', *Continuum*, 8 (1970), pp. 77–95.

Gadamer, H.-G.: *Philosophical Hermeneutics*, ed. D. E. Linge (University of California Press, Berkeley, 1976).

Gadamer, H.-G.: *Truth and Method*, 2nd rev. edn, trans. J. Weinsheimer and D. G. Marshall (Continuum, New York, 1989).

Gaggi, S.: *Modern/Postmodern: A Study in Twentieth-Century Arts and Ideas* (University of Pennsylvania Press, Philadelphia, 1989).

Gasché, R.: *The Tain of the Mirror: Derrida and the Philosophy of Reflection* (Harvard University Press, Cambridge, Mass., 1986).

Gatens, M.: *Feminism and Philosophy* (Polity Press, Cambridge, 1991).

Geuss, R.: *The Idea of a Critical Theory: Habermas and the Frankfurt School* (Cambridge University Press, Cambridge and New York, 1981).

Giddens, A.: *Social Theory and Modern Sociology* (Stanford University Press, Stanford, and Polity Press, Cambridge, 1987).

Gilmore, M. P.: *Arguments from Roman Law in Political Thought 1200–1600* (Harvard University Press, Cambridge, Mass., 1971).

Gobineau, A.: *The Inequality of the Human Races* (1853–5) (Noontide Press, Los Angeles, 1966).

Godwin, W.: *Enquiry concerning Political Justice* (1793), ed. I. Kramnick (Penguin Books, Harmondsworth, 1976).

Goffman, E.: *Asylums: Essays on the Social Situation* (Penguin Books, Harmondsworth, 1974).

Goldman, L.: *Immanuel Kant*, trans. R. Black (New Left Books, London, 1971).

Gombrich, E. H.: *Symbolic Images: Studies in the Art of the Renaissance* (Phaidon, London, 1972).

Gramsci, A.: *Selections from the Prison Notebooks*, trans. Q. Hoare and G. Nowell Smith (Lawrence & Wishart, London, 1971).

Gray, C., ed.: *Leaving the 20th Century: The Incomplete Work of the Situationist International* (Free Fall, London, 1974).

Grosz, E.: *Sexual Subversions* (Allen & Unwin, Sydney, 1989).

Gutting, G.: *Michel Foucault's Archaeology of Scientific Reason* (Cambridge University Press, Cambridge and New York, 1989).

Habermas, J.: 'On Systematically Distorted Communication', *Inquiry*, 13 (1970), pp. 205–18.

Habermas, J.: 'Summation and Response', *Continuum*, 8 (1970), pp. 123–33.

Habermas, J.: *Über Sprachtheorie: Vorbereitende Bemerkungen zu einer Theorie der kommunikativen Kompetenz* (Handblume, Vienna, 1970).

Habermas, J.: *Toward a Rational Society*, trans. J. J. Shapiro (Heinemann, London, 1971).

Habermas, J.: *Knowledge and Human Interests*, trans. J. J. Shapiro (Heinemann, London, 1972).

Habermas, J.: 'Wahrheitstheorien', in *Wirklichkeit und Reflexion: Walter Schulz zum 60. Geburtstag* (Neske, Pfullingen, 1973).

Habermas, J.: *Zur Rekonstruktion des historischen Materialismus* (Suhrkamp, Frankfurt, 1976).

Habermas, J.: 'New Social Movements', *Telos*, 49 (1981), pp. 33–7.

Habermas, J.: *Theory of Communicative Action*, 2 vols, trans. T. McCarthy (Beacon Press, Boston, 1984; and Polity Press, Cambridge, 1991).

Habermas, J.: *Autonomy and Solidarity* (Verso, London, 1986).

Habermas, J.: *The Structural Transformation of the Public Sphere*, trans. T. Burger (MIT Press, Cambridge, Mass., and Polity Press, Cambridge, 1989).

Habermas, J.: *Moral Consciousness and Communicative Action*, trans. C. Lenhardt and S. W. Nicholson (MIT Press, Cambridge, Mass., and Polity Press, Cambridge, 1990).

Habermas, J.: *Philosophical Discourse of Modernity* (Polity Press, Cambridge, 1990).

Halperin, D.: *Saint Foucault: Towards a Gay Hagiography* (Oxford University Press, Oxford and New York, 1995).

Hampshire, S.: 'The Social Spirit of Mankind', in E. Förster, ed., *Kant's Transcendental Deductions: The Three* Critiques *and the* Opus postumum (Stanford University Press, Stanford, 1989), pp. 145–56.

Hannay, A.: *Kierkegaard* (Routledge, London and New York, 1991).

Harman, C. and Callinicos, A.: *The Changing Working Class* (Bookmarks, London, 1987).

Harvey, D.: *The Condition of Postmodernity: An Inquiry into the Origins of Cultural Change* (Basil Blackwell, Oxford, 1990).

Hegel, G. W. F.: *The Philosophy of Right* (1821), trans. T. M. Knox (Oxford University Press, Oxford and New York, 1952).

Hegel, G. W. F.: *Lectures on the History of Philosophy*, 3 vols, trans. E. S. Haldane and F. H. Simson (Routlege, London, 1955).

Hegel, G. W. F.: *The Phenomenology of Mind* (1807), trans. J. B. Baillie (Harper & Row, New York and London, 1967).

Hegel, G. W. F.: *Phenomenology of Spirit*, trans. A. V. Miller (Oxford University Press, Oxford and New York, 1977).

Hegel, G. W. F.: *The Philosophy of History* (1822), trans. J. Sibree (Prometheus, New York, 1991).

Heidegger, M.: *Discourse on Thinking: A Translation of* Gelassenheit (1955), trans. J. M. Anderson and E. H. Freund (Harper Torchbooks, New York and London, 1966).

Heidegger, M.: *Being and Time*, trans. J. Macquarrie and E. Robinson (Basil Blackwell, Oxford, 1967).

Heidegger, M.: *Basic Writings*, ed. D. Farrell Krell (Harper, San Francisco, 1977).

Heidegger, M.: *Nietzsche*, trans. D. Farrell Krell (Harper & Row, San Francisco, 1979).

Held, D.: *Introduction to Critical Theory: Horkheimer to Habermas* (University of California Press, Berkeley and Los Angeles, 1980; and Polity Press, Cambridge, 1990).

Hempel, C. G.: *Aspects of Scientific Explanation, and Other Essays in the Philosophy of Science* (Free Press, New York, 1965).

Henrich, D.: 'Kant's Notion of a Transcendental Deduction and the Methodological Background of the First *Critique*', in E. Förster, ed., *Kant's Transcendental Deductions: The Three* Critiques *and the* Opus postumum (Stanford University Press, Stanford, 1989), pp. 29–46.

Herder, J. G.: *Discourse on the Origin of Language*, ed. J. H. Moran (F. Unger, New York, 1967).

Hobbes, T.: *Leviathan* (Dent, London, 1973).

Hobsbawm, E. J. et al., eds: *The Forward March of Labour Halted* (New Left Books, London, 1981).

Hodges, H. A.: *Wilhelm Dilthey: An Introduction* (Kegan Paul, Trench and Trubner, London, 1944).

Hodges, H. A.: *The Philosophy of Wilhelm Dilthey* (Routledge, London, 1952).

Hoffmeister, J.: *Wörterbuch der philosophischen Begriffe*, 2nd edn (Felix Meiner, Hamburg, 1955).

Hollingdale, R. J.: *Nietzsche* (Routledge and Kegan Paul, London and Boston, 1973).

Holub, R. C.: *Jürgen Habermas: Critic in the Public Sphere* (Routledge, London and New York, 1991).

Horkheimer, M.: *Critical Theory: Selected Essays*, trans. M. J. O'Connell et al. (Continuum, New York, 1992).

Howard, M. C. and King, J. E.: *The History of Marxian Economics* (Macmillan, Basingstoke, 1989–92).

Hoy, D.: 'Foucault – Modern or Postmodern?' in J. Arac, ed., *After Foucault: Humanistic Knowledge, Postmodern Challenge* (Rutgers University Press, New Brunswick, 1988).

Hume, D.: *A Treatise of Human Nature*, ed. L. A. Selby-Bigge (Clarendon Press, Oxford, 1888).

Hume, D.: *Enquiries Concerning Human Understanding and Concerning the Principles of Morals*, ed. L. A. Selby-Bigge (Clarendon Press, Oxford, 1902).

Hume, D.: *Dialogues Concerning Natural Religion*, ed. M. Bell (Penguin Books, Harmondsworth and New York, 1990).

Husserl, E.: *Cartesian Meditations: An Introduction to Phenomenology*, trans. D. Cairns (Nijhoff, The Hague, 1960).

Husserl, E.: *Ideas: General Introduction to Phenomenology*, trans. W. R. Boyce Gibson (London, Collier-Macmillan, 1962).

Husserl, E.: 'Philosophy as Rigorous Science', in *Phenomenology and the Crisis of Philosophy*, trans. Q. Lauer (Harper Torchbooks, New York and London, 1965).

Husserl, E.: *The Crisis of European Sciences and Transcendental Phenomenology*, trans. D. Carr (Northwestern University Press, Evanston, 1970).

Husserl, E.: *Logical Investigations*, 2 vols, trans. J. N. Findlay (Humanities Press, New York, 1970).

Husserl, E.: *Philosophie der Arithmetik*, in *Husserliana*, vol. 12 (Nijhoff, The Hague, 1970). (I am not aware of an English translation of this work, which is named in the text *Philosophy of Arithmetic*.)

Irigaray, L.: *This Sex which is Not One*, trans. C. Porter and C. Burke (Cornell University Press, Ithaca, 1985).

Irigaray, L.: *The Irigaray Reader*, ed. M. Whitford (Basil Blackwell, Oxford, and Cambridge, Mass., 1991).

Jameson, F.: *Postmodernism, or, The Cultural Logic of Late Capitalism* (Duke University Press, Durham, NC, 1991).

Jay, M.: *The Dialectical Imagination: A History of the Frankfurt School and the Institute for Social Research, 1923–1950* (Little, Brown, Boston and London, 1973).

Jessop, B.: *The Capitalist State: Marxist Theories and Methods* (New York University Press, New York, and M. Robertson, Oxford, 1982).

Jessop, B.: *State Theory: Putting the Capitalist State in its Place* (Polity Press, Cambridge, 1990).

Jung, C. G.: *The Integration of the Personality*, trans. S. M. Dell (Farrar & Rinehart, New York, 1939).

Kamenka, E.: *The Philosophy of Ludwig Feuerbach* (Routledge & Kegan Paul, London, 1970).

Kant, I.: *Critique of Pure Reason*, trans. N. Kemp-Smith (Macmillan, London and New York, 1933).

Kant, I.: *Critique of Judgement*, trans. J. C. Meredith (Clarendon Press, Oxford, 1952).

Kant, I.: *Critique of Practical Reason*, trans. L. White Beck (Bobbs-Merrill, Indianapolis, 1956).

Kant, I.: *Groundwork of the Metaphysic of Morals*, ed. H. J. Paton (Harper & Row, New York, 1965).

Kant, I.: 'An Answer to the Question: What is Enlightenment?' in *Perpetual Peace and Other Essays*, trans. T. Humphrey (Hackett, Indianapolis, and Cambridge, 1983).

Kaufmann, W.: 'The Hegel Myth and its Method', *Philosophical Review*, 60 (1951), pp. 459–86.

Kaufmann, W.: *Nietzsche: Philosopher, Psychologist, Antichrist*, 4th edn (Princeton University Press, Princeton, 1974).

Keane, J.: *Public Life and Late Capitalism* (Cambridge University Press, London and New York, 1984).

Kellner, D.: *Jean Baudrillard: From Marxism to Postmodernism and Beyond* (Stanford University Press, Stanford, and Polity Press, Cambridge, 1989).

Kennedy, P. M.: 'Idealists and Realists: British Views of Germany, 1864–1939', *Transactions of the Royal Historical Society*, 5th series, 25 (1975), pp. 137–56.

Kierkegaard, S.: *The Concept of Dread*, trans. W. Lowrie (Princeton University Press, Princeton, 1946).

Kierkegaard, S.: *Repetition*, trans. W. Lowrie (Oxford University Press, London, 1946).

Kierkegaard, S.: *Either/Or*, 2 vols, trans. D. F. Swenson and L. M. Swenson (vol. 1) and W. Lowrie (vol. 2) (Princeton University Press, Princeton, 1959).

Kierkegaard, S.: *Selections from the Writings of Kierkegaard*, ed. L. M. Hollander (Doubleday, New York, 1960).

Kierkegaard, S.: *Philosophical Fragments or a Fragment of Philosophy*, trans. D. F. Swenson (Princeton University Press, 1962).

Kierkegaard, S.: *Fear and Trembling: Dialectical Lyric by Johannes* de silentio, trans. A. Hannay (Penguin Books, Harmondsworth and New York, 1985).

Kierkegaard, S.: *The Concept of Irony, with Continual Reference to Socrates*, trans. H. V. Hong and E. H. Hong (Princeton University Press, Princeton, 1989).

Kierkegaard, S.: *The Sickness unto Death: A Christian Psychological Exposition for Edification and Awakening by Anti-Climacus*, trans. A. Hannay (Penguin Books, Harmondsworth and New York, 1989).

Kierkegaard, S.: *Concluding Unscientific Postscript to* Philosophical Fragments, vol. 1, trans. H. V. Hong and E. H. Hong (Princeton University Press, Princeton, 1992).

Kirk, W.: 'The Introduction and Critical Reception of Hegelian Thought in Britain, 1830–1900', *Victorian Studies*, 32, 1 (Fall 1988), pp. 85–111.

Kohlberg, L., Levine, C. and Hewer, A.: *Moral Stages: A Current Formulation and a Response to Critics* (Karger, Basle and New York, 1983).

Kojève, A.: *Introduction to the Reading of Hegel: Lectures on the Phenomenology of Spirit*, trans. J. H. Nichols (Basic Books, New York, 1969).

Körner, S.: *Kant* (Penguin Books, Harmondsworth, 1955).

Kristeva, J.: *The Kristeva Reader*, ed. T. Moi (Basil Blackwell, Oxford, 1986).

Kuhn, T.: *The Structure of Scientific Revolutions* (Chicago University Press, Chicago, 1970).

Laclau, E. and Mouffe, C.: *Hegemony and Socialist Strategy* (Verso, London, 1985).

Lacoue-Labarthe, P.: *Heidegger: Art and Politics*, trans. C. Turner (Basil Blackwell, Oxford, 1990).

La Mettrie, J. O. de: *Man a Machine*, ed. G. C. Bussey (Open Court, Chicago, 1927).

La Rochefoucauld, F., Duc de: *Maximes et réflexions diverses*, ed. J.-P. Caput (Larousse, Paris, 1975).

Lash, S. and Urry, J.: *The End of Organised Capitalism* (Polity Press, Cambridge, 1987).

Lash, S. and Whimster, S., eds: *Max Weber, Rationality and Modernity* (Allen & Unwin, London and Boston, 1987).

Le Doeuff, M.: *The Philosophical Imaginary* (Athlone Press, London, 1989).

Le Doeuff, M.: *Hipparchia's Choice: An Essay concerning Women, Philosophy etc.*, trans. T. Selous (Basil Blackwell, Oxford, 1991).

Lenin, V. I.: *What is to be Done? Burning Questions of Our Movement* (Foreign Languages Press, Peking, 1975).

Levinas, E.: *Time and the Other, and Additional Essays*, trans. R. A. Cohen (Duquesne University Press, Pittsburgh, 1987).

Levinas, E.: *The Levinas Reader*, ed. S. Hand (Basil Blackwell, Oxford, and Cambridge, Mass., 1989).

Lévi-Strauss, C.: *The Savage Mind* (Chicago University Press, Chicago, 1966).

Lévi-Strauss, C.: *Structural Anthropology*, trans. C. Jacobson and B. G. Schoepf (Penguin Books, Harmondsworth, 1968).

Lévi-Strauss, C.: *The Elementary Structures of Kinship*, trans. J. H. Bell et al. (Eyre & Spottiswoode, London, 1969).

Lewis, A. D. E. and Ibbetson, D. J., eds: *The Roman Law Tradition* (Cambridge University Press, Cambridge and New York, 1994).

Locke, J.: *Essay concerning Human Understanding*, 2 vols, ed. J. W. Yolton (Dent, London and New York, 1965).

Locke, J.: *Political Writings*, ed. D. Wootton (Penguin Books, Harmondsworth and New York, 1993).

Lorenzer, A.: *Kritik des psychoanalytischen Symbolbegriffs* (Suhrkamp, Frankfurt, 1970).

Lukács, G.: *History and Class Consciousness*, trans. R. Livingstone (Merlin Press, London, 1971).

Lukes, S.: *Émile Durkheim: His Life and Work, a Historical and Critical Study* (Harper & Row, New York, 1972).

Lukes, S.: *Marxism and Morality* (Oxford University Press, Oxford, 1987).

Lyotard, J.-F.: *The Postmodern Condition: A Report on Knowledge*, trans. G. Bennington and B. Massumi (Manchester University Press, Manchester, 1984).

Lyotard, J.-F.: *Heidegger and the Jews*, trans. A. Michel and M. S. Roberts (University of Minnesota Press, Minneapolis, 1990).

MacCabe, C., ed.: *The Talking Cure: Essays in Psychoanalysis and Language* (Macmillan, London, 1981).

McCarthy, T.: *The Critical Theory of Jürgen Habermas* (Polity Press, Cambridge, 1984).

McCarthy, T.: 'The Politics of the Ineffable: Derrida's Deconstructionism', *Philosophical Forum*, 21 (1989–90), pp. 146–68.

Machiavelli, N.: *The Prince* (Penguin Books, Harmondsworth and New York, 1961).

McLellan, D.: *Karl Marx: His Life and Thought* (Macmillan, London, 1973).

McLellan, D.: *Marx* (Fontana, London, 1975).

McLuhan, M.: *The Gutenberg Galaxy* (Routledge & Kegan Paul, London, 1962).

Macquarrie, J.: *Martin Heidegger* (Lutterworth Press, London, and John Knox Press, Richmond, Va., 1968).

Macquarrie, J.: *Existentialism* (Penguin Books, Harmondsworth, 1973).

MacRae, D. G.: *Weber* (Fontana/Collins, London, 1987).

Mandel, E.: *Late Capitalism*, trans. J. De Bres (New Left Books, London, 1975).

Marcuse, H.: *One-Dimensional Man* (Sphere Books, London, 1968).

Marcuse, H.: *Eros and Civilization* (Sphere Books, London, 1969).

Marcuse, H.: *Soviet Marxism* (Penguin Books, Harmondsworth and New York, 1971).

Marcuse, H.: *Counterrevolution and Revolt* (Allen Lane, London, 1972).

Marcuse, H.: 'Sartre's Existentialism', in H. Marcuse, *Studies in Critical Philosophy* (New Left Books, London, 1972; and Beacon Press, Boston, 1973).

Marx, K.: *Critique of the Gotha Programme* (Foreign Languages Press, Peking, 1972).

Marx, K.: *Grundrisse* (Penguin Books, Harmondsworth, 1973).

Marx, K.: *The Civil War in France* (Progress Publishers, Moscow, 1974).

Marx, K.: *Capital: A Critique of Political Economy*, vol. 1, trans. B. Fowkes (Penguin Books, Harmondsworth and New York, 1976).

Marx, K.: 'Critique of Hegel's Doctrine of the State', in *Karl Marx: Early Writings*, trans. R. Livingstone and G. Benton (Penguin Books, Harmondsworth, 1976).

Marx, K.: 'Economic and Philosophical Manuscripts' (1844), in *Karl Marx: Early Writings*, trans. R. Livingstone and G. Benton (Penguin Books, Harmondsworth, 1976).

Marx, K.: 'On the Jewish Question', in *Karl Marx: Early Writings*, trans. R. Livingstone and G. Benton (Penguin Books, Harmondsworth, 1976).

Marx, K.: 'Theses on Feuerbach', in *Karl Marx: Early Writings*, trans. R. Livingstone and G. Benton (Penguin Books, Harmondsworth, 1976).

Marx, K. and Engels, F.: *The Communist Manifesto*, in *Essential Works of Marxism* (Bantam Books, New York and London, 1961).

Marx, K. and Engels, F.: *The German Ideology*, ed. C. J. Arthur (Lawrence & Wishart, London, 1977).

Merleau-Ponty, M.: *The Phenomenology of Perception*, trans. C. Smith (Routledge & Kegan Paul, London, 1962).

Merleau-Ponty, M.: *The Structure of Behaviour*, trans. A. L. Fisher (Beacon Press, Boston, 1963).

Meszaros, I.: *Lukács' Concept of Dialectic* (Merlin Press, London, 1972).

Michelfelder, D. P. and Palmer, R. E., eds: *Dialogue and Deconstruction: The Gadamer–Derrida Encounter* (State University of New York Press, Albany, 1989).

Mill, J. S.: *A System of Logic, Ratiocinative and Inductive*, 2 vols, 10th edn (Longmans Green, London, 1879).

Mohanty, J.: *Edward Husserl's Theory of Meaning* (Nijhoff, The Hague, 1964).

Morris, M.: 'Operative Reasoning: Michèle Le Doeuff, Philosophy and Feminism', *Ideology and Consciousness*, 9 (Winter, 1981/2), pp. 71–101.

Mortley, R.: *French Philosophers in Conversation: Levinas, Schneider, Serres, Irigaray, Le Doeuff, Derrida* (Routledge, London and New York, 1991).

Nicholson, L. J., ed.: *Feminism/Postmodernism* (Routledge, New York and London, 1990).

Nietzsche, F.: *Twilight of the Idols and The Anti-Christ*, trans. R. J. Hollingdale (Penguin Books, Harmondsworth, 1968).

Nietzsche, F.: *On the Genealogy of Morals and Ecce Homo*, trans. W. Kaufmann and R. J. Hollingdale (Vintage Books, New York, 1969).

Nietzsche, F.: *Thus Spake Zarathustra*, trans. R. J. Hollingdale (Penguin Books, Harmondsworth, 1969).

Nietzsche, F.: *Beyond Good and Evil*, trans. R. J. Hollingdale (Penguin Books, Harmondsworth and New York, 1973).

Nietzsche, F.: *Gay Science*, trans. W. Kaufmann (Vintage Books, New York, 1974).

Nietzsche, F.: *Untimely Meditations*, trans. R. J. Hollingdale (Cambridge University Press, Cambridge and New York, 1983).

Nietzsche, F.: *Human, All Too Human* (Cambridge University Press, Cambridge and New York, 1986).

Nietzsche, F.: *Birth of Tragedy*, trans. S. Whiteside (Penguin Books, Harmondsworth and New York, 1993).

Norman, R.: *Hegel's Phenomenology: A Philosophical Introduction* (St. Martin's Press, New York, 1976).

Norris, C.: *Derrida* (Fontana/Collins, London, 1987).

Oakeshott, M.: *Rationalism in Politics, and Other Essays* (Methuen, London, 1962).

Oakeshott, M.: 'Michael Oakeshott on Marx on Hegel', *Spectator*, 6 February 1971, pp. 192–3.

Oakeshott, M.: *On Human Conduct* (Clarendon Press, Oxford, 1975).

O'Brien, C. C.: *Camus* (Fontana/Collins, London, 1970).

Ollman, B.: *Alienation: Marx's Conception of Man in Capitalist Society* (Cambridge University Press, Cambridge, 1971).

Outhwaite, W.: *Habermas: A Critical Introduction* (Polity Press, Cambridge, 1994).

Oxford Dictionary of Quotations, 4th edn (Oxford University Press, Oxford and New York, 1992).

Palmer, R. E.: *Hermeneutics: Interpretation Theory in Schleiermacher, Dilthey, Heidegger, and Gadamer* (Northwestern University Press, Evanston, 1969).

Pascal, B.: *Pensées*, ed. J. Chevalier (Gallimard, Paris, 1962).

Pascal, B.: *The Provincial Letters*, trans. A. J. Krailsheimer (Penguin Books, Harmondsworth, 1967).

Passmore, J.: *A Hundred Years of Philosophy*, 2nd edn (Penguin Books, Harmondsworth and New York, 1978).

Passmore, J.: *Recent Philosophers* (Duckworth, London, 1985).

Pateman, C.: 'The Fraternal Social Contract', in J. Keane, *Civil Society and the State* (Verso, London, 1988).

Pateman, C.: *The Sexual Contract* (Polity Press, Cambridge, 1988).

Patton, P., ed.: *Nietzsche, Feminism and Political Theory* (Routledge, London and New York, 1993).

Pedersen, H.: *The Discovery of Language: Linguistic Science in the Nineteenth Century*, ed. J. W. Spargo (Indiana University Press, Bloomington, 1967).

Pettit, P.: *The Concept of Structuralism* (University of California Press, Berkeley, 1975).

Piaget, J.: *Structuralism*, trans. C. Maschler (Routledge & Kegan Paul, London, 1971).

Pivcevic, E.: *Husserl and Phenomenology* (Hutchinson University Library, London and Sydney, 1970).

Pivcevic, E., ed.: *Phenomenology and Philosophical Understanding* (Cambridge University Press, Cambridge, 1975).

Plato: *Meno*, in *Protagoras and Meno*, trans. W. K. C. Guthrie (Penguin Books, Harmondsworth, 1956).

Plato: *Phaedo*, in *The Last Days of Socrates: Euthyphro, The Apology, Crito, Phaedo*, trans. H. Tredennick (Penguin Books, Harmondsworth, 1969).

Popper, K.: *The Poverty of Historicism* (Routledge & Kegan Paul, London, 1957).

Poster, M.: *Sartre's Marxism* (Pluto Press, London, 1979).

Rasmussen, D. M.: *Reading Habermas* (Basil Blackwell, Oxford, 1990).

Rée, J.: *Descartes* (Allen Lane, London, 1974).

Reich, W.: *The Invasion of Compulsory Sex-Morality* (Souvenir Press, London, 1972).

Rieff, P.: *The Triumph of the Therapeutic: Uses of Faith after Freud* (Penguin Books, Harmondworth, 1973).

Rohde, P.: *Kierkegaard* (Allen & Unwin, London, 1959).

Rorty, R.: 'Postmodernist Bourgeois Liberalism', *Journal of Philosophy*, 80, 10 (1983), pp. 583–9.

Rorty, R.: 'Is Derrida a Transcendental Philosopher?' in David Wood, ed., *Derrida: A Critical Reader* (Basil Blackwell, Oxford, and Cambridge, Mass., 1992).

Rose, G.: *The Melancholy Science: An Introduction to the Thought of Theodor W. Adorno* (Macmillan, London, 1978).

Rossi, I.: 'Intellectual Antecedents of Lévi-Strauss' Notion of Unconscious', in *The Unconscious in Culture: The Structuralism of Claude Lévi-Strauss in Perspective*, ed. I. Rossi (Dutton, New York, 1974).

Rousseau, J.-J.: 'Discourse on the Origin of Inequality', in *The Social Contract and Discourses*, trans. G. D. H. Cole (Dent, London, 1973).

Rousseau, J.-J.: *Émile*, trans. B. Foxley (Dent, London, 1974).

Ryan, M.: *Marxism and Deconstruction* (Johns Hopkins University Press, Baltimore, 1982).

Ryle, G.: *The Concept of Mind* (Penguin Books, Harmondsworth, 1976).

Said, E.: *Orientalism* (Routledge & Kegan Paul, London, 1978).

Sartre, J.-P.: *What is Literature?* trans. B. Frechtman (Methuen, London, 1950).

Sartre, J.-P.: *Being and Nothingness*, trans. H. E. Barnes (Routledge, London, 1958).

Sartre, J.-P.: *The Age of Reason*, Book I of *The Roads to Freedom* (Penguin Books, Harmondsworth, 1961).

Sartre, J.-P.: *Imagination: A Psychological Critique*, trans. F. Williams (University of Michigan Press, Ann Arbor, 1962).

Sartre, J.-P.: *Sketch for a Theory of the Emotions*, trans. P. Mairet (Methuen, London, 1962).

Sartre, J.-P.: *Saint Genet: Actor and Martyr*, trans. B. Frechtman (George Braziller, New York, 1963).

Sartre, J.-P.: *Nausea*, trans. R. Baldick (Penguin Books, Harmondsworth, 1965).

Sartre, J.-P.: *L'Imaginaire* (Methuen, London, 1972).

Sartre, J.-P.: *Between Existentialism and Marxism*, trans. J. Matthews (NLB, London, 1974).

Sartre, J.-P.: *The Wall (Intimacy) and Other Stories*, trans. L. Alexander (New Directions, New York, 1975).

Sartre, J.-P.: *Existentialism and Humanism* (Haskell, New York, 1977).

Sartre J.-P.: *Critique of Dialectical Reason*, vol. 1, trans. A. Sheridan-Smith (Verso, London and New York, 1991).

Saussure, F. de: *Course in General Linguistics*, trans. W. Baskin (McGraw-Hill, New York and London, 1959).

Schiller, F.: *Über die ästhetische Erziehung des Menschen*, in E. Ackerknecht, ed., *Schillers Werke*, vol. 2 (Knaur Klassiker, Munich, 1953).

Schiller, F.: *On the Aesthetic Education of Man*, ed. and trans. E. M. Wilkinson and L. A. Willoughby (Clarendon Press, Oxford, 1967).

Schnädelbach, H.: *Philosophy in Germany 1831–1933*, trans. E. Matthews (Cambridge University Press, Cambridge and New York, 1984).

Schopenhauer, A.: *The World as Will and Representation*, 2 vols, trans. E. F. J. Payne (Dover, New York, 1966).

Schütz, A.: *The Phenomenology of the Social World*, trans. G. Walsh and F. Lehnert (Northwestern University Press, Evanston, 1967).

Scruton, R.: *Kant* (Oxford University Press, Oxford and New York, 1982).

Scruton, R.: *A Short History of Modern Philosophy: From Descartes to Wittgenstein* (Routledge, London, 1984).

Sheridan, A.: *Michel Foucault: The Will to Truth* (Routledge & Kegan Paul, London, 1990).

Sigmund, P.: *Natural Law in Political Thought* (Winthrop, Cambridge, Mass., 1971).

Singer, P.: *Hegel* (Oxford University Press, Oxford and New York, 1983).

Skinner, Q.: *The Foundations of Modern Political Thought* (Cambridge University Press, Cambridge, 1978).

Smart, B.: *Foucault, Marxism, Critique* (Routledge & Kegan Paul, London, 1983).

Smart, B.: *Postmodernity* (Routledge, London and New York, 1993).

Smith, A.: *An Inquiry into the Nature and Causes of the Wealth of Nations*, ed. R. H. Campbell and A. S. Skinner, 2 vols (Clarendon Press, Oxford, 1976).

Solomon, R. C.: *Continental Philosophy since 1750: The Rise and Fall of the Self* (Oxford University Press, Oxford and New York, 1988).

Soper, K.: *Humanism and Anti-humanism* (Hutchinson, London, 1986).

Steiner, G.: *Heidegger* (Fontana/Collins, London, 1992).

Stern, J. P.: *Nietzsche* (Fontana/Collins, London, 1978).

Strawson, P. F.: *The Bounds of Sense: An Essay on Kant's* Critique of Pure Reason (Methuen, London, 1966).

Strawson, P. F.: 'Sensibility, Understanding, and the Doctrine of Synthesis', in E. Förster, ed., *Kant's Transcendental Deductions: The Three* Critiques *and the* Opus postumum (Stanford University Press, Stanford, 1989), pp. 69–77.

Strawson, P. F.: *Analysis and Metaphysics: An Introduction to Philosophy* (Oxford University Press, Oxford, 1992).

Sturrock, J.: *Structuralism*, 2nd edn (Fontana, London, 1993).

Taylor, C.: *Hegel* (Cambridge University Press, Cambridge and New York, 1975).

Taylor, C.: *Sources of the Self* (Cambridge University Press, Cambridge and New York, 1989).

Thody, P.: *Jean-Paul Sartre: A Literary and Political Study* (Hamish Hamilton, London, 1960).

Thompson, E. P.: *The Poverty of Theory* (Merlin Press, London, 1978).

Thompson, J. and Held, D.: *Habermas: Critical Debates* (Macmillan, London, 1982).

Thompson, R.: *The Pelican History of Psychology* (Penguin Books, Harmondsworth, 1968).

Tong, R.: *Feminist Thought: A Comprehensive Introduction* (Westview Press, Boulder, 1989).

Touraine, A.: *The Voice and the Eye: An Analysis of Social Movements*, trans. A. Duff (Cambridge University Press, Cambridge, 1981).

Touraine, A.: 'Introduction to the Study of Social Movements', *Social Research*, 52 (Winter, 1985), pp. 749–87.

Tuck, Richard: *Natural Rights Theories: Their Origin and Development* (Cambridge University Press, Cambridge, 1979).

Warnke, G.: *Gadamer: Hermeneutics, Tradition and Reason* (Polity Press, Cambridge, 1987).

Warren, M.: *Nietzsche and Political Thought* (MIT Press, Cambridge, Mass., 1988).

Weber, M.: *Sociology of Religion* (Methuen, London, 1965).

Weber, M.: *Economy and Society: An Outline of Interpretive Sociology*, ed. G. Roth and C. Wittich, 2 vols (University of California Press, Berkeley, 1978).

White, S.: *Political Theory and Postmodernism* (Cambridge University Press, Cambridge and New York, 1991).

Whitehead, A. N. and Russell, B.: *Principia Mathematica*, 2nd edn, 3 vols (Cambridge University Press, Cambridge and New York, 1950).

Whitford, M.: *Luce Irigaray: Philosophy in the Feminine* (Routledge, London and New York, 1991).

Wiggershaus, R.: *The Frankfurt School*, trans. M. Robertson (Polity Press, Cambridge, 1994).

Willard, D.: *Logic and the Objectivity of Knowledge: A Study in Husserl's Early Philosophy* (Ohio University Press, Athens, Ohio, 1984).

Williams, B.: *Descartes: The Project of Pure Enquiry* (Penguin Books, Harmondsworth, 1978).

Williams, R.: *The Long Revolution* (Penguin Books, Harmondsworth and New York, 1961).

Williams, R.: *Keywords* (Fontana/Collins, London, 1976).

Williams, T. C.: *The Concept of the Categorical Imperative* (Clarendon Press, Oxford, 1968).

Wittgenstein, L.: *Philosophical Investigations*, trans. G. E. M. Anscombe (Basil Blackwell, Oxford, 1974).

Wollheim, R.: *Freud* (Fontana/Collins, London, 1971).

Woodcock, G.: *Anarchism: A History of Libertarian Ideas and Movements* (Penguin Books, Harmondsworth, 1975).

Young, I. M.: 'The Ideal of Community and the Politics of Difference', in L. J. Nicholson, ed., *Feminism/Postmodernism* (Routledge, New York and London, 1990).

Young, I. M.: *Justice and the Politics of Difference* (Princeton University Press, Princeton, 1990).

Zuidervaart, L.: *Adorno's Aesthetic Theory* (MIT Press, Cambridge, Mass., 1991).

Index